THE WORKS OF SRI CHINMOY

POETRY

VOLUME IV

THE WORKS OF SRI CHINMOY

POETRY

VOLUME IV

TOME I

★

SEVENTY-SEVEN THOUSAND
SERVICE-TREES

PART 1 TO 7

LYON · OXFORD

GANAPATI PRESS

LXXXVII

ISBN 978-1-911319-14-6

See appendix for notice regarding this edition.

FIRST EDITION WENT TO PRESS ON 13 NOVEMBER 2017

POETRY

VOLUME IV

SEVENTY-SEVEN THOUSAND SERVICE-TREES

PART 1 TO 7

1.

My Lord,
You have commanded me
To offer You
Seventy-Seven Thousand Service-
    Trees.
I shall obey Your absolute
    Command.

2.

My heart
Is one of my homes,
But my heart's only Home
Is God.

3.

To see the Face of God,
First I must devour
The Nectar-Dust
Of God's Feet.

4.

To see the Eye of God,
First I must become
The Heart of God.

5.

Earth's cry ascends,
But before it touches Heaven's
    Eye,
It returns.

6.

Heaven's Smile descends,
But before it feels earth's heart,
It returns.

7.

My God-gratitude-heart
Is my soul's
Rainbow-dance-ecstasy.

8.

My Lord Supreme,
Do expedite the birth
Of my gratitude-heart.

9.

Today my heart and I
Are exceedingly happy,
For we are seeing my mind's
Ego-balloon
Losing its altitude very rapidly.

10.

My Beloved Supreme,
I do not want to become
A computer-brain.
I wish to become only
A devotion-chain.

11.

A sincerity-mind
Is a long road.
A purity-heart
Is a longer road.
A divinity-life
Is the longest road.

12.

When the mind does not aspire,
It becomes a victim
To devastating and damaging
    thoughts.

13.

It is not at all a difficult task
For the mind to become
Deliberately anti-divine.

14.

O my mind,
How long will you enjoy
Your lame arguments
Against God's Compassion-Eye?

15.

An Avatar is he
Who receives from God Himself
The world-purifying breath.

16.

An Avatar is he
Who receives from God Himself
The world-saving fingertips.

17.

An Avatar is he
To whom God Himself tells
The world-illumining secrets.

18.

An Avatar is he
Who receives from God Himself
God's own Dreams
For God's full manifestation
Here on earth.

19.

An Avatar is he
Who gladly stoops beneath
The weight of world-sorrows.

20.

Abiding satisfaction
Lies only
In the roots of faith.

21.

The suspicious mind
And the sagacious heart
Can never amicably agree.

22.

My Lord,
Do You really see and feel
My throbbing heart's deep sobs
    for You?
"My child, I do, I do,
And I claim them
To be absolutely Mine!"

23.

Each day with a spiritual Master
Is a life-saving
And
Life-shaping opportunity
For the disciple.

24.

Every day my Lord passes
My frustration-examination.
Every night my Lord passes
My exasperation-examination.

25.

O God-seekers,
How can you be such fools
That you do not realise
That each God-given task
Is a golden opportunity
For you to expedite
Your Godward journey?

26.

O seeker,
Your soul is extremely
    embarrassed
To introduce you to God.

27.

O seeker,
I feel extremely sorry for you!
Your entire life has become
A box of mind-worries.

28.

I want to become
The beauty and fragrance
Of a self-disciplined life.

29.

If you lack sincerity
In your spiritual life,
Then you will be heading
Towards NOTHING.

30.

May my love of God
Swing
Into full action.

31.

No more shall I allow
The temptation-snake
To bite my life.

32.

I shall always
Feast my eyes
On God's Lotus-Feet.

33.

When I have a deep meditation,
I feel that my life is blossoming
Into a tree of paradise.

34.

My sleepless surrender-heart
Is the official residence
Of my Lord's Satisfaction-Eye.

35.

To reach God's Palace
You do not need an outer guide,
But you do need an inner cry.

36.

Aspiration becomes frustration
When we want to fulfil our lives
In our own desperate way.

37.

Every rule admits of exception
Under the law
Of supreme necessity.

38.

When our surrender is complete,
We are able to fly
At a meteoric aspiration-speed.

39.

You profess yourself
To be a wise seeker.
Then how is it that you still live
In your mind-desire-jungle?

40.

His heart-aspiration-volcano
Has destroyed the bridge
Between his mind
And the vital world.

41.

Do not worry,
My seeker-friend.
God has not told you
That you are a finished product.

42.

Every night my soul comes
And tells my heart
To sleep in a field
Of dream-flowers.

43.

God is so proud of me
Because I am totally lost
Inside my gratitude-heart.

44.

You are saying that you have
    received
A new hope-supply.
That means God is dreaming
Through your new dreams.

45.

God's Compassion-Eye intervened
And prevented him
From needing mind-surgery.

46.

Lovingly and compassionately
My soul is asking my heart
To immigrate
To God's Satisfaction-Country.

47.

Alas, why am I not allowing God
To handcraft my life
Inch by inch
According to His sweet Pleasure?

48.

I have completely withdrawn my
    loyalty
To my doubting mind.
All my loyalties have now gone
To my aspiring heart.

49.

Even if you sing prayerful songs
To an imaginary audience,
Your soul becomes
Extremely proud of you.

50.

If you sincerely love this world,
Then no proof is necessary.
But if you do not love the world at
    all,
Then no proof will be sufficient.

51.

Some are of the opinion
That God-manifestation
Is an impossibility,
While others think
That God-manifestation
Is a remote possibility.
Still others think that God-
    manifestation
Is a living reality.
I proudly and happily
Belong to the last category.

52.

My perfection-loving heart
Is the personal secretary
Of God.

53.

My mind's hope
Comes and goes,
But my heart's promise
Will never leave me.

54.

True, I want to be a God-speaker,
But I want to be a God-seeker
Infinitely more.

55.

God wants
Each and every aspiring heart
To be a universal peace-shrine.

56.

God wants me to be a passenger
On His own Train,
And He Himself wants to take me
To His absolute Perfection-
    Station.

57.

I have three places to meditate:
I meditate inside
My God-searching mind.
I meditate inside
My God-yearning heart.
I meditate inside
My God-serving life.

58.

Most special souls
Love and treasure
God's most simple Life.

59.

Do not allow
Your anxiety-arrows
To pierce
Your aspiration-heart-blossoms.

60.

Your blind imitation-mind
Can bring about for you
A life of tragedy.

61.

My silence-heart
Has silenced
My mind's loudspeaker-sound-
    pride.

62.

A true God-seeker
Can enjoy
A divine symphony
With every breath.

63.

I see a soulful song
Taking birth
In each heartbeat of mine.

64.

May my failure-desire-life
Set
With the setting sun.

65.

May my soul-fountain-hopes
Never become
A weeping heart.

66.

All seekers are accepted
By God happily,
Even the ones who come to God
At the very last moment.

67.

The promise-power
Of a positive thought
Cannot be measured.

68.

Just listen to your soul's
Charming whispers.
You can easily overthrow
Your mind-dictator.

69.

A soulful hope
And a beautiful dream
Live together.

70.

I value and treasure God's Hope
Inside my heart's garden
Infinitely more than I value and
    treasure
Anything else.

71.

Life collects
Infinity's
Smiling songs.

72.

Death collects
Eternity's
Sad stories.

73.

The mind's death-demolition
Can take place
When the seeker becomes
A God-gratitude-heart.

74.

Hesitation not only
    unconsciously,
But even consciously,
Takes the longest road.

75.

If you are a part-time seeker,
Then God will nowhere be
    discovered
By you.

76.

Only a rank fool
Can indulge
In future phantom worries
And anxieties.

77.

I implicitly trust the peace-
    seekers,
For I know that one day
They will become the peace-
    bringers.

78.

When I become
A sincere God-seeker within,
God turns me into
A truth-seer without.

79.

Each aspiration-heart
And each dedication-life
Is an exclusive God-
    Responsibility.

80.

God invites only those
To dine with Him
Who have developed
A genuine God-hunger.

81.

I must never allow
My God-manifestation-dream-
    blossoms
To wither.

82.

Your stupidity knows no bounds!
You rely on your heart's
Insecurity-tears.

83.

The mind does everything wrong.
The poor heart, on behalf of the
    mind,
Has become a perpetual apology!

84.

O my mind,
It is high time for you
To veer away
From the dark ignorance-path.

85.

Always aim directly
At perfection-target
And at nothing else.

86.

O seeker,
Do not allow your purity-heart
To be shrouded
By fear, doubt and anxiety.

87.

No matter how hard we try
To be indifferent to our doubting
   mind,
The doubting mind monopolises
Our lives.

88.

My Lord Supreme,
Do give me the capacity
Plus opportunity
To put an end
To my arrogance-ego-talk.

89.

A devotion-flooded heart
Can easily avoid
The mind-trickster.

90.

A staunch God-lover knows
That his heart has the capacity
To go far beyond
His mind's authority-limits.

91.

When you join the spiritual life,
You must consciously brace
   yourself
Against destructive ignorance-
   blows.

92.

You and your heart-garden-
   beauty
And fragrance
Will always prevail.

93.

God wants us to rise high
In our heart's sky
To transform our earth-bound
   lives.

94.

Long, long ago
I lodged my life
In God's Heart-Home.

95.

You absent yourself
From God's Presence.
Poor God does not know
How to retaliate!

96.

His inner life is nothing other
Than a beautiful harvest
Of prayers and meditations.

97.

My beautiful meditation-birds
Fly before me
Before dawn arrives.

98.

A hope-plant
Grows faster
Than any other plant.

99.

Who can penetrate
The jungle-jumble-mind
That has no aspiration-cry?

100.

You must never trivialise
Your God-given
Spiritual life.

101.

Why are we such fools?
How is it that we do not feel
That we are privileged
To perform our God-given duties?

102.

Pride
In any promise
Is simply intolerable.

103.

I can clearly see
That the breath of Heaven
Every day
Feeds my God-surrender-soul.

104.

It is not an impossibility
To have a pyramid-high dream
Every day.

105.

Nobody can appreciate you
And nobody will
If you deliberately become
The destruction-cloud
Of disobedience.

106.

We do not want to claim time.
But we do not realise
How time claims everything.

107.

Do you want to enjoy a miracle?
It is very simple.
Always say "Yes!" to God!

108.

O my mind,
Do not waste precious time
Making gigantic master plans.

109.

The sun is in the west,
A rainbow is in the east,
But I am neither in the sun
Nor in the rainbow.
I am only in God's Satisfaction.

110.

The tears of my eyes
Are forced to live
In a chorus of clouds.

111.

I pray to God every day
To make my mind
The brightest God-vision-star.

112.

If you do not dare to stop
Your meandering thought-train,
Your goal will always remain
A far cry.

113.

To hear God's secret Whispers
Is to drink
Ecstasy-flooded dreams.

114.

If you are indifferent
To name and fame,
Then certainly you are
Pleasing God
In a very special way.

115.

Finally I have demolished
My mind's
Doubt-tower.

116.

God can easily answer
All our questions.
But He deliberately
Does not answer
Some of our questions
So that we can make
The fastest progress.

117.

Forgiveness is a supreme virtue,
And this particular virtue
Can be practised by anybody.

118.

Do not think!
Do not think!
The more you think,
The more you generalise
And categorise.
Thinking is of no avail
In the spiritual life.

119.

A constantly questioning
And analysing mind
Does not even have the speed
Of an Indian bullock cart.

120.

If there is no love-foundation,
There cannot be
Any perfection-edifice.

121.

Each service-opportunity
Is, indeed,
A progress-joy.

122.

Every day
God's Compassion-Eye
Forgives our wild blunders.

123.

O seeker, if you have
A non-stop
Enthusiasm-eagerness,
Then for you there can be
No goal unattainable.

124.

Criticism decreases
The beauty and fragrance
Of the God-searching mind.

125.

The seeker who has
Angel-soft eyes of sweetness
Makes very fast progress
In the spiritual life.

126.

God's Compassion
Is always eager
To carry us beyond our life's
Self-styled limitation-zone.

127.

Let your mind's discipline
And heart's patience
Perform their miracles for you.

128.

No more shall I permit myself
To be buffeted
By my life's desire-surges.

129.

In the bloom of early hours,
God Himself comes
And takes
My meditation-attendance.

130.

My debate with God
Is not only shameless
But also useless
In every possible way.

131.

Every morning
God gives me an opportunity
To fly upon the wings
Of my devotion-songs.

132.

Before leaving,
Try loving more,
Infinitely more.

133.

Alas, how many God-dreams
Are waiting inside me
For their full manifestation!

134.

I am determined
To make the fastest progress
In my spiritual life
And not be satisfied with my years
Of ping-pong progress.

135.

Even the tiniest aspiration-tear
God treasures
In His Satisfaction-Heart.

136.

In the morning,
I wish to be the sunrise-beauty
Of a climbing heart.
In the evening,
I wish to be the sunset-beauty
Of a sailing heart.

137.

No more shall I allow
My life to be eclipsed
By failure-darkness
And failure-sadness.

138.

Today's
Peace-bloom-dreamer
Will become
Tomorrow's
Peace-blossom-bestower.

139.

My mind, you are versed
In the science of self-deception.
Can you not get a new life
By becoming versed
In self-illumination?

140.

The birth-cry
Is Infinity's beauty.
The death-cry
Is Eternity's duty.

141.

My Lord does not come alone
When He visits
My gratitude-heart.
He comes
With His Satisfaction-Embrace.

142.

A God-seeker is he
Who has a prayerful song
In his heart
All the time for everyone.

143.

I am kept alive
Only by
My God-hope-fragrance.

144.

Do not allow
Your tomorrow's unborn sorrows
To destroy your today's
Fully-blossomed happiness.

145.

The doubting mind
Will eventually be known
And convicted
As a misleader of mankind.

146.

When impatience becomes
A God-seeker,
It will definitely meet its end
In a great disaster.

147.

If we have soulfulness
Inside our heart,
Then we shall appreciate
And admire
The fulness of each moment.

148.

Begin your spiritual life
By totally forgetting
Everything
That has disappointed you.

149.

Be careful, O seeker!
Your every wasted opportunity
May cost a lifetime.

150.

My Lord Supreme,
Do come and steal
All my heart-blossoms.

151.

My Lord Supreme,
Do come and steer my heart-boat
In accordance with Your sweet
     Will.

152.

I am eager
To take the earliest flight
From ignorance-land
To the land of wisdom-light.

153.

Your self-help-quest
Will not lead you
A great distance.

154.

Your weak and cowardly faith
Will not receive
A God-Palace-entrance-ticket.

155.

Readiness, willingness
And eagerness
Can bless your life
With a new God-viewpoint.

156.

I can hide everything,
Save and except
My mind's frustration-tears.

157.

I want to explore
The sacred secrets
Of my aspiration-heart.

158.

Happily and proudly
I have relinquished
At long last
My ego-throne.

159.

Purity in boundless measure
Resides inside the lotus
Of our aspiration-heart.

160.

I am overwhelmed with joy
To see my real spiritual life
Blossoming again.

161.

I am expediting
My life-journey
With beams of hope.

162.

The power
Of the spiritual current
From his eyes
Cannot be fathomed.

163.

His heart is seated
On the rose petal
Of sweetness, newness
And fulness.

164.

A seeker's heart
Sparkles
With beauty's wisdom-stars.

165.

O Pilot of my heart's dreams,
You are the breath
Of my Godward journey!

166.

I clearly see that my soul
Is in the galaxy
Of star-dreams.

167.

If you do not aspire,
One day
You will find yourself
In dark thought-tunnels.

168.

Each aspiring moment
Is Divinity's
New birth.

169.

Do not allow your heart
To be a trembling leaf
Of insecurity-night.

170.

My soul tells my mind
That it has no right to mar
The beauty of my heart's
Rising sun.

171.

Each truth-seeker
Must make his heart-muscle
Stronger than the strongest.

172.

O doubting mind,
I shall not allow you
To eclipse all my heart-dreams.

173.

Forgiveness-flower
Is infinitely more beautiful
Than anything else.

174.

He is so stupid!
He is enjoying
His self-congratulation-
     indulgence.

175.

God's Compassion-Eye
Has put me back
On the aspiration-road.

176.

God is telling me
That I will do Him a big favour
If every day,
In the small hours of the morning,
I think of Him, pray to Him
And meditate on Him.

177.

My searching mind
Is born to succeed.
My aspiring heart
Is born to proceed.

178.

You can be
A personal relation to God
If you can raise
Your God-aspiration-standard.

179.

I gave a special surprise to God
On His Birthday
By awakening from
My spiritual coma.

180.

I have a very special surprise
For God's Birthday:
My absolutely unconditional
Surrender-life.

181.

God's Compassion-Eye
Has taught me
How to become
A sleepless God-obedience-server.

182.

I shall not allow
Even one ego-plant
To grow alongside
My heart-blossoms.

183.

My Lord Supreme
Is heaving a sigh of relief
Because I am no longer
A friend of ignorance-night.

184.

If God is our only escort
In our aspiration-dedication-life,
Then we shall arrive
At the destination safely.

185.

Until we see the invisible
Inside the visible,
We must not be satisfied.

186.

Each day God gives me
The capacity to offer humanity
A stream of inspiring
And aspiring deeds.

187.

I am fully determined
To dismantle
All my evil thought-buildings.

188.

God's Satisfaction-Heart
Clears the path
For peace-pilgrims.

189.

Every morning
When I pray and meditate,
God's Compassion-Eye
Plucks the strings
Of my inner harp.

190.

Delay not!
Immediately break
The age-old ignorance-chain
Of your mind.

191.

Every morning
God deposits
His special Blessings
In your heart-safe.

192.

We have to ascend
To our summit-heights
To transcend and transform
Our mind.

193.

My mind,
Enough of your arrogance!
Enough of your self-indulgence!

194.

I am so happy
That my mind's
Temptation-indulgence-days
Are numbered.

195.

He has an overwhelming urge
Not to speak
To God,
But to speak
For God.

196.

God is holding back
His real Smile
Until the boundaries of the world
Are no more.

197.

Only God-lovers are entitled
To be members
Of the perfection-assembly
Of the cosmic gods and goddesses.

198.

Today's beautiful gratitude
Will become
Tomorrow's powerful surrender.

199.

No matter which country
We go to,
God-surrender-lovers
Are extremely rare.

200.

God's Pride
In His cheerful surrender-
   children
Is unimaginable.

201.

God did not mean
To frighten your mind.
He just wanted
To enlighten your mind.

202.

To become flawless children
Of God,
We must remain firmly seated
In His Compassion-Sailboat.

203.

Too often we neglect
Our God-ordained tasks;
Therefore, our perfection-life
Remains a far cry.

204.

I see God on rare occasions.
But I keep meeting
His Compassion-Eye
And Forgiveness-Heart
Every day.

205.

I cannot believe
That today my mind
Is singing soul-carols.

206.

Our heart's purity
Embodies
Measureless strength.

207.

There is always a choice for me:
Either to place my life
At the Feet of God
Or to place my life
In the hands of my mind.

208.

The only way
To sing God's Victory
Is to sing the songs
That my soul sings.

209.

I know, my Lord,
How much You love me.
But do You know
How much I love You?

210.

A long string of successes
In his outer life
Has extinguished his heart's
God-loving aspiration-flames.

211.

If you have the power
In your mind
To rule the world,
Never use it!
If you have the love
In your heart
To become the world itself,
Then use it!

212.

When I am inside my mind-
    prison,
I serve time.
When I am inside my heart-
    garden,
I love time.

213.

His tranquillity-mind
Is not affected,
Although problems are tumbling
One on top of another.

214.

Not only unconsciously
But also consciously
My God-doubting mind
Is in league
With the hostile forces.

215.

If you have an iota of peace
In your mind,
Then you cannot snarl
And growl
At other seekers.

216.

Nothing can ever
Compensate God
For His infinite Compassion
For us.

217.

We must be always
On the royal road
To the palace
Of God-manifestation.

218.

When I lost contact
With my soul,
I became as destitute
As a street beggar.

219.

You are absolutely wrong
When you expect God
To placate you.

220.

Our Beloved Lord cries and cries
When He sees
That we are consciously allowing
Impatience to assail us.

221.

The smallest act
Of self-offering
Can give us
An ocean-vast joy.

222.

To smite our doubt-foe,
Let us bring to the fore
Our faith-sword.

223.

When our soul-birds carry us
On their blue-gold wings,
They take us directly to paradise.
There is no stopover on the way.

224.

You too can be
A great God-manifestation-hero,
If you can specialise
In sterling devotion.

225.

My Lord Supreme took me aside
For a moment
To speak to me in a silence-
    whisper:
"My child, I desperately need
Both your love and concern."

226.

You do not need a high soul
To embark on your God-journey.
What you need is a high goal.

227.

My mind admits
That it arrives nowhere
When it deliberately speaks ill
Of my heart.

228.

A God-loving seeker
Has a lifetime supply
Of God-Smiles.

229.

When God is really pleased
With our aspiration and
    dedication,
He shows us the private entrance
To His celestial Abode.

230.

At the beginning of time,
God gave us a route
To reach Him.
Those who think
They have discovered
A new route to God
Are all mistaken.

231.

There are some people
Who enjoy having a face-lift.
I am not one of those!
But please give me
A faith-lift,
Which I desperately need.

232.

If your life-breath
Is in your devotion-tears,
Then your Goal
Is within your reach.

233.

Everything in his life
Is weakened
By his long ignorance-
    imprisonment.

234.

Constant disobedience-fire
Within –
Total destruction-smoke
Without.

235.

Man's constant ingratitude
Is God's
Everyday experience.

236.

Nobody has forced me
To play the sad flute
Of a failure-life.

237.

Even my soul-stirring
Heart-peace-melody
Cannot satisfy my mind.

238.

A God-lover's obedience
Crowns his days
With boundless satisfaction.

239.

God tells me that
My love-devotion-surrender-
    letters
Do not need perfect grammar.

240.

If you live in your mind-jungle
All the time,
You are bound to suffer
From God-disobedience-
    blunders.

241.

God will come and embrace you
Only if you are prepared
To throw yourself headlong
Into the aspiration-sea.

242.

My aspiration-heart-room
Is always
Impurity-proof.

243.

I am constantly searching
For my heart's
Blissful peace-hermitage.

244.

Desire-fed worldly people
Are definitely
Homeless wanderers
In the inner life.

245.

God says to me
That He has read
More than He needed to
Of my promise-failure-letters.

246.

My willingness-heart-wealth
Is my soul's
Very special treasure.

247.

You are bound to arrive
At your Goal
If you continue to follow
God's discipline-schedule.

248.

A purity-heart
Is entitled to have
Sacredness-breath.

249.

My God-faith
And my God-devotion
Are my two most reliable oars.

250.

Nothing is incurable!
Nothing is unchangeable!
This should be the slogan
Of the God-believer.

251.

To his great shock and surprise,
Man chains himself
To the pillar of suffering.

252.

Every day my aspiration-heart
Makes a soulful flute
For me to play.

253.

Whenever I have a deep
   meditation,
I hear God's Nectar-Messages
Resonate in my delight-heart.

254.

My soul is using
All its divine light
To unearth my mind's
Doubt-landmines.

255.

Every morning
I deeply enjoy
My soul-fragrance-walk
Through my heart-garden.

256.

If you want to make
The fastest progress,
Try to stay as long as you can
In the sweet presence
Of a God-lover.

257.

Bind God's Feet
With your heart's love.
You will see your soul
Blinding your desire-eyes.

258.

The step from God-realisation
To God-manifestation
Can be infinitely longer
Than you can ever imagine.

259.

After staying on the spiritual path
For a long time,
If you leave the path,
Your life becomes a compendium
Of spiritual disasters.

260.

To pilot our aspiration-plane,
We need
A God-lover-pilot.

261.

O unfortunate seeker,
Do not worry.
God Himself will come
To take you out of your mind's
Impurity-tragedy-school.

262.

Alas, what has happened to me?
How is it that I have all of a
    sudden
Become a victim
Of my doubt-dominated mind?

263.

This morning God planted
Inside my heart
A special kind of faith-tree
That will climb far above
My mind's doubt-clouds.

264.

I am determined
To stop living
Inside the forest
Of my God-forgetfulness-mind.

265.

If we do not aspire
And offer our love to God
In the morning,
Then the whole day
Becomes a dull monotony
Of mechanical efforts.

266.

Those who do not get
Spontaneous joy
From the rainbow-dawn
Will find the day
A total failure.

267.

I plan to restart
My spiritual life anew.
This time my spiritual life
Will be "God for God's sake."

268.

May my life become
The goodness
Of a newness-hope
And the greatness
Of a fulness-promise.

269.

As soon as you enter
Into the spiritual life,
You must kindle
The flame of self-awareness.

270.

Truth has the capacity to shatter
And it ultimately does shatter
The pride of cynicism.

271.

My soul is advising me
To smile
As if I never had
A darkness-mind.

272.

The beauty of peace
And the fragrance of bliss
Shall remain together forever.

273.

Why should God's Compassion-
   Eye
Wait for you?
Walk, march, run and sprint
Towards God!
What for?
For your own satisfaction!

274.

Once I saw an inspiration-sun
Inside my eyes.
But now I see a destruction-
   volcano
Inside my eyes.

275.

To our great sorrow,
Our mind quite often enjoys
A hesitation-festival.

276.

My Supreme tells me
Again and again
That His Promise-Land
Is inside my fragrance-heart
And nowhere else.

277.

My mind enjoys
Competition-fire.
My heart enjoys
Cooperation-stars.

278.

The security of the heart
Longs for God's Command.
Insecurity seeks its own company.

279.

My heart lives
On God's
Compassion-Protection-Smiles.

280.

My Lord, every day
At every moment
I implore Your absolute
    Command.

281.

If you claim any superiority
Over others,
Then you are nowhere
Near perfection.

282.

To serve one's Master
With sterling devotion
Is, indeed, the fastest way
To arrive at God's Palace.

283.

I do not look
For a man-made crown,
But I sleeplessly and breathlessly
    long
For God's Compassion-Eye.

284.

When I do not aspire,
When I do not pray
And when I do not meditate,
My mind becomes the heavy
    weight
Of futile frustration.

285.

Alas, my mind
Is a blighted dream
And my heart
Is a dashed hope.

286.

To become an excellent
    instrument
Of my Lord Supreme,
At every moment I must offer Him
My heart's delight-tears.

287.

I do not know when and how
Depression has found a home
In my vital.

288.

No matter how hard we try,
It is almost impossible
To escape our desire-prison.

289.

God has kept in front of you
Both desire-wings and aspiration-
    wings.
Why are you not using aspiration-
    wings
To fly to God's Summit-Palace?

290.

My mind
Is trained on God,
But my heart
Was trained by God.

291.

Every day
I want to hear
God's Victory-celebration-drums.

292.

Only the music
Of the aspiration-heart
Can unlock the door
Of Heaven.

293.

My heart dresses
In rainbows
To pay a visit
To my Lord Supreme.

294.

If you ever lose your life's
God-surrender-keys,
Then how will you unlock
God's Heart-Door?

295.

To know what is destined
Is unnecessary.
But to know what role
You are supposed to play
In God's Cosmic Play
Is absolutely necessary.

296.

Together they went to God:
My aspiration-heart
And my dedication-life.

297.

Do not expect God
To approve everything you do
And everything you say.
Just pray to God
To give you the capacity
To do the right thing always.

298.

God does not always want you
To come Home immediately.
If you are totally exhausted,
Then take rest
Until you can resume your
    journey.

299.

There is every possibility
That one day our mind-
    knowledge
Will explode
And our heart-wisdom
Will expand.

300.

Our high-altitude God-visions
Will ultimately transform
The four corners of the globe.

301.

The computer-mind-speed
Will never be able
To save the world.

302.

The oneness-heart-speed
Will definitely be able
Not only to save the world
But to elevate the world.

303.

There is no reason
Why your aspiration-decline
Has to last
For such a long time.

304.

O my doubt-enemy,
I never thought
That you would be
So formidable.

305.

There is nothing wrong
With each and every generation
Defining God.

306.

As we are addicted
To outer rules and regulations,
Even so,
We should be devoted
To our inner laws and ordinances.

307.

May each newborn thought
In my mind
Open immediately its eyes
To my heart's inner light.

308.

I do not know
If any great soul
Does not suffer
From oppressive
And weighty problems.

309.

God wants me to destroy
My mind-computer completely
To avert my spiritual disaster.

310.

If your aspiration-heart
Is devoid of intensity,
Your God-realisation
Will always remain a far cry.

311.

To begrudge the happiness
Of others
Is to delay one's own happiness
Indefinitely.

312.

To my great joy,
My mind's doubt-interest
Is rapidly waning.

313.

Each human life
So often is found
In a bewildering sea
Of uncertainty.

314.

O my mischief-making mind,
One day you are bound
To sit at the Feet
Of my God-loving heart.

315.

I am so proud to see
That all my doubts
Are proudly finishing
Their last acts.

316.

I tried to please man
In his own way.
I have failed!
Now I am trying to please God
In His own Way.
My Lord says to me:
"My child, you have already done
    it!"

317.

Alas, in vain I am trying and
    trying
To come out of my medley
Of confusing and confused
    thoughts.

318.

When the simplicity-safeguard-
    life,
The sincerity-safeguard-mind
And the purity-safeguard-heart
Work together,
They prove that they are
    invincible.

319.

The fog of our uncertainty-mind
Does not dare to come
Near our soul
When it whispers
To our heart.

320.

My expectation-boat has capsized.
Therefore, I am now ready
To embark on the real spiritual
    life.

321.

My soul has come forward
To train my life
To the highest pitch
Of God-reliance.

322.

My Lord's unconditional
Compassion-Eye
Is bulldozing all my doubts
Out of the way.

323.

God and God's Concern
Always escort me
All the way
To my Divinity's Home.

324.

My paradise is only inside
My God-gratitude-heart,
And nowhere else.

325.

God has told my surrender-life
And gratitude-heart
That they can enter
The court of Heaven
At any time that they want to.

326.

If you can please God
In God's own Way
Here on earth,
Then instead of trembling,
You will be dancing
When you arrive at the gate of
    death.

327.

May my aspiration-heart-speed
Be faster than
The fleetest of horses.

328.

Each time I sing
A God-Victory-song,
God asks me to mount
His own
World-manifestation-chariot.

329.

God loves only
The love inside me
That He has already
Given me.

330.

So far,
Nobody has discovered
A successful remedy
For an ingratitude-mind.

331.

No matter what I do,
God always keeps me
In His Heart-Embrace.

332.

For a human mind
Not to have restless thoughts
Is almost an impossibility.

333.

To sit on the throne of time,
Our life has to be armed
With prayers and meditations.

334.

My heart enjoys
Regular adventures
In my soul's country.

335.

God's Grace embodies
Not only enlightenment
But also enchantment.

336.

By staying always
In a state of depression,
You make your Lord Supreme
Extremely unhappy.

337.

Each time you deliberately
Do something wrong,
You must realise
You are sinking once more
Below the waves of ignorance-sea.

338.

The mind has to be freed
From unlit thought-hunger
Every day.

339.

The soul invites
The heart, mind, vital and body
To accompany it
While it is swimming
In God's Ocean of Bliss.
Only the heart at times
Accepts the invitation.

340.

God's Forgiveness-Power
Is the magic touch
Of God's Compassion-Eye.

341.

Disobedience does not know
That it will be chased
By destruction.

342.

O my mind,
God's Will is not
An object of frustration,
But it is
An object of adoration.

343.

My Lord's Satisfaction-Smile
Is within easy reach
Of my gratitude-heart.

344.

Tears stream
From the Heart-Eye of God
When I say that
I am not meant for
The spiritual life.

345.

May my aspiration-heart-tree
Every day offer
Fresh and sacred blossoms.

346.

Without faith,
A man is like
A waterless cloud.

347.

God does not mind
If I quarrel with Him,
As long as I agree
At the end of the quarrel
That I am wrong and He is right.

348.

God is so pleased
That I have requested Him
To undertake
My mind-transformation-task.

349.

My purity-heart
Is my only
Safe shelter.

350.

You get no satisfaction-result
From your spiritual life
Because for you
God is only a word,
Nothing more.

351.

You must increase
Your imagination-height,
Your inspiration-height
And your aspiration-height
All at the same time
Every day.

352.

If you want to sit
In the front seat of God's Car,
Then you must offer Him first
The beauty and fragrance
Of your aspiration-heart-flower.

353.

A soulful question
Always receives
A blessingful answer.

354.

I am so happy
That my mind
Is totally disappointed
With playing with doubt.

355.

I have replaced most happily
My mind-victory-thirst
With my God-Victory-hunger.

356.

When the oneness-heart
Comes to the fore,
Victory cannot remain invisible.

357.

To me, a powerful
And blessingful Smile
From my Lord
Is far more significant
Than the Bliss of Heaven.

358.

I am always hungry
For God's Peace-Breakfast
And not man's power-lunch.

359.

O my mind,
Do not remain anymore
A spirituality-spectator,
But become
A spirituality-participant!

360.

Only when I become
A sacred mind
Does God share with me
His secret Thoughts.

361.

To seal all the ignorance-holes
Of the mind
Is imperative.

362.

My life becomes a wave of joy
When my heart
Is armed with faith.

363.

Because of your
Devouring doubt-mind,
God does not want
To be visible to you.

364.

I am truly, powerfully
And endlessly proud
Of my oneness-blossoming
And oneness-spreading heart.

365.

My Lord's
Forgiveness-Heart-Nest
Has captured me and my all.

366.

My Lord's Satisfaction-Smile
Is my only reason
For living on earth.

367.

Three things have to be done
Sooner than at once:
My God-aspiration,
My God-realisation
And my God-manifestation.

368.

I need only
God's Compassion-Eye
To remain in
My life's control-tower.

369.

Each time my life makes progress,
God sings a special Pride-Song
For me and my life.

370.

Man's faith-gift-offering
To God
Is man's highest achievement.

371.

My Lord,
Do show me the way
To undo the wrongs
That I have already done.

372.

My Lord,
From this very moment
I shall destroy my age-old
Ignorance-attachment.

373.

My Lord,
Come quickly and break my head
Into millions of pieces
To save my poor heart!

374.

Encouraging
Is my God-search.
Inspiring
Is my God-chosen path.
Fulfilling
Are my God-offering-cries.

375.

Secretly I wait
In my Lord's Heart-Room,
Devotedly to serve Him
When He is in need.

376.

The finish line is at once
Blissful to see
But painful to reach.

377.

The more I am generous
With my heart,
The more I am precious
In God's Heart.

378.

When we are our indomitable
    will,
The temptation-wall falls down
At our feet.

379.

Do not enter into
The temptation-tunnel.
It is inexplicably dark.

380.

Nobody can force you
To have doubt
On every page
Of your life-book.

381.

The mind is satisfied
With good fortune.
The heart is only satisfied
With God-fortune.

382.

O seeker, no more rest!
It is high time for you
To resume your aspiration-ascent.

383.

Only with your heart's
Devotion-tears
Can you sound
God's Victory-Trumpet.

384.

My Lord,
In my inner world,
You are my secret hope.
In my outer world,
You are my sacred promise.

385.

You say that
You do not know
When God is pleased with you.
I am telling you the supreme
    secret:
God is pleased with you
Only when you are pleased with
    Him.

386.

One by one
The soul offers its divinities
To the Absolute Supreme.

387.

My Lord, my Lord,
It is only at Your Compassion-Feet
That my gratitude-heart's bumper
    crop
Grows.

388.

There is a constant
Affection-play
Between my soul and my heart.
There is also a constant
Attachment-play
Between my mind and my vital.

389.

My bleeding heart
Has the prayerful capacity
To touch the pinnacle
Of God's Compassion-Eye.

390.

The world mistrusts you
And mistreats you.
But love the world all the more,
For that is what God expects
From you.

391.

My Lord,
You never waste
Even an iota of time.
May I not be
Your most devoted follower?

392.

The doubting mind does not
    realise
That it is engaged in a headlong
    rush
Towards its own destruction.

393.

God wants both God-lovers
And God-servers
To remain always on the alert.

394.

My heart strongly feels
That there are more God-yearning
    lovers
Than God-manifesting servers.

395.

Be careful of your
Overconfidence-sermon!
God is listening.

396.

Each sincere prayer
Is a sincere effort
To catch the doubt-thief
In our mind.

397.

I am so proud
Of my aspiration-heart
For radiating sunshine-beauty
Around my life.

398.

Unlike the mind,
No matter how weak the heart is,
It does not betray God's Trust.

399.

Do not hide from the eye
Of criticism.
Face it and disgrace it!

400.

True, obstacles may seem to be
Insurmountable,
But they are no match
For God's Compassion-Eye.

401.

Ask not:
"Why?"
Say:
"It is all done!"

402.

God's faith
In me
Admits of no doubt.

403.

The mind
Is a world-peace-stranger
And
A world-peace-strangler.

404.

The heart
Is a world-peace-dreamer
And
A world-peace-lover.

405.

The inevitable necessity
Must
Be fulfilled.

406.

Man-question
Is a soldier.
God-answer
Is a singer.

407.

Regret-torture
Can easily
Be avoided.

408.

Nothing can resist the mind
When it becomes
A God-determination-
    manifestation-rock.

409.

The tears of my heart
At every moment cherish
God-Affection-Smiles.

410.

In vain the computer-mind
Tries to silence
The oneness-beauty
Of the aspiring heart.

411.

The athlete of the heart
Runs and jumps
Inside the soul's
Illumination-garden.

412.

God blesses
Doubt-conquering faith
With peace-sun-satisfaction.

413.

Every Avatar
Is a new
God-Arrival-announcer.

414.

My God-expansion-heart and I
Are enjoying
My mind's ego-explosion.

415.

My intense and unreserved
Love of God
Has many times surpassed
The speed of time.

416.

The light in the heart of man
Can easily guide
The eyes of man.

417.

Life's tasteless fruits
Can be turned into sweetness
    itself
By God's Compassion-Touch.

418.

O my mind,
What makes you think
That you can always sit
In the judgement seat?

419.

My soul's voiceless voice
Always remains
Close to my heart.

420.

The stars of the sky
Always adorn
Only the brave.

421.

An Avatar is he
Who lovingly and faithfully
Brings the longing of man
To the Absolute Supreme.

422.

Be on the alert always!
At any moment
You can stumble
On the way to Heaven.

423.

God treasures
Your gratitude-tears
More than anything else.

424.

How beautiful, charming,
Illumining and fulfilling
Is my rising moon
Above the horizon!

425.

Be careful
Of your dissatisfied mind.
It can before long
Become rebellious.

426.

God blows His Joy-Whistles
In the child-heart
Of the seeker.

427.

The ecstasy-flooded flute
Of the soul
Never stops playing.

428.

At last
My mind is freed
From desire-headaches!

429.

Do not forget
To keep your vital-tiger
On a very short leash.

430.

He is really fortunate
Who does not have to carry
Excess attachment-weight.

431.

Worries, anxieties and
    frustrations
Are found in abundant measure
On the temptation-road.

432.

Change your inner attitude first!
Your outer environment
Will automatically change.

433.

I have two rooms to live in:
My illumining mind-room
And
My beautifying heart-room.

434.

My soul is teaching my heart
How to climb up
To the very summit of self-giving.

435.

Rich imagination you need.
Richer inspiration you need.
Richest aspiration you need.

436.

It seems each and every
Individual mind
Is susceptible
To frustration-torture.

437.

Man's desire-story
Will become
A fable.

438.

Man's aspiration-songs
Will become
A legend.

439.

To desire God
Is a common
Hunger.

440.

To satisfy God
Is an exquisitely uncommon
Meal.

441.

In my own life
I shall become
A God-satisfaction-tower
That can never be tarnished.

442.

Offer a smile-gift
To every eye.
Your God-hunger-heart
Will be nourished.

443.

The neutral moment
And
The compromising hour
Will never succeed.

444.

Heartily embrace
The challenge
Of human nature-transformation.

445.

My heart and I proudly observe
The funeral procession
Of my ignorance-mind.

446.

The earth-bound desire-mind
Is apt to swim
In a goalless circle.

447.

My pure soul
Receives undeserved
   mistreatment
From my body, vital and mind.

448.

My soul is my perfect
Mind-purification-
Counsellor.

449.

My heart is my strict
Mind-ignorance-appointment-
Canceller.

450.

Every morning
God blesses me
With a new aspiration-tear
And a new dedication-smile.

451.

Every day
I expand my tiny heart
With streaming tears
To please my Lord Supreme.

452.

Every day try to feel
The blossoming goodness
Of others
As your very own.

453.

Your heart's God-surrender-joy
Can easily conquer
Your mind's doubt-thoughts.

454.

If you are looking for peace,
Then look for it
Inside your oneness-heart-depth,
And nowhere else.

455.

The beauty of newness
And
The fragrance of willingness
Can easily be found
Inside the eagerness-heart.

456.

Tears of joy
Can purify and illumine
The sorrows of the heart.

457.

Deep meditation
Does have the power
To remove all mind-barriers.

458.

My God-willingness-heart
Has melted
All my mind-resistance.

459.

God is ready to speak to me
Only when I offer Him
My silence-heart.

460.

God tells His Life-History in full —
Lovingly, affectionately
And self-givingly —
To the unconditional surrender-
    life
Of a seeker.

461.

My aspiration, my dedication
And my realisation—
Everything that I have and I am—
Is in the ever-blossoming process
Of God's Will-fulfilment.

462.

May my life be full
Of everything
That is spiritually beautiful,
Soulful and fruitful!

463.

If you have patience
In abundant measure,
You can succeed
In your outer life.

464.

If you have surrender
In boundless measure,
You can succeed
In your inner life.

465.

It seems that we all have
Two hearts within us:
One heart is for God-adoration
And
One heart is for man-admiration.

466.

My negativity-mind disappears
The moment I accept
God's Will as my own will.

467.

My gratitude-heart
Always bears testimony
To my Lord's Compassion-Flood.

468.

A sleepless gratitude-heart
Is tantamount
To a great miracle.

469.

The Smiles that we receive
From our Lord Beloved Supreme
For manifesting Him on earth
Can never be calculated
By our human mind.

470.

God feasts His Eyes
On the happiness-news
That my heart offers to Him.

471.

The exquisite beauty of the soul
Can never be robbed
By human desires.

472.

My Lord, like You
I do not want to spend
Even a fleeting moment
Complaining.

473.

My Lord, like Your Heart
I want my heart also
To be empty of anger
And frustration.

474.

Alas, my uncertainty-mind and I
Have been living together
For a very long time!

475.

Even though I do not have
Any right,
God does not mind
If I ask Him for a favour.

476.

God tells me
That if I want to start again
With my spiritual life,
Then I must abandon
    immediately
All my guilt-miseries.

477.

I treasure every peace-thought
Of my mind
Inside my God-gratitude-heart.

478.

One single God-Compassion-Look
Is the master-key
That unlocks and discards
All my mind-problems.

479.

Not the happiness
That comes and goes,
But the silence-fulness
That comes and never goes
Is what I need.

480.

Today we can avoid God's Will,
Perhaps even tomorrow,
But we cannot forever and forever
Avoid God's Will.

481.

You may not believe
In the power of your prayer,
But God firmly believes in it.

482.

The destined Hour has struck!
I must place
My disobedience-insolence-mind
At the Feet
Of my Lord Beloved Supreme.

483.

All the beauty
Of the world within
And the world without
Has the same Source:
God's Compassion-Eye.

484.

O my devotion-heart-fountain,
Where are you?
I have been searching for you
For such a long time!

485.

I must obliterate
My past
Failure-life-torture.

486.

The hostile forces
Fail to catch me
When I become a completely
God-dependent seeker.

487.

I enjoy Immortality's Nectar-Bliss
The moment I receive
From my Master
A sweetness-affection-smile.

488.

When I pray and meditate
To please God in His own Way,
He tells me:
"My child, I am giving you
A mind inundated with silence-
    peace."

489.

O seeker, do not waste your time
Thinking of the distance
To your destination.
I tell you in secrecy supreme
That your destination
Is much closer than you think.

490.

My Lord, my only desire:
The capacity
To devotedly blossom
At Your Lotus-Feet.

491.

To reach your loftiest
Aspiration-summit-height,
Offer all your gratitude-tears
And gratitude-smiles
Simultaneously
To God's Compassion-Eye.

492.

My humility-mind
And my purity-heart
Are my life's real safeguards.

493.

Finally my heart's wisdom-key
Has unlocked all my mind's
Obstruction-doors.

494.

Let my mind
Be as old as the world itself,
But I want my heart
To be as young as a bud.

495.

The heart that is inspired
By God's Compassion-Eye
Does not need wings to fly.

496.

May my mind
Be fully aware
Of disobedience-disasters.

497.

Quite often the enthusiasm
Of the human mind
Is next to zero.

498.

It is an easy task
For the doubting mind
To be a gossip-collector.

499.

Under God's Protection-Eye,
Not even a weakling
Can stumble.

500.

With my soul's adamantine
Will-power,
I have trampled my disobedience-
    mind
Into the dust.

501.

My soul has made
A blessingful promise
To my heart, mind
Vital and body
To show them God's Face.

502.

My Lord has kept His Promise.
All Heaven-born dreams
Are flowering
Inside my life.

503.

Avoid
The confusion-life-abyss
All the time!

504.

I have buried
My yesterday's mind
Completely.

505.

It is unnecessary to be
Today
What we were yesterday.

506.

God's unconditional Grace
Has descended.
My desert-mind is blooming
And blossoming.

507.

Anything unconditional
Surprises
Everybody.

508.

When aspiration
Is tired of aspiring,
Confusion comes to the fore
And becomes the ruler.

509.

My Lord,
Your express Command
I humbly take
As my life-heart-song.

510.

A genuinely aspiring heart
Asks everything for God
And nothing for itself.

511.

May my heart every day
Become
A God-satisfying prayer.

512.

O my mind,
Finally your total
Transformation-time
Has arrived!

513.

Just one Compassion-Smile
From my Lord Supreme
Is needed
To change my mind's bitterness
Into my heart's sweetness.

514.

To my greatest joy,
Meditation-silence once more
Is rising in my heart.

515.

The human mind
Is terribly afraid
Of the presence
Of divine Love.

516.

God loves immensely
Even my amateur
God-aspiring heart
And God-serving life.

517.

Every day I pray to God
To bless me with the capacity
To offer Him a sumptuous
Gratitude-meal.

518.

No mind can come
To God's Country
Without crossing
God's Silence-Bridge.

519.

If you are not one hundred
    percent
On God's side,
God will not give you His Ladder
To climb up to His highest
    Height.

520.

For the poor seekers
Vacation is granted,
But not for the rich seekers.

521.

God is extremely fond
Of my life's
Pilgrim-progress-smile.

522.

My joy knows no bounds
Because today I have turned over
A new
Love-devotion-surrender-leaf.

523.

Desire-fulfilment
And life-enlightenment
Are never allowed to meet
    together
By my Lord Supreme.

524.

In the morning
I take two deep breaths:
A blossoming hope-breath
And a fulfilling promise-breath.

525.

To silence my desire-storm,
My life and I
Have prayerfully placed our
    surrender
At the Feet
Of our Lord Beloved Supreme.

526.

God asks
My desiring mind
To leave Him alone.

527.

God is making
My aspiring heart
Ready to be
His Divinity's Throne.

528.

All my world-fears have vanished
Into thin air
Since I have taken shelter
Inside my God's Smile.

529.

Every morning
God blessingfully helps me
To be on the same wavelength
As His Sweetness-Compassion-
    Whispers.

530.

The stronger your
God-obedience-loyalty,
The faster you will run
Towards God's Palace.

531.

God gives us the capacity
To be uniquely qualified
Not only for His infinite Grace,
But also for His immortal Pride.

532.

Every day,
Each and every inspiring,
Aspiring and self-giving thought
I celebrate
With my God-gratitude-joy.

533.

I shake my head in utter disbelief
When my Lord tells me
I am a choice instrument of His.

534.

How beautiful and how powerful
Is the silver whisper
Of a golden dream!

535.

If our God-gaze is fixed
And unwavering,
Then God invites us
To come and play with Him
For as long as we want to.

536.

My soul does not believe
In games of secrecy.
My soul believes only
In games of ecstasy.

537.

My soul's two favourite pastimes:
Self-offering
And God-manifestation.

538.

O my willingness, do not delay!
Eagerness is waiting for you
At your door
So both of you can start
Your Godward journey.

539.

Every morning I offer two songs
To my Lord Beloved Supreme:
My mind's enthusiasm-song
And my heart's gratitude-song.

540.

My soul is fully confident
That eventually my doubting
    mind
Will surrender
And follow my aspiring heart.

541.

Alas,
I am totally shocked to see
That my aspiration-credit card
Expired long ago.

542.

Invariably my soul caters
To my heart's
God-hunger.

543.

O my mind, be not a fool!
Do not swing all the time
On your indecisiveness-
    pendulum.
Like my heart, swing on
Your God-devotion-pendulum.

544.

Be strong, be brave, be perfect
In every way
So that no unaspiring human
    being
Can drag you
And your aspiration down!

545.

My aspiring heart
And my serving life
Are finally enjoying
The surrender of my God-
    doubting
And God-denying mind.

546.

May my obedience-mind
Stand like an immortal statue
In my heart-garden.

547.

My Lord wants me
To chat with Him
More than He wants me
To sing for Him.

548.

My Lord,
When I deliberately absent myself
From Your Presence,
My life becomes
A living nightmare.

549.

My Lord Supreme
Wants me to believe
That I am infinitely higher
And stronger
Than I imagine.

550.

God-realisation
Is far beyond
The flight of imagination.

551.

Satisfaction shall greet
All your efforts
If surrender looms large
In your life.

552.

He started with willingness,
But on his way to God,
Eagerness met him
And accompanied him.

553.

Life's experiences
Roam
On zigzag roads.

554.

You do not have time,
But God has plenty of time.
Therefore, He does not mind
Crying for you.

555.

Sleepless faith is necessary
To nurture
One's fastest aspiration-speed.

556.

God gives His private number
Only to the aspiring heart
And not to the torturing mind.

557.

What you need
Is the beauty of discipline
And not the storm
Of self-indulgence.

558.

The mind's sunrise
Is quite baffling.
The mind's sunset
Is so inspiring.

559.

My mind,
Have nerves of steel!
Doubt is fast approaching you.

560.

Although I meet my Lord
Only on rare occasions,
I love Him more
Than I could ever imagine.

561.

I thought my journey
Towards God's Palace
Would be quite short.
But now I see that
This was a tragic miscalculation.

562.

God asks me
To come to Him
With sacred steps,
And not with secret steps.

563.

The human mind
Is so often afraid
Of striking out
Against injustice-night.

564.

A purity-heart just loves
To embrace God's Will
All the time.

565.

You just become
A total surrender-life.
God Himself will hoist
Your victory-banner.

566.

My soul tells me
That God will succeed
Only when I proceed.

567.

My Lord, do You really
Care for me?
"My child, I do!
I do not have anything better
To do."

568.

My Lord, do You really
Care for me?
"My child, I do!
I feel this is the best thing
I can do
For our inseparable oneness."

569.

My Lord, do You really
Care for me?
"My child, there was a time
When I cared for you,
But not now!
Do you know why?
In those days you claimed Me
As your own.
Alas, now your soul tells Me
That this is a long-forgotten
    story."

570.

God tells me
To stay at His Feet
Not only devotedly
But also proudly.

571.

There is no stormy day
In human life
That cannot be transformed
Into the brightest sunrise.

572.

Peace is within your reach.
Do not be afraid
Of touching it,
Feeling it
And claiming it.

573.

Two key questions
Of human life:
Does God really care
For humanity?
Does God really need humanity?

574.

An unbearable disaster:
The Master asked the disciple
To leave.

575.

An unthinkable disaster:
The disciple left
The Master.

576.

When the Master
Asks the disciple to leave,
He may give the disciple another
    chance
In the course of time.

577.

When the disciple
Leaves the Master,
The Master is under no obligation
To take the disciple back.

578.

Somehow we allow
Untold sufferings
To loom large
On our heart's horizon.

579.

God expects everybody
To be an excellent learner
In His Heart-School.

580.

No more
Shall I remain
A world-compliment-begging
Mind.

581.

Every day I pray and pray
And pray to God
To bless me
With a oneness-blossoming heart.

582.

Your willingness-signal
Has made God
Immensely happy.

583.

My Lord,
I am praying to You
For Your inner Affection
And not for Your outer Attention.

584.

A sweetness-heart
Has a free access
To God's Satisfaction-Heart.

585.

Like my heart,
I shall make my mind also
A hallowed purity-shrine.

586.

In spirituality
The inner oneness
And outer fulness
Must go together.

587.

A God-blossoming heart
I sleeplessly longed for,
And now I have it.

588.

Where do I live?
I live in between
My mind's ingratitude-jungle
And my heart's gratitude-garden.

589.

An insincerity-mind
Must be kept
Under control.

590.

True, I have done many things
Uninspiring, unillumining
And unfulfilling,
But I feel that I am
Accountable
Only to my Lord Supreme.

591.

My soul is telling my heart
That it will be very happy
Only if my heart lives
In God's Neighbourhood.

592.

Alas, I have been fighting
And fighting
With my stubborn mind!

593.

God is working day and night
To establish His permanent
   friendship
With my mind.

594.

I am happy when I have
God's Eye
Inside my heart.

595.

I am happier when I see
God's Heart
Inside my heart.

596.

I am happiest when I feel
God's Feet
Blessing my heart.

597.

My heart's faith
Chased my mind's doubt,
Finally caught it
And disarmed it completely.

598.

An unaspiring mind
Is a perfect stranger
To hope and promise.

599.

In life's tug-of-war,
Paradise is nowhere
To be found.

600.

May my aspiration-heart
Every day, without fail,
Rise like the morning sun.

601.

My gratitude-heart
And my surrender-life
Are two God-microphones.

602.

If you would like to be
God's first-class server,
Then be simplicity incarnate,
Sincerity incarnate
And purity incarnate.

603.

My Lord, what shall I do
When the whole world
Speaks ill of me?
Shall I laugh or shed tears?
"My child, just remain silent!"

604.

God finds gold
Inside our smiles.
He finds diamonds
Inside our tears.

605.

In the world
Of dissatisfaction-frustration
My mind roams and roams.

606.

I do not have to prove anything
To God,
But I have to prove each and every
    thing
To myself.

607.

Each seeker has
Two far-away dreams:
His God-realisation-dream
And his God-manifestation-
    dream.

608.

My aspiration-heart
Is the only reality
That I call my own.

609.

May my aspiration, dedication
And surrender
Speed up to thwart ignorance.

610.

There is no such thing
As a maximum
Aspiration-speed limit.

611.

Every day our complaint-volume
For God
Is becoming larger and larger.

612.

Finally I have forced
My desire-dragon
To leave me
And live inside the darkness-
   abyss.

613.

O my seeker-friend,
You must realise
That God never wants you
To lament the past.
He wants you to go forward
Faster than the fastest.

614.

I love
My God-ordained burdens
And not my self-styled burdens.

615.

Regularly, devotedly and
   faithfully
You must weed out
All impurity-thoughts
From your mind.

616.

May my everyday life
Be a roaring waterfall
Of creativity.

617.

There is a constant interaction
Between my mind's doubts
And my life's worries.

618.

If you want to be happy,
Really happy,
Then you must needs keep
Simplicity, sincerity and purity
In your life-environment.

619.

A strong desire
Has not only a voracious
But also a ferocious
World-devouring hunger.

620.

A desire-mind
Is terribly afraid
Of sunshine-transformation.

621.

The mind's reasoning power
Has considerably weakened
The aspiration-world.

622.

The insecurity of the heart
Is born
Out of the jealousy of the mind.

623.

Life's uncertain directions
Are meant only for those
Who have not entered
Into the spiritual life.

624.

The aspiration-heart must take
Longer than the longest
And faster than the fastest steps.

625.

Every day your Master
Blessingfully supplies you
With a gold compassion-coin.
Use it with wisdom-light!

626.

If you have sincerity in your
    obedience,
Then you will, without fail,
Not only follow
But also understand God's Will.

627.

Alas, I am expert at seeing
The things wrong in others
That have been looming large
Inside my own life.

628.

To the extreme sorrow
Of my aspiration-heart,
The gratitude-world
Still remains unexplored.

629.

I am helplessly and hopelessly
Devastated
By my mind's disobedience-
    insolence.

630.

A life of unconditional surrender
Is God's only prescription
For humanity's imperfection-life.

631.

Alas, there are very few students
Who are eager to study
At God's Heart-School.

632.

A superiority-sneer
Will never be able
To endear itself to God's Heart.

633.

God has a habit of repeating
    Himself
So that nobody remains
With His Philosophy unlearned.

634.

My Lord, I have nothing else
Save and except
My heart-rending cries,
Which I place devotedly
And self-givingly at Your Feet.

635.

Alas, how desperately
My God-doubting mind
Is trying to obliterate
My heart's fountain-love for God!

636.

Never allow your mind's
Darkness-pride
To eclipse your oneness-heart-sky.

637.

To find
An equanimity-mind
Is almost an impossibility.

638.

A seeker's unconditional
Gratitude-heart to God
Definitely has a place
In the galaxy of stars.

639.

I want to worship the God
Who is singing, playing and
    dancing
Right in front of me,
And not an aloof God.

640.

It is I who am responsible
In every way
For my doomed failure-life.

641.

The fragrance of my soul
Comes from its constant
And unreserved
God-satisfaction.

642.

My louder than the loudest
    laughter
Is, indeed,
One of my life-preservers.

643.

May my life be blessed
Every day
With new God-gratitude-heart-
    petals.

644.

God has blessingfully sent
His Protection-Wings
To carry me to His highest
    Heaven.
But alas,
Where is my readiness,
Where is my willingness,
Where is my eagerness,
Where?

645.

Before I walk along
The sunlit Path to God,
I must first ring my heart's
Devotion-bell.

646.

My Lord Supreme,
Why do You allow me
To forget You so often?
"My child, I fearfully obey
Your mind's express order."

647.

Alas,
I am forced to live
Between my impatience-torture-
    mind
And my patience-rapture-heart.

648.

He has cast aside
His doubting mind.
Lo, the beauty of his soul
Is dancing on his face
Once again.

649.

Not a forced surrender
But a prayerful and cheerful
   surrender
Is the winner
Of the divine race.

650.

God blesses
The gratitude-heart-sky
Of each seeker
With His own Victory-Flag.

651.

God-centredness
Is the source
Of universal oneness.

652.

The heights of Heaven
Remain far beyond the reach
Of human expectation.

653.

Do not delay, my seeker-friend!
Immediately start steering
Your God-Destination-boat.

654.

My soul's adamantine will
Helps me all the time
To break through the stormy
   obstacles
Created by my mind.

655.

If falsehood
You keep out of your mind,
Peace will hasten towards you.

656.

Do not catch depression!
It will before long
Turn into something fatal.

657.

To unleash the divine power
Within you,
Make your inner faith
Complete and perfect.

658.

He who is reluctant
To break stones
Will never be able to become
A path-maker.

659.

The mind always tries
To heap doubt-clouds
Upon the aspiring heart.

660.

Do not allow yourself
To be tempted
To visit your past life.
You may be voraciously devoured
By the tiger of your past!

661.

Smile, always smile!
You will be able to disarm
Even your worst foe.

662.

Be careful!
Do not allow
Your vital-depression-flames
To spread
Into your God-searching mind.

663.

The seeker in me
Is now enjoying
My mind's volcano-doubt-
	explosion.

664.

Every God-experience
Has the capacity
To move and shake the whole
	world.

665.

Obey implicitly and devotedly
The dictates
Of your all-illumining soul.

666.

At God's choice Hour,
Everybody's God-love awakens.
Nobody can be either too soon
Or too late!

667.

Every day
My mind starts praying
And my heart starts meditating
When dawn starts showing
Its beautiful and cheerful
Rainbow-colours.

668.

Your unbending and unwilling
   mind
Is taking you
Farther than the farthest
From your own inner divinity.

669.

Never surrender
To your unready mind
If you want to succeed
In your spiritual life.

670.

God's Heart
Is always expecting
Your safe and cheerful return.

671.

The cosmic gods
Love to live
On the fragrance of Mother Earth.

672.

My Lord Supreme,
I am so grateful to You
For blessing me and my life
Every day
With a new dream.

673.

My Lord, do bless me
With ever-quickening steps
Towards my supreme
   Destination.

674.

God always wants me
To take shelter
Under the canopy
Of His unconditional Love.

675.

Do not suffocate your life
With your mind's insincerity
And your heart's insecurity.

676.

Arrogance, insolence
And intolerance
Are three intimate roommates.

677.

Artificial sincerity
Cannot avoid
Imminent disaster.

678.

Because outer prosperity
You have amassed,
Your inner prosperity
Has disappeared.

679.

Is there any place on earth
Not swarming
With insincere seekers?

680.

No matter how insincere
And impure we are,
God still remains His Forgiveness-
    Heart.

681.

Remorse is not the answer!
Determination
To do the right thing
Is the answer of answers.

682.

Not an aspiring
But an unaspiring human being
Has to depend totally on his fate.

683.

The purity in our mind
Passes away
As swiftly as a shooting star.

684.

Human life
Is nothing short of
An insane chase
After earthly pleasures.

685.

Disobedience means
Being deliberately deaf
To God's Nectar-Message.

686.

My prayers and my meditations
Are the shields
That protect me
From ignorance-attacks.

687.

Each God-loving thought
Is an antidote
For our mind-miseries.

688.

The rising sun
Tells me where to go.
The setting sun
Tells me where to stay.

689.

A truly aspiring heart
Does not want to be
A citizen of frustration-country.

690.

My mind,
What a fool you are!
You do not care to answer
Our Lord's
Blessingful and powerful Knock.

691.

My heart's tears and smiles
Have, indeed,
God-pleasing capacities.

692.

Only a oneness-heart
Can swim in the fulness
Of the universal sea.

693.

The soul of the morning
Every day sings
A new song
For Mother Earth.

694.

Every day
I cheerfully and proudly
Participate in two races:
Aspiration-race
And dedication-race.

695.

We must obliterate
All the fingerprints
Of doubt
From our mind!

696.

Meditation is
Our heart's secret
And sacred treasure.

697.

O seeker-friend,
I clearly see
How sincerely you are trying
To free yourself
From your mind's notorious
Doubt-obstinacy.

698.

To the heart's determination-rock
The body, the vital and the mind
Have to flock.

699.

My Lord unreservedly
    sympathises
With the sadness
That devastates my heart.

700.

My prayerfully smiling gladness
Gladdens
My Heavenly soul.

701.

Humanity's
Pilgrim-sunrise-days
Will never be over.

702.

Surrender is a prayerful, cheerful,
    Sleepless and breathless
God-commitment.

703.

Disobedience is not
A mere incident,
But a serious accident.

704.

No spiritual Master
Wants his life
To be thronged
By curiosity-mongers.

705.

The lives of so many human
    beings
Are governed
By superficial happiness.

706.

Pride says to God,
"I do not need You.
That is an understatement!"

707.

Insolent disobedience
Is followed by
Endless disaster.

708.

Impurity of the mind
Is an inner cancer
In a seeker's life.

709.

Seekers are expected to be
Divine swimmers
And swim against the stream
Of past bad habits.

710.

I have come to learn
That all short cuts to God-
    realisation
Are not only fruitless but also
    futile.

711.

Is there any human being
Who does not surf
On God's
Concern-Compassion-
    Forgiveness-Waves?

712.

If you do not carefully listen
To God's Lectures,
Your life will not be adorned
With the beauty of self-
    transcendence.

713.

Only for God-disobedient human
    beings
Does God use His
Thunder-Command-Roar.

714.

Those who are clad
In the armour of divine love
Will be able to expedite
Humanity's outer success
And inner progress.

715.

Each divine thought
Is a most beautiful
Angel.

716.

The Master's footprints
Show the brightest way
To Heaven.

717.

Try to live
In the eternal springs
Of enthusiasm and eagerness.

718.

No matter where I live—
Inside my body, inside my vital,
Inside my mind
Or even inside my heart—
I meet with uncomely thought-
    intruders.

719.

My aspiration-heart
Is the sworn enemy
Of my desire-life.

720.

I desire only
A God-blessed life,
And nothing else.

721.

Spirituality enjoys
Accepting the challenge
Of temptation-forces.

722.

We are always in the prison
Of our self-styled ideas
And ideals.

723.

O my mind,
Do not sleep and snore anymore
Beneath the blankets
Of illusion and delusion.

724.

God tells us
We have to make the choice:
Whether we want to wear
An aspiration-garland
Or a desire-python
That will strangle us.

725.

Depression
In the unaspiring vital
Will never die.

726.

His mind's goalless boat
Is wandering in the ocean
Of life's ignorance-night.

727.

The desire-world
Is nothing short of
A suffocating prison-life.

728.

To my extreme joy,
My disobedience-mind-tower
Has totally collapsed.

729.

Today's unwillingness
Will be forced to enter
Into the abysmal abyss
Of nothingness.

730.

My high-soaring dreams
Are embraced
By God's own Realities.

731.

You have to come and sit
With your heart's streaming tears
At the Feet of God
To see God's highest Satisfaction-
    Smile.

732.

God's Victory-Trumpet
Sounds absolutely the best
Inside my surrender-heart-
    garden.

733.

To my greatest satisfaction,
My life and my heart
Have been captured by Eternity's
    Love
And not by Infinity's Power.

734.

The dearer than the dearest choice
Of my aspiration-heart
Is God's Satisfaction in God's own
    Way.

735.

Looking at my aspiration-failure-
    life,
My soul and my Lord Supreme
Are together crying and weeping.

736.

A life of purity-breath
Is always
For the divine in us.

737.

Tear-flooded
Is man's outer life.
Rapture-flooded
Is man's God-surrendered inner
    life.

738.

We must study lovingly,
Devotedly and self-givingly
Our heart's aspiration-pages.

739.

Day and night I am searching
Lovingly, devotedly, prayerfully
And self-givingly
For only one thing: God's
    Footprint.

740.

You refuse to accept
God-aspiration-opportunity,
Yet you are longing for
The God-realisation-award.

741.

You fool!
How do you expect to succeed
In your spiritual life
If you put God at the very bottom
Of your priority list?

742.

If you do not want to love God
For God's sake,
Eventually you are bound to give
    up
Your spiritual life.

743.

Have God-enlightenment first,
Then think of God-establishment
In your life.

744.

If God is just a word to you,
Then you will not be able
To come out of your mind-jungle.

745.

You have to tame your vital
Every single day.
Otherwise, any day you may suffer
From an emotion-explosion.

746.

Consciously and bravely
Cast aside all insecurity-thoughts
And feelings
From your heart.

747.

My soul insists and insists
On only one thing:
God's Way is the only way.

748.

Why do you think
That God considers your case
Utterly hopeless and useless?
You are absolutely wrong!

749.

To see complete Satisfaction
In God's Eye,
Your heart must muster lion-
courage
To defeat the pride
Of ignorance-night.

750.

God wants to be visible,
But He is afraid
His Power-flooded Visibility
Will cause your immediate
collapse.

751.

God's Compassion
Can never
Be bribed.

752.

God was shocked
When He heard that I had given
my mind
His World-Transformation-
Message
To deliver to the world.

753.

No matter how many times
My roguish mind
Changes its telephone number
After committing serious crimes
Against God,
My God-oneness-heart
Somehow finds it out.

754.

Successful negotiation
Begins with the illumination
Of two totally different forces.

755.

The small "I"
Has man-thirst.
The big "I"
Has God-hunger.

756.

I want my mind
To be filled with God's Sound,
But God wants to fill my heart
With His Silence.

757.

My heart-sky
Is not only wakeful
But God-full.

758.

Be the perfect embodiment
Of sincerity.
God will, without fail,
Listen to your heart-cries.

759.

I am in the same boat
As my silence-starved
Heart.

760.

If you allow disobedience
To get a foot in your mind-door,
Then that is the beginning
Of your destruction-hurricane.

761.

Alas, I do not know
Why I am forced
To wander in my thought-
    wilderness
So helplessly!

762.

Every day I pray to God
To turn my mind into a serenity-
    flower,
My heart into a purity-flower
And my life into a simplicity-
    flower.

763.

Whatever directs
Your one-pointed attention
To the Divine
Is not only perfect
But most perfect.

764.

God wants me to cry
On His Shoulder,
But I prefer to cry
At His Feet.

765.

My Lord, do give me the capacity
To wipe every tear
From every heart.

766.

Countless God-seekers
Are shedding tears every day
For the betterment of the world.

767.

God will befriend you
And claim you as His own
If you unleash
A new spirit of humility.

768.

Because I have become
A sincere God-lover,
My days of gloom and doom
Are all over.

769.

Because my mind talks
    incessantly,
My inner Guide
Has taken a vow of silence.

770.

Do not sell
Your aspiration-heart
For worthless earthly pleasures.

771.

God dearly loves
Your constant refusal
To be unhappy.

772.

If love prompts
Your God-obedience,
Only then are you
Absolutely perfect.

773.

It does not take
More than a modicum of effort
To please our Beloved Lord
   Supreme.

774.

I deeply admire
Your devoted cheerfulness,
O God-seeker,
Although your Goal
Is a billion miles away.

775.

If you are not fully prepared,
Then do not embark
On your aspiration-expedition,
For you will not arrive at
Your ultimate Goal.

776.

God wants me to hide
My sound-mind
Inside my silence-heart.

777.

A wide-open heart
And a sunshine-smile
Are enough to conquer
The heart of humanity.

778.

I offer my humility-life
To my Lord Supreme.
He showers me
With His boundless Pride.

779.

My Lord, please tell me,
What is left for me
If You leave me alone?

780.

My mind's ego every day
Comes to the fore
To ruthlessly torture
My poor heart.

781.

My heart was swimming in tears
When it saw how badly my mind
Was disobeying God.

782.

The dreamers of Paradise
Have to be heart-weepers
And heart-smilers.

783.

There is so much disparity
Between the mind's
    possessiveness
And the heart's submissiveness!

784.

O my mind,
Why do you allow yourself
To be haunted by fear and doubt?

785.

O my vital,
Why do you allow yourself
To be assailed by depression
And frustration?

786.

O my heart,
Why do you allow yourself
To be ruthlessly strangled
By insincerity and impurity?

787.

O my body,
Why do you allow yourself
To be devoured
By lethargy-sleep?

788.

Each meditation-breath
Is the flowering
Of our inner divinity.

789.

You are badly mistaken
When you say that spirituality
Is empty of practicality.

790.

The outer life
Likes to dwell
In the mind of possibility.

791.

The inner life
Loves to dwell
In the heart of inevitability.

792.

Slowness begets unreadiness.
Unreadiness begets
    unwillingness.
Unwillingness begets
    uneagerness.

793.

As there is no end
To our sound-prayers,
Even so there is no end
To our silence-meditations.

794.

My intense God-love
Is my life's
Deep God-satisfaction.

795.

The mind's brooding cares
Disappear
When the heart's tranquillity
Dawns.

796.

There was a time
When I lived inside
My mind's uncertainty-cave,
But now I live
In my heart's certainty-palace.

797.

With imperfection I went
To see God's Eye;
With perfection I sat
At God's Feet.

798.

God tells me
That He does not need
My perfection-life.
He needs only
My willingness-heart.

799.

Devotion is frustration
Only when expectation
Looms large.

800.

"Tomorrow I shall become
    perfect!"
Is the absurd philosophy
Of the idle.

801.

There is definitely a dividing line
Between goodness and greatness,
And this line is quite distinctive.

802.

You will always miss peace
If you remain inside
Your unaspiring mind-room.

803.

Do not indulge
In temptation-game!
It never wants to stop.

804.

His mind's persistent
   disobedience
Has taken him away
Farther than the farthest
From God's Compassion-Eye.

805.

Purity-exercises give us
Very quick results.
Our inner existence becomes
Extremely powerful.

806.

God is bound to disappear
If you surrender
To your depression-frustration-
   vital.

807.

When your aspiration rises,
Do not look at desire's face
Anymore.

808.

You are trying to do an impossible
   task!
Your cleverness will never be able
To fool your soul.

809.

The mind wants to exploit the
   heart,
But the mind does not know
That the heart is always assisted
   by God.
Therefore, the heart will brook
No exploitation.

810.

Our outer life is conversant
With the complicated mind-
   schemes.
Our inner life is conversant
With the beauty of heart-dreams.

811.

God wanted me to have
An ego-free life.
Alas, what am I doing?
I am enjoying an ego-fat life.

812.

When you give an inch
To disobedience,
It immediately demands a long
    mile.

813.

If you want to enjoy God-
    nearness,
Then develop sweetness
In your entire being.

814.

Not self-infatuation but self-
    expansion
Can and shall lead us
To our God-Destination.

815.

When God's Grace rushes towards
    you,
God expects from you
A receptivity-heart.

816.

It takes enormous courage
To have implicit faith
In God's outer operations.

817.

Life's turbulence cannot frighten
    you
If your mind longs for God's
Immortal Opulence: Peace.

818.

If you do not give
Your wholehearted loyalty
To your own soul,
How can you expect to have
A life of real satisfaction?

819.

Ignorance eagerly waits
For your surrender
In the sound of your outer life
And in the silence of your inner
    life.

820.

The fear of the mind
Can easily petrify
The vital and the body.

821.

Keep your intensity-heart alive
No matter how many times a day
You meet with your Master.

822.

May your prayerful and soulful
   smile
Embody man's perfection-dream
And God's Satisfaction-Reality.

823.

My surrender has always been
My life's most powerful
Safety-haven.

824.

God-Satisfaction-dreamers
And servers
Know no rest.

825.

Your mind's determination-stride
And your heart's aspiration-stride
Every day must increase.

826.

The mind
Is always fond
Of ever-changing forecasts.

827.

Every day at least once
God goes through His Family
   Album,
Which contains
The Beauty and Fragrance
Of His Universal Dream.

828.

God has no intention of
   threatening you
In any way.
He only wants to enlighten
Your body, vital, mind and heart
In every possible way.

829.

Every day
God is eager to see a new record
Set by His chosen seekers
On His Heart-Track.

830.

God has
His Compassion-Eye
And His Satisfaction-Heart
For the aspiring world.

831.

God has His Forgiveness-Heart
For the unruly, unaspiring
And self-centred world.

832.

God tells me that I always know
Right from wrong,
But I do not want to take the
    trouble
To do the right thing.

833.

A self-giving life
Is God's
Best amplifier.

834.

God is
His Employer-Eye.
God is
His Employee-Heart.

835.

God the Creator
Is prone to smile.
God the creation
Is prone to cry.

836.

The supermarket-mind
Of unaspiring human beings
Every day
Demands extra supplies.

837.

God's great Justice-Light
Is always
Up to date.

838.

God's Protection-Eye
Stays on twenty-four-hour duty
To protect the lives
Of His chosen children.

839.

God's Heart
Knows how to whisper.
Man's mind
Knows how to whimper.

840.

The mind-batteries
Never work properly.
The heart-batteries
Never run low.

841.

My desire-fulfilment
Is not
God's priority.

842.

My aspiration-awakening
And aspiration-blossoming
Are God's top priorities.

843.

When I am on God's Compassion-
    Wings,
I fly not only the highest
But also the farthest.

844.

Pure dreams
Import and export.
Impure dreams
Only explode.

845.

Every day my heart
Gives my mind God-lessons
In vain!

846.

God is always ready
To secretly cover all my faults,
But my enemies at every moment
Point out each and every fault of
    mine.

847.

Alas, when will my mind smile?
When?
Alas, when will my heart cry?
When?

848.

The dust-tornadoes of the mind
Do have the power
To destroy the inner poise of our
    heart.

849.

God the Mother
Teaches me how to look upward
And ceaselessly cry.

850.

God the Father
Teaches me how to dive deep
    within
And sleeplessly smile.

851.

I want the wisdom of my heart
To be the source
Of my freedom-loving mind.

852.

God asks my heart
To tell Him its mantra.
My heart replies,
"My Lord, my only mantra is,
'I sleeplessly and breathlessly love
Only You.'"

853.

Alas,
How long shall I remain
A totally vision-blind mind?

854.

His God-denying mind
Could not foretell
His imminent perdition.

855.

His God-loving heart
Could foretell
God's imminent Satisfaction-
   Smile.

856.

The indolence of the body
And insolence of the vital
Are two destructive hostile forces.

857.

Your ignorance-night will be
   thickened
If you enjoy the presence
Of a God-denial-mind.

858.

God tells us
That ultimately
Nobody will fail His final Test.

859.

The power-hungry mind
Deliberately rejects
God's Compassion-Eye-Nest.

860.

Do you want to offer delight to
   God?
Then steal His Light
As much as you want to
At your sweet will.

861.

Unimaginable delight awaits him,
For his life has become
A surrender-breath.

862.

When we do not pray and
     meditate Regularly,
God's heavy Sighs
Devour His living Breath.

863.

If you do not nurture your divine
     life,
Your animal life will, without fail,
Return.

864.

When we live in our restless mind,
No matter what God gives us,
We immediately reject it.

865.

Not by crying and crying,
But by singing and dancing,
His life came out of his darkness-
     mind.

866.

Alas, he never realised
That his computer-brain
Would steal the beauty and
     fragrance
Of his happiness-heart.

867.

God the Satisfaction came down
Happily and proudly
To greet his gratitude-heart.

868.

Before trying to embrace God,
Humanity should try to trace
God's Footprints.

869.

God is at a loss
When He stands in between
The complexity of science
And the simplicity of spirituality.

870.

God tells me
That He is giving me
A full-time job:
Aspiration.

871.

Worries and anxieties
Are the faithful messengers
Of death.

872.

I pray to God every day
For the victory of my heart's
    happiness
Over my mind's unhappiness.

873.

To defeat the commotion-mind
Once and for all,
Our heart needs sleepless
And breathless God-devotion.

874.

Weak disciples do not believe
In their Master
When he says that he has
    shortened
The distance.

875.

Not the abnegation
But the illumination
Of our desire-life
We need.

876.

God wants our mind to be
    authentic,
Our heart to be sympathetic
And our soul to be prophetic.

877.

God's Greatness frightens us.
God's Goodness enlightens us.
God's Fulness feeds us.

878.

Two things I dearly love:
My God-obedience-heart
And my God-surrender-life.

879.

My heart is always eager
With all its affection
To teach my mind, vital and body.
But, alas, its eagerness-sun
Turns into frustration-night.

880.

Does the human mind
Have the opportunity to excel?
Yes, it does!
But unfortunately the mind
Does not apply itself.

881.

The secret is out:
The desiring mind
Does not want to room
With the aspiring heart.

882.

The undivine mind does not
    believe
In practising.
It only believes in preaching.

883.

The joyful tears of our soul
Nurture and support
Our God-fulfilling oneness-heart.

884.

God Himself
Is enjoying the resurrection
Of the long-lost aspiration-cries
Of my heart.

885.

The heavy pressure
Of hidden anxieties
Can never be adequately
    described.

886.

God begs me to see sense
And not nonsense
In everything.

887.

Rest assured,
God is not going to cheer up your
    mind
If you carry fear with you
When you visit God's Palace.

888.

For an unaspiring mind,
It is impossible to sacrifice
The pleasure-life
For a supreme cause.

889.

Never allow
Your heart to surrender
To the feeling of unworthiness.

890.

Try to be pacified
By hope
And fortified by promise.

891.

Finally,
Your suspicion-mind
Enters into the abyss
Of nothingness.

892.

The old millennium says
To the new millennium:
"My Brother,
Do not commit the same mistakes
That I made!"

893.

God wants my heart
To enjoy every day
The bounty of aspiration
And my life,
The bounty of dedication.

894.

The aspiration-heart-life
Will sooner or later, without fail,
Thrive.

895.

I have nothing to do with
The mind that desires
World-domination.

896.

If you maximise,
God will immortalise
The tears of your aspiration-heart.

897.

I tell my mind
That it can never overestimate
The capacities of my soul.

898.

I beg my mind
Not to underestimate
The capacities of my heart.

899.

There can be
No adequate replacement
For God's Compassion-Eye-
    Touch.

900.

To try to define illumination
Is to feed the hunger
Of frustration.

901.

Our mind, our heart
And our earth-existence
Will be glorified
If we feel that our Lord Supreme
Has an iota of faith in us.

902.

I clearly see that my aspiration-
   heart
Is being cradled
By God's Compassion-flooded
   Eye.

903.

O my mind,
Your stupidity knows no bounds!
Look how far you have gone away
From God's Heart-Home.

904.

My Lord,
Break my life into millions of
   pieces
Since it is still unwilling
To sit at Your Lotus-Feet.

905.

God wants me to give Him
Only one thing
To make Him supremely happy:
My heart-beauty-smile.

906.

Every day I surrender
My life's limited sighs
To God's unlimited Compassion-
   Breath.

907.

God is not satisfied
In seeing me close to His Heart.
He wants me to be deep inside
His Heart-Home.

908.

My life moves at bullock-cart
   speed.
Time does not wait for me.
My nature's transformation, alas,
Will remain always a far cry.

909.

I shall no more blow
My mind-trumpet.
From now on I shall only blow
My soul-trumpet.

910.

God wants my willingness
And not my capacity
To love Him and serve Him.

911.

Every day I feel miserable
To see and feel
That my desire-life
Is expanding its boundaries.

912.

Alas, what do I see
When I dive within?
I see a sea of sadness
And a mountain of failure.

913.

Each time you climb up
To a new aspiration-height,
Your realisation-stars
Come near you and perform
A new God-Victory-dance.

914.

My seeker-friend, you are telling
    me
That you have nothing.
But I clearly see that wherever you
    go
You radiate Infinity's blue Light.

915.

Not an easy task
To throw insecurity
Completely out of one's life.
But I have done it!
Yes, I have done it!

916.

My confusion-mind
And my dissatisfaction-life
Are intimately fond of each other.

917.

Like a postage stamp,
Stick only to God's Heart
Of infinite Love.

918.

A life without ups and downs
May not be
So completely fulfilling.

919.

True happiness does not spring
From the mind's
World-possession-thirst,
But from the heart's
God-surrender-hunger.

920.

Opportunity
Makes the undivine in us a thief
And the divine in us a saint.

921.

A big mouth
Is not always accompanied
By a big heart.

922.

The heart-torch shines
Most powerfully
Inside the darkness of the mind.

923.

The joy of the heart
Belongs to nobody
Until it belongs to everybody.

924.

Prayers and meditations
Are citizens
Of God's Heart-Country.

925.

Share a smile of your heart
With humanity.
Lo, you have become
Divinity's pride!

926.

Impurity's very presence
In anybody's life
Is a real threat to everybody's
    purity
Everywhere.

927.

Knowledge we acquire
By working hard.
Wisdom we acquire
By surrendering ourselves
To God's Will.

928.

Your sterling devotion
To God's Will
Tells you what true love
And what false love are.

929.

Ignore your vital-dog,
Which is always barking
Inside your heart-garden.

930.

He who smiles sleeplessly
Lives in the Eye of the Supreme,
And he who cries breathlessly
Lives in the Heart of the Supreme.

931.

The sound of my mind
Can be quoted and misquoted,
But not the silence of my heart.

932.

There is always
Plenty of room
At the highest Heights.

933.

To love your heart of love
Is to love its Source:
God.

934.

Do not worry
About your future.
Pay all attention
To the Eternal Now.

935.

Never too late
To practise your spiritual life
And to please God
In God's own Way!

936.

Indecision forces your mind
To remain inside
A darkness-cave.

937.

You must give up
Once and for all
Your mind's anxiety-indulgence!

938.

Your emotion-life
Must totally surrender
To your vision-eye.

939.

God is a Sweetness-Whisper
And not a loudness-trumpet
Inside your heart-temple.

940.

My Lord's Sunshine-Heart-Eye
Has been beckoning me
For centuries!

941.

There is always
An unseen light
Inside our heart-hope.

942.

Our teeming hopes
And glowing promises
Must needs be harmonised.

943.

My Lord always lives
Inside the secret and sacred
   chamber
Of my silence-heart.

944.

Unlike us,
God loves to sing two songs:
A heart-oneness-song
And a life-fulness-song.

945.

My devotion is the golden bridge
Between my aspiration-heart
And God's Satisfaction-Smile.

946.

We simply have no idea
How often
We dare to throw God forcefully
Out of our hearts.

947.

Love is not a business deal
Of the mind.
It is a oneness-skill
Of the heart.

948.

Modern science is foolishly
   making
Attempt after attempt
To replace
God's Compassion-flooded Heart.

949.

If my surrender-heart blossoms,
Then I know my happiness-
    destination
Will be within my easy reach.

950.

My Lord Supreme,
Do bless me with a lifelong
Gratitude-heart-plant.

951.

My heart's
Aspiration-attendance
Is quite satisfactory,
But, alas, not my life's
Dedication-attendance.

952.

You must discard immediately
Your mind's old, unhealthy
And unaspiring thoughts.

953.

I must save
My earth-existence
From constant self-abnegation.

954.

My Lord Beloved Supreme
Suffers and suffers
When my mind discourages and
    belittles
The beauty and fragrance
Of my blossoming heart.

955.

The doubting mind
Finally dies
Of its own monotony-life.

956.

Do not believe the falsehood-
    carriers
Who inform the world
That the God-thirst
Can never be fully appeased.

957.

A peaceful mind
And a blissful heart
Are Eternity's twins.

958.

My heart and I know for certain
That God's Compassion-Eye
Is the source of God's Life.

959.

Perseverance
Eventually shall arrive
At the Golden Shore.

960.

Two doors—
God's Compassion-Door
And God's Forgiveness-Door—
God keeps always open.

961.

My God-dependence-wings
Invariably shall take me
To God's highest Palace.

962.

Day after day
God continues to warn us
Not to be at all friendly
With ignorance-night.

963.

God wants everybody to be
    familiar
With the length and breadth
Of His Will.

964.

God tells me that
His Philosophy is:
Man's mind has to unlearn;
Man's heart has to learn.

965.

For years and years
I have been planning and
    planning
To offer my gratitude-heart
To my Lord Supreme.
Alas, my success
Still remains a far cry.

966.

The difference between
My own desire and God's desire
Is this:
I want to bind God,
And God wants to liberate me.

967.

Every day
With a new happiness-heart
I try to reach
My aspiration-mountain-heights.

968.

God tells me that
I do not have to make up
For lost time.
It will be perfectly all right
If I run faster
Right from here and now.

969.

A stupidity-mind's
Best friend
Is an absurdity-thought.

970.

The mind's ambition-tower
Is
Always overcrowded.

971.

What am I?
I am my heart's helpless cry
To reach my God-Destination.

972.

When I look upward,
I become
My life's prayer-beauty.
When I look inward,
I become
My heart's meditation-fragrance.

973.

My heart-alarm
Not only awakens me
But also guides me
All the way to my Destination.

974.

Sing prayerfully and self-givingly!
God Himself will come down
To establish His Oneness-
    Friendship
With your life.

975.

The torturing mind
Gets malicious pleasure
When it sees the suffering heart.

976.

We must ignite our minds
With the beauty of new hopes
And the fragrance of new ideals.

977.

My heart's inner aspiration-tears
Will unmistakably and easily
    outlast
The wrong actions of my outer
    life.

978.

Each time I dive deep
In my meditation,
My heart starts singing
Peace-melodies.

979.

So often my expectation-mind
Gives heart attacks
To my God-surrender-life.

980.

O God-seeker, rest assured,
Nobody will erect a monument
To your hostile critics.

981.

The curiosity-mind
Never sees
The face of Reality
And never feels
The heart of Divinity.

982.

Have a mind of imagination.
Have a heart of aspiration.
Have a life of dedication.
You need nothing more!

983.

My Lord, how I wish
You would make my life
A perfect perfection,
Even for a fleeting second!

984.

You can have no inspiration
To serve God the creation
If you have no aspiration
To realise God the Creator.

985.

I have been developing
An indomitable will
To fulfil
My God-manifestation-promise
Since the moment
I saw the light of day.

986.

Human life is nothing but
A series
Of unfulfilled desires.

987.

I shall never allow
My aspiration-heart
To be defeated
By my desire-mind.

988.

The heart's oneness-game
I enjoy
And not the mind's
Competition-division-game.

989.

From each small God-devotion-
    step
There comes into existence
A giant God-surrender-step.

990.

To hope against hope
Can eventually become
A positive reality.

991.

Our Lord Beloved Supreme
Will unmistakably fulfil
His Peace-Promise here on earth.

992.

Spirituality is full of
Astonishing promises
And assurances.

993.

Expectation-misery covers
The length and breadth
Of the mind.

994.

A sleepless God-gratitude-heart
Will always be blessed
With Divinity's Peace and Bliss.

995.

My mind wants
To import greatness.
My heart wants
To export goodness.

996.

Only the invited God-pleasing
    guests
Are allowed to enter
Into God's Heart-Room.

997.

My God-surrender-light-wings
Fly me happily and proudly
To the Shores of the Beyond.

998.

My Lord, do fulfil
My snow-white desire:
May my heart become
The perfect embodiment
Of Your Immortality's Goodness.

999.

Two things are never out of
    season:
God's Compassion-Eye
And God's Forgiveness-Heart.

1000.

My Lord,
My Absolute Lord Beloved
    Supreme,
You have commanded me to write
Seventy-seven thousand service-
    tree-poems.
I have just completed one
    thousand.
My heart, my mind, my vital, my
    body
And I
Are most sincerely tired.
"My child, My own Divinity's
    child,
Tiredness is unacceptable."

1001.

My Lord Supreme,
I was born to love You only.
I was born to place myself
At Your Feet only.
I was born to please You
In Your own Way only.

1002.

O my mind,
You may wander in all directions,
But I am settled here
At the Feet of my Lord Supreme.

1003.

My Lord Supreme tells me
That to remain seated
At His Feet
Is the only task
I have to perform.

1004.

O my heart,
Without God's Presence
Inside you and inside me,
We are nothing, absolutely
    nothing!
I am making it known.

1005.

Finally my God-love has arisen
Inside my heart,
And all my earthly sorrows
Are flying away.

1006.

I have placed my head
At the Feet of my Lord
For Eternity.
I am not going to lift it up again.

1007.

My Lord tells me
That if my heart and I
Live together
And try together to catch Him,
Only then shall we succeed.

1008.

Each time
My devotion for my Lord
    increases,
I see a flood of tears filling my
    heart.

1009.

My Lord, I know, I know
That I am unable to love You
Dearly enough,
But I beg You not to vanish
From my heart or from my eyes.

1010.

My Lord, do show me the way
How I can claim You
As my only dream-fulfilled
    Reality.

1011.

Not only my mouth,
But even my heart
Is not sufficient
To praise my Lord Supreme.

1012.

My Lord dwells
On the tip of my tongue.
I cannot and I shall not
Speak of anything else.

1013.

When I live
Inside my jungle-mind,
God's Compassion-flooded Eye
Is a stranger to me.

1014.

My Lord supports me
And every step forward I take
Towards perfection.

1015.

In the mortal world,
My God-aspiring heart
Has become one
With God's all-pervading Spirit.

1016.

O my doubting mind,
Within and without
You are useless.
I shall never want you
As a companion.

1017.

God can never dismiss
Even an unaspiring
Human being.

1018.

My Lord Supreme,
My only task is to love You
And clap my hands ceaselessly
In adoration of You.

1019.

At long last
I am able to place
At my Lord's Feet
My burden of giving and taking.

1020.

I must keep my mind
Empty of doubts
To remain free
From all Heaven-criticism.

1021.

Every good seeker
Is an embodiment
Of God's Goodness.

1022.

Our progress-journey
Will be most remarkable
If we keep devotion and surrender
In our heart-home.

1023.

An unceasing flow of devotion
Is needed
To return
To our God-realisation-home.

1024.

A sleepless self-offering
Will eventually be able
To reap the God-manifestation-
    harvest.

1025.

It is only when
I pray most sincerely
That God invites me
To enter into His Heart-Room.

1026.

My soul is begging
My heart, mind, vital and body
To come and live with God
The way my soul has been living
With God
From time immemorial.

1027.

Our God-realisation-hope
Has to be kept always young
In every possible way!

1028.

My heart's God-love-step
Is followed by
My life's God-surrender-step.

1029.

God Himself
Holds His Protection-Umbrella
Over each genuine seeker.

1030.

God feeds on
The sun-smile-blossoms
Of truth-seekers
And truth-lovers.

1031.

God loves to turn the lives
Of genuine seekers
Into a daily celebration
Inside His Heart-Home.

1032.

Every day
My heart accompanies
The God-loving sun
On its way
To the Golden Shore.

1033.

God is extremely happy
When He can blessingfully supply
More and more hope
To the hopeful.

1034.

God asks me
To live with Him proudly
When He sees my crying heart.

1035.

God asks me
To breathe with Him
When I become
My smiling soul.

1036.

God looks extremely beautiful
When I see Him inside
My searching mind.

1037.

God looks extremely bountiful
When I see Him inside
My aspiring heart.

1038.

Do not keep your eyes closed!
Keep them
Prayerfully and soulfully open
If you want to be embraced
By God's Satisfaction-Heart-
    Smile.

1039.

Our desire-life becomes
A destruction-reality
Even before we finish
Looking all around.

1040.

All the cries of my heart
Are not the same.
All the smiles of my soul
Are not the same.
But all the surrender-songs
Of my life
Are not only the same,
But also all-illumining
And all-fulfilling.

1041.

The God-Summit-Goal
Is inside your heart,
And nowhere else.

1042.

O my heart, wake up
And speed towards
The ever-transcending Beyond!

1043.

If you stand firm
Like a rock,
Nothing undivine shall dare
To challenge you.

1044.

The tired eyes
Long for
Perfect sleep.

1045.

The tired heart
Longs for
Immediate God-rescue.

1046.

God and His self-giving children
Every morning and every evening
Sing together
In God's Heart-Home.

1047.

Every day God asks me
To sail and sail
My happiness-heart-boat
Towards the Golden Shore.

1048.

My God-disobedience
Has left my heart, mind,
Vital and body
Completely empty.

1049.

My Lord's Compassion-Eye
And my own gratitude-heart
Can never be parted.

1050.

When my heart pines
And longs for God,
God tells me, "My child,
I shall reach you
In the twinkling of an eye!"

1051.

The inspiration of the mind
Sings.
The aspiration of the heart
Cries.
The realisation of the soul
Whispers.

1052.

The unaspiring mind
Feasts on doubt, suspicion
And criticism.

1053.

The insecurity of the heart
Is a huge stumbling block
On the way to God-realisation.

1054.

My soul shows me
The path of Divinity's Light.
In return, I show my soul
The path of humanity's night.

1055.

To have an abiding Spring
In his life,
The seeker must have
An inner devotion-spring.

1056.

I want to live
In the shadow of God's Feet,
But God wants me to live
In the Light of His Heart.

1057.

When my heart sings
Silence-songs,
My Lord Supreme enters into
His highest Self-amorous Trance.

1058.

The body thinks that death
Is a ruthless torturer.
The soul knows that death
Is an Unknown Way-revealer.

1059.

The evening stars
Have a very special fondness
For my heart.
They invite my heart to come
And play, sing and dance
With them.

1060.

My soul cries and cries
If I do not have
God-hunger
For even one solitary day.

1061.

The doubting mind
Does only one thing:
It always turns its back
On the inner sun.

1062.

If you have
A life of total surrender,
Then God will prove to you
That He is your only Friend
In all circumstances.

1063.

I am absolutely sure
That my soul and my Lord
    Supreme
Applaud me far beyond my worth
Whenever I do something
Inspiring, aspiring and
    illumining.

1064.

God asks me
To come to His Heart-Home
Not as a beggar and visitor,
But as a real friend of His.

1065.

The angels come to me
To enchant my eyes.
The cosmic gods come to me
To enlighten my life.
God comes to me
To fulfil His Eternity's Dream.

1066.

Today my joy
Knows no bounds,
For I am seeing the ashes
Of my mind-edifice.

1067.

You have to devour
Your ego first
Before you can be drunk
With a God-Vision.

1068.

O my seeker-friend,
To my extreme sorrow,
What you have is
A mind of jealousy,
And what you are is
A vital of depression.

1069.

Do not allow your life
To be paralysed
By your absurd expectations
Of what should come from Above.

1070.

God definitely wants you
To cherish
Your lofty God-manifestation-
    dreams.

1071.

My Lord, the world blames me
For many things.
Will You not tell the world
Once and for all
That You are not only my Creator
But also my life-violin-Player?

1072.

You have to make the choice:
The thunder-voice
Of your mind
Or the silence-voice
Of your heart.

1073.

Disappointments
Sprout during the day
When in the morning
We cancel our God-appointments.

1074.

O my aspiration-heart,
When the evening stars
Invite you to ride with them
On their God-paved path,
Do not miss the opportunity.

1075.

My Creator-Lord,
Do You feel sorry for me
When the world chides me
For my imperfection-life?
"My child,
I shall be extremely proud of you
If you do not play the same game."

1076.

My Lord,
Now that I have embraced Your
    Feet
With all the devotion
That You have bestowed upon me
Over the years,
I feel that I am completely
    liberated
From the snare of earthly desires.

1077.

There is only one way
To please God in His own Way:
We must cast aside
Our desire-life altogether.

1078.

Alas, how blind I have become!
I have allowed myself
To be completely entangled
In earth-life-pleasure.

1079.

I have realised
That our life on earth is short,
And death will come soon.
How I wish the death of our
    ignorance
To come sooner than the soonest!

1080.

My Lord,
I shall not give You
My heart's harrowing pain.
I shall give You only
My heart's ever-blossoming
    smiles.

1081.

My Lord,
Please do not forget
That You have promised me
That my life shall never suffer
Separation from Your Nectar-Feet.

1082.

My Lord, I am alone
Not because I cannot bear
Anyone's company,
But because I want only to walk
In Your Footsteps.

1083.

My Lord,
Please do not appreciate me.
I mean it!
Your appreciation will make me
Proud beyond measure,
And this pride-burden
Will keep me away from
Your Protection-Feet.

1084.

I have annihilated
My desire-life
As it was decreed long ago
By my Lord Supreme.

1085.

My Lord's Eye
Knows the meaning
Of my meditation-whispers.

1086.

I know the meaning
Of the Blessing-Touch
Of my Lord's Feet.

1087.

I am not what I seem to be.
I am my Lord's
Supremely chosen child,
For His full manifestation
On earth.

1088.

To my extreme happiness,
My Lord has come to tell me
That from now on
I must stand apart from my
    actions,
Divine and undivine.
He alone is the Doer;
I am a mere observer.

1089.

My seeker-friend,
When I see God on your face,
I become truly proud of you.
But when I feel God inside your
    heart,
I become soulfully one with you.

1090.

My Lord Supreme,
Do bless me
With a new cry
For a totally new start.

1091.

My heart is madly in love
With God.
It is begging me
To be the same.

1092.

The mind has many necessities.
The heart has only one:
God's Love.

1093.

If you want to conquer
All your weaknesses,
Then you must face them
One at a time.

1094.

May my Goal
Be an ever-rising dawn
Inside my aspiration-heart.

1095.

For a genuine seeker,
The inner world
Is infinitely more real
Than the outer world.

1096.

My soul wants me
To spread its light
Everywhere
And offer it to
Everyone.

1097.

My Lord, You have suffered
So many sad experiences.
I assure You
From me, at least
You will have none!

1098.

There was a time
When God used to ask
My doubting mind to halt.
Now His Request
Has been replaced
With His Command.

1099.

I beg God to repeat
Again and again
That I am a choice instrument
Of His.

1100.

The day I do not pray
And meditate,
I feel like a blind man
Lost in the thick
Of the forest.

1101.

How long
The mind-negativity-tower lasts!
But eventually
It has to crumble.

1102.

I feel my nature's transformation
Is even far beyond
God's Vision-Eye.

1103.

How I wish my life
To sing and dance
On the road
Of God's special Delight.

1104.

God never asks me
For my life-history.
He asks me only
For my heart-song.

1105.

Alas, I have been strangled
So ruthlessly
By desire-serpent!
I do not know
How I am still alive.

1106.

Every morning
The smiling Beauty of the
    Supreme
Awakens me
To participate in His Cosmic Play.

1107.

My inner heart
Is dreaming
Only real God-manifestation-
    dreams.

1108.

My life's hope-seed
Has now grown into
A reality-tree.

1109.

If you do not accept
The spiritual life,
Nothing can move you away
From the yoke of Fate.

1110.

I wish to be another sun.
The sun not only loves,
But also serves humanity
Unconditionally.

1111.

Divinity's Message for humanity:
Light, more Light, abundant
    Light,
Light infinite.

1112.

Our self-imposed God-blindness
Definitely hinders and delays
God's Arrival.

1113.

Everything needed
Is here inside
My heart's aspiration-flames.

1114.

I am praying to God
To bless me with
Some beautiful, meaningful
And fruitful days
In my crowded life-market.

1115.

We all sleep
On idleness-bed
And dream
Of a star-flooded sky.

1116.

Cheerfulness in the mind
Begins
My God-satisfaction-day.

1117.

Every day God inspires me
To run an ultramarathon
In my inner life
So I shall arrive at my Destination.

1118.

God is not compelling me,
But it is I who am
Sharing with humanity
My God-realisation-light
On my own.

1119.

God the Mother
Has a very special love
For the crying child
Inside my heart.

1120.

God the Father
Has a very special love
For the awakening child
Inside my heart.

1121.

Each morning
Greets my aspiration-heart
With a rainbow-beauty.

1122.

God is dying to hear from me
My God-realisation,
God-revelation
And God-manifestation-promises.

1123.

God says to the mind,
"I have tolerated you
For a very long time!
No more doubt,
No more suspicion,
No more hesitation
Shall I accept from you!"

1124.

Only my God-obedience
Can smash the pride
Of my mind's insolence.

1125.

God wants my mind
To observe silence-hours
Exactly the way my heart does.

1126.

My Lord Supreme,
Do You have
A minute to spare?
Please tell me
How I can totally destroy
The pride-crown of my mind.

1127.

O my mind,
How long do you want to remain
A perfect stranger
To softness, tenderness, sweetness
And soulfulness?

1128.

My life-boat and I
Are fully determined
To arrive at the Golden Shore.

1129.

My Lord, with His Compassion-
   Eye,
Lovingly and regularly
Prunes
My aspiration-heart-garden.

1130.

In my God-service-life
What I need is
God-Thunder-Will-
   manifestation.

1131.

God says to me,
"My child,
Give Me your desire-life
And take from Me
My Satisfaction-Heart.
Delay not!"

1132.

The moment the doubting mind
Sinks,
The aspiring heart
Rises.

1133.

My God-searching mind
Is for myself.
My God-loving heart
Is for all.

1134.

Everybody's love of God
Blooms and blossoms
In the heart-garden
Of faith.

1135.

My mind challenges
The face of truth.
My heart embraces
The life of truth.

1136.

Can you imagine!
I get tremendous joy
Even when I keep thinking
That my Lord does not care for me.

1137.

I know every burden
Will be lessened
If I hasten towards
God's Compassion-Eye.

1138.

My mind cares
Only for my self-esteem.
My heart cares
Only for my soul-esteem.

1139.

My doubting mind
Eats everything
That is forbidden.

1140.

My aspiring heart
Eats only the things
That are God-given.

1141.

May I be the possessor
Of the lustre
That shines forth
From Divinity's Eye.

1142.

I just would like to know
What my life means
To God,
And not to anybody else!

1143.

If my hands
Are not exclusively
For God-service,
Then what are they for?

1144.

If my heart
Is not sleeplessly
For God-worship,
Then what is it for?

1145.

May my heart not change
Its God-loving nature,
As fire does not change
Its burning nature.

1146.

God tells me
That He does not need me
To defend Him.
He just does not want me
To offend Him.

1147.

I do not know
If I will ever be able
To have a doubt-free
Mind-dream.

1148.

A true God-lover
Is an earth-made cry
And a Heaven-made smile.

1149.

The smiling Supreme
Tells me
That I have everything
I need.

1150.

The dancing Supreme
Tells me
That I have everything
He needs.

1151.

The difference between God and
    me:
I take God's help
When I need it;
God takes my help
Even when He does not need it.

1152.

My Lord,
I know You are tired of my
    complaints.
One more complaint, and no
    more:
If You are not planning to release
    me
From my bondage-shackles,
Why do You inspire me inwardly
To pray to You every day?

1153.

The aspiration-flames of the heart
Must eventually burn
The desire-house completely.

1154.

My Lord, You do not like it
When I turn my thoughts to
    austerity,
And You do not approve of
My self-indulgence-life.
Please show me the way
Between the two extremes.
I am all ready!

1155.

I know why God is so reluctant
To come to me.
My life is totally devoid of faith.
What can poor God do?

1156.

My Lord, I entreat Your
    Forgiveness
For everything bad that I do and
    say.
Do accept the little I have to offer:
My feeble breath.

1157.

Do not use your old eyes.
Use your new eyes.
You are bound to appreciate
The beauty, fragrance and
    soulfulness
Of Mother Earth.

1158.

My Lord, I am ready
For You to break my heart
As many times as You want to
To compensate for the suffering
I have caused You.

1159.

Every day
My heart's blossoming faith
Is being destroyed
By my mind's brooding doubt.

1160.

My God-realisation tells me
That God lives only for humanity
Happily, proudly and self-
    givingly.

1161.

Not only do I fail,
But my poor Lord also fails like
    me.
In vain He has been trying
To make my heart
His permanent Abode.

1162.

Even the very thought
Of my separation
From the Feet of my Lord
    Supreme
Ruthlessly shakes my entire
    being.

1163.

If you want a vacation from God,
God will definitely grant it.
But rest assured,
You will not remain the same.

1164.

O my mind,
Do not disturb my heart.
My heart is all attention
To my Lord's Nectar-Speech.

1165.

I do not want freedom.
I want my Lord's Compassion-Eye
And His Forgiveness-Heart
To govern my life.

1166.

The best day of my life
Was the day when my Lord
Cooked a special Meal for me
And fed me with His own Hand.

1167.

In spite of my countless blunders,
God blesses me
With His ambrosial Embrace.

1168.

When I tell God
That I am hungry for His Love,
He tells me that
He would be equally happy
Even if I were greedy for His Love.

1169.

My Lord, I did not know
That You are hard of hearing.
Otherwise, instead of addressing
My mind's sound-prayers to You,
I would have offered You
My heart's silence-meditation.

1170.

Both my gratitude-heart
And my surrender-life
Have developed such measureless
God-hunger!

1171.

I knew I was not good,
But I never knew
That I would be so bad
As to disobey and displease
My Lord Supreme
On an everyday basis.

1172.

My Lord,
Now that I am the possessor
Of the dust of Your Feet,
My inner world's beauty and
    divinity
Have increased immeasurably.

1173.

Do not dismiss God's Love.
It is His Love that is sustaining
Your earth-hope and Heaven-
    promise.

1174.

Today my aspiration-heart
Is embodying God's Face.
Tomorrow my dedication-life
Will reveal God's Heart.
The day after tomorrow
My illumination-soul
Will manifest God's Heartbeat.

1175.

To my extreme happiness,
My heart and I have revived
Our long-forgotten God-longing.

1176.

When I look at God's Eye,
He immediately makes my life
Divinely beautiful.
When I feel God's Heart,
He immediately makes my life
Supremely fruitful.

1177.

An awakened heart
Is entitled to
Blissful peace.

1178.

An iota of peace in the mind
Can expedite
Our inner journey.

1179.

Heaven showers its bliss-petals
On those who sleeplessly
Love God.

1180.

I would like to become
A member
Of the world-peace-heart-
        committee.

1181.

My Lord's great need
Is my mind.
My Lord's greater need
Is my heart.
My Lord's greatest need
Is my soul.

1182.

Immortality always dances
On the face
Of a newborn child.

1183.

Millennia have come and gone,
But humanity still takes
Infant-steps
On the road to its God-
    Destination.

1184.

O my mind,
While trying to define God,
Can you not see that
You are confining Him?

1185.

A genuine seeker knows
That an insecurity-heart
Is in no way less frightening
Than an impurity-mind.

1186.

Eternity and Infinity
Are two friends of ours.
They give our life a chance
To run towards God,
But they do not wait
If we delay.

1187.

The Cosmic Game
Is never meant for
Faint-hearted seekers.

1188.

O my sorrowful heart,
What can give you joy?
Believe me,
I am all for you.

1189.

I need the beauty
And fragrance
Of a child's surrendered heart.

1190.

Creativity needs
A mind of inspiration,
A heart of aspiration
And a life of dedication
To succeed.

1191.

If I do not lose myself
While searching for
God's Compassion-Eye,
Then I will never succeed.

1192.

Sincerity is the heart's
Most reliable
God-remembrance-capacity.

1193.

Only a perfection-seeker
Is invited by God Himself
To carry His Heart
As a shrine
Wherever he goes.

1194.

There was a time
When I travelled the whole way
With my self-assertion.
Alas, joy was not to be found.
Now I am travelling the whole
    way
With my self-denial.
Alas, joy is still not to be found.
God tells me that both ways are
    wrong.
I have to travel my life-journey
Only with God-dependence.

1195.

My Lord, Your Name is
Compassion-Forgiveness-Ocean.
I have committed a million
    blunders.
Do justify Your Name!

1196.

My Lord,
All my wrongdoings
Throw fetters upon my life.
If there is a way to escape,
Please show me.
I solely depend upon You.

1197.

My Lord,
When You think of me,
I call You great.
When You love me,
I call You good.
When You fulfil me,
I call You perfect.

1198.

Realisation, my Lord,
You have given to many.
Is there no place for me,
Even as the very last?
If You say "No,"
I shall fully understand You.

1199.

My Lord,
I pretend that I know everything
About You.
You pretend that You know
   nothing
About me.
Both of us are clever
In our own way.

1200.

My Lord of Compassion,
Do You not feel disgraced
When Your Compassion-Light
Surrenders to our darkness-night?

1201.

My Lord,
Have You asked everyone
Not to bring me news about You?
If so, then kindly do me a big
   favour:
Do put an end to the anxiety and
   eagerness
Of my heart-world.

1202.

My desire-life continues,
Unsatisfied.
Yet what compels me to pray to
   You
I do not know.

1203.

My Lord,
Do You mind if I mix with
The uninspiring and unaspiring
Human beings
Before You come to see me?
I shall be all ready
The moment You come.
"My child,
Thinking of future perfection
Is, indeed, absurdity's height."

1204.

My Lord,
I have taken hours and hours
To make a most delicious meal
For You
With my heart of love.
Is it so distasteful
That You do not want to touch it?
How do You know it is so?
My Supreme says:
"My sweetness-child,
No comment!"

1205.

My Lord,
I have spent half my life
Away from You
In my mind's wild jungle.
Now I feel it is high time
For me to leave the jungle
And enter into my heart-garden,
To see Your Eye
And gladden Your Heart.

1206.

It is easy for me to believe
That a seed can grow into a tree,
But how can the tree
Become the seed?
The finite can grow into Infinity,
But how can Infinity breathe
In the heart of the finite?

1207.

My Lord,
My heart is filled
With trembling fear.
When and how will I be able
To beg You
To come to my rescue?

1208.

My past does not control me.
My past only extols
My present-day spiritual life.

1209.

When day is done,
Night comes to prevail.
Before the night's arrival,
My Lord,
Will You not grant me
Your safest Protection?

1210.

My Lord,
I hope You do not mind
If I sit by Your Feet
And ask my eyes
To feast on their Beauty.

1211.

My Lord,
Everything goes well
In my life
Until You reveal my faults
To the world at large.

1212.

My Lord,
My doubting mind is all ready
To take away Your Forgiveness-
    title
If You do not forgive my wretched
    life
Once and for all.

1213.

My Lord,
How do I dare to call You
My own, very own,
When I displease You
At every moment?

1214.

My Lord,
I know You are proud of me
Not because I am great,
But because You are able to make
    me
Humility incarnate.

1215.

My Lord,
You are telling me
That my sinful life
Is not as powerful
As Your Forgiveness-Heart.
If it is true, then prove it!

1216.

My Lord,
I have never disobeyed
Your divine Authority.
So why is it
That You are not blessing me
With more responsibility
To manifest You?

1217.

My Lord,
Is it true that You bring things
To a crisis
So that eventually You can
    perform
Your Safety-Miracles?

1218.

My Lord,
Is there any special reason
Why You are taking such a long
    time
To transform my tragedy-heart
Into a happy ending-life?

1219.

My Lord,
I have only two prayers:
May my mind run away from me;
May my heart always remain with
    me.

1220.

My Lord,
In the morning
I do not succeed in running
    towards You.
In the evening
I also have the same problem.
Is it destined that my desire
Has to remain unsatisfied?

1221.

My Lord,
Sometimes I think
How unkind You are to me
For allowing me,
For such a long time,
To roam idly in indulgence-land.

1222.

My Lord,
I am praying to You
Not for universal authority
But for universal unity.

1223.

My Lord,
Is it true that a falsehood-mind
Carries a heap of sin?
"My child, true, absolutely true!"

1224.

My love of God
May not last forever,
But God's need for me
Forever lasts.

1225.

The divine warrior
May have a very poor start,
But he is bound to win
Eventually.

1226.

My Lord,
Please make me
Even the tiniest star
In Your galaxy of immortal stars.

1227.

I am determined
To arrive at my Goal,
Even through thick forests
Of blunders.

1228.

Delay,
Either necessary or unnecessary,
Dampens our inner joy.

1229.

Since the beginning of human
   incarnation,
Humanity's God-thirst
Has remained unquenchable.

1230.

Truth does not force us,
Truth does not beg us,
Truth just inspires us.

1231.

Either my Lord Supreme
Or His blessingful and watchful
Eye of Love
Follows me wherever I go.

1232.

I do not know
Why and how I allow myself
To remain caught
In entangling, futile and useless
Worldly activities.

1233.

Tragedy
Deadens my heart.
Comedy
Lightens my mind.

1234.

My Lord is so compassionate to
    me!
Every day He allows my devotion
To encircle His Lotus-Feet.

1235.

My Lord asks me
To sing His Heart-Songs
Not only inside my heart-garden,
But also inside my mind-jungle.

1236.

Every day
I release hoards of doubts
From my prison-mind.

1237.

Every day
My soul, my heart and I
Collect a very rich harvest
Of our Master's nectar-utterances.

1238.

To make a friendship perfect,
First it has to be
Sincere, hallowed and self-giving.

1239.

May my aspiration-heart
Every day
Play, sing and dance
With new devotion-blossoms.

1240.

God wants from your life
Divine prosperity,
And not your self-created pride
In your spiritual poverty.

1241.

God does not mind
When I enjoy comfort
At His expense,
But my soul vehemently does.

1242.

At long last,
My smiling soul, my crying heart
    and I
Are returning to our
Divinity's Immortality-Home.

1243.

How can my deaf mind, blind eye
And weak heart
Appreciate the soul-stirring Songs
Of my Lord's Heart?

1244.

My Lord, do You not see
That I am completely exhausted
And totally lost
From playing hide-and-seek with
    You
For centuries,
Uninterrupted!

1245.

To me,
Not the Smiles of my Lord's Eye,
But the Tears of my Lord's Heart
Are my heart's peerless treasures.

1246.

May my mind be full of
    inspiration-leaves,
My heart be full of aspiration-
    flowers
And my life be full of satisfaction-
    fruits.

1247.

O my mind,
God definitely loves you dearly.
Do not allow yourself
To get lost
In the thickest fog of disbelief!

1248.

God tells me
That I have come into the world
To enjoy the sweetness of His
    Heart
And not the bitterness of my life.

1249.

How stupid I am
When I allow my insect-mind
To try to inject wisdom
Into my heart!

1250.

My Lord,
I need silence and silence and
    silence.
Do silence the drumbeats
Of my outer life.

1251.

May each thought of my life
Be blessed with a new throb
Of my heart.

1252.

The world of my mind
Is smaller
Than the tiniest hole.

1253.

The world of my heart
Is vaster
Than Vastness itself.

1254.

My Lord,
I am so grateful to You
For giving me a heart
That accepts Your Praise-Fountain
And the world's blame-mountain
With equanimity.

1255.

My mind's newness, my heart's
    oneness
And my life's fulness
Live together inside my Lord's
Heart-Home.

1256.

I must develop an adamantine
    will
To become the sacred fire
Of ceaseless God-remembrance.

1257.

My Lord,
I do not like Your Divinity's
    suggestions,
But I appreciate, admire, adore
    and love
Your Divinity's assertions.

1258.

If my heart is not a God-prayer,
Then how can my life ever be
A God-lover?

1259.

When I do not aspire,
I surrender my mind
To my preoccupations.
When I aspire,
I surrender my heart
To my God-service-occupation.

1260.

My life's self-control
Has made my eyes
Infinitely more beautiful
Than I ever could imagine.

1261.

The further I keep away from
The sound-life of the finite,
The closer I shall come to
The Silence-Heart of the Infinite.

1262.

It is dangerous
To bind oneself
In self-opinion.

1263.

I beg God
To give my mind a little freedom.
God begs me
To accept His Heart's unbounded
    Kingdom.

1264.

My Lord's Grace has descended.
I shall now be able to fell
The tall trees of my God-denial-
    mind.

1265.

How beautiful I look
When I live in the daylight
Of my heart's blossoming smiles!

1266.

My Lord,
I do not want You to respect my
    sleep,
But I want You to expect
The acceleration of my readiness.

1267.

In God's entire creation,
There can be no heart
That will ever be deserted
By God's Love.

1268.

O my heart's dream-angels,
Where are you?
Do appear and play
Your God-Victory-trumpets!

1269.

God definitely does not want me
    to live
Inside an unhappy corner of my
    mind.
It is I who have chosen to live there
Unfortunately and blindly.

1270.

The silence of my heart
Reverberates
In the happiness-flooded Heart
Of my Lord Supreme.

1271.

Every day
In my heart-temple
I drink the Foot wash
Of my Beloved Supreme.

1272.

Do not forget
That you are your Lord's chosen
    child.
It does not become you
To mix with ignorance-soldiers.

1273.

Humanity is humanity's
Utter shamelessness.
Divinity is Divinity's
Helpless sorrow.

1274.

My mind wants God
Unmistakably
To be proud of my mind.
My heart wants God
Throbbingly
To be fond of my heart.
My life wants God
Desperately
To be the only Ruler of my life.

1275.

My Lord,
My mind's sincerity,
My heart's purity
And my life's surrender
Are only for You to enjoy,
And for nobody else.

1276.

If you want to enjoy
The pleasure-life,
Then you do it
At your own inner expense.
Destruction will soon start
Running after you!

1277.

I wanted to have an inner
    conversation
With my Lord Supreme.
He said to me,
"My child,
You have to wait
Until we meet face to face."

1278.

The mind cannot give us peace
Because the mind
Does not have peace.
God's Feet have peace,
And God is telling us
That His Feet are all ready
To bless us with peace.
We have just to touch Them.

1279.

To my aspiring heart,
Faith is not something
That I have to discover
Inside God's Heart.
My breathless faith
Is itself God.

1280.

Faith can be achieved
Only from God-experience
And not from mind-information.

1281.

The verbosity of the mind
Drowns the veracity
Of the heart.

1282.

I have come to realise
That talking without loving
Is merely barking.

1283.

End your conversation
With ignorance-night.
Lo, God's Illumination
Is speeding towards you.

1284.

If you do not allow your mind
To disobey God,
You and your heart
Will be able to feed each other
Sumptuously.

1285.

My Lord, now that You know
That my heart
Is all sincere love for You,
Can You not expedite
My God-realisation-hour?

1286.

Desire tortures us
Infinitely more than
It gives us happiness.

1287.

When we do away with
Our doubt and suspicion-mind,
God teaches us
The language of sweetness,
Affection and devotion
So we can converse with Him.

1288.

If our mind is all hesitation,
Then God-experience-hope
Will never be able to come near us,
Not to speak of clasping us.

1289.

Wisdom is not self-imposition.
Wisdom is not self-mortification.
Wisdom is not smearing oneself
    with ashes.
Wisdom is not the forest-life.
Wisdom is not self-abnegation.
Wisdom is God's Shelter.

1290.

You say that
You are a God-listener.
Then how is it that you are not
A good God-lover?

1291.

My Lord,
My desire-life is so tiny.
Your Compassion-Heart is so
    huge.
Why do You refuse to satisfy
My poor little desire-life?

1292.

My Lord,
Why do I have to wait for joy
From the fulfilment of my desire-
    life?
Can You not bless me with
    unbounded joy
Even before I show You my desire-
    list?
If You do so,
I can easily discard
My desire-list.

1293.

My Lord,
To protect my body, vital, mind
And heart,
I beg of You not to allow
Your Compassion-Eye
To sleep anymore.

1294.

Faith we need
To love God permanently.
Surrender we need
To satisfy God fully.

1295.

My Lord,
Can You not be
As fond of Your Generosity
As I am fond of my cravings?
In this way,
You can solve all my problems.

1296.

When I do not think of God,
I am a stranger to God.
When I pray to God,
I become His neighbour.
When I surrender
My very existence-life to God,
I become a member
Of His immediate Family.

1297.

My Lord,
Can You not count and count and
    count
All the good things
I have done for You?
I am sure that while counting,
You will fall fast asleep.
Then You will not be able
To count all the bad things
I have done to You.
God smilingly says to me,
    "Amen!"

1298.

My Lord,
When I place my head
At Your Feet,
You say to me, "Not enough!"
When I place my life
At Your Feet,
You say to me, "Not enough!"
My Lord, when will it be enough?
"It will be enough
When you can assure Me
That you will not take them back."

1299.

My Lord,
Can You not see
That I am suffering
From a life-threatening doubt-
    stroke?
Where is
Your Compassion-Emergency
    Room,
Where?

1300.

May my gratitude-heart-flower
To my Lord Supreme
Forever and forever remain pure.

1301.

My prayer, my meditation,
My aspiration and my dedication
Together are on
A world-peace-tour.

1302.

O seeker,
Be fully determined
Not to allow your mind
To collapse
Under its doubt-burden.

1303.

I am astonished
That I have
A shameless desire-mountain-life.

1304.

I have taken a short cut
By avoiding my mind's
Desire-forest
To enter into my heart-garden.

1305.

My Lord,
I do not know how You do it.
You never count it
When You give me anything
Unreservedly and
    unconditionally.
But whenever I give you
    something,
You not only count it
But also add infinitely more.

1306.

The power of humility
Has the capacity to simplify
The mind's complicated ego-life.

1307.

My life's devotional gratitude
To my Lord Supreme
Revives my heart-flower.

1308.

God is always eager
To eat
Humanity's oneness-meal.

1309.

God likes to read
Our gratitude-heart-letters
Long before He reads
Any other letters.

1310.

Those who want to explore the
    heart
Will have no time
To indulge in the thought-world.

1311.

Every day
I decorate my shrine
With the tears
Of my devotion-heart.

1312.

Yes, you can silence your mind
With the aspiration, beauty,
Purity and divinity
Of your heart.

1313.

Every day a new, illumining
And fulfilling life
Must come into existence
From our aspiration-heart.

1314.

Every day my Lord Supreme
Wants me to feed my heart
With devotion-tears,
And I do it readily, willingly
And eagerly.

1315.

What is enthusiasm?
Enthusiasm is something
That immediately activates
Our God-satisfaction-willingness.

1316.

Every day we must increase
Our heart's devotion-tears
To enjoy the delight
Of God-satisfaction.

1317.

My soul wants me every day
To aim at
A perfection-life
And a God-satisfaction-heart.

1318.

Oneness has the magic power
To remove our insecurity-barriers
In the twinkling of an eye.

1319.

A God-disobedience-mind
Will never realise
How happy and fulfilled
A God-obedience-heart is.

1320.

God wants to give my mind
Infinity's freedom.
My mind immediately rejects it,
And my heart gets terribly
   frightened.

1321.

My soul tells my heart
That if I want to make
Rapid progress
In my spiritual life,
Then I have to look at
The brightness only
In every little thing
That I see and do.

1322.

I tell God,
"My Lord, I am not in a hurry.
I can linger indefinitely
In expectation of Your Arrival."

1323.

Self-indulgence-fire
Is unimaginably difficult
To extinguish altogether.

1324.

If you are not on speaking terms
With your soul,
Then every day your God-
    disappointment
Will loom large, larger, largest
Inside your heart.

1325.

Every time I have a good thought
In my mind,
God blesses me with a new
    bodyguard
To protect my life.

1326.

Alas, when shall I realise
That human friendships
Are extremely, extremely fragile?

1327.

Each dedication-life
Is a soul-stirring piece
Of God's Music.

1328.

My outer life is governed
By my restless thoughts.
My inner life is regulated
By my God-feelings.

1329.

Nothing is as valuable
As my heart's cry
For my Lord Beloved Supreme.

1330.

Every day I pray to God
To give me the capacity to fulfil
  Him,
And not for a happiness-harvest-
  life.

1331.

When my heart and I
Fail to smile at each other,
I see my life is completely
Upside down.

1332.

Love-devotion-surrender-flowers
Are available in our life-trees.
But alas, we do not pluck them
And place them at the Feet
Of our Lord Supreme.

1333.

God's Compassion-ringing Bell
Awakens
My morning prayer-heart.

1334.

God tells me that
My searching mind is reliable,
But my crying heart is not only
  reliable
And dependable,
But also extremely valuable.

1335.

If you live with your doubting
  mind,
Then sooner or later
You are bound to take the exit
To destruction-abyss.

1336.

Do not argue
With your suspicion-mind.
You will add only more ignorance
To your life.
Be wise.
Just ignore it!

1337.

God wants me to smile
Not as His slave,
But as a choice representative
Of His Satisfaction-Heart.

1338.

There are many games
God plays with me,
But He loves most
The hide-and-seek game.

1339.

My Lord, I love Your Lotus-Feet
Infinitely more than I love
Anything else of Yours.

1340.

God tells me
That He will withdraw
His Forgiveness
If I do not totally forget
My Himalayan blunders.

1341.

Today's determination
Is definitely strong enough
To bury my deplorable past.

1342.

God does not care for
My heart's trembling fears.
But He loves and loves and loves
My heart's beaming smiles.

1343.

My heart's aspiration-flames
Are blazing
My life's transformation-path.

1344.

My inner vision far supersedes
The calculation
Of my outer achievements.

1345.

Because of my undivine mind,
No matter what God does,
I fail to appreciate it.

1346.

Because of my divine heart,
No matter what God does,
Not only do I appreciate
But I also heartily admire it.

1347.

Where do I come from?
Alas, I come from
Lethargy's unlimited
Indulgence-fund.

1348.

Where am I going?
I am going
To Infinity's unknowable
Ecstasy-Blossoms.

1349.

The specially blessed ones
Love to walk together
Towards their Destination.

1350.

Self-glory or God-discovery:
Make your choice,
Here and now!

1351.

My Lord, look, look!
My mind's hesitation-fog has
    vanished.
Please, please book me
On the next boat
To Your Golden Shore.

1352.

My Lord's Compassion-Eye
And my own aspiration-heart
Every day dine
In the Heart-Garden of my Lord.

1353.

Even the convictions
Of the human mind
Are more fickle
Than the wind.

1354.

My seeker-friend,
Look how beautiful
Your aspiration-tree is
And how powerful
Your dedication-branches are!

1355.

Our desire-life
Never takes 'no'
As an answer
From God.

1356.

Ego, you must go, you must!
"Tell me, where?"
None of my concern;
Only you must go, you must!

1357.

If you can sincerely say and feel
That God-obedience is your life-
    breath,
Then your heart's aspiration-
    plants
Will grow by leaps and bounds.

1358.

My Lord, I am sleeplessly
And breathlessly grateful to You
For blessing me
With a heart-pleasing mind.

1359.

I have changed my mind totally!
I shall never again walk
On my desire-life-street.

1360.

A Heaven-aspiring dream
I have.
A Heaven-manifesting reality
I am.

1361.

I long to live between
My Eternity's heart-cries
And
My Infinity's soul-smiles.

1362.

Can you imagine
What God's Grace can do!
I cannot even remember
Where the desire-road is.

1363.

Each aspiration-dream
Of my heart
Is the beginning
Of a reality-manifestation
In my life.

1364.

No more shall I surrender
To my mind's labyrinthine
    thoughts,
No more!

1365.

A clever man relies on nothing.
A wise man relies on everything.
A God-loving man relies on God
In everything.

1366.

I offer my heart's gratitude-breath
To my Lord Supreme
Before the birth of my prayer-
    hour.

1367.

I have regained
My God-faith completely.
My doubting mind
Is thunderstruck!

1368.

My ego-satisfaction
And my soul-frustration
Are always at war.
My Lord, please come
And take my soul's side.

1369.

May my bitterness-mind
And my sweetness-heart
Both take shelter at the same time
At the Feet of my Lord Supreme.

1370.

Alas, in vain
I have been in search of
New tomorrows!

1371.

The philosophy of the mind
Can confine you, bind you
And even blind you.

1372.

God touched the false seeker's
Desire-hands
And smashed them asunder.

1373.

God touched the genuine seeker's
Aspiration-hands
And blessingfully and proudly
Clasped them.

1374.

If you always want to justify
Whatever you do and say,
Then the spiritual life
Is not meant for you.

1375.

If you take spirituality
As your expectation-fulfilment-
    smile,
Then you are feeding absurdity.

1376.

Do not retire.
Desire to be great,
Aspire to be good,
Surrender to be perfect.
Do not retire.

1377.

My heart-tears discover
God the Emperor.
My life-smiles discover
God the Supreme Lover.

1378.

All I need
Is an inspiration-encouragement-
    Smile
From my Lord Supreme
To run the fastest in my inner life.

1379.

My mind,
Are you not tired of
Your hostile monster-atrocities?

1380.

Every day I pray to God
For a oneness-vision,
But alas, division-realities
Come and threaten me.

1381.

If I do not obey God's Call,
Who can bless my mind with
    peace?
Nobody!

1382.

My tearful devotion-songs
Are dissolving the sorrows
Of my heart.

1383.

Quite often God asks
My aspiration-heart to smile,
My gratitude-heart to sing
And my surrender-heart to dance
For Him.

1384.

My Master's outer strictness-face
Frightens me.
My Master's inner sweetness-
    heart
Enlightens me.

1385.

The road of service can be
A two-way street,
But the road of surrender has to be
A one-way street.

1386.

Do not try to escape
From doubt and fear.
Challenge them and conquer
  them
If you really want to be
A choice instrument of God's Will.

1387.

Aspiration is difficult to choose.
Dedication is a hundred times
More difficult.
Manifestation is a million times
More difficult.

1388.

My heart has always
A blissful dialogue with God.
My mind has always
A painful dialogue with God.
I have always
A fruitful dialogue with God.

1389.

I love those
Who live for God-realisation,
But I love infinitely more
Those who live for God-
  manifestation.

1390.

When the giver gives you
Happily and unreservedly,
You receive a double amount.

1391.

A self-giving heart
Is God's
Compassion-Wisdom-publisher.

1392.

The moment he left
His desire-mansion,
His riot of wild thoughts
Immediately stopped.

1393.

As the doubting mind
Is always blameable,
Even so the God-searching heart
Is always laudable.

1394.

A self-proclamation-mind
And a self-dedication-heart
Are eternal rivals.

1395.

Aspiration's best friend
Is not pleasure.
Aspiration's best friend
Is not comfort.
Aspiration's best friend
Is God's Compassion-bestowing
     Eye.

1396.

Love expands,
Love magnifies,
Love beautifies
And love unifies
A seeker's heart.

1397.

The joy of manifestation
Is not a duty
And not a responsibility,
But a supreme opportunity
To bring to the fore
One's own divinity.

1398.

When I bend my heart to God,
He blesses me with His magnetic
     Smile.
When I bend my mind to God,
He sings, He runs, He jumps
And dances all-where.

1399.

The calculation-mind
And the compassion-heart
Are always far apart.

1400.

Self-doubt weakens
Our God-manifestation-
     possibilities
Most tragically.

1401.

My God-hunger
And my God-love
Are the two most
God-pleasing twins.

1402.

True, to come out of
The desire-mind-jungle
Is not an easy task,
But not an impossible task either.

1403.

My heart is crying
And crying
In the land of deaf ears.

1404.

The mind's attachment-forest
Is extremely
Life-threatening.

1405.

God does not come down to
    frighten,
But to enlighten
His insecurity-children.

1406.

Every morning,
When you pray most self-givingly,
You are bound to be embraced
By God's Delight-Heart.

1407.

Your God-fulfilling dreams
Are founded upon
Your life's goodness-heart.

1408.

A good seeker is the result
Of God's
Compassion-Blessing-Eye.

1409.

God takes me
Under His Protection-Wings
When I aim at
My personality-perfection.

1410.

Even my Lord's Compassion-Eye
May not accompany me at times,
But His Forgiveness-Heart
Always accompanies me.

1411.

When your heart
Is all readiness,
God the Fulness
Proudly arrives.

1412.

Aspiration is my heart's
God-climbing certitude.
Dedication is my life's
God-spreading certitude.

1413.

Do not weep
In the despair-night of your heart.
It does not become you.

1414.

I never listen
To humanity's thunder-march,
But I do devotedly listen
To Divinity's Silence-Steps.

1415.

My Lord, I feel it is high time
For me to know
When my life's bondage-chains
Will be broken.

1416.

Wisdom
Can cross all boundaries
At its sweet will.

1417.

Knowledge quite often
Ends up in
A dead-end street.

1418.

Every morning my Lord comes
To bless my mind
With a silence-sea,
But my sleeping mind
Rejects His Offering.

1419.

Sweeter than the sweetest
And richer than the richest
Are our gratitude-tears.

1420.

Alas, how can I make progress
In my inner life
When I clearly see
That my heart is made of tears
And my life is made of sighs?

1421.

God's first Smile was born
The day humanity awoke
To His Light.

1422.

Desires roam
In the pathless
Jungle-mind.

1423.

Every day Heaven whispers
God-manifestation-messages
To my aspiration-heart.

1424.

God smiles
To inspire the outer world
To sing His Glory.

1425.

God sings
To inspire the inner world
To proclaim His Victory.

1426.

A gratitude-heart
Is the master key
That opens up all the rooms
Of God's Heart-Palace.

1427.

Static spirituality
Is an antique spirituality,
And my aspiration-heart
Wants nothing to do with it.

1428.

The mind's possession-obsession
Is the spiritual life's
Gradual destruction.

1429.

Human love
Is quite often
A pretense-specialist.

1430.

Divine love
Is God's
Compassion-invocation-
     specialist.

1431.

Because of his purity-heart,
He has the Heaven-smile
In his eye.

1432.

O my mind,
Do not remain any longer
     addicted
To the path of vanity's unreality.

1433.

O my heart,
Forever remain devoted
To the path of reality's beauty.

1434.

I adore
My Master's
Temper-proof poise.

1435.

I worship
My Master's
Infinity's Silence-Heart-Sky.

1436.

A simplicity-mind
And a sincerity-heart
Are the two most loyal subjects
In God's Heart-Kingdom.

1437.

I have emptied
The sorrows of my heart
Into my Lord's Sympathy-Heart-
    Sea.

1438.

A goodness-heart
Is definitely entitled
To sweet dreams.

1439.

God wants from me
A service-life
And not a servility-mind.

1440.

No matter how thorny,
How arduous and how
    challenging
The road is,
I shall never, never fail
My Lord Supreme again!

1441.

The outer riches –
Prosperity, name and fame –
Have limits.

1442.

The inner riches –
Poise, peace and delight –
Have no limits.

1443.

I am enraptured
By the Silence-Sound
Of my Lord's Forgiveness-Feet.

1444.

Insignificant thoughts
Aimlessly and foolishly
Rule the outer world.

1445.

Look forward!
Run and run towards your Goal!
You have no time to lament
Your past lethargy-life.

1446.

As long as there is breath
Inside my heart,
I shall devote myself only
To my God-manifestation-task.

1447.

The more I use
My God-obedience-life,
The brighter I see
My Lord's Satisfaction-Smile.

1448.

God always tells me
Smilingly and proudly
To do anything that expedites
My inner and outer progress.

1449.

Disobedience is nothing other
   than
A downhill race
To the abysmal abyss.

1450.

God finds it impossible
To be near my idle mouth
And empty hands.

1451.

The happiness of my today's heart
Cannot be preserved
For tomorrow.
Tomorrow I must pray
For a new happiness-heart.

1452.

I know, I know
My present failure-life
Will before long vanish
Inside the beauty
Of my heart's new dreams.

1453.

A hero-God-warrior
Is he whose temptation-life
Dies untested.

1454.

When my mind suffers,
I use different kinds of painkillers.
But my Lord's smiling Eye
Not only is by far the best,
But also is an immediate cure.

1455.

I have given my Lord Supreme
The copyright for my life.
Therefore, like a free bird,
I am flying in the vastness-sky.

1456.

Only to the aspiring heart
Does God choose to teach
His own Heart-Language.

1457.

The mind's complacency
And the life's failure
Always live together.

1458.

When God comes
To say something to my mind,
Immediately my mind
Resonates with the sound of "No!"

1459.

When God comes
To say something to my heart,
My heart first breathes in
The dust of God's Feet,
And then resonates with the
    sound
Of "Yes, yes, yes!"

1460.

Alas, will there ever come a time
For earth to celebrate
Its peace-victory-festival?

1461.

O my ignorance-night-life,
Sleep no more!
It is high time
For you to wake up.

1462.

The mind's
God-dedication-car
Stalls more often
Than it ever runs.

1463.

My heart's devotion
Is the perfect multiplication
Of my God-love.

1464.

A true compassion-heart
Will never run short
Of love.

1465.

O my disobedience-mind,
Look what you have done!
You have smashed
All my God-fulfilment-dreams
Into pieces.

1466.

My mind's hesitation-torture-life
Has devoured
All my God-fulfilment-promises.

1467.

An unconditional surrender-path
My Lord Supreme
Has already paved for me.

1468.

The brilliance
Of my intelligence-mind
Is no match for
The radiance
Of my aspiration-heart.

1469.

My God-unwillingness-mind
Is a serious threat
To my heart's golden future.

1470.

A true prayer
Always enters into
Its heart-home,
Smiling and smiling and smiling.

1471.

Can you imagine!
Even my mind
Is exceedingly happy
With my constant
God-satisfaction-choice.

1472.

For a seeker,
God's Standard
Is the only standard
To live by.

1473.

My Lord, I beg of You
A million times
To steal my desire-eyes
And replace them with
My aspiration-heart.

1474.

My God-surrendering heart,
I adore you,
I love you –
Far beyond your imagination.

1475.

O my Master,
When I see tears in your eyes,
I see that you are
My only Way.
When I see smiles in your eyes,
I realise that you are
My only Goal.

1476.

My Lord, You think I cannot,
But I am sure I can.
One day I shall make You love
My wish.
And my Lord, what is my wish?
My wish is to please You
And fulfil You unconditionally
In Your own Way.

1477.

My Lord, the world thinks
That I am mad.
You know and I know
That my madness is only my cry
To be at Your Feet.
My Lord, I pray to You
Not to take away this madness.

1478.

My Lord, I thought that by
    fulfilling
My desire-life,
I would become extremely strong.
But now I see that by taking away
My desire-life,
You have made me stronger
Than the strongest.

1479.

My Lord, when I do not please You
In Your own Way,
Do make me feel only one thing:
That I am a mere nothing.
This feeling of nothingness
Will wake me up.

1480.

My Lord,
Without Your unconditional
    Compassion,
I could not have separated
My heart-dreams
From my mind-nightmares.

1481.

My Lord,
How can I destroy
My insincerity-mind?
"My child,
Forget about your insincerity-
    mind.
Just think of the beauty and
    fragrance
Of your sincerity-heart
All the time."

1482.

My Lord,
How can I make my life sweet?
"My child,
Just sing the Glory of My Name.
Your life, inner and outer,
Will be sweeter than the
    sweetest."

1483.

My Lord,
My heart wants me to kiss Your
    Feet,
But my soul wants me to embrace
    You.
What shall I do, my Lord?
"My child,
Always listen to your soul.
Your soul is My direct
    representative
On earth."

1484.

When I touch my Lord's Feet,
Lo and behold,
All my mind's desires
And all my heart's aspirations
Run away together
Faster than the fastest,
And Infinity's Satisfaction smiles
    and sports
Inside my life.

1485.

My Lord,
By Your Grace I have many good
    things
In my life.
But now can You tell me
If by offering only one particular
    thing
I shall be able to please You
    forever?
"My child,
There is such a thing,
And that thing is your sleepless
And breathless faith in Me."

1486.

When my sincerity-heart
Loves God,
My life cannot measure
My joy.

1487.

God's Compassion-Eye
Has led my life to my Master.
My Master's eagerness-heart
Will carry me to God's Feet.

1488.

My Lord Beloved Supreme,
The very thought of You
Is the treasure chamber
Of all my happiness.

1489.

Sufferings chase me
When I forget my Master's heart.
But when I remember my Master's
    heart,
My Master chases away my
    sufferings.

1490.

My Lord tells me that silence-joy
Is not only the right thing,
But also the only thing to embody,
    reveal
And manifest
Here on earth.

1491.

My Lord quite abruptly
Entered into my mind,
Caught my pride
And threw it away.

1492.

My Lord quite unexpectedly
Entered into my vital,
Caught my impurity
And threw it away.

1493.

My Lord, with no warning,
Entered into my heart,
Caught my insecurity
And threw it away.

1494.

My Lord on tiptoe
Entered into my body,
Caught my lethargy
And threw it away.

1495.

My Lord threw away
My pride, impurity, insecurity
And lethargy
Only to replace them
With His Pride supreme.

1496.

My Lord gave me a worshipping
    heart.
But when He realised
That I was not complete,
He gave me a surrendering life
To make me
Complete and perfect.

1497.

My Lord tells me
That He gets joy only twice:
Once when I preach to His Mind
And once when He teaches my
    heart.

1498.

Each enlightened soul
Shortens the distance
Between humanity
And the God-Satisfaction-Shore.

1499.

Alas, when my Lord says nothing
To my heart,
My heart feels miserable,
And when my Lord says
    something
To my mind,
My mind feels miserable.
I ask my Lord,
"How can I have such a miserable
    fate?"
My Lord tells me
That I have such a miserable fate
Because my heart has not studied
Oneness-lesson,
And my mind has not studied
Illumination-lesson.

1500.

Inactive faith
Sleeps inside our minds.
Active faith
Lives inside our hearts.

1501.

Poor God every day
Begs us to allow Him
To arrest all the evil forces
That are ruthlessly torturing us.
But we do not allow Him
Because we are somehow enjoying
The wild temptation-bond
Of the evil forces.

1502.

When we soulfully pray
And self-givingly meditate,
Our prayer-universe
And meditation-universe
Immediately expand.

1503.

A God-server is, indeed,
A supreme hero
Of both the inner world
And the outer world.

1504.

Early in the morning
God rings only three doorbells—
My life's readiness-doorbell,
My mind's willingness-doorbell
And my heart's eagerness-
      doorbell.

1505.

The twentieth century is
      undoubtedly
An age of self-imposed worries
And anxieties.

1506.

I actually cannot measure
My heart-joy
When I touch the Lotus-Feet
Of my Lord Supreme.

1507.

The devotion of the heart
Unmistakably indicates
The blossoming of the seeker's
God-satisfaction-life.

1508.

I am applying myself
To the life of perfection.
I shall never deviate
From the path
Of my determination.

1509.

The sufferings of my heart
In no time vanish
When I remember the
    Compassion-Eye
Of my Absolute Lord Supreme.

1510.

I have found peace,
Not in my feeble attempt
To perfect the world,
But in my daring attempt
To silence my mind.

1511.

The silence of the mind
And the peace of the heart
Are inseparable.

1512.

I was drowning
In my mind's ignorance-sea
Until I bravely and safely reached
My Lord's Compassion-Heart-
    Shore.

1513.

If we have a sleeplessly self-giving
    life,
Then no special effort is needed
To be in the Presence
Of our Lord's Satisfaction-Heart.

1514.

Human beings praise me and
    blame me
In accordance with their sweet
    will,
But my Lord is the only one
Who claims me smilingly, proudly
And unconditionally.

1515.

God can expedite His Hour.
He can even bring His Hour
And place it right here and now.
But alas, where is my receptivity,
Where?

1516.

If you want to enjoy world-
   pleasures,
Then enjoy them to your heart's
   content.
But remember,
Destruction-night shall start
   chasing you
Before long.

1517.

We get tremendous pleasure
Speaking to our friends,
And we forget to speak to God.
But God exists in the very breath
Of our life,
And when God stops talking to us,
We get frightened.
Then we start speaking to Him,
Only to Him.

1518.

The sacred and secret Truth
Can be discovered
In the God-blossoming heart
Of the seeker.

1519.

Remain seated at God's Feet
While serving
The omnipresent Vision-Eye
Of the Lord Supreme.

1520.

Delight will dawn upon you
When you consciously and
   deliberately
Stop conversing
With your God-doubting mind.

1521.

Peace of mind
Is bound to be there,
Where the faith of the heart
Reigns supreme.

1522.

If only once
I can convince my mind
That I am only of God
And I am only for God,
Then there will be nothing left
   undone.

1523.

My Lord, I have renounced
My earthly desire-life.
Now I have taken You
As my only desire.

1524.

Who says that we have no
    authority
Over time?
God's Compassion-Eye
Can easily sanction it.

1525.

When I forget to think of myself,
God not only thinks of me
But also talks about me.

1526.

Alas, my Lord, how many things
I have said and I have done
To remove myself
From Your Heart-Garden!

1527.

Hard it was for me to find You,
    Lord,
Harder to receive Blessings from
    You.
But now my hands and my heart
Are full of Your Blessing-
    Blossoms.

1528.

Before I was nothing at all.
But now that I am at Your Feet,
You make me feel
That I am Your Dream-Reality's
    all.

1529.

My Lord says to me,
"My child,
Now that I have burnt up
Your past life-history,
Can you not come and be with Me
As My Heart's
Perfection-Satisfaction-Smile?"

1530.

The path that leads me back to life
For God-manifestation
I shall follow happily and proudly.

1531.

My Lord asks me:
"My child,
Since your love of Me costs
    nothing,
Why do you not love Me?"

1532.

My Lord asks me:
"My child,
Since your God-realisation-dream
Costs nothing,
Why do you not apply yourself
To your God-realisation-dream?"

1533.

I am weeping and sobbing
Not because God has rejected
My life,
But because I have deserted
God's Heart.

1534.

My Lord has promised me
That not only His Compassion-
    Eye,
But also His Forgiveness-Heart
Will follow me,
No matter where I go.

1535.

God has no time
To think of my ascetic mind,
But He has all the time
To bless my self-giving heart.

1536.

I am a beggar,
And I am proud of my beggar-life.
But what do I actually beg for?
God's Compassion-flooded Smile.

1537.

I know the sacred meaning
Of what God says to me.
God knows the secret significance
Of what I do not say to Him.

1538.

My Lord always encourages me,
Inspires me and feeds me
By saying that I am not
What I seem.
According to Him,
I am another blooming,
    blossoming God.

1539.

When I enjoy idle words,
My Lord immediately becomes
A sea of tears.

1540.

Finally, I have stilled
My flying desires.
My Lord tells me
That I am a supreme authority
On the desire-rejection-life.

1541.

God wanted me to be
His devoted listener.
I obeyed Him.
Now He wants me to be
His world-lover, His world-server
And His world-transformer.

1542.

O seeker, do not miss the road.
Do not enter into your mind-
    jungle.
Be careful, be cautious, be
    watchful,
Be mindful!
Take the right path.
Your heart-garden is eagerly
Waiting for you.

1543.

My Lord,
I have come crying to You.
I want to love You once more.
Do give me a chance.
Do turn me into Your Eternity's
Smiling self-giver.

1544.

My Lord, once upon a time
My heart was faithful,
My mind was dependable,
My life was serviceable.
Do tell me, who has robbed me
Of those virtues?

1545.

When my mind spends time
Studying the differences
Between the scriptures,
The seeker in me
Gets painfully and completely
    lost.

1546.

When my heart spends time
In meditation,
God's Heart proudly claims me
And God's Life blessingfully
Appoints me.

1547.

The secret desire of my mind
Is to dominate the world.
The sacred desire of my heart
Is to love the world.
The perfect desire of my soul
Is to become inseparably one
With the world.

1548.

May every human being
Tell every other human being
How close he feels to God.

1549.

My Lord,
Since I cannot govern my desires,
Can You not, on my behalf,
Govern them
With Your absolute Authority?

1550.

My Lord tells me
That He will protect me
From all future entanglements
If I can place,
Once and for all,
My information-head
And my confusion-mind
At His Feet.

1551.

It may be difficult
To accept God's Justice-Eye,
But it is extremely easy
To love God's Forgiveness-Heart.
Let nobody hesitate.

1552.

Alas, I have become
My heart-night's
Helpless cry.

1553.

God tells the doubting mind
That He will never give it
His Home Address.

1554.

Every morning my prayer-tears
Most soulfully worship
The Feet of my Lord Supreme.

1555.

O my mind, go forward!
Go forward!
Stop counting your days of
    miseries.

1556.

The rejection of God's Will
Eventually becomes itself
The most furious punishment.

1557.

Our ceaseless cries for power
Compel God
To sigh and sigh.

1558.

What makes us
A real loser?
Our height and depth
Of pride!

1559.

What is patience?
Patience is
An illumining inner light.

1560.

If you lose
Your heart's devotion-tears,
Then all the fears of the inner
    world
Will attack you.

1561.

Do not exercise
Your authority-power,
Do not!
There are superior powers
That will compel you ruthlessly
To surrender to them.

1562.

If it is wrong,
Your sincere heart
Is always ready to admit,
Instead of justifying.

1563.

Lethargy is, indeed,
A force undivine, uninspiring
And unfulfilling.

1564.

Nothing can protect you
As adequately and as perfectly
As your obedience-heart.

1565.

Self-sufficiency
Eventually ends
In the most deplorable misery.

1566.

One Compassion-flooded Smile
From my Lord Supreme
Changes my inner world.

1567.

I challenge my mind's
Negativity
With my heart's
Rainbow-beauty.

1568.

If there is real love
For God,
Then obedience
Has to follow.

1569.

We have many enemies,
But our worst enemy
Is our vital depression.

1570.

God's blessingful and poignant
    Song
Echoes and re-echoes
Inside my aspiration-heart-
    garden.

1571.

A seeker must devotedly live
In the hope of arriving
At his destined Goal.

1572.

My Lord, save me!
Save my life
From my constant refusals.

1573.

My Lord,
If You really love me,
Then do not make any Request.
Just command
And command
And command!

1574.

My Lord,
When others blame me
    unjustifiably
And even unnecessarily,
Do give me the capacity
To be perfect
In Your own Way.

1575.

My Lord,
Do not give me freedom!
Do not give me freedom!
I am apt to misuse it,
And then my doom chases me.

1576.

You cannot and you must not
Avoid reality.
You must face reality
And cast forth your reality
In accordance with God's Will.

1577.

O mind, my restless mind,
Right now stop here!
Stop and offer your prayerful
    gratitude
To our Lord Supreme.

1578.

When my mind comes to me,
I tell my mind
That I am extremely busy.
"Come later! Come later!"
This is the game
That I play with my mind.

1579.

I pray to my Lord Supreme
To give me news.
It does not have to be good news.
Any news from Him
Enlightens me and satisfies me.

1580.

Ignorance-night
Is curious to know
What the seekers are doing
In the small hours
Of the morning.

1581.

Lord Buddha saw
Over two thousand years ago
What I am seeing now.
Lord Krishna saw
Over five thousand years ago
What I am seeing now.
What am I seeing?
I am seeing
The beauty, the harmony
And the fragrance
Of Infinity's Vision-Delight-Light.

1582.

Each desire of our mind
Leads us with tremendous
    eagerness
To more and more and more
    desires.

1583.

An inner revolution
Is of paramount importance
To shatter the ignorance-pride
Of humanity.

1584.

Who chooses what?
God chooses
My mind's ignorance-night
For transformation.
I choose
My Lord's Compassion-Eye
For satisfaction.

1585.

My Lord,
If You do not love me,
Tell me the truth.
I shall become a better person
So that You can love me.

1586.

My Lord,
Once more invent my soul,
Invent my heart,
And invent my life
To please You in Your own Way.

1587.

To succeed and to proceed,
I must reconcile first
My outer life and my inner life.

1588.

At long last
I have restored
My long-lost heart-shrine.

1589.

My Lord, I beg of You
To stop my insatiable
Power-hunger.

1590.

My mind,
I shall be so happy
And so proud of you
If you allow me to enjoy
A longer than the longest
Vacation from you.

1591.

When disaster strikes,
It never, never gives us
Any notice.

1592.

The human mind
Does not mind
When contradictions
Become its ruler.

1593.

When we pray and meditate
Soulfully and ceaselessly,
We enter into a world
Where Divinity blooms
And blossoms.

1594.

The purity, fragrance, light
And power
Of a prayerful action
Are unimaginable.

1595.

You say that you have nothing to
   do.
But I tell you,
You have something to do
That you are not aware of.
You have to bury your fear,
Bury your self-doubt
And bury your God-doubt
Here and now.

1596.

A citizen
Of the inner world
Is anxiety-proof.

1597.

My Lord,
How long do I have to continue
Wrestling with wicked fears?

1598.

God speaks to us most clearly
Through each and every
   experience
That we receive from Him.

1599.

Every day God invites us
To enter into a divine partnership,
But fear tortures us,
And we do not accept His
   Invitation.

1600.

Patience lengthens my time
And shortens the distance
To my Destination.

1601.

A self-oriented mind
Will never be able
To please God.

1602.

A God-surrendered heart
Always pleases God
In His own Way.

1603.

Although it was
An extremely difficult task,
I did finally bid adieu
To my suspicion-mind
And my frustration-vital.

1604.

Why does God keep countless
   secrets
From us?
He does it so that we will value
   them
And be worthy of them,
And one day be able to manifest
These secrets,
Which are nothing other than
His blossoming Dream-Realities.

1605.

When all else fails,
Try only two things:
Your heart's gratitude-tears
And
Your life's surrender-smiles.

1606.

I have not only diminished,
But also totally destroyed
The forces of my desire-greed.

1607.

A willingness-mind
And an eagerness-heart
Are two reciprocal supporters.

1608.

In my aspiration-heart,
My motto is:
Tears, tears and tears alone!

1609.

In my dedication-life,
My motto is:
Smiles, smiles and smiles alone!

1610.

How I wish
That no human being would
    suffer
The ruthless tragedies
Of a wasted life!

1611.

My Lord asks me
To offer my heart
Sleeplessly
To please Him always
In His own Way.

1612.

My Lord asks me
To offer my life
Unconditionally
To become another God.

1613.

Lavish your affection and
    fondness
On the Lord Supreme.
Behold, ecstasies from Heaven
Are fast approaching you!

1614.

To make yourself truly happy,
See what you have already
    received
From God.

1615.

Never, never try to imagine
What you deserve from God,
Or you will immediately become
A victim to unhappiness.

1616.

The God-searching mind
Is apt
To plan.

1617.

The God-loving heart
Is apt
To execute.

1618.

Reject
Life's superficiality-stupidity,
Reject!

1619.

Accept
Life's spirituality-necessity,
Accept!

1620.

Accept without reservation
God's Justice-Light
For your mind's transformation
And your life's perfection.

1621.

The remote future
Can be a future unknown,
Even unknowable.

1622.

God is partial.
This is, indeed,
The mind's useless understanding
Of God.

1623.

My Lord says to me:
"My child,
Humility is what you need.
But on the way,
If humiliation precedes humility,
Do not lose faith in Me.
I shall adorn you
With My Divinity's Pride."

1624.

Aspiration is not
My thinking process,
No, never!

1625.

Aspiration is
My self-offering progress
For my Lord Supreme.

1626.

The unanswered question
Of my life
Destroys my inner joy:
Will I ever be able
To please God
In God's own Way?

1627.

O my mind, I warn you!
Do not interrupt me
When I speak to my heart.

1628.

O seeker, do not fool yourself
By thinking and feeling
That you do not have to
Bear responsibility
For God-manifestation here on
    earth.

1629.

God sheds ceaseless Tears
When I resort to crushing others
For my own advancement-
    satisfaction.

1630.

We must live the inner life
Of soulfulness
And not the outer life
Of swiftness.

1631.

After visiting Heaven,
My mind says to me
That Heaven
Is not as beautiful
As it thought.

1632.

After visiting hell,
My heart says to me
That hell
Is not as frightful
As it imagined.

1633.

An aspiration-heart
Is the only gateway
To an illumination-soul.

1634.

May every morning
Become a new, inspiring
And fulfilling
Blossom of my heart.

1635.

Nature's beauty
Teaches optimism
To the aspiring heart.

1636.

Our mind tries
To inject pessimism
Into Nature,
But it fails.

1637.

Anything that you do for God
Can be done not only divinely
And perfectly,
But also easily.

1638.

When we do not pray and
    meditate,
We see the two worst possible
    rivals
In our own life-family:
Our frustration-mind
And
Our depression-vital.

1639.

What your mind
Thinks is great
May not necessarily
Be great.

1640.

What your heart
Feels is good
Is unquestionably good.

1641.

Be not discouraged!
Today you may be a novice
In your aspiration-life,
But in the near future,
You can become
A super-excellent aspirant.

1642.

When we live in the mind,
Then everything new
Is a wonder of wonders.

1643.

When we live in the heart,
Then everything new
Is a natural and spontaneous
    expression
Of our inner divinity.

1644.

Every human being
Is worthy of being loved,
For he is a unique
God-blossoming life.

1645.

What can our meditation
Do for us?
Our meditation can prevent
Worries and anxieties
From flocking to us.

1646.

God gave us the heart
To use for prayers,
But we are using our lips
Instead.

1647.

O my mind,
I shall tame you,
Not hurt you.
You will never be hospitalised.

1648.

Change yourself.
Lo, the world
Is already changed!

1649.

Do not evade
The hostile forces.
You have to invade their domain
To declare God's Victory supreme.

1650.

If you cherish doubt,
Then you have a serious deficiency
In your spiritual life.

1651.

Jealousy's head
Is longer than the longest.
It can reach anywhere.

1652.

God does not mind
If you want to negotiate
With Him.
But it is you who will be
The most deplorable loser.

1653.

Your neutrality
Destroys the joy
Of both parties
In a dire disagreement.

1654.

Keep your mind far above
The domain of criticism,
Just or even unjust.

1655.

Let your faith
Govern your life.
To your great satisfaction,
You will tame your doubt.

1656.

How can you have happiness
If your mind is buried
In indifference-cave?

1657.

I shall leave nothing undone
To discover my Lord's
Compassion-flooded Footsteps.

1658.

Do not worry!
Do whatever you are expected
To do.
The inner joy will start
Accompanying you.

1659.

Exclude doubt and exclude fear
The moment you feel
That you are ready to offer
    yourself
To your Lord Supreme.

1660.

Old, uninspiring thoughts
Can be resisted and replaced
By new, inspiring ones.
A true seeker is fully aware of this.

1661.

You fold your hands
In supplication,
But your mind is engrossed
In self-aggrandisement.
How then can you please
Your Lord Supreme?

1662.

You can be a free
And exalted soul
If you study
At God's Surrender-School.

1663.

You have carefully educated your
    mind
In greatness
For a long time.
Now you must devotedly educate
    your heart
In goodness.

1664.

Export your heart to God.
He will allow you to import
Everything from Him
Unreservedly.

1665.

For a God-realised soul,
Nothing can ever be
Insoluble.

1666.

The doubting mind
Is apt at grumbling—
Not only audibly,
But loudly.

1667.

I am so happy
That my mind is at last
Developing the habit
Of obeying God.

1668.

You have no idea
How deplorably you weaken
The power of your creativity
By thinking and thinking.

1669.

You must accept your fate
Bravely,
And then master it
Slowly, steadily
And unerringly.

1670.

Every day we must pray
And meditate
In the light-flooded garden
Of our heart.

1671.

Man's oft-repeated conversation
With God:
"God, do You love me?
Do You need me?
If so, then prove it!"

1672.

Immortality befriends
The beauty of our aspiration-heart
And
The fragrance of our dedication-
    life.

1673.

God gave you the capacity
To create Heaven,
But He never, never imagined
That you would create hell
    instead.

1674.

Associate with God-dreamers.
God-lovers will come
And associate with you.

1675.

Our weak mind, weak heart
And weak life
Do not agree with God
When He tells us
That each of His children
Is unique.

1676.

When we completely surrender
To God's Will,
We see God Himself
Cutting the long arms
Of our misfortune-life.

1677.

Our conscience tells our mind:
"Compromise is the height
Of stupidity,
And the life of futility."

1678.

Say "Yes" to God quickly
Before He turns
His Back.

1679.

Alas, will we ever realise
How often we consciously
And deliberately
Give unnecessary pain
To the ones around us?

1680.

Every day
My heart's promise-tree
Gets stronger and stronger
To satisfy God
In God's own Way.

1681.

Our undivine life
Can never intrude
On the ecstasy-life
Of our soul.

1682.

If we do not develop
The power of discrimination,
We will not be able
To proceed successfully
In our spiritual life.

1683.

Every night
I commit myself
To a God-satisfying dream.

1684.

Eternity's Silence
Is awaiting our mind.
Infinity's Joy
Is awaiting our heart.
But we do not know
Where they are.

1685.

If we do not aspire,
We shall not be able
To keep ourselves away
From brooding fears
And doubts.

1686.

Sleepless love of God
Is the true measure
Of a real devotee.

1687.

Those who at every moment
Overestimate themselves
Deserve to be underestimated
By all and sundry.

1688.

Learn the art
Of investing your service-time
Wisely.
God will proudly claim you
As His very own.

1689.

Your God-given talents
Are for your God-service only
Here on earth.

1690.

Unwillingness says:
"I have done enough
Both for earth
And for Heaven!"

1691.

The road
Least travelled
Is the gratitude-heart-road.

1692.

The clever, nay, the stupid mind
Purposely skips
The love-devotion-surrender-
    classes.

1693.

If you do not have
Love, devotion and surrender
In your inner life,
Then your outer life and your
    inner life
Will both suffer
From chronic disobedience-
    illness.

1694.

Nobody can forecast
The daily mind-weather,
Nobody.

1695.

My doubting mind
Is at odds
With each and every
Human being.

1696.

My aspiring heart
Is at peace
With the whole world.

1697.

Each seeker must know
That there can be no overdose
Of aspiration, dedication
And God-manifestation.

1698.

My soul says to my heart:
I shall train you to be divinely
And supremely brave.
You will never be paralysed
With fear.

1699.

Do not sacrifice
Your heart's goodness-diamond
For your mind's greatness-
    balloon.

1700.

Do not neglect
The inner voice.
The inner voice
Is God's perfect Choice.

1701.

Every day my soul amplifies
My Lord's Silence-Messages
For my aspiring heart.

1702.

Self-importance is, indeed,
A distorted,
Perverted inner will.

1703.

What I like most
Is my heart's endless pilgrimage
To my soul-destination.

1704.

My Lord tells me
That each prayerful song
Of my heart
Gives Him enormous comfort.

1705.

A great expectation
Does not know that
It will be chased
By a greater frustration.

1706.

Is it possible
For my soul to sleep?
I do not believe it,
But alas, it is true.

1707.

My inner life
Is not only my real reality,
But also the only reality
That can please my Lord Supreme
In His own Way.

1708.

My Lord Supreme
Is pleased with me
Only when I breathe
My heart's ecstasy-flooded breath.

1709.

My God-surrender
Is the most meaningful
And most fruitful necessity
In my aspiration-life.

1710.

I prayerfully follow
My Lord's every Footstep.
My Lord proudly follows
My heart's every smile-step.

1711.

My Lord,
I am offering You
Everything that I have,
Including my impossible
Ingratitude-heart,
For Your Forgiveness,
For Your Perfection
And for Your Transformation.

1712.

Only one individual can change
My life entirely,
And that is
My Lord Absolute Supreme.

1713.

My Lord,
I am begging You,
From the very depths of my heart,
To revive my God-loving life.

1714.

Nobody has compelled me
And nobody can compel me
To love God.
I am loving God
Because it is my free choice.

1715.

God is not a policeman,
But God is an ever-serving
Volunteer Watchman.

1716.

The mind likes to be always
In a whirlwind of activities
Without any destination.

1717.

How I believed
In my spiritual life once!
Alas, what has gone wrong
With me?
I have lost my spirituality.
I have lost everything
That was divine in me.

1718.

God wants me to fly and fly
To Him
In His Compassion-Benediction-
  Chariot.

1719.

If you start crying in repentance
For every mistake
That you have committed,
Then there will be no time
For you to pray to God
For a new life of illumination.

1720.

Hesitation prevents us
From doing anything
That is illumining and fulfilling.

1721.

I am determined
Not to neglect anymore
My gratitude-heart-field.

1722.

No discipline,
No determination,
No goal,
No satisfaction
From my heart
To God's Heart.

1723.

My Lord,
Speed up, speed up!
Do deface my pride-drunk mind
And my pride-drunk life.

1724.

This moment
Life is a broken hope.
Next moment
Life is a God-fulfilment-promise.

1725.

O my soul's rainbow-smile,
I am prayerfully yearning
For you to appear before me
For the illumination of my life.

1726.

Where is safety?
Safety is in our prayer-cries.
Safety is in our meditation-smiles.
Safety is in our surrender-dance
To God's Will.

1727.

Be wise! Be wise!
Be not a self-imposed barrier
On your way
To your God-realisation-life.

1728.

Aspiration, realisation,
God-manifestation
And life-transformation
Are cherished children of God.

1729.

Finally my mind
Is surcharged with peace,
To weather all trials
Successfully.

1730.

When you become
Your heart's soulfulness,
The whole world will love you
Far beyond your imagination.

1731.

Optimism, optimism!
Keep a profound optimism.
Bow to your future Goal.
Your Goal will not fail you,
And you will not fail your Goal.

1732.

May my heart's determination,
Devotion and surrender
Forever remain unbroken.

1733.

Alas, we do not know
How and why
We keep our heart's aspiration-car
So often in reverse.

1734.

Approach
Each and every second
With a God-surrendering heart.

1735.

God does not care for
Your mind's loneliness.
He cares only for
Your heart's selflessness.

1736.

God Himself has come down
To celebrate my mind's
Bondage-independence day.

1737.

God's Forgiveness, God's
    Compassion
And God's unconditional Self-
    Giving
Are everybody's
Unimaginable possessions.

1738.

We need
An ultramarathon of patience
Every day
To fulfil the divine in us
Perfectly.

1739.

Do not be doomed to
    disappointment!
Today your love-devotion-
    surrender-steps
May be awkward and
    disheartening,
But tomorrow they are bound to
    be
Charming, astonishing and
    perfect.

1740.

My soul has
What my heart needs,
And not what my mind wants.

1741.

Go deep within.
To your great surprise,
All obstacles
Will turn into opportunities.

1742.

My mind,
You have been torturing me
For years.
Can you not leave me alone?
I want you to shut up
For good!

1743.

The inspiration of the mind
And the aspiration of the heart
Together fight
Against the frustration of the
    vital.

1744.

I have cast aside
My mind's complaint-daggers.
I have now become
My heart's aspiration-tower.

1745.

What you immediately
And desperately need:
A desire-rejection-project.

1746.

If you aspire most soulfully,
Then you do not have to grope
In the shadows of doubt.

1747.

My unconditional God-surrender
Is the new language
Of my aspiration-heart.

1748.

If you follow a spiritual path,
Then you must deepen constantly
Your love of God.

1749.

Invited or uninvited,
You must place
Your entire earth-existence-life
At the Feet of your Lord Supreme.

1750.

God-denials
Increase my heart's
God-hunger.

1751.

God-delays
Excite my mind's
God-thirst.

1752.

I have only two dreams:
My life-transformation-dream
And my God-satisfaction-dream.

1753.

If you have humility,
Then you are advanced
In the spiritual life.

1754.

Each one is trying to offer light
To the world.
But, alas, we are all ending up
Gathering darkness for the world.

1755.

Illumination comes from
    experiences
And not from discussions.
Discussions are nothing short of
    futilities.

1756.

Constant surrender
To God's Will
Is the most momentous choice
A seeker can make.

1757.

With my heart's certainties
I make my fastest progress,
And never with my mind's
    curiosities.

1758.

A seeker's God-surrender-life
Will always remain
The most ancient and most
    perfect language
Of his heart.

1759.

Humanity has given me
Heavy burdens,
But God has given me
Two strong shoulders.

1760.

I hinder not only my growth,
But also the growth of the entire
    world,
When I do not feed God
With my love, devotion
And surrender.

1761.

My mind,
God is talking to you.
Why are you so careless and
    callous?
Take heed!

1762.

How can you neglect
The inner voice
When you tell the world
That God is your only choice?

1763.

Are you waiting for an invitation
From God?
He may not invite you at all.
The best thing is for you to go to
    Him
Uninvited.
I assure you, He will not mind.

1764.

Break
The exorbitant pride
Of your sound-mind!

1765.

Make friends
With the silence-beauty
Of your heart.

1766.

Worthless and useless words
Produced by the mind
Are weakening
The life-climbing aspiration
Of the heart.

1767.

Be always generous
With your soul's
Compassion-delight.

1768.

Be always generous
With your heart's
Affection-light.

1769.

Be always generous
With your life's
Concern-assurance.

1770.

Do not feed your anxieties
With your attention,
But starve them to death
With your determination.

1771.

If I have to wait for my perfection
Before I can present myself
At God's Feet,
Then this process will be
    deplorably
And absurdly long.

1772.

Surrender yourself to God
    unreservedly
And unconditionally.
Your mind is bound to obtain
    peace
In the shortest time.

1773.

From God's point of view,
No human being is disheartening
Or even discouraging.

1774.

How long will the mind's
Negativity-poison last,
How long?
Definitely not for good!

1775.

If we prayerfully sit at God's Feet,
He immediately shows us
The direct road
For His manifestation.

1776.

We can be perfect
If we are willing to learn
    everything
From the illumining experiences
Of our inner life.

1777.

As the rising sun is of no value
To the blind,
Even so, a faithful heart is of no
    value
To the doubting mind.

1778.

My Lord,
There are many people on earth
Who steal things from others.
Can You not steal my heart?
Please do!

1779.

My life and I are determined
To make full use
Of our Lord's Forgiveness-Heart.

1780.

My mind and I are determined
To make full use
Of our Lord's Compassion-Eye.

1781.

God has many Palaces,
But He advises me
To visit His Peace-Palace
And live there permanently.

1782.

My heart and I every day
Pray to God
To make us the perfect slaves
Of His Will.

1783.

The lion-souls
Are God's most precious
   manifestations
On earth.

1784.

To me, my faith is not something
That I have inside
To carry me to God.
My faith is the manifestation
Of God's Will in me.

1785.

Do not be frightened of your ego's
   death.
Your ego's death is the beginning
Of your Infinity's smile.

1786.

Devotion
Is not to be found
In the mind's market-confusion.

1787.

Every day
God's Silence-Messages
My heart prayerfully and soulfully
Obeys.

1788.

My mind tells me
That my dreams are as fragile
As a mirror.

1789.

My heart tells me
That my lofty dreams
Shall eventually become
God-manifestation-realities.

1790.

My Lord Supreme,
In all sincerity,
I am begging You
To humiliate me
And my endless ignorance-pride!

1791.

The seeker's negativity-mind
Is to be fully blamed
For his sad failure-life.

1792.

My Lord,
Please take me wherever You go,
Even if You go to hell.
"My child,
Where am I now?"

1793.

My Lord,
Can You make my life a little
    better?
"Of course, My child,
If you seriously want Me to."

1794.

My Lord,
I am with You twenty-four hours a
    day
In my thoughts and in my deeds.
I beg of You only one thing:
Allow me never to feel
That I have had enough
Of Your company.

1795.

We commit countless sins,
But when we recite Your very
    Name
With our gratitude-heart-tears,
You burn all our sins to ashes.

1796.

My Lord,
You have saved my life
Countless times
With Your Greatness-Power.

1797.

My Lord,
You are loving my heart
At every moment
With Your Goodness-Delight.

1798.

My Lord,
When I do not fulfil my promise,
Do not think that I love You less.
It is only because I am weak.
My Lord,
Will You not give me more
    capacity
So that I never fail You?

1799.

My Lord,
I have shown You what I have:
My dissatisfied mind.

1800.

My Lord,
Will You not show me what You
    are:
Your Forgiveness-Heart.

1801.

The exploration
Of the aspiration-heart
Always remains limitless.

1802.

The tears of our heart
Brighten and strengthen
Our love-devotion-surrender-
    smile.

1803.

Two doors God never locks:
His Compassion-Eye-Door
And His Forgiveness-Heart-Door.

1804.

We should not be discouraged.
Our desire-life does not die
All at once.
Slowly, steadily and unerringly
We can put our desire-life
To death.

1805.

Our adamantine determination-
    power
Can easily tame
All our stray and unwilling
    thoughts.

1806.

Eventually,
Each human being will be able
To discover his heart's
Oneness-peace-bliss-treasure.

1807.

Our souls are on the alert
To see if our aspiration-supplies
Are running low.

1808.

There is a constant battle going on
Between the stupid mind's
Unwillingness-night
And the wise heart's
Willingness-light.

1809.

My heart's prayerful soulfulness
Has brought down a special power
From Above
To force my desire-tigers
To leave.

1810.

Aspiration-cries
And dedication-smiles
Can easily uproot
Our desire-life-tree.

1811.

May positive thoughts
Sing and dance
Right in front of
My aspiration-heart-cries.

1812.

The heart-host takes very special
   care
When simplicity, sincerity and
   purity
Arrive.

1813.

Meditation helps the heart
To empty
Its insecurity-purse.

1814.

I appreciate most sincerely
And most proudly
My readiness-mind.
I admire and love
My willingness-life.
I love and love
My eagerness-heart.

1815.

Who is fit for the spiritual life?
Anyone who chooses the spiritual
    life
Is more than fit,
For God has already chosen him
To be His choice instrument.

1816.

God has given me full
    responsibility
To take care of
My aspiration-heart-flames.

1817.

God has given me full
    responsibility
To take care of
My dedication-life-blossoms.

1818.

May my aspiration-cries
Fly and fly
In the sky of Infinity's Light.

1819.

Every day my life
Swims and swims
In the sacred Compassion-Sea
Of my Lord Supreme.

1820.

May each thought
In my mind
Become a prayer
Of God-love.

1821.

O seeker,
Do not be doomed
To disappointment.
Behold,
The sunny sky of your soul
Is beckoning you.

1822.

May each aspiration-heart
Fly high, higher, highest
To reach God's Compassion-Sky
And become a member
Of God's inner circle.

1823.

My morning prayer
And Nature's morning song
Begin at the same time.

1824.

Each soul is selected
By God Himself,
And each soul is shaped and
    moulded
By God Himself.

1825.

Sweeter than the sweetest,
Stronger than the strongest
Are the teardrops of surrender-
    light.

1826.

God has just touched
My gratitude-heart.
I shall never forget,
NEVER,
This hallowed moment!

1827.

Each time I pray and meditate,
I am blessed with sunlit blossoms
In my heart-garden.

1828.

I clearly see that
My life's prayerful moments
Are skyrocketing to God.

1829.

I vehemently disdain
The collaboration
Of my doubting mind
And angry vital.

1830.

The more my mind
Invokes newness,
The sooner my life
Shall grow into fulness.

1831.

Each warrior-soul
Is a most beautiful picture
Of God's future Victory.

1832.

I must rediscover
The beauty and fragrance
Of my aspiration-life.

1833.

I must never pay any attention
To the ever-changing weather
Of my mind.

1834.

Forgiveness
Is the birthless and deathless Song
Of my Lord Supreme.

1835.

My heart's obedience
And my mind's interruptions
Must be kept apart.

1836.

You certainly can
And happily will
Have a life of unconditional
    surrender.

1837.

Where is the jungle
That we talk about,
If it is not within?

1838.

Your God-dependence
Is so endearing
To God.

1839.

Just wait!
There is a most special message
    afoot
For you from God.

1840.

The moment God saw
My obedience-heart
And my surrender-life,
He started singing, dancing
And flying.

1841.

My mind,
If you want to make the fastest
    progress,
You ought to see and feel
That you are smaller than the
    smallest,
Humbler than the humblest—
A most insignificant speck of dust!

1842.

Falsehood and sin
Love each other,
Live together
And die together.

1843.

Be not afraid of the thickest
    darkness
Of your mind.
The tears of your heart
Will eventually prevail.

1844.

The confession of the mind
Does not solve any problem.
It is the invocation of God
That solves all our problems.

1845.

Human friendship
Secretly enjoys
Rivalry-boats.

1846.

God's Permission
Is of paramount importance
At every second
If you are a true seeker.

1847.

The stronger
The computer-mind,
The louder
The heart's pitiful cries.

1848.

A happiness-heart
Is, indeed,
Another name for meditation.

1849.

Alas, I am lost
In between my creation-heart
And my destruction-mind.

1850.

Be extremely careful, O seeker!
At any moment
Your love-devotion-surrender-
    birds
May fly away.

1851.

God wants me to drive
His Compassion-Chariot
To be victorious
In the battlefield of life.

1852.

O my doubting mind,
Enough!
I shall not remain anymore
At your mercy.

1853.

It is our human mind
That holds our gratitude-heart
    cheap –
Not God, never!

1854.

Blow your readiness-conch
On your way
To God's Palace.

1855.

Play your willingness-violin
On your way
To God's Palace.

1856.

Play your eagerness-flute
On your way
To God's Palace.

1857.

At every moment
Use the smile-weapon
That you were born with
To conquer the pride
Of ignorance-night.

1858.

Quite often
Love does not succeed
When it comes to clasp hatred.

1859.

A great mind
May extol itself to the skies,
But never a good heart.

1860.

The soul lives
Inside the heart-shrine,
And not in the sealed mind-box.

1861.

God's dreaming Smiles
Shall abandon
Your doubt-cherishing mind.

1862.

A self-giver
Is, indeed, another name
For a God-lover.

1863.

A sleepless God-server
Unmistakably expedites
God-manifestation
Here on earth.

1864.

Now that you are in the spiritual
    life,
Your ego will make you constantly
    cry,
Unless you smash its pride.

1865.

A life of discipline
Is not a matter of punishment.
It is a matter of wisdom-love.

1866.

There can be no adequate reason
For you to feel
That a life of transformation
Is not indispensable.

1867.

If you forget God
Because you are too busy,
Then God also can play
The same game.

1868.

A life of seclusion
Does not necessarily mean
A life of illumination.
It can easily mean
Either a life of self-oblivion
Or a life of self-mortification.

1869.

Remember,
When you do not care for peace,
You do not care for God as well.

1870.

A greatness-mind
We ourselves can achieve,
But a goodness-heart
We receive from God.

1871.

Alas, when shall we realise
That we have infinitely more
    important
Things to do
Than dance with desires?

1872.

The soul does not come alone.
It brings delight with it
When it pays its blessingful visits
To the aspiring heart.

1873.

I become the possessor
Of a oneness-heart
Only when I become the
    renouncer
Of the division-mind.

1874.

God waits and watches me
To see if I have really thrown
All my doubts out of my mind
So He can come in.

1875.

If you can be the conqueror
Of the dividing mind,
Then God will make you the lover
Of uniting hearts.

1876.

Spiritual success, spiritual
    progress,
Spiritual victory and spiritual
    satisfaction
Will never be found
In the cave of oblivion.

1877.

The moment my little "I"-ness
Goes out,
God with His Fulness
Comes in.

1878.

When you give joy to others,
You automatically see
The multiplication of joy
For yourself.

1879.

God asks me to concern myself
With the immediate,
And not with the ultimate.

1880.

What is jealousy,
If not the ruthless chaser
Of happiness?

1881.

God's Compassion-Eye
Is always lovable,
Yet it remains unfathomable.

1882.

God's Will-Wheel
Eternally spins
World-transforming Messages.

1883.

When your goodness
Is for others to use,
Then only is your goodness
Absolutely true and perfect.

1884.

Only a heart of beauty
Can offer
A face of sanctity.

1885.

When my gratitude-heart and I
Walk together towards our Goal,
Divinity's beauty accompanies us.

1886.

When we talk, we do not realise
That God's Compassion-Eye
Is the speaker,
And God's Satisfaction-Heart
Is the listener.

1887.

If you have a readiness-mind,
A willingness-life
And an eagerness-heart,
Then nobody will be able to equal
    you.

1888.

In the spiritual life,
If you crave friends to chat with,
Then you are bound to lose
Your hard-earned friendship
With God.

1889.

Poor God,
In vain He tries to pour Light
Into my darkness-mind.

1890.

The mind that can catch easily
Others' thought-waves
Is a spiritually awakened
And advanced mind.

1891.

Alas,
Will I ever believe God
When He tells me
That my negativity-mind
Will produce nothing good for
    me?

1892.

My today's hope-bird
Will be tomorrow's
Promise-blossom.

1893.

God's Compassion-Eye
Is all for us.
God's Forgiveness-Heart
Is all for us.
When God comes to us,
What is there to be nervous about?

1894.

While my disobedience-mind
    broods,
God Himself
Cradles my obedience-heart.

1895.

My desire-mind
Has binding eyes.
My aspiration-heart
Has liberating smiles.

1896.

From the beginning to the end,
A disobedience-mind is a
    nightmare.
From the beginning to the end,
An aspiring heart
Is God's own flying Kite.

1897.

My Lord,
Do You love me still,
Even when I do not love You at all?
"My child,
What have I been doing so far?"

1898.

My Lord,
Can You not do something better
Than thinking of me all the time?
"My child,
I simply do not want to do
Anything else."

1899.

My Lord,
What were You doing
When I was shedding
Such sad heart-tears
For You?
"My child,
Did you not see Me
Devouring greedily and proudly
Your heart-tears?"

1900.

The moment I touch the Lotus-
 Feet
Of my Lord Supreme,
My desire-life gets frightened
And runs away.

1901.

There can be no
Totally threatening eclipse
Of the aspiration-heart.

1902.

The aspiring heart
Is often a victim
To the mind's prejudice
And indifference.

1903.

The mind refuses to commit itself
To anything
That is not of immediate profit.

1904.

May my God-awareness-faith
Be
A universal citizen.

1905.

When God Himself
Puts His Arm around you,
Touch immediately
His Compassion-Feet
To get the utmost from Him.

1906.

I see no difference
Between my life's expectations
And my mind's demands.

1907.

My mind's ignorance-night
Veils my inner beauty.
My heart's wisdom-life
Unveils not only my inner beauty,
But also my God-representing
    divinity.

1908.

Equanimity is
Far beyond the snares
Of pleasures and pains.

1909.

If we love God only
And if we need God only,
Then God's Compassion-Eye
Will definitely smash the clinging
    chain
Of our doubting mind.

1910.

His unconditional surrender-life
Is completely lost
In his soul's boundless
Amazement-ecstasy.

1911.

Do not allow your indifference-
    mind
To close
Your God-longing mind.

1912.

Both the superior mind
And the inferior mind
Have divided and ruined
Our beautiful world.

1913.

Alas, what am I doing?
I am promoting my mind
By demoting others' hearts!

1914.

Your aspiration-life will be
    impoverished
If you fail to appreciate
Others' inspiring, aspiring
And self-giving capacities.

1915.

Each opportunity is, indeed,
A special blessing from Above
For the effacement
Of our undivine qualities
And the advancement
Of our divine qualities.

1916.

There is nothing in God's creation
That God loves so well
As the transformation of human
     nature.

1917.

Do not underestimate
Your undivine qualities,
And do not overestimate
Your divine qualities,
If you want to meet with
God the Satisfaction-Delight.

1918.

If we have complacency,
Whether in the mind or in the
     vital,
Then our spirituality's death
Is fast approaching.

1919.

Human life is governed by
Dark doubts, darker suspicions
And darkest misunderstandings.

1920.

I believe in present heroism
And not in future victory
Or defeat.

1921.

Your borrowed happiness
Will someday be swallowed
By your own giant despair.

1922.

When I pray to God,
My aspiration-heart
And God's Compassion-Eye
Together win.

1923.

If we do not continue aspiring,
We are bound to fall
From the pinnacle of our
     spirituality.

1924.

Mine is the adamantine
    determination
To set my past ablaze,
Like a wildfire.

1925.

It is an insult to our spiritual life
When we say
Even God cannot inundate our
    mind
With abundant peace.

1926.

God feels He has given us
Infinitely more opportunities
Than our mind's readiness,
Our life's willingness
And our heart's eagerness deserve.

1927.

We can hide from
The curses of earth,
But not from
The Blessings of Heaven.

1928.

I am struggling and struggling
To free my life
From my mind-entanglements,
And I am sure my victory is
    certain.

1929.

My mind's selfishness
Is fully responsible for
My life's ugliness.

1930.

Humility feeds the divine in us
And starves
The undivine in us.

1931.

Alas, I do not know when and how
I shall be able to free myself
From the torture of my prison-
    mind.

1932.

The surrender-beauty
Of a dedication-life
Can never be adequately
    described.

1933.

A devotion-heart
Is
A God-expansion-life.

1934.

Every day
I enjoy spending long hours
Removing my mind-thorns
From my heart-garden.

1935.

Alas,
Are we really destined to lead
Day to day
A life of ignorance?

1936.

Everybody's life
Has to face
Countless desire-obstacles.

1937.

O God!
Had I been wiser,
I would have accepted
The life of aspiration
Long ago.

1938.

Lord, save me once again
So that I can love You
Self-givingly
For Your enormous Satisfaction.

1939.

To enjoy God's infinite Beauty
In the garden of our aspiration-
     heart,
We must go beyond the territory
Of our superficial and commercial
     mind.

1940.

God's Compassion-Eye
Does not have to remain
Always open,
Especially when we deliberately
     misuse
The freedom bestowed upon us.

1941.

God's Smiles are irresistible.
So are God's Tears.
Whatever God has and is
Is irresistible.

1942.

To enjoy a moment
Of God-receptivity
Is all I need.

1943.

Not because God exists,
But because God's Dream exists,
Do we hope to become one day
Perfect citizens of the world.

1944.

A glamorous vital,
A humorous mind
And a superfluous life —
Alas, this is all we have,
Nothing more!

1945.

If you depend all the time
On self-effort,
You will never be able to discover
God's effective Way
Of selfless effort.

1946.

Our greatness
Can at times be
Our life's frustration-reality.

1947.

God compassionately and
    emphatically
Tells me
That to increase the beauty
Of His universe,
He unmistakably depends on
My heart's aspiration-flames.

1948.

When calamity is asleep,
Do not arouse it
To see how destructive it is.

1949.

Anything inspiring and
    illumining
Will definitely make you
A better God-lover
Than you were yesterday.

1950.

A desire-life
Is undoubtedly
A misguiding light.

1951.

You are not
The complexity of your mind.
You are the unparalleled
Simplicity, sincerity and purity
Of your heart.

1952.

There was a time
When I wanted to know
What I could do for humanity.
But now I want only to know
Who I truly am.

1953.

If you want to think of Heaven,
Then think of Heaven's
    encouragement.
If you want to think of earth,
Then think of earth's patience.
This is how you can be
A perfect instrument of God.

1954.

If you are afraid of the
    consequences
Of your God-dedication-life,
Then your life can do nothing
And you will be nothingness
    itself.

1955.

It is not the doubting mind
Or even the searching mind,
But the aspiring mind
That can switch back and forth
From Heavenly Smiles to earthly
    cries.

1956.

When you come to realise
That this world has nothing for
    you,
Then only will you be able to
    follow
The Real in yourself.

1957.

Doubt does not know
And does not understand
What doubt actually is.

1958.

Faith does not believe
In understanding.
It only knows self-giving
And God-becoming.

1959.

The firmness of a spiritual Teacher
Clearly indicates
His genuine compassion-concern
For his devotees.

1960.

If you have peace of mind,
Then you can easily escape
From the noisy world around you.

1961.

If we fearfully cling
To what we have,
We will never be able to discover
Who we truly are.

1962.

Do not ask God
What you are supposed to do.
Ask yourself
Why so far you have remained
Totally inactive.

1963.

There is no difference
Whatsoever
Between self-mastery
And God-discovery.

1964.

Because you are a problem
To yourself,
No matter how sincerely
God tries to please you,
Your doubting mind
Will not be satisfied.

1965.

The ignorance of the world
Is threatening you at every
    moment.
But a day will come
When your heart-tears
Will be able to drown and devour
That threat.

1966.

O my mind and vital,
Do not join the world's
Discouragement-committee.
O my heart, may you be
The flower-beauty-
    encouragement
Of the worlds within and without.

1967.

If you adore your aspiration-heart
And dedication-life,
Then your mind's cleverness
Will be turned into
Your heart's ever-willing
    eagerness.

1968.

Do not try to repair
Your mind-cottage,
But build anew your heart-palace
For God to give you
His God-fulfilment-instructions.

1969.

If you are always
In the world of self-concern,
Then poor God has to remain
Outside your life's boundary.

1970.

I call it my self-awakening,
But God says that very thing
Is the beauty of His own
Blossoming Smile.

1971.

If you think and feel that you are
A problem-illumining child of
    God,
Then, indeed, you are so.

1972.

The misguiding cleverness
Of the mind
Takes me everywhere
To get a glimpse of God.

1973.

The readiness, willingness
And eagerness
Of the heart
Take me everywhere
To be the Pride of God.

1974.

Each time I justify my weakness,
I lower the perfection-quality
Of the whole world.

1975.

Do not retreat
From your attempt to perfect
Your outer world.
Just entreat God
To perfect both your inner
And outer worlds.

1976.

The noisy mind-office
Can easily be silenced
By the poise of your heart-home.

1977.

Now that you are participating
In God's Cosmic Game,
You must never anticipate failure.

1978.

God wants you to be
An exceedingly happy recipient
Of His Blessing-Light.

1979.

To tame my monkey-mind,
What I need
Is the longest length of patience.

1980.

God wants your new
God-awakening-life
To divinely bloom
And supremely blossom.

1981.

God-fulfilment-promises
Always run short
Here on earth.

1982.

The cries of our heart
Embody the answers
To all the questions
That our mind can ever have.

1983.

With God-obedience,
We embark
On our God-aspiration-journey –
Only to continue forever.

1984.

God needs you
As a God-serving lover
And not
As a silence-practising recluse.

1985.

Only the life of a self-giving heart
Is cherished by both God the
    Creator
And God the creation.

1986.

You take your life
As a life of disgrace,
But God takes it
As another important way
To look at your face.

1987.

As long as I am blessed
With an eventful life,
I shall not be doomed
To disappointment
If I have an uneventful death.

1988.

What has blindfolded your vision-
    eye,
If not your mind's measureless
Pride-luxury?

1989.

May time be
My God-denying
Mind-killer.

1990.

May time be
My God-worshipping
Heart-temple-builder.

1991.

My mind's God-searching smiles
Are
Supremely beautiful.

1992.

My heart's God-longing tears
Are
Absolutely perfect.

1993.

My heart is permitted to join
My Infinity-winging soul
When it becomes the life
Of a ceaselessly God-longing cry.

1994.

Two truths I unmistakably know:
My mind is not worthy
Of God's Forgiveness-Ocean;
My heart is not worthy
Of God's Compassion-Sun.

1995.

God wants me to perform
My aspiration-task
Lovingly and self-givingly
And not to be involved in His
    Task:
My perfection-dream-fulfilment.

1996.

The moment I fall flat
At the Feet of God's Will,
My life becomes
Ecstasy's thrill.

1997.

God's enduring and endearing
    Affection,
Tears and Smiles
Have changed my unchangeable
    life.

1998.

To adorn my Lord's Heart
With joy,
I must turn my life
Into humility-grass.

1999.

To collect my heart's gratitude-
    tears
And place them at the Feet
Of my Lord Supreme
Is my only task.

2000.

I feel that I can be perfect
If I adore, love and obey
God's Blessing-flooded
Commands.

2001.

Now that I have entered
Into the kingdom of ecstasy,
My God-manifestation-life
Is my topmost priority.

2002.

Upward I fly
To see my Lord's Feet.
Inward I dive
To become my Lord's Heart.

2003.

You will have a complete
And satisfactory answer
To your life's questions
If you every day open your heart-
    book
And read the love-page.

2004.

God tells me that
My mind's love-letters
Are sweet,
My heart's devotion-letters
Are sweeter
And my life's surrender-letters
Are sweetest.
He also tells me that
Every day
He expects at least one letter
From me.

2005.

Finally I have become
An ever-climbing aspiration-
    heart.
Therefore,
God has blessingfully made me
A choice instrument of His Vision-
    Eye.

2006.

If only one man
Can satisfy God unconditionally,
Then he expedites humanity's
    evolution.

2007.

Because of my heart's gratitude-
    tears,
My life is ever so close
To my Lord Beloved Supreme.

2008.

Just by imagining
That my every breath
Is a beautiful flower,
I enjoy tremendous satisfaction-
    delight.

2009.

My life's each forward step
Is a special Blessing
From my Lord Supreme.

2010.

When you have
A sincerity-purity-flooded
Devotion-heart,
God will beckon you to join Him
In His Heart-Garden.

2011.

Prayerfully and soulfully
My service-trees
Feed my Lord Supreme.

2012.

The life
Of an unconditionally
    surrendered seeker
Happily and unreservedly enjoys
Mountain-zenith-joy.

2013.

The doubting mind
Has to be totally obliterated
If you want to make satisfactory
    progress
In your spiritual life.

2014.

May my life grow into
My Lord's
Compassion-Manifestation-
    Breath.

2015.

Be wise!
If you cannot illumine
Your past misdeeds,
Then completely forget them,
For they are worse than useless.

2016.

At every moment
My spiritual life depends on
My Lord's
Compassion-Miracle-Smile.

2017.

My mind desires
Thunderous success-applause.
My heart desires
A running river of progress.

2018.

O my heart's ever-blossoming
    faith,
You are my life's
Pole-star.

2019.

I never knew
That insecurity-thorns
Are so destructive.

2020.

By praying to God,
I deliberately avoid drinking
My mind's doubt-poison.

2021.

By meditating on God,
I soulfully drink deep
My heart's faith-nectar.

2022.

Before I wanted sound
To capture my life.
Now I need silence
To embrace my heart.

2023.

God wanted us to obey
Our higher Self.
But, alas, we are doing
Just the opposite!
We are obeying the commands
Of our lower self.

2024.

My mind and I are determined
Not to be vulnerable anymore
To jealousy-invasion.

2025.

God has already given us
A free access to His Heart-Garden.
We do not know why, but alas,
We hesitate and delay entering.

2026.

There was a time
When the sadness of failure
Tortured my life.
But alas,
Now the gladness of success
Is also torturing me
In a peculiar way.

2027.

An act of God-defiance
Has completely uprooted
His God-service-tree.

2028.

You will not be able to enjoy
God's infinite Affection and Love
If your life remains
A deep-rooted insecurity.

2029.

Purity
Is a perfect stranger
To a jungle-mind.

2030.

God wants from my body, vital,
Mind and heart
An unselfish love
And not a slavish devotion.

2031.

The divine in me
Is simply shocked
To see my cheerful and complete
Identification
With my pseudo-self.

2032.

O seeker,
How can you be such a fool
To cater to the proud demands
Of your vital?

2033.

A self-imprisoned mind
Knows
No hope.

2034.

A breath that knows
No love of God
Is not a real breath.

2035.

My mind's marching thoughts
I shall turn into
A God-loving will.

2036.

O my God-loving heart,
You are infinitely stronger
Than my God-doubting mind.
I want you to conquer my mind
Once and for all,
Here and now.

2037.

No human heart
Can forever escape
Ruthless anxiety-tortures.

2038.

Even his outer life
Has become one with
His inner life's
Deeply rooted God-faith.

2039.

God looks for me
Only inside
My gratitude-heart-tears.

2040.

My heart uses
Devoted whispers
To speak to God.

2041.

My mind uses
Proud drumbeats
To speak to God.

2042.

In the spiritual life,
A wild ambition-destination
Is lifeless and useless.

2043.

The God-serving heroes
Will definitely be honoured
By God Himself
At His choice Hour.

2044.

God has made
A new invitation list.
He has added my life
Of unconditional surrender.

2045.

O universal peace-dreamers,
My mind wants to know
If you are real.
If so, where are you?
How are you?

2046.

To the aspiring heart only,
God's Compassion-Eye
Is always visible.

2047.

Aspiring souls
Always hunger for God's Love—
More, ever more.

2048.

A God-dreaming heart
Embodies
A God-living life.

2049.

Alas, most human beings
Either consciously or
    unconsciously
Forget
Their gratitude-prayers.

2050.

Although poor God ceaselessly
 knocks
At my mind-door,
My mind is utterly complacent
And reluctant to answer.

2051.

My love of God
Not only silences
But also slices my mind.

2052.

A God-loving heart
Knows
What intensification is.

2053.

A God-searching mind
Knows
What clarification is.

2054.

My ignorance-freedom-fighter-
 heart,
You are my soul's
Hero supreme.

2055.

I shall not try to escape
From my mind.
I want to be brave
And fight for
My jungle-mind-forest's
Complete transformation.

2056.

I prayed to God
To bless me
With an invisible mind,
But God blessed me
With an invincible heart instead.

2057.

Alas,
A lonely heart
Longs for a hope
That is not yet born.

2058.

Our heart's streaming tears
Play hide-and-seek
With the blossoming Smiles
Of Heaven.

2059.

Within, the invisible acts
Of God-Compassion.
Without, the visible acts
Of God-Satisfaction.

2060.

O seeker,
Lengthen and strengthen
Your God-devotion-tears.

2061.

Finally I am able
To awaken
My God-denying mind.

2062.

From my heart-room,
One by one I release
My God-manifestation-promises
Here on earth.

2063.

God is forced to live
Behind the curtain
Of our mind.

2064.

God gives your heart humility
To increase
Your God-manifestation-abilities.

2065.

An indolence-life
Cannot easily be transformed,
Even by the astonishing power
Of miracles.

2066.

Every day
God gives you a new opportunity
To please Him,
But because of your faith-empty
    heart,
You may not recognise it.

2067.

Earth-born knowledge
Is afraid
Of God.

2068.

Heaven-born wisdom
Is fond
Of God.

2069.

Inside the body of time,
Nothing can ever
Be perfect.

2070.

Beyond the mind of time,
Perfection grows, glows
And flows.

2071.

My aspiration-heart
Deeply values
Even a fleeting Smile
From God's Eye.

2072.

No matter how beautiful
And how long-lasting
God's Smile is,
My dissatisfaction-mind disdains
    it.

2073.

God's Compassion-Height
And His Forgiveness-Delight
Shall always remain
    unfathomable
And, therefore, unteachable.

2074.

If happiness-sky you want,
Then gratitude-tears
You must first become.

2075.

Alas, my ego and my pride
Feel that whatever they do
Is always right and just.

2076.

My desire-life
Does not know
What real happiness is.

2077.

My aspiration-heart
Shall never surrender
To a failure-life.

2078.

O God,
Had I been wise,
I would not have played, sung and
    danced
With ignorance-king.

2079.

A surrender-life
Does not take it as a challenge,
But as a blessing,
To live up to God's Standard.

2080.

Do not blame your life
And do not blame your mind,
But only blame yourself
For all the bad choices you have
    made
Over the years.

2081.

A regularity-attendance-seeker
I appreciate.
A punctuality-attendance-seeker
I admire.

2082.

God wants you to stop
Immediately
Your unaspiring train of thought.

2083.

I am so fortunate
That I cannot even remember
When I was an ingratitude-mind.

2084.

Your heart-tears are so powerful
That they can easily drown
Your mind's fears.

2085.

My happiness
Is
My God-ascending dream.

2086.

My promise
Is
My God-descending reality.

2087.

My Lord has promised
That the next time He visits,
He will bring me
His Silence-Sunrise-Beauty.

2088.

It is not the quantity,
Not even the quality,
But the sincerity
Of my surrender-life
That pleases my Lord most.

2089.

Every day
My life-boat plies
Between my God-realisation-
    shore
And
My God-manifestation-shore.

2090.

Sincerity makes my life
God-lovable.
Purity makes my heart
God-enjoyable.

2091.

Falsehood fearfully accepts
The challenges of life.
Truth smilingly accepts
The challenges of life
And declares its victory supreme.

2092.

If we can peacefully live
In our inner self,
Then we can proudly live
With our outer self.

2093.

The Enlightened Ones
Do not import and export
    Divinity.
They just spread Divinity
All-where.

2094.

Desire is a bird
That we can never
Actually catch.

2095.

Aspiration is a bird
That offers its wings
So that we can
Proudly fly.

2096.

The doubting mind
And the strangling vital
Will never be able to see
The face of happiness.

2097.

God has some
Supremely chosen instruments
Who can definitely turn
The ignorance-tide.

2098.

You are a rank fool
If you expect the whole world
To follow you all the time.

2099.

You are wisdom incarnate
If you do not lead,
If you do not follow,
But side-by-side
Walk with the rest of the world.

2100.

O my aspiration-flames,
Because of you
My heart is divinely beautiful
And my life is supremely fruitful.

2101.

Every morning
When I wake up,
My Lord Supreme blesses me
With a new happiness-heart-flute.

2102.

Every day
New blooms and new blossoms
Take birth
In our God-serving life.

2103.

My Lord tells me
That if I do not unlearn
My earthly information-book,
Then He will not bless me
With His Illumination-Smile.

2104.

If you are rich in faith,
Then God Himself comes down
To show you the way
To your Destination.

2105.

My Lord, when You allow me
To sit at Your Feet,
I never question You.
But when You allow me
To look at Your Eye,
I do question You.
My Lord, then why do You allow
    me
To look at Your Eye?

2106.

God has given me
His full Assurance
That nothing in my life
Will ever be expelled
From His Grace.

2107.

Frustration angrily chases
My greatness-mind.
Satisfaction proudly follows
My goodness-heart.

2108.

By virtue of my prayer-life,
All my sweet dreams of God
I shall turn into
God-Victory-Songs.

2109.

O seeker,
Do not allow depression
To come into you.
Even your yesterday's failure-life
You must take as a remote
    incarnation.

2110.

My prayers are my tears,
And my tears
Are my only satisfaction.

2111.

I give my Lord
My aspiration-cries.
My Lord gives me
His Satisfaction-Harvest.

2112.

Today's patience-heart
Will become
Tomorrow's peace-life.

2113.

A oneness-life
Has always proved to be
The victor over insecurity.

2114.

When we speak ill of others,
We definitely enter into
Our mind's darkest abyss.

2115.

Each time I satisfy my Lord
    Supreme
In His own Way,
I become my soul's
Rainbow-beauty-smile.

2116.

A disobedience-mind
Is forced to walk
Along the destruction-road.

2117.

I always try to listen
To my heart's
Sweetness-flower-beauty-
    whispers.

2118.

If we do not aspire,
Then we remain
A useless, empty vessel-life.

2119.

O my mind,
Wake up, wake up!
Do you not think
That it is too late to continue
    sleeping?
Wake up
From your eyeless ignorance-
    sleep!

2120.

A difficult task, indeed,
But I have done it.
I have thrown insecurity
To the winds.

2121.

Self-offering is the master-key
That can open up
Each and every human heart.

2122.

Even the unutterable mistakes
In our lives
Can be rectified and illumined.

2123.

Everything can be achieved
If we can have sterling faith
Both in God and in ourselves.

2124.

God is
A twenty-four-hour
Compassion-Server.

2125.

If you do not surrender your life
    to God
Happily and cheerfully,
Then your life will always be
    found
In the dust.

2126.

The sooner you close your eyes
To darkness,
The better you will be able to see
The beauty and divinity of Light.

2127.

Desire-drum
I was.
Aspiration-whisper
I am.

2128.

If you really want to succeed
In your spiritual life,
Then you must not dance
With hesitation-legs.

2129.

God-obedience-seekers
Are the products
Of God's own Hands.

2130.

What you should be looking for
Is not God's Compassion,
Not even His Forgiveness,
But His Oneness-Delight.

2131.

O seeker,
Do not waste time!
God's Patience-Clock
May, before long, stop.

2132.

God keeps His choice Hour-Door
    open
All the time
Only for those who deeply
And unreservedly value
His Compassion-flooded Eye.

2133.

When I pray and meditate
    sleeplessly
And breathlessly,
God blesses my mind
With a moonlit sea of peace.

2134.

God is always ready
To feed my hungry heart,
Not my greedy mind.

2135.

A doubt-treasuring mind
I was.
But now a faith-blossoming heart
I am.

2136.

God is extremely fond
Of my heart-tears,
No matter how short-lived they
        are.

2137.

God-dreams do not allow God
To walk alone.
They most faithfully follow Him
Wherever He goes.

2138.

I wanted to sail on a cruise ship,
But my Lord said to me,
"My child, what you need
Is an aspiration-sailboat."

2139.

Now that my heart
Is replete with faith,
Doubt is extremely eager to leave
        me
Once and for all.

2140.

I do my job:
I greedily cling
To my desire-life.
God does His Job:
He sleeplessly dreams
Of my perfection-life.

2141.

God tells me
That if I feel I am really great,
Then I must face my own face,
Not others' eyes.

2142.

Yesterday
I threatened my anxiety-mind
So that it would leave me alone.
Alas, today my pride-mind
Is telling me
That it will never let me live alone.

2143.

My mind,
It is high time for you
To look for a new place to live.
For such a long time
You have been living
In your old despair-house.

2144.

Yesterday
I thought that my desire-life
Was stronger than the strongest.
Today
I am convinced that my
    aspiration-life
Is sweeter than the sweetest.

2145.

My Lord, I beg of You,
Do come and fix my will-power.
How long will You allow it
To remain out of order?

2146.

My soul is cautioning my heart
Not to wear out
My Lord's Compassion.

2147.

Wake up, wake up,
O my sleeping mind!
Can you not hear
God's Compassion-Concern-
Alarm Clock
Ringing and ringing?

2148.

Watch out!
The doubt-tiger is running fast,
Very fast,
To devour your aspiration-heart
And dedication-life.

2149.

Do not worry about your
    connection
With Heaven.
Worry only so long as it is
    necessary
To revive your aspiration.

2150.

Now that I have cornered
My doubting mind,
Nothing in my life can remain
Unattainable.

2151.

Hesitation obstructs
Our forward-looking vision
More than we can ever imagine.

2152.

Alas,
Anticipation of failure
Is devouring his life-breath.

2153.

May my world-transformation-
    promises
Devotedly and powerfully
Thrive.

2154.

O seeker, you fool!
You must always pay attention
To your soul's sweet whispers
And not to your mind's loud
    drumbeats.

2155.

You want God to be proud of you,
But can you supply Him
With even one solitary reason?

2156.

If your heart accepts God
On His own terms,
Then He will immediately give
    you
His private Telephone Number.

2157.

God tells me
That each approach I make to Him
Is, indeed, unique.

2158.

O seeker,
You suffer precisely because
You do not keep your heart-
    engine
All the time running.

2159.

The mind's obscurity
Either hides or always speaks ill of
The heart's humility.

2160.

An unaspiring life
Is nothing other than
An insignificant ant-promise.

2161.

You are apt to misunderstand
Your third eye.
Therefore, God is compelled
To blindfold it.

2162.

A hopelessly useless day
Is the day that I do not offer
My gratitude-heart
To my Lord Supreme.

2163.

God tells me
That He will be highly pleased
   with me
If I pay all attention
To my own divinity's reality
And not to my mind's false
   specialty.

2164.

How can there be any willingness
In the mind
When there is no soulfulness
In the heart?

2165.

You will never be able
To succeed triumphantly
In your spiritual life
Until you feel God's Heart
Is your only home.

2166.

Each God-manifestation-dreamer
On earth
Is a supreme herald
Of a new age.

2167.

Keep asking whomever you meet
For directions to God's Heart-
   Home.
Someday,
Someone will definitely be able
To help you.

2168.

Simplicity, sincerity and purity
Are God-messengers.
They are not supposed to play the
   role
Of actors.

2169.

If you want to enjoy
The thrill of silence,
The thunderous sound-life
You must shun.

2170.

Do not try to correct
People who do wrong things.
It will be worse than useless.
Only support and help
Those who are doing the right
   thing.

2171.

When my desire-life sees
God's Light-flooded Palace,
It gets frightened to death.

2172.

When my aspiration-heart sees
God's Light-flooded Palace,
It just runs there
And becomes a permanent
    resident.

2173.

God suffers more than you do
When you think of your failure-
    life.
You love God.
Why, then, torture poor God?

2174.

May my heart every day
Swim in the sea
Of my God-longing tears.

2175.

Alas, my doubt-mind-patient
For years and years
Has been hiding
From my faith-heart-doctor.

2176.

God's Compassion-flooded Will
Will never be understood
By humanity's mind.

2177.

The unavoidable consequences
Of our actions
Can be avoided
If we can bring down the Smiles
Of God's Compassion-Eye.

2178.

God immediately rewards my
    heart
Lovingly, cheerfully and
    abundantly
Whenever my heart offers
    something
Prayerfully and soulfully
To Him.

2179.

Our search for world-peace
Will one day
Be crowned with success,
Without fail.

2180.

My Lord tells me,
"My child, I have come to you
With My most blessingful Gift:
Poise."

2181.

Peace
Is not a new invention.
Peace
Is a very, very old discovery.

2182.

God's Forgiveness-Heart-Door
Is open every day
For twenty-four hours.

2183.

A God-surrendered life is blessed
With unparalleled capacities
For God-manifestation.

2184.

My heart's ever-increasing tears
And my soul's ever-blossoming
    smiles
Have pleased my Lord Supreme
Far beyond my imagination.

2185.

If we do not use the aspiration-
    cries
Of our heart,
Then we are bound to lose them.

2186.

He who always follows closely
God's Will
Will succeed in his outer life
And proceed in his inner life.

2187.

Nothing good and divine
Can ever be accomplished
Without God's Compassion-Sea,
Or at least God's Co-operation.

2188.

The very nature
Of the unaspiring mind
Is to misunderstand and belittle
    others.

2189.

How stupid the human mind is!
It does not even mind being
    buried
Under an avalanche of worthless
And useless facts.

2190.

Each disobedience-breath
Is extremely dangerous
To the God-longing aspiration-
    heart.

2191.

Today I am so happy and proud
Of myself
For telling the world
That my very breath
Is only for God to use.

2192.

O my mind,
What are you doing?
How do you dare to dance
With the doubt-dragon?

2193.

If we worship God's Will
As our own, very own,
Then God will declare us
His choicest representative
On earth,
Him to please and fulfil
In His own Way.

2194.

God-realisation and God-
    manifestation
Have to be for God's Satisfaction,
And for nothing else.
This divine message has been told
And retold
Down through the centuries.

2195.

God's Compassion knows only
    nearness,
Oneness and fulness,
And never aloofness.

2196.

Disobedience belongs to those
Who are already lost
Or going to be lost
In the battlefield of their spiritual
    life.

2197.

When I use God's Forgiveness
Inside my mind-jungle,
It is perishable.
When I use God's Forgiveness
Inside my heart-garden,
It is imperishable.

2198.

Each time I become the possessor
Of a divine thought,
I immediately jump
Into the cosmic Beyond.

2199.

To my greatest joy,
My God-willingness-heart
Is blooming and blossoming
With sweetest fragrance.

2200.

Sympathise only with those
Who are weak
Yet, at the same time,
Are trying to be strong
In their spiritual life.
But never sympathise with those
Who treasure their disobedience-
    life.

2201.

Only a very poor seeker
Keeps his aspiration-heart
Always under construction.

2202.

God claims us as His own,
Very own,
Not only when we are at the
    summit
Of our aspiration-height,
But also when we and our
    consciousness
Live together in the abysmal
    abyss.

2203.

My marathon boasting
Puts my Lord Supreme
To most peaceful sleep.

2204.

Carelessness is not only painful
But also destructive –
Far beyond our imagination.

2205.

Just a fleeting Smile
From my Lord Supreme
Has built a new foundation
For my aspiration-life.

2206.

God's Forgiveness-Heart
And His Compassion-Eye
Are infinitely dearer and closer
Than our breath.

2207.

Neither the God-reasoning mind
Nor the God-doubting mind
Will ever be able to understand
    God.

2208.

Secretly, happily and proudly
God uses His private Door
To enter into my aspiration-heart.

2209.

May my life grow
Into the beauty
Of a rainbow-dawn.

2210.

God
Never pays any attention
To the God-hesitating mind.

2211.

In the spiritual life,
An aspiration-power failure
Is so common!

2212.

You have simply no idea
How powerful a single doubt can
    be.
It can destroy our sterling faith
In the twinkling of an eye.

2213.

A self-giver
Is God's
Own extended Hands.

2214.

The more tears you shed for God,
The sooner you will be able
To please Him
And claim Him.

2215.

God and God's Ears
Eagerly wait for
Your love-devotion-surrender-
    whispers.

2216.

Since God has come to you,
Make up your mind!
Give Him either your crying heart
Or your doubting mind –
Or you can give Him both!

2217.

God the Mother you can please
    easily
With your soulful smiles
And tearful eyes.

2218.

When I finally claimed God
As my own, very own,
Heaven stood up
With roaring applause.

2219.

I frequent my Lord's House
And take His Newsletters
To distribute to the world.

2220.

You can expect a heavy downpour
Of Grace from Above
If you give God implicitly
The beauty, purity and divinity
Of your heart.

2221.

My Lord, only one thing
I need from You:
A moment of bliss-flooded peace.

2222.

His mind's doubt-storm
Has ruthlessly shocked
His faith-built heart-foundation.

2223.

Humanity and unfulfilled
God-manifestation-promises
Shall always be found together.

2224.

It is never too late
To sit for
Our God-satisfaction-
    examination.

2225.

My whole being is drawn into
The beauty and fragrance
Of a new age.

2226.

My heart is resolved
To be more devotedly involved
In God-manifestation-activities.

2227.

You can climb up the highest
   heights
Provided you do not forget
To take your Lord's immeasurable
   Help.

2228.

All our differences disappear
When our mind's readiness,
Life's willingness
And heart's eagerness
Work together.

2229.

May each breath of my heart
Help me turn my life
Into a God-temple.

2230.

We must learn once more
That human life
Is the melody of a universal song.

2231.

God's unconditional Grace
Has transformed his barren
Nothingness-life
Into a colourful and powerful
God-manifestation-smile.

2232.

Every day I would like to be
A new-born devotion-creation
Of God.

2233.

The life of a seeker
Has to be guarded
Every day, without fail,
Against impurity-attacks.

2234.

I want to enshrine my life
Not by continual sacrifices,
But by constant love of God.

2235.

Never too late to regain
One's aspiration-cries
And dedication-smiles!

2236.

If you forget to offer
Your morning tears and cries
To God,
Then you will sigh the entire day.

2237.

The more he increased
His faith in God,
The more soulfully his heart
Was able to worship God.

2238.

Whenever there is a sad dispute
Between my mind and my heart,
God always takes the side
Of my heart,
For God knows that the heart
Has a clear vision of reality's life.

2239.

Poor seeker!
At long last you feel and believe
That God has a special Blessing,
Special Love and special Concern
For you.

2240.

Do not give up!
God will definitely
One day come to you
And clasp your eyes
With His Fondness-Smile.

2241.

Can you win your life's battle
Against the undivine forces?
Yes, you can,
If you say "Yes" to God
Long before the battle begins.

2242.

My soul has drawn
My body, vital, mind and heart
Into the beauty of a new dawn.

2243.

Our longing for God
Has to be
Both urgent and permanent.

2244.

O seeker, you cannot have
A God-smiling heart
If you enjoy
A man-hating mind.

2245.

Alas, in vain I say
Good-bye and good-bye and good-
    bye
To my God-disobedience-mind.

2246.

It is not enough
To trim negative thoughts.
Negative thoughts have to be
    buried!

2247.

O my mind, you can easily escape
At every moment
From the clutches of giant doubt
By taking shelter at the Feet
Of our Lord Beloved Supreme.

2248.

God-fulfilment-opportunities
Will arrive at our aspiration-door
Again and again every day,
If we can keep our heart's
    devotion-cries
On the increase.

2249.

His sleepless aspiration
Has pleased God to such an extent
That God Himself has built
A God-Satisfaction-Nest
For him to live in.

2250.

If you are a sincere seeker,
Then fear and anxiety
Are bound to chase
All your pleasure-indulgence-
    thoughts.

2251.

The human life has its ups and
    downs,
But the divine life is blessed
Only with God's ever-brightening
    Smiles.

2252.

You are good when you strive
For your perfection,
But you are infinitely better
When you strive for God-
    Satisfaction
Only.

2253.

No matter what happens,
Today I am determined
To bid farewell
To my mind's brooding doubts.

2254.

When my life is only for God,
I clearly see
That God is ready to feed
All my needs.

2255.

O seeker, do not despair,
Do not despair!
Despair is an all-devouring,
Ferocious tiger.

2256.

Meditate on God's Compassion-
    Eye
While you are driving
Through the streets of life.
Lo, God will not allow
Fear, doubt and anxiety
To accompany you.

2257.

God is always eager
To crown us with His divine Love,
Joy and Pride.
But, alas, we are never ready!

2258.

The deplorable fate of humanity
Is that it is apt to bathe
In a sea of unfulfilled promises.

2259.

May my life become
A perfect slave
To my God-fulfilment-desire.

2260.

My God-satisfaction-life
Is made by
The Tears of God's Heart
And the Smiles of His Eye.

2261.

There is no difference,
Absolutely none,
Between a desire-land
And a wasteland.

2262.

All my God-fulfilment-promises
Were born from my heart's
Heaven-climbing hopes.

2263.

We know that our lives
Are made of endless
    shortcomings.
But do we know or even care to
    know
That God's Life is made of
Endless and endless Forgiveness?

2264.

The more I pray and meditate,
The clearer I hear God's Voice
Saying that I am a choice
Manifestation of His Will.

2265.

When I pray soulfully,
I unmistakably see
That God's Compassion-Eye
Is watching me, protecting me
And guiding me
All the time.

2266.

Without God's unconditional
    Grace,
I could not have even dreamt
Of terminating my age-old
    relationship
With the darkness-ignorance-
    prince.

2267.

Negativity's turbulent sea
You can easily escape
By taking shelter inside
Your faith-heart-fort.

2268.

Beauty is our face
When our life becomes
Its purity-heart.

2269.

Alas, we do not know
Why somehow we enjoy
Our life's sorrow-bound journey.

2270.

When God and God's
  Compassion-Eye
Come to visit me in my heart-
  room,
I immediately enjoy
An indescribable ecstasy-thrill.

2271.

In a twinkling,
The disobedience-mind
Has the capacity to capsize
Our life's God-happiness-boat.

2272.

The soul is the only
God-representative-singer
Authorised by God Himself.

2273.

I am perfectly fine
Only when I realise
That God is not only mine,
But everybody's.

2274.

Every single Smile from God
Shortens the distance
To my God-Destination-Shore.

2275.

Only a God-Satisfaction-dreamer
Can be
A universal oneness-lover.

2276.

Obedience and surrender
Are lesser-known
Virtues.

2277.

He has made the fastest progress
On the strength of his inner poise
And outer courage.

2278.

Familiarity with God's
Compassion-Eye
Is sweetness indescribable.

2279.

We fail to make the fastest
  progress
In our spiritual life
Because so often we oscillate
Between inner strength
And outer weakness.

2280.

Our academic accomplishments
Quite often stand in our way
When we want to dive deep
Into the spiritual life.

2281.

We must not try to escape
The mind-abyss.
We must illumine the mind-abyss
For peace and bliss to live in.

2282.

I strongly feel that
When I lose the riches
Of the outer world,
I shall gain the riches
Of the inner world.

2283.

My Lord Supreme
Is extremely proud
Of my soul's limitless harvest
Of His God-Smiles.

2284.

The undivine forces give us
Disobedience-lessons
And compel us to walk along
The destruction-road.

2285.

May my aspiration-heart
Remain ever-beautiful
And my dedication-life
Remain ever-bountiful.

2286.

God wants me to take
My past mistakes
As remote incarnations,
And pay no attention to them.

2287.

God tells me that if I sing
My aspiration-songs well,
Then He will be inspired
To teach me
Realisation-dances.

2288.

My Lord Supreme,
Never allow my mind
To suffer from
Inspiration-exhaustion.

2289.

My Lord Supreme,
Never allow my heart
To suffer from
Aspiration-shortage.

2290.

Do not depend
Either on time or space.
Depend only
On God's ceaseless Grace.

2291.

O seeker, do not be a fool!
Never, never dispute
With God's Compassion-Eye
On any subject.

2292.

He who turns away from God's
    Grace
And thinks he can protect himself
In the inner life by his own efforts,
Will meet with perdition –
To his great shock.

2293.

Jealousy, insecurity and impurity
Have no access
To my heart-home.

2294.

Smile, smile, O world, smile!
You have to replace your heart-
    tears
With your soul-smiles.

2295.

Our frightening and threatening
    destiny
We must challenge and transform
Into an enlightening destiny.

2296.

As our enthusiasm and success
Live together,
So also do our obedience and
    progress.

2297.

Life's sorrows and joys
Are but
Revolving doors.

2298.

My Lord tells me
That my task is to satisfy Him
With my surrender-heart,
And His Task is to perfect my life
With His Compassion-Sea.

2299.

My readiness-mind, my
    eagerness-heart
And my willingness-life
Have won today
God's Victory-Chariot.

2300.

I shall never return
To my mind's
Depression-frustration-country!

2301.

Without loving God first,
If you try to improve the world,
Then you are only going
To prolong the life
Of your own stupidity-mind.

2302.

You do not have to go
To the forest.
Only keep your mind
Out of the forest.
Your heart-garden is beckoning
    you.
Immediately respond.

2303.

Do not feed
Your fawn-curiosity.
Feed your genuine
Aspiration-necessity.

2304.

At last I am so happy
Because I am returning everything
To its real Owner:
God.

2305.

It depends entirely
On us
Whether we make our body
A friend or an enemy.

2306.

My Lord Supreme,
I am unimaginably happy
When I sincerely feel
That I am a slave of Your slave.

2307.

Out of His infinite Compassion,
My Lord Supreme has allowed me
To touch His Feet.
Therefore, all my desires
And earthly wishes
I have totally forgotten.

2308.

Your false spirituality
Can govern only
Your outer life of doubt,
And never your inner life
Of faith.

2309.

If you want God's Grace
More than anything else,
Then happily and proudly
Remain seated at God's Feet.

2310.

If your mind is not caught
By pleasure and pain,
Then God Himself will come
    down
And unchain your life.

2311.

My hungry desire-life
Has ceased.
I am now ready for
The real spiritual life.

2312.

How can I have any fear and doubt
Now?
I clearly see my Lord Supreme
Is coming –
Singing and dancing.

2313.

God tells me to be wise
And to welcome smilingly
Whatever befalls me.

2314.

We came into the world
To enjoy the beauty and fragrance
Of calm delight
While manifesting God's Light
On earth.

2315.

My Lord,
Do You really love me?
Then do not allow me
To part from You.
From now on, I shall gladly
And proudly
Do Your Bidding.

2316.

I have unmistakably departed
From my desire-life.
My soul is the witness.

2317.

My Lord says to me:
"My child,
You are under no obligation
To allow your desire-mind
To torment your life."

2318.

I have replaced my illusion-mind
With my aspiration-heart—
To my greatest joy!

2319.

O my Inner Pilot Supreme,
Do allow not only my heart,
But also my eyes,
To rest at Your Compassion-Feet
Forever.

2320.

Only one Compassion-Touch
Of my Lord Supreme
Has changed the course of my life
Altogether.

2321.

The moment I woke up,
I saw my soul
Singing and dancing
In ecstasy.

2322.

We usually do not mind
When our Heavenly visa expires,
But we feel miserable
When our earthly visa expires.

2323.

O my mind, come with me!
Let us both retire
Into the heart of silence.

2324.

An aspiration-heart
Is the brightest Smile
Of God.

2325.

God does not mind
Giving us repeated chances
If He sees each time
That our sincerity increases.

2326.

Every day we must clean
Our mind-room
In the hope that our Lord
    Supreme
Will pay a short visit.

2327.

The moment our mind
Became a victim to insecurity,
We were thrown off
The spirituality-track.

2328.

The divine in us
Smilingly wants to serve.
The human in us
Proudly wants to be served.

2329.

O seeker,
Do not let your insincerity-mind
Try to escape from the world-eye,
If you long for perfection.

2330.

As an encouragement-flower
Inspires all,
Even so, a criticism-thorn
Hurts all.

2331.

The more worries and anxieties
Speak about God,
The more they get lost
In the land of nowhere.

2332.

My mind's bitterness-hatred
Cannot help loving
My heart's sweetness-smile.

2333.

When my aspiration-heart
Sleeps,
My illumination-soul
Helplessly weeps.

2334.

Man quite often forgets
The consequences
Of his tempting and tempted fate.

2335.

God keeps His Promise:
He comes down
With His Compassion-Smile.
Man does not keep his promise:
He does not go up
With his aspiration-cry.

2336.

The very nature of obstacles
Is to mount.
But who asked you not to
    surmount?

2337.

God's Compassion-Eye
Becomes His Sadness-Heart
When His lost children
Do not care for
His all-illumining Light.

2338.

My God-aspiration-cries
Are, indeed, beautiful and
    fruitful.
But my God-manifestation-life
Is all satisfaction.

2339.

My heart-approach to God,
I feel,
Will definitely allow me to avoid
Future Himalayan blunders.

2340.

My heart-peace-home
Is deep inside
My soul-power-fortress.

2341.

The unaspiring mind always
    thinks
That God's Standard
Is unnecessarily high.

2342.

The aspiring heart feels
That God's Standard
Could have been infinitely higher
If God's Justice-Light
Had prevailed.

2343.

A blessingful God-Touch
Powerfully awakened
My sleeping life.

2344.

God asks me to judge everything
With my heart's tears
And not with my mind's frowns.

2345.

May each heartbeat of mine
Be a sacred Dream
Of my Absolute Lord Supreme.

2346.

A sincerity-mind
And
A purity-heart
Are truly fond of each other.

2347.

A man of prayer
Eventually becomes
A heart of silence-delight.

2348.

Today's God-Compassion-
    dreamer
Will be tomorrow's
God-Satisfaction-achiever.

2349.

My heart's ceaseless tears
And my life's sorrowless smiles
Are making a passport for me
To enter the highest Heaven
When the final hour strikes.

2350.

I want to listen to God
Not with my mind-disobedience-
    ear,
But with my heart-obedience-
    smile.

2351.

My Lord,
How can I touch Your Feet
With my impure mind?

2352.

God is stretching out
His Oneness-Heart
To me.

2353.

Desire-trips
Are always
Unbelievably dangerous.

2354.

God's Compassion-Eye
Is always eager
To navigate our life-boat.
But where is our readiness?

2355.

God's Lion-Victory
Shall dawn in our life
When we long for
His Omnipresence-Love,
And not His Omnipotence-Power.

2356.

My Lord's Forgiveness-Smile
Is the pole-star
Of my aspiration-life.

2357.

God asked me if I needed anything
From Him.
I said to Him,
"My Lord, only one Boon:
While repeating Your Name,
I want to declare my journey's
    close."

2358.

O my seeker-friend,
God can definitely erase
All your past failures.
I am, indeed, a radiant example!

2359.

A God-realised person
Is he who can inundate
The whole world
With His God-realisation-light
And delight.

2360.

One seeker says to another,
"My friend, be not discouraged
On the way.
I have taken millions
Of faltering steps
To arrive at the Feet
Of my Lord Supreme."

2361.

Hope,
My secret and sacred hope,
Let us ascend together
For God-realisation.

2362.

Promise,
My challenging and daring
    promise,
Let us descend together
For God-manifestation.

2363.

Nobody is condemned
To be a victim
To spirituality-drought.

2364.

Nobody is condemned
To a slow and dangerous
Spirituality-voyage.

2365.

To insulate ourselves
From the outer world
Is definitely not the right way
To please God.

2366.

God is extremely proud of him
Because his days and nights
Are punctuated by prayers
And meditations.

2367.

My lotus-heart
Has only one place
To bloom and blossom:
At my Lord's Compassion-Feet.

2368.

Infinity's silence sleeps inside
The beauty and fragrance
Of my aspiration-heart.

2369.

I am so happy and excited
That my Lord Supreme and my
    soul
Have arrived together
To unveil my heart-shrine.

2370.

The God who has given you
The capacity to dream
Has also given you
The capacity to execute.
So begin your task here and now!

2371.

Give and give and give
Ever-increasingly
If you do not want to
Impoverish yourself.

2372.

The beauty of my outer smile
Entirely depends on
The fragrance of my inner faith.

2373.

May my soul's delight
Reign supreme
In my life.

2374.

We must realise that our inner
    strength
Is infinitely stronger
Than any outer incidents.

2375.

My forgiveness-heart
Is always rewarded
By my Lord Supreme
Far beyond my imagination.

2376.

Is there a single aspiration-heart
That does not long for
Peace?

2377.

Is there a single desire-mind
That ever longs for
Peace?

2378.

I have made my life
Happy and peaceful
By expecting the unexpected.

2379.

Do not look out;
There is nothing.
Turn within;
There is everything.

2380.

My prayer-heart
Has finally transformed
My barren desert-life
Into a blossoming heart-garden.

2381.

In God's Eye,
Everything is His own
Beauty's Touch.

2382.

It is the same God
Who decreases my desire-life
And increases my aspiration-
    heart.

2383.

Our God-obedience in small
    things
Makes big things
Infinitely easier to achieve.

2384.

My Lord,
May I claim everybody's heart-
    beauty
As my own?
"My child,
Certainly you can and you must."

2385.

God gives me His Inspiration,
And I give Him my heart-song
In return.

2386.

Alas, every day I argue
With my mind.
My mind wants nothing
But new degrees of greatness-
    height.
What I want my mind to have
Is goodness-depth.

2387.

The difference between
My mind and my heart
Is this:
My mind is a self-styled
God-talker,
And my heart is an accomplished
God-lover.

2388.

My greatest discovery
Was my love-devotion-surrender-
    recovery
From ignorance-night.

2389.

The distant shore
Towards which we sail our life-
    boat
Is within, and not without.

2390.

If you are planning to graduate
From your desire-course
And go on to a higher aspiration-
    course,
Then immeasurable will be
God's Joy.

2391.

Ineffable
Are man's ascending tears
And God's descending Smiles.

2392.

From now on I shall cherish
My new blossoming
And blossomed dreams,
And not remain in the valley
Of my forgotten dreams.

2393.

Once you enter into the spiritual
    life,
You must take your life as God-
    belief,
And your heart as the God-
    believer.

2394.

A love of beauty
I was.
The beauty of love
I am.

2395.

Peace-dreamers and peace-lovers
Are God's first-class
    representatives
On earth.

2396.

May my aspiration-heart
Become once more
An earth-illumining lamp.

2397.

Be not afraid of the storms of life.
The rainbow of time
Will soon be visible.

2398.

When you aspire,
You bring to the fore from within
The celestial beauty of your
    future.

2399.

My heart's pitiful tears
Are my life's questions.
My soul's bountiful smiles
Are my life's answers.

2400.

Why do I not listen to my Lord
    Supreme?
Is it because He is too familiar,
Or too unfamiliar?

2401.

What kind of seeker are you
If you are not blindly,
Sleeplessly and breathlessly
For God?

2402.

Even when sorrows cloud his
    heart,
He meditates on God's
    Compassion-Eye
And Protection-Feet.

2403.

We are totally mistaken
If we feel that God has disowned
    us
For our impossible misdeeds.
He has not yet learnt the art
Of disowning His creation.

2404.

Be not proud!
If you think your aspiration
Is unsinkable,
You may be utterly mistaken.

2405.

We must wash our suspicion-
    mind
With our heart's tears
If we want to see rainbow-beauty
In our spirituality-sky.

2406.

My Lord Supreme
Is extremely proud of me
Because my heart is no longer
Attacked by insecurities.

2407.

Alas, the desire-mind
Has no inkling
Of the aspiration of the inner life.

2408.

Frustration-days and nights
Are so familiar
To the unaspiring mind!

2409.

God's unconditional Compassion
Has taken away completely
My desire-hunger.

2410.

My joy knows no bounds
Now that I have become
A newborn
God-fulfilment-eagerness-child.

2411.

I am so grateful to my soul
For never allowing me
To neglect my heart-shrine.

2412.

I must never forget
That God wants me to have
    friends,
And not fans.

2413.

I have come to realise
That there are many things
    invisible
That can play the roles
Of invincibilities.

2414.

God is not at all impressed
With my outer success.
What He wants from me
Is perfection-flooded progress.

2415.

When saints and sinners mix
    together,
God becomes His Heart's
Ecstasy-Song.

2416.

I have known
Since the beginning of time
That God never gives up on us,
No matter how worthless and
    useless
We are.

2417.

Be not proud
Of your mind-jungle.
Can you not see that
You have lowered
The God-aspiration-standard
Of humanity?

2418.

God's express Compassion-Train
Knows no
Ultimate station.

2419.

God wants to bless each human
    being
With a perfection-tower,
But alas, our receptivity
Is nowhere to be found.

2420.

When we embark
On our spiritual journey,
We embody the beauty
And reveal the fragrance
Of our own divinity.

2421.

If you cannot break through
Each and every ego-obstacle,
Then you will not be able
To place the victory-crown
At the Feet of your Lord Supreme.

2422.

God tells me to be a volunteer
In the battle for
God-manifestation-height
And God-satisfaction-depth.

2423.

Without serving mankind,
You can never become a member
Of God's immediate Family.

2424.

His sleepless devotion
To his Lord Supreme
Has devoured
All his doubt-anxiety-enemies.

2425.

O my mind,
How long do you want God to
    wait
For you to launch your life-boat
On His Compassion-Love-Sea?

2426.

The seeker's God-satisfaction-
    attempts
Cannot forever remain
Unfulfilled.

2427.

Do not expect
The outer world's sympathy
To liberate you.
It is unmistakably absurd!

2428.

Once a self-giving heart
Starts giving,
It only continues and continues,
And never stops.

2429.

I am winging and winging
The vault of the blue sky
To hear God's Victory-Song.

2430.

Humour
Is my life's
Fear and tear-killer.

2431.

I have finally liberated
My insecurity-heart
To walk, march and run
Along God's sunlit Road
To arrive at the Destination.

2432.

Success comes from
Enthusiasm.
Progress comes from
Self-giving.

2433.

The only solace
In my anxiety-ridden life
Is that my Lord Supreme
Truly and sleeplessly loves me.

2434.

He who holds goodness in his
    heart
Feels at once
God's Fondness and Fulness.

2435.

Human life
Desperately tries to keep
The flickering hope-flame
Alive.

2436.

God wants my inspiration-mind
To patronise my aspiration-heart.
But what my mind is doing,
Instead of patronising,
Is antagonising.

2437.

Alas, I claim to be a God-lover,
Yet so often
I dare to disagree with Him.

2438.

My heart's aspiration-song of
    today
Will tomorrow turn into
My life's dedication-dance.

2439.

You must become a God-dreamer
First.
Then you can become a God-lover.

2440.

A God-lover is
A blooming and blossoming
God-representative on earth.

2441.

If I really feel
God's Love for me,
Who or what
Can ever disturb me?

2442.

The mind definitely needs
Divine Illumination.
The heart unmistakably needs
Universal Oneness.

2443.

In the spiritual life,
Nothing can be as valuable
As unconditional surrender
To God's Will.

2444.

If you cannot claim others'
    happiness
As your own,
Then you will not be able to enjoy
Your own happiness unreservedly.

2445.

If there is a competition between
A God-questioning mind
And a God-aspiring heart,
I am sure the heart will prevail.

2446.

Each moment can be
The blossoming
Of a new life.

2447.

Obedience
Paves the way
To ecstasy-sea.

2448.

The mind can conceive
Great things.
The heart can do
Good things.

2449.

I am happy
When I can sincerely believe
That my Lord Supreme is for me.

2450.

I am perfect
When I can prayerfully
And devotedly feel
That I am for God only.

2451.

A genuine prayer carries in itself
Joy in abundant measure.
It does not have to wait
For its fulfilment.

2452.

I am praying to God
For my aspiration, dedication,
Surrender and gratitude
Always to remain in full measure.

2453.

Unless you have
A fulness-heart-fragrance,
You cannot have
A newness-life-beauty.

2454.

I am praying to God
Not for a mind-exciting
Experiment,
But for a life-illumining
Experience.

2455.

Since life itself is an art,
We must pray to God
To make us His choice artists.

2456.

Nobody really likes to mix with
    doubt,
Yet we are neither brave
Nor eager enough
To cast aside all doubts
From our mind.

2457.

When I lose sight of
God's Compassion-Eye
And His Forgiveness-Heart,
I am hopelessly lost –
Like a street beggar!

2458.

To a certain extent,
My mind can tolerate the person
Who does not appreciate
Anything great in others.

2459.

It is impossible
For my heart to tolerate anybody
Who cannot admire
The good things in others.

2460.

Your receptivity-heart
Must never give shelter
To your negativity-mind.

2461.

Our unwillingness to accept
The world as it is,
Is an unnecessary extra obstacle
That stands in the way of
Our happiness-life.

2462.

I am determined to transform
My heart's pitiful tears
Into my life's blissful smiles.

2463.

My Lord,
Please do not forget to do one
    thing:
Do give me the capacity
To enter into the storms of time
To proclaim Your supreme
    Victory.

2464.

If you can fill the day
With devotional songs,
Then God promises to strike
His Victory-Gongs.

2465.

When we criticise others,
We mistakenly feel that we are
Mature adults.
When we try to understand
    others,
We unmistakably feel that we are
Younger than an infant.

2466.

The outer music
Can at times puzzle our heart,
If not our mind.
But the inner music
Is our life's invaluable strength
And treasure.

2467.

God has given my soul
A very special task:
Wherever God goes
My soul smilingly and dancingly
    carries
The Keys to God's Kingdom.

2468.

God's Compassion-Heart-Door
Remains always wide open.
Alas, everybody comes in,
Save and except
The intellectual giants.

2469.

If you can respect and love
The present hour,
Your future years will fly towards
    you
With confidence-delight.

2470.

We really do not know
What we do and why we do it.
This moment we see that our life
Is nothing other than an endless
    sleep.
The next moment we feel that our
    life
Is an aimless run hither and
    thither.

2471.

A self-giving heart
Constantly bubbles
With ecstasy's height
And ecstasy's depth.

2472.

May my life's cry
Fly
With my heart's prayer.

2473.

My soul's God-manifestation-
  dream
Is immortalising
My life.

2474.

My God-willingness only
Has the capacity to challenge
The pride of disobedience-wall.

2475.

My fountain-flow-meditation
Is inspiring me to sing
The song of self-transformation.

2476.

My God-gratitude-heart
Has said a determined good-bye
To ignorance-night.

2477.

If you are wallowing
In the pleasures of ignorance
On earth,
How do you expect a front row
  seat
In Heaven
At your journey's close?

2478.

God wants you to sow
Aspiration-dedication-seeds.
Is there any reason
Why you are not abiding
By His Request?

2479.

May every second of my earth-life
Be transformed into
A self-offering-song.

2480.

Self-doubt is
The drowning moment
Of our spiritual life.

2481.

My Lord,
Your divine Greatness
Is trying to save me.

2482.

My Lord tells me
That I must offer Him
Every single day
My devotion-intensity-heart.

2483.

My Lord,
When You do not fulfil my desires,
Somehow I accept my fate.
But when You pretend
That You do not know me,
I just swim in the sea of despair.

2484.

My Lord, You are proud of me
When my humility is sincere.
My Lord, You are proud of me
When my gratitude is pure.

2485.

My Lord, my heart is full
Of anxious longing.
Do You get pleasure
By remaining always beyond my
    reach?

2486.

My Lord,
Detachment is what You want
From me.
But I also want something
From myself:
Patience.

2487.

My Lord,
It seems that You love
To bring things to a crisis.
"My child,
Your intuition needs immediate
    repair."

2488.

My Lord,
My austerities do not please You.
My repetition of Your Name
Does not please You.
What, then, will please You?
"My child, your sleepless,
Smiling surrender to My Will—
That is all!"

2489.

My Lord, it is up to You
To accept me or reject me,
But until You decide,
My eyes are going to feast
On Your Feet.

2490.

I deeply enjoy
My Lord's Sweetness-Smile.
My Lord blessingfully enjoys
My openness-heart.

2491.

As it is true that I have spent
Most of my life
Away from my Lord,
It is equally true that I shall spend
The rest of my life
At my Lord's
Compassion-Forgiveness-Feet.

2492.

Alas, I have increased my earthly
    ties
To make me happy,
And my Lord has decreased
His Heavenly Smiles
To make Him happy.

2493.

I have come to realise
That my mind's false gladness
And my heart's true sadness
Are not far apart.

2494.

My doubting mind,
Why do you torment me
When I sing my Lord's high
    praises,
Why?

2495.

"My Lord,
What do You think of my two
    resolves:
I want to love You sleeplessly;
I want to serve You breathlessly."
My Lord smiles and smiles
And smiles.

2496.

My Lord,
I have only one desire,
And that desire
Is to be in Your blessingful
    Presence
Once a day.
Since it is a good desire,
May I not expect a positive
    response?

2497.

My Lord repeatedly asks me
Not to subscribe to the view
That something will definitely
    happen
Because it is so destined.

2498.

Because of my unaspiring mind,
My life and I were doomed
To suffer.

2499.

Because of my aspiring heart,
My life and I are destined
To prosper.

2500.

When I do not aspire,
Time chases me ruthlessly.
When I aspire,
The same time surrenders to me
Smilingly.

2501.

God loves me,
But He loves my child-heart-smile
Infinitely more.

2502.

Divine love
Eventually becomes
Illumination-perfection.

2503.

If you really love God,
Then you cannot remain a
    stranger
To God-manifestation.

2504.

In the beginning,
We think that God-realisation
Is impossible.
But after some time,
We feel that God-realisation
Is inevitable.

2505.

I asked God
The actual meaning of devotion.
His immediate reply was
"Life-breath."

2506.

God wants a personal answer
From us.
He does not believe in
Answering machines.

2507.

An obedience-mind
And a gratitude-heart
Epitomise and immortalise
Our God-necessity-life.

2508.

I studied at belief and faith-
    school.
Therefore, it is extremely easy for
    me
To welcome God the Compassion.

2509.

Alas,
My heart has been crying and
    crying
And crying
Through the darkness of my
    mind.

2510.

If we are able
To love God inwardly,
Then we shall be able
To manifest God outwardly
Also.

2511.

God's Forgiveness-Heart
Knows no foreigner
And has no stranger.

2512.

God never forces us
To do anything.
He only waits and waits and waits
Until we wake up.

2513.

If you do not take exercise
To develop your oneness-muscle,
Who can and who will do it for
    you?

2514.

We must offer our Heaven-born
Oneness-heart
Here, there and all-where.

2515.

I have no idea
When satisfaction will dawn.
But I do know that someday,
Somehow,
It will dawn on earth.

2516.

You can easily ignore
All doubt-suspicion-
Phone calls.

2517.

When I go to God
To make an appointment,
He says to me:
"My child, you do not need
An appointment.
Just come and talk to Me
And unburden all your problems."

2518.

A wisdom-flooded heart
Does not mind waiting
For satisfaction to dawn.

2519.

O seeker,
Open the door and see who is
    knocking.
"I am the doubt-marcher."
"I am the faith-singer."
Command the doubt-marcher:
"Off with you!"
Embrace the faith-singer
And invite him to come in.

2520.

My heart-home has two names:
God's Tears
And God's Smiles.

2521.

We must offer God
Our most significant
And our most insignificant
    moments
Happily.

2522.

We are supposed to work only
And not judge the value
Of our work.

2523.

Every atom
Embodies the smiles and tears
Of the whole world.

2524.

The human question is:
"My Lord, do You really love me?"
The divine Answer is:
"You are the only one whom I
    love."

2525.

I really do not know
How long I shall have to remain
A perfect slave to my earthly tears.

2526.

It is quite common
For the unaspiring mind to reject
All the invitations that it receives
From God.

2527.

On the whole,
Humanity's suspicion-mind
Roams in the abysmal abyss.

2528.

If I have to make a choice
Between my heart-cottage
And my mind-mansion,
I shall immediately choose
My heart-cottage.

2529.

God's Heart does not measure
Anything.
It only treasures
Everything.

2530.

On a regular basis,
My Lord consoles, feeds and
    strengthens
My orphan-hope.

2531.

I asked God
If I should stay at His Door,
Like a dog,
Or if I should sit beside His
    Throne,
Like a prince.
He said to me:
"If you claim Me to be your own,
Then you must sit beside Me."

2532.

O Time,
The great devourer,
Do come and devour
My heart-sorrows.

2533.

I never allow my heart
To remain in the prison-cell
Of expectation.

2534.

I have been trying and trying
To replace my desire-mind
With my aspiration-heart.
I do not know why I am not
    succeeding.

2535.

My heart expects,
My mind demands
And my soul surrenders—
Surrenders to God's Will.

2536.

In my Lord's
Compassion-Heart-Garden,
I enjoy tomorrow's
Perfect freedom.

2537.

Every day
I wish to fly in the sky
Of my imagination-beauty-heart.

2538.

Always be careful!
Doubt can at any moment
Lord it over you.

2539.

My acceptance of the spiritual life
Is not a whim,
But a supreme necessity.

2540.

My Lord Supreme Himself
Has paved
My heart-walkway.

2541.

Every day
I must use my will-power
To keep my mind and vital
Under full control.

2542.

I am desperately trying
To regain my heart's
Simplicity-sincerity-purity-touch.

2543.

The mind wants to free us
With its counterfeit wisdom.
The heart wants to free us
With its snow-white love.

2544.

I want to have a sleepless
Thought-evolution-life,
And not an endless
Thought-revolution-mind.

2545.

We are mistaken
If we think that certain human
   beings
Have a monopoly
On God's Compassion-Affection.

2546.

God's most favourite
Food:
Man's gratitude-heart-smile.

2547.

O my Lord,
Do come and bring me out of
My heart's insecurity-cave.

2548.

We never realise
That desire-disasters
Can be so imminent.

2549.

I seek Grace
In every step I take
To see the Face
Of my Beloved Supreme.

2550.

O seeker,
If you really dislike
Your doubting mind,
Then why do you give
Your doubting mind
Your company?

2551.

You are a failure
Because you are not turning
In the direction
Of the all-illumining Light.

2552.

How can I express any concern
For humanity
Before I show my sleepless
   concern
For God?

2553.

If you do not resist
Your own divinity,
Then your life is bound
To have a smooth sailing.

2554.

If you are a sincere seeker,
Sooner or later
You are bound to get
A sincere Master.

2555.

A real God-lover
Does not find it difficult at all
To cling to his Master's feet.
But to abandon his Master's feet
Is, indeed, an impossible task for
    him.

2556.

Even when your inner poise
Is shattered,
Do not give up!
At God's choice Hour
God will definitely come
To your rescue.

2557.

If you want to remain happy
    always,
Then do not tell the world
What you want,
Or even what you need.

2558.

If you feel you are coming
To your Master on equal terms,
Then you have not found a real
    Master
Or your Master has not found
A real student.

2559.

If you beg a Master to lift you up,
Be careful!
If he is a false Master,
He may drag you down.
Have faith in yourself first,
And also have faith in your Master.

2560.

A spiritual Master is he
Who scatters confidence-light
Throughout the length and
    breadth
Of the sinking world.

2561.

In Heaven God always smiles.
It is the bounden task
Of the spiritual Masters
To make God smile on earth.

2562.

A spiritual Master
Says to his spiritual children:
"I have changed my name for you.
My name has become
Compassion-height.
Now I want to change your name
For humanity.
Your new name will be tolerance-
    light."

2563.

We must never hide
From good people,
For their very nature
Is to help us
And not chide us.

2564.

If we love God wholeheartedly,
Then His invisible Forces
Will prove to us
That they can be visible as well.

2565.

The more I can give myself
To my inner life,
The more I can expect
From my outer life.

2566.

If God the inner Voice
Is your only choice,
Then God will bless you
With His outer Voice
As well.

2567.

God asks me to uncover myself
First,
Before I try to discover myself.

2568.

The unaspiring mind
Enjoys
Bewilderment-thunder.

2569.

The aspiring heart
Loves
Enlightenment-flute.

2570.

To show a confidence-smile
Without first establishing your
    oneness
With God's Will
Is empty bravado.

2571.

How do I prove
That I do not desire desires
    anymore?
Just by accompanying aspiration
Wherever it goes.

2572.

If you do not conceal or protect
Your insincerity-life,
Then God Himself will come
And embrace your sincerity-heart.

2573.

If you desperately need God's
    Help,
Then wait for His Help
Before you take it upon yourself
To solve your problem.
If you do not wait for God's Help,
He may not value your future
    requests.

2574.

If you all the time pretend
To love the world,
You may never get the chance
To love the world sincerely.

2575.

Try to prove
To your outer life
That you are not
An insincerity-mind.
God's Compassion-Eye
Will definitely support you.

2576.

Until we have developed the
    capacity
To proclaim victory over
    ourselves,
It is sheer stupidity
To declare victory over others.

2577.

God tells the seeker
That His Task is to invent
And the seeker's task is to
    discover.
Therefore, the seeker must not
Reverse the game.

2578.

If you have an inner
Profundity-heart,
Then you cannot have an outer
Futility-life.

2579.

Do not ask truth to understand
    you.
Truth has already understood
    you.
It is you who are unwilling
To understand the truth
The way it is supposed to be
    understood.

2580.

I give my Lord what I have:
My obedience-heart.
My Lord gives me what He is:
His Pride-Breath.

2581.

The human mind
Loves
Even distant thunder.

2582.

The divine heart
Loves
Only instant silence.

2583.

His vital is afraid of saints.
His mind is afraid of sinners.
God tells him:
"My child,
Do not be afraid of either.
Both saints and sinners
Are My own creations."

2584.

We come to a spiritual Master
For him to take care of us.
Alas, very soon we feel
That we can deal with our own
    lives Better.
But we do not forget to keep him
As a figurehead.

2585.

The divine in us says "Hello!"
Even to the undivine
Around us.

2586.

The undivine in us
Has only two words in its
   dictionary
For the divine:
"Good-bye!" and "Begone!"

2587.

The mind's separation-worlds
Exist
Because we do not persist
In bringing to the fore
Our unification-hearts.

2588.

"I do not believe in ignorance-
   night!"
Just repeat this mantra
Day in and day out.
Soon there shall come a time
When the pride
Of Himalayan ignorance-night
Will force it to leave you.

2589.

The Inner Pilot is eagerly waiting
To whisper something to you.
Just give Him a chance
Only once.

2590.

The higher life says
To the lower life:
"Please follow me.
I want both of us to come
To our Lord Supreme
To make Him supremely happy."

2591.

The lower life says
To the higher life:
"Either follow me blindly
Wherever I go,
Or I shall chase you
To your destruction-doom!"

2592.

Even to feel
That you can one day become
A good God-seeker
Is, indeed, a most remarkable
   start.

2593.

Modern doctors
Are
Experiment-lovers.

2594.

Ancient doctors
Were
Experience-dreamers.

2595.

Success and progress can go
     together
Provided success sincerely longs
     for
Progress,
And progress sincerely admires
Success.

2596.

You want to lead?
Easy!
Just read the self-discovery-book
First.

2597.

We think that we can change the
     world.
God tells us:
"My children, certainly you can.
But do Me a favour first.
Just love the world unreservedly."

2598.

I am so surprised to see
That my soul does not believe in
My mind's interpretation of truth.

2599.

I am simply astonished
That my Lord does not believe in
My imperfection
At all.

2600.

My ability to hear God,
My ability to follow God,
My ability to surrender to God
And my ability to become one
     with God
Are definitely my birthrights.

2601.

My hopeful heart
Secretly
Beckons me.

2602.

My hopeless mind
Openly
Marshals me.

2603.

You may succeed in deceiving
The minds of the world-citizens,
But you will never be able to
    deceive
The God-oneness-child
Of your own heart.

2604.

Damaging thoughts
Think they can destroy the world
If they want to.
God says to them:
"Is that so?
Just try and prove it!"

2605.

Aspiring thoughts
Feel they can at least
Try to unburden the world.
God says to them:
"My children, amen!"

2606.

You have become
Your life's streaming tears
Because you have neglected
Your God-dreaming heart.

2607.

We try to judge
Right and wrong,
Good and evil.
God tells us:
"My children,
Why bother?
I have plenty of time
To do My own Work."

2608.

What does a wrong thought do?
It darkens our mind
And imprisons our life
Immediately.

2609.

What does a right thought do?
It inspires our heart
And liberates our life
Unmistakably.

2610.

If your life is touched
By Divinity's Compassion-Eye,
Then your life will remain
    untouched
By humanity's frustration-vital.

2611.

Surrender, God will embrace you.
Surrender, God will need you.
Surrender, God will claim you
As His own.
Surrender, God will fulfil
All His infinite Dreams
In and through you.

2612.

Sometimes I wonder
When I say that I need God's Help,
Do I really mean it,
Or would I even welcome it?

2613.

If you want to create
A new Divinity for the world
By dint of your personal will,
You are definitely going to be
The most deplorable failure.

2614.

If you want to reveal yourself
Again and again as a new Divinity
By obeying God's Will,
You are bound to succeed.

2615.

The doubting mind says:
"Not only are human beings
My problem,
But God is also.
Perhaps He is my problem
Number one!"

2616.

The aspiring heart says:
"O world, because I have accepted
All your problems as my own,
God is so kind to me, proud of me
And fond of me.
Therefore, O world, my heart is
All gratitude to you."

2617.

Imaginary happiness tells me
That there shall come a time
When I shall unmistakably
    become
Real happiness
In all its beauty and splendour.

2618.

Real happiness tells me
The secret of secrets:
God the infinite Happiness
Is constantly knocking
At my heart's door.
I just have to open it.

2619.

My mind is sad
That it cannot possess
The world.

2620.

My heart is extremely sad
That it has not yet allowed God
To be its sole possessor.

2621.

Can you imagine!
Even fear thrills me
When I am about to open
God's Heart-Door.

2622.

God has only two Commands for
    me:
He commands my soul to come
    down
To spread
His two Delight-flooded Wings
All over the world.
He commands my heart to climb
    up
High, higher, highest,
As fast as possible,
To feed His own Heart.

2623.

Concentrate.
Nothing will remain
Unattainable.

2624.

Meditate.
Nothing will remain
Unimaginable.

2625.

Self-enlightenment
Purposely remains
A perfect stranger
To self-aggrandisement.

2626.

Human self-aggrandisement
Is an instant
Balloon-burst.

2627.

Divine contentment
Is a God-prepared
Feast.

2628.

When I declare that my way
Is the only way,
God pleads with me
To see if His Way
Is a little better.

2629.

The darkest night
Wants to convince the world
That it is the brightest light.

2630.

The brightest light
Enjoys a vow of silence,
And in silence reveals
Its God-bestowed
World-transformation-promise.

2631.

The doubting mind has played
Its role:
It has veiled the Truth.
The aspiring heart is now
About to play its role:
It shall unveil the Truth.

2632.

Anxiety gets frightened
And leaves the mind
When you one-pointedly try to
    discover
Who you really are.

2633.

I depend heavily on my friends
Who thrust courage upon me
For God-manifestation here on
    earth.

2634.

You think that you know
Everything about everything.
But a day shall dawn
When you will realise
That you know nothing about
    anything.

2635.

Your mind-jungle remains
    dangerous
Just because you do not dare
To come out and run
Into your heart-garden.

2636.

Poor God does not know
What to say or what to do
When we unnecessarily blame
    others
For our own misdeeds.
He is totally lost
Between our ignorance
And their innocence.

2637.

My mind and I have decided
To explore the world
Outside us.

2638.

My heart and I are resolved
To discover the Real
Within us.

2639.

The divine in us invites
The human and the animal in us
To come to it
For their transformation.
The human in us says:
"I do not trust you."
The animal in us says:
"I am perfectly all right.
My big brother,
What you should worry about
Is your own satisfaction."

2640.

Real delight comes into existence
Only when the human in us
Gladly and unreservedly wants to
    play
With the divine in us.

2641.

The human in us
Cannot become divine
If the soul loses its sovereignty.

2642.

It seems that the more I give
Freedom to my mind,
The quicker I imprison
My spiritual life.

2643.

My God-disobedience-mind
Tells me that I do not need
The spiritual life.

2644.

My God-obedience-heart
Tells me that the spiritual life and
    I
Need each other at every moment.

2645.

The mind-train usually travels
   downhill
And arrives at
A nowhere-station.

2646.

In the inner world,
Happiness-runners are by far
The fastest runners.

2647.

The more I love
The beauty of the inner world,
The less I need
The wealth of the outer world.

2648.

"Love me, my Lord! Love me
At every moment!"
This is how I begin my prayer,
And this is how I end my prayer.

2649.

If you have not studied the first
   lesson,
How will you succeed in learning
The last lesson?
The first lesson is
Your sleepless love of God.
The last lesson is
Your unconditional surrender
To God's Will.

2650.

Cry, cry,
At every moment cry
For God's Compassion
And God's Satisfaction.
Otherwise, your life-vessel
Will always remain empty.

2651.

O seeker, since you have not
Cried for God,
How do you expect to be able
To smile at God?

2652.

My fearless vital
Is not challenging the ignorance
Of the outer world,
But is only attacking
Day in and day out
My poor aspiration-heart.

2653.

Negative thoughts are so powerful
That they can easily turn back
Our heart's aspiration-clock.

2654.

To reach the Goal,
You must here and now
Start celebrating
The divinity of the Goal.

2655.

My gratitude-heart
Keeps my dedication-life
Active and dynamic.

2656.

The obedience of the mind
And the enthusiasm of the vital
Are two inseparable,
God-cherished friends.

2657.

Although the body, vital and mind
Work together,
They want to maintain
Their individuality.
But when the heart and soul
Work together,
The heart simply swims and
    swims
In the sea of the soul's light and
    delight.

2658.

Disobedience-pleasure
Is always
Unimaginably shallow.

2659.

Insecurity does not have
The capacity
To walk happily
Around the life-track.

2660.

Every day I take
A morning walk
With my faithful heart-dog:
Obedience.

2661.

A day of unconditional obedience
Is the most perfect day
To sow peace
Inside our heart-garden.

2662.

How I wish my mind
Would commit to the prayer-life
The way my heart
Has committed to the meditation-
    life!

2663.

I feast on the beauty
And fragrance
Of my soul's peace-song.

2664.

My heart's aspiration-strides
And my life's dedication-strides
Are extremely exhilarating.

2665.

We need aspiration-flames
That cannot be touched
By wild emotions
In order to run the fastest
In our spiritual life.

2666.

When there is any dramatic battle
Between darkness and Light,
Darkness may win in the
    beginning,
But the ultimate victory
Goes to Light.

2667.

You are unwilling to leave
Your Master's protection-feet.
Indeed, this is an achievement
Of achievements.

2668.

The Master unfolds his Divinity
According to the disciple's
Readiness, willingness
And eagerness-life.

2669.

Why do you search
For an ideal hero?
Is not your faith in God
By far the best
Of all heroes?

2670.

Pray and meditate,
Meditate and pray
For as many hours as you can
Every day.
If not, you will be doomed
To a life of self-oblivion.

2671.

The loveliness of your face
Comes from the God-nearness
Of your heart.

2672.

God tells me
That my heart-tears
Are purer than purity itself.

2673.

When I have to make a choice
Between a blameless life
And a fearless heart,
I will always choose a fearless
    heart.

2674.

O my heart, if you are willing
To manifest your soul's smile,
Then start doing it—
Immediately and dynamically!

2675.

We have to entirely depend on
Our eagerness,
And not our restlessness,
For the Vision of God.

2676.

O seeker,
When your Master's words
Pierce your heart,
You are fully accepted
By your Master.

2677.

Every morning God comes in
And rings my faith-bell
To awaken my heart.

2678.

The clearer I see
The beauty of my soul,
The easier it becomes for me
To manifest my Lord's Light
On earth.

2679.

My soul tells me
That while I am indulging
In ignorance-sleep,
It will keep intact
My heart's great yearning
To reach God's
Transcendental Heights.

2680.

I ask God to end
His Silence-Vow.
God tells me to plough
My heart-garden first,
And then He will listen
To my prayer.

2681.

My Lord, You know how I love
Your Sweetness-Whisperings.
How is it that You forget me
So often?

2682.

Alas, will my striving
To conquer all my doubts
Ever end?
When will success-sun
Dawn on me?

2683.

O my mind, if you do not pass
Your sincerity-test,
Then God will never trust you
In the spiritual life.

2684.

My heart, your long absence
From the meditation-life
Is destroying all my love for God.

2685.

I keep my mind under control.
Therefore, I do not allow
Wild desire-wind
To blow through it.

2686.

We can never buy spirituality
With our material wealth.
We can only acquire spirituality
With our inner wealth:
Love, faith and obedience.

2687.

Once and for all,
My mind and I
Have stopped crossing
The doubt-strait.

2688.

Satisfaction comes to me
Automatically
When I listen devotedly
To my obedience-heartbeat.

2689.

May the river of my hope-dreams
Carry me every day
Towards the ever-increasing
     beauty
Of the Golden Shore.

2690.

O my insecurity-heart,
Can you not do anything better
Than cry, weep, moan
And sigh?
I am sure you can!

2691.

When I asked my soul
If I should start taming my mind,
I received from my soul
And my soul's friends
Roars of approval.

2692.

If I allow my doubting mind
And my strangling vital
To remain as they are,
Then I know I am foolishly risking
My soul's disfavour.

2693.

Your mind is ignorant,
Your heart is wise.
Therefore, God teaches only your
     heart
How to read His Handwriting.

2694.

God sings and dances
Right in front of me
When I study
The self-improvement books
Written by Him.

2695.

I do not trust my mind;
I do not trust even my heart.
I trust only my soul.
Therefore, I beg my soul
To coordinate my day.

2696.

My gratitude-heart-bird
Has two
God-happiness-wings.

2697.

Learn by heart
Your life-surrender-prayers.
God will lift you up immediately
To His own Transcendental
    Heights.

2698.

God secretly tells
His unconditionally surrendered
    seekers
How to spread His Manifestation-
    Light
Throughout the length and
    breadth
Of the world.

2699.

If you are ready to cry at God's
    Feet,
Then God will be ready to bring
    you
Inside His Heart
To smile.

2700.

Time hangs heavily
Only on those who have not learnt
How to use it properly.

2701.

My Lord Supreme,
My ever-blossoming surrender-
    life
Bows to Your birthless Cry
And deathless Smile.

2702.

My Lord Supreme,
My ever-increasing gratitude-
    heart
Bows to Your birthless Silence
And deathless Sound.

2703.

If one has a devotion-heart,
Then an iota of God's Compassion
Can create a miracle.

2704.

To become a choice instrument
Of God,
I must become an expert
In the love-devotion-surrender-
    game.

2705.

The third-class disciples
Receive a special message
From their Master:
"God is in Heaven.
I am His sole representative on
    earth
For you."

2706.

The second-class disciples
Receive a very special message
From their Master:
"God and I are eternally
And absolutely one."

2707.

The first-class disciples
Receive a very, very special
    message
From their Master:
"I am the Way; I am the Goal."

2708.

God's Heart-Door
Is always wide open
For our humility-life
To enter.

2709.

Intensity is the secret of secrets
To expedite the seeker's journey
Towards his destined Goal.

2710.

Oneness with humanity,
Minus God,
Is, indeed, a most miserable
Frustration.

2711.

I am God's; God is mine:
This feeling comes
From our lofty awareness
Of God's Transcendental Will.

2712.

Sweetness
Is the outer name
Of a gratitude-heart.

2713.

Fulness
Is the inner name
Of a surrender-breath.

2714.

Let us cultivate faith
More and more
In our everyday life,
So that God can illumine
Our jungle-minds.

2715.

My heart's determination
Will forever remain
Far beyond the boundaries
Of joy-devouring frustrations.

2716.

The heart's aspiration
And the life's dedication
Do have the capacity
To please God in His own Way.

2717.

I love to love my little "i".
But then what happens?
Lo, I am millions and billions of
    miles
Away from God.

2718.

I love to love my big "I".
And then what happens?
Lo, my Lord Supreme
Embraces me.

2719.

You will never miss
The God-track
If your heart is flooded
With devotion.

2720.

Once aspiration disappears,
We become
Veritable beggars
In the inner world.

2721.

Without devotion,
You can never succeed
In touching God's Feet
Or in clasping God's Eye.

2722.

When we live in our mind,
We haughtily expect God to
    surrender
To our commands and demands.

2723.

When we live in our heart,
We cherish only one code of life:
We are of God and we are for God
Only.

2724.

My Master asks me:
"Where is your past?"
Master, I do not know.
"How can you know, my child?
I have cast it aside."

2725.

My Master asks me:
"What is your present doing?"
Master, to be honest,
I really do not know.
"My child, how can you know?
I keep it inside my heart."

2726.

My Master asks me:
"Where is your future?"
Master, how can I say
Where my future is?
"My child, that is not your
    problem.
Leave it to me.
Happily I shall deal with it."

2727.

It is a real insult
That we hurl upon our soul
When we worry about our future
While sailing in our Master's
Golden Boat.

2728.

Become a God-devotion-heart.
Yours is the life
That will grow into
The fastest progress-delight.

2729.

When I am with my devotion-
    heart
At God's Feet,
The sweetness and fulness
Of the universe
Immediately embrace me.

2730.

My prayer-life and my
    meditation-heart
Have taken full responsibility
For placing me permanently
At the Feet of my Lord Supreme.

2731.

God asks the Master
To exercise his full Divinity
Only in the lives of those
Who believe in him implicitly.

2732.

Self-doubt and God-doubt
Are the most deplorable results
Of God-disobedience-thoughts.

2733.

God tells the Master
That he has to perform
Miracle after miracle in the inner
    world
Secretly
To keep the world-aspiration
In perfect order.

2734.

Alas, how often I see my Lord
    Supreme
Touching not just my heart,
But even my feet,
To make me do the right thing
And become the right person.

2735.

The devotee who inspires
Other devotees
Becomes infinitely more devoted –
An immediate reward from God
    Himself.

2736.

I hear the sweetness-whispers
Of the New Millennium
Inside my Heaven-climbing heart.

2737.

My Lord, do give me the capacity
Every day
To renew my promise
To accept You and fulfil You
In Your own Way.

2738.

Spirituality is never a matter
Of mind-understanding,
But it is ever a matter
Of heart-feeling.

2739.

O world-mind, I beg of you,
Do keep inside your mind-cave
Your God-criticism-poison!
Do not spread it
Inside my heart-garden.

2740.

God's chidings
Are only for those devotees
Who beg God to help them
Make the fastest progress.

2741.

My God-commitment
Is the only commitment
That I must embody, reveal
And manifest.

2742.

Golden opportunities
Are God's unconditional Gifts
To mankind
For mankind's immediate outer
    success
And immediate inner progress.

2743.

Spirituality has always been
A one-way ride.
There is no round-trip ticket.

2744.

Sincerity must always be fed
By faith –
Faith in our God-hunger,
Faith in our God-banquet.

2745.

At the dawn of each day,
Let us make our hopes
And promises
As sincere and powerful
As possible.

2746.

We must not misunderstand
The role of discipline.
Discipline is not torture.
It is our most reliable
Safeguard.

2747.

Discipline at once illumines
The unlit in us
And fulfils the unfulfilled in us.

2748.

Every day you must repeat,
Prayerfully and soulfully,
One thing:
"There is no such thing
As insignificant disobedience."

2749.

Each aspiration-song
Of our heart
Embodies fragrance exquisite.

2750.

The Master tells us,
And we must believe him,
That he is nothing but a
    mouthpiece
For the Absolute Lord Supreme.

2751.

If you have
A beautiful hope,
Make it sleepless.

2752.

If you have
A powerful promise,
Make it breathless.

2753.

God inundates our life
With opportunities.
Either we do not value them,
Or we are afraid of their enormity.

2754.

Often we take God's blessingful
    Requests
Very lightly.
Therefore, our spiritual life
Has become most painful
And difficult.

2755.

To become a perfect instrument
Of my Lord Supreme,
I must harmonise my outer
    dedication
And inner aspiration.

2756.

We suffer from excruciating pangs
Because harmony is nowhere
To be found —
Either in our inner life
Or in our outer life.

2757.

When we become spiritually
    weak,
Our very first love-step
Is extremely difficult.

2758.

If I love my Master
Sincerely and self-givingly,
Then my obedience-life
Is bound to follow him.

2759.

My God-obedience-eagerness
Is my Lord's
Fulness-Heart-Smile.

2760.

When the love-devotion-
    surrender trinity
Was ignored by us,
God was forced to add a new step,
Easier than the easiest –
Obedience.

2761.

If we lovingly and self-givingly
Place our foot
On the God-obedience-rung,
We will be able to confidently
And easily climb up
The love-devotion-surrender-
    steps
To reach the highest Height.

2762.

The mind is unable to enjoy purity
Because undivine thoughts
Every day
Supply the mind with impurity-
    food.

2763.

When we establish our oneness
With God the Power
Before we have established our
    oneness
With God the Love,
God tells us, "My children,
I am afraid you are going to
    misuse Me."

2764.

Once you establish your oneness
With God's Compassion-Eye,
God tells you that yours will be
The power infinite
To conquer the pride of
    ignorance-night.

2765.

I am happy
Because I have offered my love
To the Compassion-Heart
Of my Lord Supreme.

2766.

I am perfect
Because I have offered
My love-devotion-surrender-life
To the Forgiveness-Feet
Of my Lord Supreme.

2767.

A surrender-heart is the only
    thing
We are supposed to offer
To the Highest in us
For the transformation
Of the lowest in us.

2768.

An impurity-thought-mind-train
Is creating countless problems
For each and every human being.

2769.

A morality-bound sincerity
Is not enough.
A spirituality-bound sincerity
Placed at the Feet of God
Is what we need
To satisfy God in His own Way.

2770.

The Absolute Supreme
Is always eager to nullify
All our misdeeds,
But alas,
We are still not awakened enough
To call upon Him.

2771.

You will be not only safe,
But also fulfilled completely
If you allow God to take care of
Your constant obedience.

2772.

We must become our own
Unalloyed devotion-heart
To please our Lord's
Compassion-Forgiveness-Feet.

2773.

When we offer our sincerity-mind
And purity-heart to God,
He proudly gives us two rewards:
His Sweetness-Smile
And His Fulness-Heart.

2774.

Spirituality is infinitely higher
Than so-called morality.
God's highest Divinity works
Only in and through spirituality.

2775.

I give my Lord Supreme what I
    have:
My simplicity-life.
My Lord Supreme gives me what
    He is:
His Infinity's Heart.

2776.

We can become
Choice instruments of God
Only by
Thinking of Him alone,
Loving Him alone,
Devoting ourselves to Him alone
And surrendering our very
    existence
To Him alone,
Sleeplessly and breathlessly.

2777.

Earthly power
Consciously embodies
Separativity-supremacy.

2778.

Heavenly Power
Smilingly embodies
Oneness-fulness.

2779.

First we must touch the Feet
Of God the Creator
Before we can become the Heart
Of God the creation.

2780.

Spirituality is not
A compulsory course.
It is the blossoming
Of an inner urge.

2781.

No mind-made force
Can ever equal
A heart-born power.

2782.

You must study at your heart-
    school,
And nowhere else,
If you want to become
A universal being.

2783.

In life, there is always a challenge
When we want to do something
    great.
The challenges become
Infinitely more difficult
When we want to do something
    good.

2784.

My mind's readiness and
    willingness
I need
To prove my greatness.

2785.

My heart's eagerness and self-
    givingness
I need
To prove my goodness.

2786.

Invoke the poise of your soul
To quiet
Your restless vital-horse-life.

2787.

When luminosity enters,
The restless vital becomes
    dynamic
To fulfil God in His own Way.

2788.

Outer success can have
A very special meaning
If inner progress
Starts blossoming first.

2789.

Just repeat again and again:
"I am the soul, I am the soul."
You will definitely be able
To unburden yourself
Of anything standing in your way.

2790.

It is the Immortality of the soul
That has and is the power
To lift the burdens of humanity.

2791.

The insecurity of the heart
Makes us helpless.
The impurity of the mind
Makes us useless.

2792.

The mind wants
To teach the world
Endlessly.

2793.

The heart wants to study
At God's Heart-School
Eternally.

2794.

Name and fame can turn us insane
Long before we are fully awakened
From ignorance-sleep.

2795.

God wants me and my aspiration-
     heart
To arrive at His Satisfaction-
     Zenith
As soon as possible.

2796.

For me, an iota of peace
In my mind
Is of supreme importance,
And not a plethora
Of earthly achievements.

2797.

When I use my heart-eye,
I clearly see
That my today's destination
Is my tomorrow's starting point.

2798.

Everything in the outer life
Eventually fails,
Because the outer life does not
   have
An abiding inner hunger.

2799.

World-peace entirely depends
On our inner hunger
And outer service.

2800.

To solve any problem in life,
Do not just arrest it,
But illumine it —
Immediately!

2801.

Your own earth-knowledge
Will one day oppose
Your forward march, your upward
   flight And your inward dive.

2802.

Everybody else will be able to rise
To the heights of God-satisfaction,
But not a man of pride.

2803.

Your goodness-heart
Will bring sweetness-dreams
When sleep descends on you.

2804.

Your self-giving heart
Will be able to perform
A transformation-miracle
In your life.

2805.

A new light from within
Is embracing and illumining
His confusion-mind.

2806.

Abandon,
Abandon as soon as possible
Your jungle-mind
And attachment-life.

2807.

A spiritual Master quite often
Cries pitifully and helplessly
In the land of the deaf.

2808.

My devotion-heart every day
Decorates the Feet of my Lord
With lotus petals.

2809.

Do not ever allow your
    enthusiasm
To burn down
If you want to make continuous
    progress
In your spiritual life.

2810.

If you do not aspire,
Then your spiritual death-door
Will revolve open
Right before your inner eye.

2811.

Always remain on your guard.
Do not allow yourself to be exiled
To oblivion's cave.

2812.

Quick, march within!
Your Lord Supreme will proudly
    come
And embrace you.

2813.

Alas, I am suffering and suffering!
Is there no soul to soothe
My God-forgotten heart?

2814.

Off with you,
O my unsatisfied and dissatisfied
Vital and mind!

2815.

Every day my heart and I
Stand united against ignorance-
    enemy
To conquer it once and for all.

2816.

The sole purpose of my life
Is to find God,
For Him to bind my heart
And blind my mind.

2817.

Our life is
Divinely meaningful
Only when we soulfully pray.

2818.

Our heart is
Supremely fruitful
Only when we self-givingly
    meditate.

2819.

Physical suffering
Is not
A God-lover.

2820.

Physical suffering
Is
A ruthless invader.

2821.

Our mind can get astounding
    answers
To its questions
If it is ready to surrender
To a new light.

2822.

There are infinitely better things
    to do
Than surrender
To our lethargy-indulgence.

2823.

Our life's age-old road must
    surrender
To the new road
That is sweetly beckoning us.

2824.

If you are sincerely aware
Of your emptiness-life,
Then God's Fulness-life
Will speed towards you.

2825.

If we are divinely lovable,
Only then are we teachable
By God Himself.

2826.

God feels sad when I ask Him
How long the distance is
To the Destination.
He says:
"See not the destination-distance,
But be the destination-
    satisfaction."

2827.

Sleeplessly think
Of what you can do for God,
And never for a fleeting second
Think of those
Who stand against
Your Godward journey.

2828.

"My way is the right way!"
So does the mind
Broadcast.

2829.

"God's Way is the only way!"
So does the heart
Whisper.

2830.

God may one day come to me:
This was my old way
Of thinking.

2831.

God has already come:
This is my new way
Of feeling.

2832.

God will claim you
Only when you do not try to
    escape,
But brave the confusion-world.

2833.

Not by challenging and not by
    fighting,
But by loving the world,
We raise not only our individual
    standard
But the human standard as well.

2834.

God will ask you
To write the preface to His
    Autobiography
If you can dwell far above
Your surface mind
And sleeplessly sing the song
Of self-transcendence.

2835.

You will never be able
To love the world
With your understanding mind.

2836.

The clearness of the mind
Is, indeed,
The nearness of God.

2837.

The desire to proclaim your outer
    victory
Has extinguished
All your aspiration-heart-flames.

2838.

You want to possess the world;
The world wants to possess you.
But you do not see
That both you and the world
Are already possessed
By God's Universal Oneness-
    Heart.

2839.

The mind wants God's Help
But when God's Help arrives,
The mind does not welcome it.

2840.

To know who you truly are,
You must first claim God
To be your own, very own.

2841.

My God-worshipping days
Are coming back once more.
Therefore, I am swimming
In the sea of ecstasy.

2842.

I came into the world
For God the Lover,
And not for man
The ignorance-dreamer.

2843.

Add everything divine and
    inspiring
To your aspiration-heart
To fulfil God.

2844.

Subtract everything
Undivine and disheartening
From your division-mind
To please God.

2845.

If you are afraid of your past,
You will not be able to blossom
Beautifully and satisfactorily
In the heart-garden of your
    present.

2846.

My Lord,
Do bless me with the capacity
To fill my aspiration-heart
And dedication-life
With Your Silence-Light.

2847.

God's express Command:
"You must leave
Your ignorance-rented apartment
Immediately!"

2848.

If you are a real seeker,
You must try to realise
The unity-ocean
In the midst of diversity-waves.

2849.

If you think that by isolating
    yourself
From the world
You will make fast progress
In your spiritual life,
Then you are only blinding your
    mind
And misleading your life.

2850.

The chant of the New
    Millennium:
"The world's heart-home
Is the Beauty and Fragrance
Of the Absolute Lord Supreme."

2851.

Alas, we do not know
How we can ever succeed
In escaping
The age-old, false god:
The mind.

2852.

We must long for God
From the very dawn of our life,
If we want to realise Him
And fully manifest Him on earth.

2853.

Every day
God comes to me
With His childhood Friends:
Love and Joy.

2854.

God has been waiting for us
With infinite Patience
For a long time.
At last we are now ready
To accept Him
With our aspiration-heart
And dedication-life.

2855.

I long not for God
The limitless Power,
But for God the sleepless Presence.

2856.

Humanity's powerful
God-awareness-body
Is religion.

2857.

Humanity's spirituality
Is the express result
Of God's Self-Transcendence-
    Dream.

2858.

The mind-lord
We can never please.
The heart-lord is always
Pleased with us.

2859.

Every day we must write
A newness-mind-song
And sing
A fulness-heart-song.

2860.

In God's Eye,
Humanity's tears
And Divinity's Smiles
Are of equal importance.

2861.

Unless and until you have
    developed
A heart inundated with
    compassion,
Do not sit on the seat of
    judgement.

2862.

In the inner world,
God tells us what to do.
In the outer world,
God teaches us how to do it.

2863.

We are eager
To see God's beautiful Face.
God is eager
To give us His bountiful Heart.

2864.

Each solitary day
Is a golden opportunity
For us to make a fresh approach
To our Lord Supreme.

2865.

With our desire-hunger,
We try to capture and possess
The world.
With our aspiration-hunger,
We try to create God-hunger
For the whole world.

2866.

At the final end of our journey's
    close,
God will ask us to show Him
Only one thing:
Satisfaction.

2867.

The science-lord tells his devotees,
"My children, I shall teach you
How to perform an endless series
Of miracles."

2868.

The spirituality-lord tells his
    devotees,
"My children, let us dream
Of a higher dream
And a better creation."

2869.

If we devote ourselves
To inner exploration,
Then we shall never suffer
From outer dissatisfaction.

2870.

My outer education
Is confusing my God-searching
    mind.
My inner education
Is feeding my God-hungry heart.

2871.

Your goal is the highest
Self-transcendence-height.
No lesser goal must you accept!

2872.

God-realisation
Is an extremely difficult task.
God-manifestation
Is infinitely more difficult.

2873.

The seeker's only security
Is the Smile
Of God's Compassion-Eye.

2874.

We must shut down
Our mind's
Animal-confusion-disobedience-
    zoo.

2875.

The easiest and most effective way
To see God
Is through our soul's
God-satisfying light.

2876.

What is the source of our mind's
Inspiration-flood,
If not our heart's aspiration-sea?

2877.

Meditation
Is my heart-expansion.
My heart-expansion
Is my God-satisfaction.
My God-satisfaction
Is my life-perfection.
My life-perfection
Is the world-progression.

2878.

A simplicity-mind, a purity-heart
And a humility-life
Are of supreme importance
In expediting
Our aspiration-dedication-
    journey.

2879.

When God's Name
Resounds inside our heart,
We find peace all around us.

2880.

Although the mind lives
Inside a tiny ego-cage,
The mind acts like a sovereign.

2881.

Futility, even absurdity,
Are the products
Of intellectual discussion.

2882.

The beauty of devotion
And the fragrance of surrender
Are the two God-satisfying
    messages
Of the heart.

2883.

God had given us shoulders
Long before
Man gave us burdens.

2884.

Each purity-thought
Deepens our love
Of God.

2885.

You do not need God's invitation.
You do not need God's
    permission.
What you need is your own
    eagerness
To enter into God's Heart.

2886.

God's Forgiveness
Is my heart's only
Peace-shrine.

2887.

To see the Feet of God,
I shall have to offer
My heart's silence-tears
To God first.

2888.

My Lord, if You really love me,
Then humiliate me
Here, there and everywhere
For my fastest progress.

2889.

If you want to be familiar
With God's Will,
Then stop cherishing your mind's
Ignorance-dream.

2890.

God is not interested in counting
My years.
He is interested only in counting
My self-giving moments.

2891.

Confession does not really solve
Our problems,
But an adamantine determination
Can solve all our problems.

2892.

Determination
Can bravely and forcefully change
The deplorable past into real dust.

2893.

Quite often
Outer friendship-boats
Are nothing other than
Inner rivalry-boats.

2894.

Punishment properly used
Is the sure beginning
Of enlightenment.

2895.

Our mind needs every day
The Forgiveness
Of our Lord's Vastness-Heart-Sky.

2896.

Divinity's Touch
Is far beyond
Humanity's imagination.

2897.

The sweeter our heart-cries,
The sooner our Lord Supreme
Will arrive.

2898.

The tears of my heart-sea
Are transformed into
The smiles of my soul-ocean
By a single glance of my Lord
    Supreme.

2899.

The concern of humanity's mind
For human oneness
Is, indeed, the biggest joke!

2900.

Each seeker has many
    bodyguards,
But a one-pointed devotion
To our Lord Supreme
Is by far the best bodyguard.

2901.

My Lord smiles and smiles
When I ring my heart's
Sweetness-devotion-bell.

2902.

A surrender-life
Is the first messenger
To bring God-news
Down to earth
From Heaven.

2903.

The arrows of attachment-life
Are destroying
The real beauty and real joy
Of the whole world.

2904.

My mind, I cannot believe
That you missed deliberately
Your God-appointment-hour.

2905.

The doubting mind can enjoy
The fresh air of freedom
If it starts making excursions
Into the countryside of the heart.

2906.

Ignorance first blinded my eye
And then stabbed my heart.
Therefore, I am totally useless.

2907.

My sorrow-flooded life
Slowly and slowly dies
All day long.

2908.

My delight-flooded soul
Flies and flies
In the infinite vastness
Of the sky.

2909.

Every time the heart receives
    something
From our Beloved Supreme,
The mind shamelessly demands
A lion's share.

2910.

God-obedience is our giant
    strength
To make both God and ourselves
Supremely happy.

2911.

In each heartbeat,
My life-breath I offer
To my Lord Supreme
Through my devotion-songs.

2912.

Always encourage and inspire
Your fellow travellers
To follow their inner dictates
And abide by their soul's
    decisions.

2913.

What is my surrender,
If not my cheerful and breathless
    oneness
With God's Will?

2914.

If you claim your Master
    wholeheartedly,
He will definitely come to you,
Without fail,
When your life-boat is sinking.

2915.

If you please your Master
In his own way here on earth,
Then in Heaven,
His plane of consciousness
Will be all yours.

2916.

O seeker, you come and go
To serve God the creation
Here on earth
And God the Creator
There in Heaven.

2917.

If you remain inside
Your Master's heartbeat,
His very name will give you
Infinity's Nectar-Delight.

2918.

Today I am determined
To fly far beyond
The domain of self-criticism
And world-complaints.

2919.

Do not worry about
What people will say.
Your life is your life.
You will be held accountable
For what you do
Only to God.

2920.

If you are planning to have
A God-fulfilling future,
Now is the very best time
To embark on your new life.

2921.

If you have implicit faith
In God,
Then your God-proximity
Is assured.

2922.

You have heard God's Philosophy
Again and again,
But poor God is waiting,
With all His Patience,
For you to live His Philosophy.

2923.

My Lord, may I live every day
And every hour
In the blossoming fragrance
Of Your Heart-Garden.

2924.

By this time
You would have been
A super-excellent seeker,
If you had not alienated yourself
From your soul's company.

2925.

God is all ready to accept
Your volcano-anger,
But He begs you not to use it
Against any human being.

2926.

When your dear ones run towards
The Light infinite,
Replace your human jealousy
With your divine pride.

2927.

You may be well-established
In your outer life,
But who knows, in your inner life
You may be absolutely bankrupt!

2928.

You can embrace the outer life
Only after you have founded
  yourself
In the heart of your spiritual life.

2929.

When the Master speaks
About devotion,
A false disciple's
Disbelief-unwillingness-
  temperature
Goes sky-high.

2930.

When the Master speaks
About obedience,
The Master becomes a victim
To a false disciple's
Wild criticism.

2931.

When the Master speaks
About surrender,
A false disciple thinks
Only of forced surrender,
And not of cheerful, self-giving
Surrender.

2932.

Your outer success
Has made you enormously proud,
But do you care to know
That inwardly
You are a most deplorable failure?

2933.

Because you are not truly
Spirituality-bound,
Outer world-temptations
At a tiger's speed
Are fast approaching you.

2934.

There is no separativity
In surrender.
The finite simply
Recognises its own Infinity
And becomes inseparably one
  with it.

2935.

Do not be a member
Of a spiritual circle
That underrates the true value
Of obedience, love, devotion
And surrender.

2936.

If you are totally dedicated
To your Master's will,
Then your Master's guiding hands
You will definitely feel,
Not only in this incarnation,
But also in future incarnations.

2937.

When God created humanity,
He had the full intention
Of transforming humanity's life
Into Divinity's Heart.

2938.

At times
The affectionate emotional
    demands
God's choice children
Make on Him
Are immeasurably sweet.

2939.

Share your sorrowful heart
With God.
He will immediately
Share His blissful Heart
With you.

2940.

If you are a true God-seeker,
Then God is bound to ask you
To sow peace-blossom-plants
Here, there and all-where.

2941.

The more we can concentrate
On our inner needs,
The sooner we shall be able
To free ourselves
From our outer desires.

2942.

When you sing devotion-songs,
Try to hear your own heart-
    melodies
Resonating in your entire being.

2943.

May my life
Become
A Mother Earth-service-tree.

2944.

I do not know
When my ignorance-life
Shall die at Your Feet,
But I do feel
It will definitely die one day.
My Lord, do me the biggest
    favour:
Do expedite the hour!

2945.

The more I tell God
That I am nothing,
The more He tells me
That I am His equal –
A unique manifestation
Of His Dream-Reality.

2946.

God's Compassion
Is an ever-running river
Carrying me
To my Golden Shore-Destination.

2947.

Yesterday
My Lord Supreme came to me
As His Vision-Light.
Today
He has come to me
As His Reality-Delight.

2948.

My Lord tells me
That my gratitude-heart
His Eye and His Heart
Treasure
More than I can ever imagine.

2949.

When I talk to God,
Quite often He does not listen.
But when I sing for God,
He smilingly, lovingly and
    unreservedly Enjoys my heart-
    songs.

2950.

Every day
Has a special beauty
In my God-aspiration-dream.

2951.

When I am peaceful
In my heart-home,
My mind runs away
Through the emergency exit.

2952.

Even if you are a last-minute
    seeker,
God's Heart-Door
Will remain open to you.

2953.

My Lord, I look at Your Eye
To be divinely happy.
My Lord, I listen to Your Heart
To be supremely perfect.

2954.

My Lord is extremely pleased with
    me
Because my heart
Is a short-time speaker
And my mind
Is a long-time listener.

2955.

Negativity may not be superiority.
Negativity may not be inferiority.
But it definitely is futility.

2956.

God allows only my prayer-tears
To wash His Feet
Every day.

2957.

Spirituality is not something
We can push forward.
No, spirituality is a force
That has its own rhythm and
    course.

2958.

The mind-jungle never thinks
That there can be a heart-shrine
Anywhere on earth.

2959.

My soul has taken upon itself
A most painful responsibility:
To awaken my sleeping body
And illumine my strangling
And doubting mind.

2960.

Every day
God the Compassion
Comes to me,
But I turn Him into
God the Rejection.

2961.

When it is a matter of surrender,
I immediately feel
My surrender to God's Will
Is long overdue.

2962.

My life is the creation
Of my Lord's Vision-Eye.
Therefore, willingly or
  unwillingly,
I must abide by His Will.

2963.

If you are a true God-lover,
Then either today or tomorrow
You have to become
A self-indulgence-conqueror.

2964.

I have realised
That no matter how poorly
I behave in the spiritual life,
My Lord's Compassion-Smiles
Will never run short.

2965.

Life is not for eating and drinking.
Life is not for struggling and
  working.
Life is for God-realisation,
God-revelation
And God-manifestation.

2966.

My ever-blossoming faith and I
Are determined to dethrone
My doubt-mind-king
Once and for all.

2967.

Aspiration-heart-children
Solely live on
Good meditation-food.

2968.

Each time an Avatar
Comes into the world,
He is at least a thousand years
Ahead of his time.

2969.

My Lord Supreme tells me
That from now on
My aspiration-heart
And my dedication-life
Must be found
In the midst of the here and now.

2970.

May my heart's
God-worshipping tears
Flood my doubting mind-jungle.

2971.

My mind has a secret
And sacred name:
God-reliance.

2972.

My heart has a secret
And sacred name:
God-obedience.

2973.

My life has a secret
And sacred name:
God-satisfaction.

2974.

I have two secret
And sacred names:
God the tearful Eye
And
God the cheerful Heart.

2975.

An unconditionally surrendered
    seeker
Is the treasurer
Of God's Heavenly Dreams.

2976.

O seeker,
Be sleeplessly on your guard!
At any moment,
Your desire-mind-currents
Can carry you away
To the land of nowhere.

2977.

My mind has written
A great many books
On many subjects.
My heart has written
Only one book:
God's Earth-Tears and Heaven-
    Smiles.

2978.

My heart's happiness
Is my life's
Disobedience-bulldozer.

2979.

My self-offering
Is nothing other than
The Heaven-climbing songs
Of my heart.

2980.

My prayer-heart-tears
Come directly from the purity
Of Mother Earth.

2981.

A seed-thought
Is the source
Of a huge life-fulfilling idea.

2982.

If your faith in God
Is dwindling,
Then your spiritual life
Will suffer from total
   deterioration.

2983.

My mind's constant suggestions
I take
As giant transgressions.

2984.

God's Compassion-Eye
Tells me where to go.
God's Forgiveness-Eye
Tells me how to go.
God's Justice-Eye
Tells me why to go.

2985.

I am so happy
That I have been living
In my God-Presence-
Remembrance-moments.

2986.

My God-manifestation-promises
Are the results
Of my blooming mind
And blossoming heart.

2987.

My aspiration-heart
Is always from the country
Of God-manifestation-promises.

2988.

When God plays
His Compassion-Flute,
Man's justice-thunder
Immediately stops.

2989.

My Lord, do whatever You wish
With my heart's aspiration-cries
And my life's dedication-smiles.
Like me,
They are all ready to please You
In Your own Way.

2990.

One way I can please
My Lord Supreme
Is to devotedly and gladly bow
To His Justice-Commands.

2991.

When my soul
Is pleased with me,
My heart becomes
A garden of paradise.

2992.

When Compassion rains down
In torrents,
My hope-bird flies
In the sky of fulfilment.

2993.

Keep your consciousness high
All the time,
And then add inspiration-flight
And enthusiasm-delight.
Everything else divine will follow.

2994.

My Lord, when I look at the
    beauty
Of Your Eye,
I find it extremely difficult
To remove my eyes.

2995.

My Lord, when I smell the
    fragrance
Of Your Feet,
My heart and I are caught,
Caught forever.

2996.

My aspiration-heart
And my dedication-life
Are all excited
To see the Face of God smiling
And the Heart of God dancing.

2997.

When you whisper prayers
In God's Ears,
God swims in the sea
Of ecstasy.

2998.

Beauty non-pareil has blossomed
In the heart of
The subtle atom-tapestry.

2999.

A day shall dawn in the remote
    future
When the ignorance-darkness-ink
Of the mind
Will nowhere be found.

3000.

The zenith-glories
Of the seeker's aspiration-heart
Are only for the Absolute Lord
    Supreme.

3001.

My heart's
Willingness-eagerness-service
To humanity
Is keeping me close to the Feet
Of my Lord Supreme.

3002.

I live in between
My heart's compassion-rain
And my life's oneness-gain.

3003.

I play my role by self-giving.
God plays His Role
By Intensity-Joy-becoming.

3004.

How beautiful to look at
When my prayer
Lights a candle of hope
In my heart.

3005.

Goodness
Is oneness-love
In perfect action.

3006.

Do not forget that your heart
Has two devotion-wings.
If you are on them,
You can fly higher than the
    highest,
Farther than the farthest
And faster than the fastest.

3007.

Cultivate love, devotion
And surrender
Every day, every hour
And every minute
To see your Lord Supreme smile,
Sing and dance
Inside your own heart-garden.

3008.

If you have real love,
Devotion and surrender
To your Master,
Then your life receives
A new name from God Himself:
Sweetness.

3009.

As a lotus gives joy
To my heart and my eyes,
Even so, I would like my very
    presence
To give joy to my Lord Supreme.

3010.

If you really want to make
The fastest progress,
Then this very moment
Take a solemn oath
That your life will be
A constant and cheerful
Devotion-obedience
To God's Will.

3011.

Each day is a new opportunity
For us to look at God's Eye
Devotedly
And to place ourselves at God's
    Feet
Self-givingly.

3012.

My Lord, I pray to You
Most soulfully
To bless me with a heart
That will breathe Your Oneness-
    Smile.

3013.

What is expectation?
Expectation is something that
    limits us,
Binds us and frustrates us
Far beyond our tolerance-capacity.

3014.

My fear is nothing short of
My unrecognised separation
From God.

3015.

Once we deviate
From our spiritual life,
We fail to stop
Until we have entered into
The abysmal abyss.

3016.

You have to join
The God-aspiration-society
Before you join
The God-manifestation-club.

3017.

My Lord was so sad
To see my heart crying.
He begged my heart
To give Him a smile.
Alas, it was to no avail!

3018.

My humility-heart is embraced
By God's
Affection-Love-Joy-Pride-
    Fondness.

3019.

How surprisingly beautiful
Was the sunrise
Of my aspiration-heart!

3020.

How astonishingly peaceful
Is the summit
Of my service-life!

3021.

I thought of placing my sadness
At the Feet of my Lord Supreme.
But He grabbed it and put it
Inside His Heart-Pocket.

3022.

Our dream wants to go up
And touch God's Feet
Immediately.

3023.

Our reality is afraid of God's Feet,
And tries to remain
As far away as possible
From God's Feet.

3024.

If you want to keep
Your spiritual journey
Safe, inspiring, illumining
And fulfilling,
Then you must needs have
    devotion
All the time.

3025.

There is not a single country
That does not have
God-manifestation-armies.

3026.

The vastness-heart of humility
Immediately welcomes
The head of pride.

3027.

Pride has only one thing
To show humility:
Its thunder-feet.

3028.

After we have seen something,
We try
To believe it.

3029.

After we have felt something,
We try
To become inseparably one
With its reality.

3030.

If we can awaken the slumber
Within us,
Then we can easily claim the
    world
As our own, very own.

3031.

Human greatness
Does not mean
God-closeness.

3032.

Human beings are good
Only if God
Declares them so.

3033.

Only God-lovers and God-servers
Are God's
True inheritors.

3034.

Man says to God,
"My Lord,
Please, please deepen Your Love
For me."

3035.

God says to man,
"My child,
Please, please ripen your need
For Me."

3036.

A God-seeker says to God,
"My Lord, will my seeking
Ever come to an end?"

3037.

God says to the God-seeker,
"My child,
My seeking and your seeking
Will come to an end together –
If there will be an end at all."

3038.

Our heart-obedience
Devotedly leads us
To God.

3039.

Our mind-disobedience
Haughtily takes us away
From God.

3040.

What shall I lose through my
God-disobedience?
I shall lose the Beauty
Of God's Compassion-Eye
And the Fragrance
Of God's Satisfaction-Heart.

3041.

God-revelation awakens
The human
In us.

3042.

God-manifestation fulfils
The divine
In us.

3043.

Discouragement sets in
When we do not feed
The rainbow-beauty
Of our heart-sky.

3044.

Discouragement sets in
When we stop challenging
The mounting pressures
Of life.

3045.

When we stop feeding
Our heart's aspiration-flames,
We meet with life's obstruction-
    walls
Wherever we go.

3046.

I really do not know
How many kicks
A God-realised soul gets
From the indifference
Of Heaven
And from the heedlessness
Of earth.

3047.

If the Avatar cannot please
    humanity
In humanity's own way,
Humanity laughs and laughs at
    him.

3048.

If the Avatar cannot please
    Divinity
In Divinity's own Way,
Divinity becomes extremely sad—
Alas, alas!

3049.

For spiritual seekers,
Ignorance is never bliss,
But always something to be
Bravely conquered
Once and for all.

3050.

A God-realised soul
Is a God-ordained
Compassion-bestower.

3051.

May a new gratitude-flower
Every day blossom
In all its beauty
And fragrance
Inside my heart-garden.

3052.

If you have a devotion-heart,
You always will have a green light
On your life-highway,
And your journey
Will be all safe.

3053.

If you have no devotion to God,
You will have a red light
On your life-highway.
If you go through the red light,
Danger and destruction
Will befriend you.

3054.

When we come to realise
That nobody is insignificant
And each individual is unique
In his own way,
Our Lord reveals His Divinity's
     Pride.

3055.

If we truly love Mother Earth,
Then the weight of her children
Will not feel heavy and
     unbearable.

3056.

Good seekers are destined
To succeed in their spiritual
     journey
By virtue of their obedience-heart
And surrender-life.

3057.

Bad seekers are destined
To fail in their spiritual journey
Because of their disobedience-
     mind
And betrayal-life.

3058.

Only on the strength
Of our devotion-magnet
Can we become closer than the
     closest
To our Lord Supreme.

3059.

If you have devotion,
Then you will receive from God
His most blessingful
And most powerful Embrace.

3060.

If you have devotion,
Then love and surrender
Will gladly accompany you.

3061.

If you use your doubting mind
And not your loving heart,
You will become the world's
Shameless, number one critic,
And cynicism will garland you.

3062.

When God talks about surrender,
He meets with humanity's
Immediate inner revolt.

3063.

I want the interdependence
Of the multitude.
I do not need the independence
Of solitude.

3064.

Every day we spend our time
Complaining.
At least for one day,
Can we not try loving –
Loving the world, loving God
And finally, loving ourselves?

3065.

May the fragrance of hope
Cover the length and breadth
Of my heart-garden.

3066.

To live in the house of the mind
And not have any connection
With falsehood
Is an impossible task.

3067.

What I need is a mind
That does not dispute
My soul's supreme authority.

3068.

What I need is a life
That does not deny
God's Compassion-Eye.

3069.

Accept your own inner divinity
    first.
Then it will be extremely easy
For you to accept the divinity
Of others.

3070.

If we can shun the old way of
    thinking,
Then we will be able to escape
From the battlefields of our mind
And vital.

3071.

My Lord,
I have kept my heart-door wide
    open.
Is it such a difficult task for You
To blessingfully pay me
A very brief visit?

3072.

If you are wanting in obedience,
Love, devotion and surrender,
Then how do you expect
Your spiritual life to be safe at all?

3073.

Alas, like everything,
Obedience can come and go.
There was a time when he had
God-obedience in abundant
    measure.
But now obedience has become
A perfect stranger to him.

3074.

One can have God-realisation,
But he can be fated to
An ever-increasing number
Of disobedient disciples.

3075.

God tells each and every seeker
That the life's obedience
And the heart's devotion
Are not foreigners,
But natives to the inner world.

3076.

Love
You have cleverly forgotten.
Devotion
You have deliberately forgotten.
That is why poor God
Had to bring obedience-life
Into your aspiration-heart-breath.

3077.

Bring back
Your obedience-devotion-life.
Do not enjoy anymore
Your doubt-suspicion-mind.

3078.

It is so easy
To find God-philosophers.
But to find a God-lover
Is infinitely more difficult
Than we can ever imagine.

3079.

God's oneness-philosophy
Is the most difficult
For humanity's mind and vital
To study.

3080.

To God's greatest sorrow,
Some devotees of His
Who once implicitly believed
In His philosophy
Now feel that it is incorrect
And imperfect.

3081.

If your philosophy is
A carefree self-indulgence-life,
Then it will never fit in with
God's strict
Discipline-self-giving-philosophy.

3082.

Accept your spiritual life
In a very serious way.
Whatever is bad,
Bravely try to transform.
Whatever is good,
Slowly, steadily and unerringly
Make perfect.

3083.

God tells His seeker-students
That if they do not agree with
His love-devotion-surrender-
    philosophy,
Then they can definitely exit His
    School
To enjoy their self-chosen
    freedom-life.

3084.

O God-doubters,
Do not pollute those
Who love God
And need God desperately.

3085.

Each individual is a God-
    representative,
Accountable only to God.
If he cannot love, serve
And manifest God
    wholeheartedly,
Then he is definitely delaying
Humanity's progress-speed.

3086.

Why do you have to remain
A no-class seeker?
Do you not think
It severely pains God?

3087.

Why do some seekers year after
    year
Fail to please God?
Because they have added
Negligence and carelessness
To their spiritual life.

3088.

Life's perfection-bliss
Is the result
Of the heart's streaming tears.

3089.

Every morning
I place at the Feet
Of my Lord Supreme
A few petals
Of my heart's flower-smiles.

3090.

A disobedience-seeker
Will be compelled to run
An ultramarathon distance,
Longer than the longest,
To reach his Goal,
In comparison to the shortest
    distance
Of the obedience-seeker.

3091.

The heart longs for
The ultimate Truth.
The mind is satisfied
With its present friend:
Falsehood.

3092.

O seeker,
At every moment
You find fault with the world
When you see that God
Is not pleased with you.

3093.

Even God's small talk
Brightens my way,
Lightens my mind
And fulfils my heart.

3094.

In my case,
Before my God-realisation,
God was my Host
And I was His guest.
But now,
I am His host
And He is my Guest.

3095.

A real seeker does not care for
Outer affluence.
He cares only for
Inner assurance.

3096.

To my extreme happiness,
My heart,
You are no longer a victim
To infant insecurity.

3097.

Conquer pride, inner and outer,
To run the fastest
For God-Satisfaction
In His own Way.

3098.

My heart
Has a sleepless need
For aspiration-flight.

3099.

My life
Has a breathless need
For dedication-tide.

3100.

Because I aimlessly think,
I am unable to become
A true citizen
Of the inner world.

3101.

If you are on the spiritual path,
Then at every moment
Try to live inside
God's Heart-Temple,
Which is your only home.

3102.

Rest assured,
Eventually the divine in you
Will prevail,
The Supreme in you
Will win.

3103.

Because of your sincerity-mind,
God has a special liking
For you.

3104.

Because of your obedience-heart,
God dictates His Will
To you.

3105.

Because of your humility-life,
God takes your service
Day in and day out.

3106.

It is your mind's readiness,
Your life's willingness
And your heart's eagerness
That can make you
A first-class God-seeker.

3107.

O unfortunate seeker,
Your soul every day
Tries to teach you
The universal oneness-philosophy
Of your Lord Supreme,
But you refuse to learn.

3108.

I am absolutely certain
That God will not sail His Boat
    alone,
For there are many genuine
Aspiration-dedication-
    passengers.

3109.

Because you are cherishing
Your self-doubt-mind,
Your love-devotion-surrender-
    heart
Is buried in oblivion.

3110.

Remember, it is the Vision
And the Mission-Life of the
    Supreme
That we are all carrying
Here on earth.

3111.

Alas, how long will our solemn
    promise
To God
Remain unfulfilled?
Him to manifest, Him to please
In His own Way,
We came into the world.

3112.

Our Lord Beloved Supreme
Definitely expects, but never
    demands,
One hundred per cent
Of our loyalty and devoted
    oneness.

3113.

O impossible God-cynicism-
    mortals,
You will never succeed
In poisoning the ears and hearts
Of those who are meant for God.

3114.

My heart is desperately trying
To be in the company
Of self-giving God-seeker-
    passengers
In God's Golden Boat.

3115.

Why do you need a spiritual
    Master?
You need a spiritual Master
To carry you into
Your own heart-breath,
To watch and enjoy
Its exceptional love of God.

3116.

A sincere seeker cannot imagine
There can ever be two ways.
He is absolutely certain
That God's Way is the only way.

3117.

You will drown
In the sea of ignorance
If you keep one foot
In God's Boat
And one foot in your own
Self-styled boat.

3118.

Once you have accepted the
   spiritual life
With all the sincerity at your
   command,
Then it is a real insult
To your own soul, to your own
   Master
And to your own Lord Beloved
   Supreme
If you worry about your future.
After all,
Are you not supposed to have
   placed
Your past, present and future
In their hands?

3119.

If you once saw Light
On your spiritual journey,
But now do not see it,
Then you have definitely made
   friends
With darkness,
Either consciously or
   unconsciously.

3120.

A false seeker
Definitely is responsible
For his own future.
But a real seeker
Is not responsible,
For his future is in God's Hands.
Remembering this, he has only
To smile, sing and dance.

3121.

For me there was, there is
And there forever will be
Only one real world:
My God-obedience-
Love-devotion-surrender-world.

3122.

When my heart sings
God's Victory-Songs,
God tells me,
"My son, you are creating
My Heaven-Heart-Life
On earth."

3123.

In a soulful consciousness
Blossoms
A very deep meditation.

3124.

Your disbelief
Can never be the real judge
Of your Master's God-realisation.
If you believe in his God-
    realisation,
Then be in his boat.
If not, find your own boat.

3125.

Those who keep their hearts open
Will always hear God's all-
    illumining
And all-fulfilling Messages.

3126.

Strengthen your heart's capacity
If you want to diminish
Your ego-necessity.

3127.

If you give God
Your mind's readiness,
    willingness
And eagerness,
Plus everything that you have and
    are,
Then God will unmistakably tell
    you
That He is for you,
Only for you.

3128.

When you listen only to God,
God captures you
In His Compassion-Heart-Net.

3129.

If your heart's light
Runs through the darkness
Of your mind,
Then even your questioning mind
Will be able to fly in the sky
Of the Beyond.

3130.

Nobody can really
Satisfy himself
Without satisfying God first.

3131.

The God-realisation-dream
Is not above my head,
But inside my heart.

3132.

A prayerful heart-singer
Is, indeed,
A God-harbinger.

3133.

No matter how undivine we are,
God still wants us
To claim His Compassion-Eye
As our very own.

3134.

No matter how hostile
Some human beings are,
God's Forgiveness-Heart
Will never be able to leave them.

3135.

No matter where
An unfortunate seeker goes,
Even if he enters into
The abysmal abyss,
God's streaming Tears
Will accompany him.

3136.

Only an aspiration-heart
Can correctly answer the
    question:
"Why are we here on earth?"

3137.

God Himself gave me
My gratitude-heart,
And He expects me
To return it to Him safely.

3138.

Our heart invokes
And our mind disregards
The same thing:
God's Compassion.

3139.

My Lord, can You not guide me
Right from the very start?
"My child, can you not prove to
    Me
That you have implicit faith in Me
Right from the very start?"

3140.

Peace
Is the ultimate achievement
Of the whole world.

3141.

Faith is the power
Behind our desire-success
And our aspiration-progress.

3142.

Every morning
I am deeply touched
By angelic inspiration
From the rising sun
And the rainbow-sky.

3143.

My mind,
With all its mistakes,
Is taking shelter
In oblivion-cave.

3144.

At every moment,
A seeker must guard himself
Against doubt-destruction-
    thoughts.

3145.

How I wish to remain forever
A perfect slave
To my aspiration-necessity.

3146.

To rise above our own miseries,
We must sleeplessly live in
Our God-faith-heart.

3147.

I am ready to chant God's Name
Even a million times
To glimpse a tiny ray
Of God-Satisfaction-hope
In my heart.

3148.

My sleeplessly self-giving
Gratitude-heart
Has delighted God
Beyond measure.

3149.

My soul every day tells my heart
That my heart came into existence
Only to execute God's Will
With no delay whatsoever.

3150.

Our mind's mere belief in God
Is not strong enough
To set our life free.
What we need
Is an adamantine faith-heart.

3151.

God's Compassion-Eye
Can easily read
Infinitely more than our
   aspiration-heart
Can ever write.

3152.

The outer world is ruled
By the power
Of human thought.

3153.

The inner world is guided
By the Love
Of Divine Will.

3154.

The whispers of God
Enrapture
My aspiration-heart
And dedication-life.

3155.

It seems that earthly friendship
Will always remain
More fragile than a mirror.

3156.

There was a time when my life
Was the music of a drum.
Now my life has become
The melody of a flute.

3157.

Name, fame and glory
Are riches
Bound by limits.

3158.

Aspiration-dedication
And love-devotion-surrender
Can go far beyond
The farther than the farthest
   boundaries.

3159.

In his aspiration-heart
And dedication-life,
A man of spirituality
Has everything to gain
Both for God and for himself.

3160.

Calamities, calamities!
Is there anybody
Who can rid himself
Of calamities within
And without?

3161.

How difficult it is
For the soul
To liberate the heart
That is locked in insecurity-grip.

3162.

Our outer belief
Determines
Our true love of God.

3163.

Our inner faith
Determines
Our God-manifestation-courage.

3164.

My aspiration-heart
Never visits
My mind's pride-fed ego-house.

3165.

O my heart,
I know you love me.
But tell me,
When will you start inspiring me
To go to God's
Compassion-flooded Shore?

3166.

The more I surrender
To God's Will,
The sooner I become
The God-race winner.

3167.

If you self-givingly love God,
You will be able to swim and swim
Inside God's Heart-Ocean,
And never drown.

3168.

O world,
Your imperial pride
First confuses me
And then amuses me
In abundant measure.

3169.

The seeker's progress-journey
Will never come to an end
For God always sings ceaselessly
Inside the seeker's heart.

3170.

In the world of ignorance-night,
God calls you by your real name:
Hero supreme.

3171.

God cries and cries
And laughs and laughs
At the same time,
When a seeker
Is unbelievably afraid
Of losing his life's
Fleeting earth-bound pleasure-
    mind.

3172.

The masterpiece of life
Is founded upon
The seeker's self-giving heart.

3173.

May my aspiration-heart
Sleeplessly and breathlessly
Long for God.

3174.

O my doubting mind,
I am now my indomitable will
To challenge you and illumine you
Once and for all.

3175.

My Lord-Employer
Is extremely strict
With my punctuality and
    regularity,
But is unimaginably generous
With His Compassion-Affection-
Love-Salary.

3176.

I just learned the happiest news
Of my life!
God has finally accepted
My heart's aspiration-application.

3177.

God the Teacher
Asks me most difficult questions
In the outer life,
But God the Tutor
Immediately whispers the
    answers.

3178.

Salvation denies those
Who forcefully demand
And proudly expect it.

3179.

Salvation embraces those
Who breathlessly need it
And know no expectation.

3180.

His spiritual progress report:
One step on the Heaven-road,
One hundred steps on the hell-
    highway.

3181.

Only aspiration-chariots
Are invited to participate
In the heart-races.

3182.

May a Compassion-Glance
From my Lord Supreme
Envelop my very existence on
    earth.

3183.

We must alter the course
Of our fate
If that is the divine necessity
In our life.

3184.

Each heart-singer
Is a new harbinger
Of God-Delight on earth.

3185.

I am not for
A computer-mind.
I am all for
A lover-heart.

3186.

The smile of my flower-heart
Has awakened in me
The peace of the Beyond.

3187.

My Lord,
To You I come
With my sorrowful eyes.
To me You give
Your bountiful Heart.

3188.

My morning prayers
Are made of my heart's love
For my Lord Supreme.

3189.

When I offer my fragrance-heart
To my Lord Supreme,
I reach my soul's
Mountain-pinnacle-heights.

3190.

My aspiration is
My heart's climbing cry
To reach my Lord's
Compassion-Feet.

3191.

Whenever I have even a moment
Of aspiration,
I feel this world of ours
Is definitely the Heart-Garden
Of our Lord Supreme.

3192.

I want my heart's path
To sleeplessly
Lead inward.

3193.

I want my mind's path
To stop
Going backward.

3194.

I want my soul's path
To go upward,
Higher than the highest,
For my Lord Supreme to travel.

3195.

My God-loving surrender is the
    bridge Between my darkness-
    mind
And my happiness-heart.

3196.

The seeker has to be
Fired with determination
Every day
To manifest God's Will here on
    earth.

3197.

Yesterday's accomplishments
Are definitely meant
For yesterday only.

3198.

Today's accomplishments
Are opening a new road
To Heaven's ecstasy-flooded
    height.

3199.

My Lord's blooming faith in me
Is, indeed, the result
Of His infinite Patience-Light.

3200.

A self-giving life
Is the result
Of our soul-delight.

3201.

The ascent
Of my aspiration-heart
Is the descent
Of my ego-mind.

3202.

When we aspire
And feel exquisite happiness
In the depths of our heart,
It clearly indicates that
God's Hour
Is fast approaching us.

3203.

O seeker,
God needs no reminder.
He will definitely abide by
His Promise to you.

3204.

Nobody can ever close
The door
Of God's Heart-Home.

3205.

If I sing heart-songs,
That means God has already
    chosen me
To sing God-songs as well.

3206.

O my heart,
I want you to increase
The life span
Of your God-manifestation-
    promise.

3207.

No matter when you start,
If sincerity looms large
In your aspiration,
Then you will meet with
God's smiling Eye.

3208.

The ancient question mark of life:
Does God really have any Concern
For me?

3209.

If you can remember your Goal
Even in your stark adversity,
Then you will be able
To drive your life-car the fastest
On your divinity's highway.

3210.

Every day I am inspired
To pilot my Golden Boat
With God-hungry hearts.

3211.

Every day I need
My heart's faith-invocation
To repel
My mind's doubt-invasion.

3212.

Man's unrevealed capacity
Is the yet-unmanifested Reality
Of God.

3213.

O my mind,
Surrender yourself to the Light
For your illumination,
Long before the world of darkness
Attacks you.

3214.

O seeker,
Wherever you go,
Keep always with you
Your heart's faith-flashlight.

3215.

The stupidity of the mind
Knows no bounds!
It even tries to bind God's Infinity
With its poor imagination-flights.

3216.

Every morning try to sing
A heart-song.
It will give your life a new
    meaning.

3217.

Do not allow fear
To claim your heart
As its own home.

3218.

Alas, mine is the Goal
That is completely lost
Behind the mirage
Of the darkness-past.

3219.

Do not allow your mind
To drive you through
Dark depression-tunnels,
For these tunnels have no end.

3220.

Those who hear God's
Whisper-Messages
Try to preserve the beauty
And fragrance
Of those Messages.

3221.

God's Compassion-Eye
And His Forgiveness-Heart
Come to me
Not only unannounced,
But also unnoticed.

3222.

I must fly far beyond the mist
Of my failure-life
To manifest my inner divinity.

3223.

It is quite easy for a human being
To live between
Self-congratulation and ego-
indulgence.

3224.

We must confront
The disobedience-mind
consciously
To prove our absolute loyalty
To our Lord Supreme.

3225.

Even when we stand face-to-face
With God's Justice,
We feel God's Compassion
Inside the heart of God's Justice.

3226.

Unless we have full control
Over our unruly and doubting
mind,
We cannot bring to the fore
All our goodness-qualities.

3227.

God knows our frailties,
But He also shows us
How to conquer them
For His complete Satisfaction.

3228.

My Lord,
Do give me the capacity
To capsize my doubt-mind-boat
Once and for all.

3229.

We can enter into anybody's
Heart-garden.
There is no fee.

3230.

When I commanded my mind
To observe silence,
My Lord showed me immediately
His huge relief.

3231.

My Lord,
May my prayer-heart
Climb up to the skies
To touch Your Forgiveness-Feet
Every day.

3232.

Not my calculation-mind
But my devotion-heart
Has a free access
To my Lord's Heart-Home.

3233.

My Lord,
If only I could see the world
Through Your Eyes,
I am sure I would see the world
As absolutely perfect.

3234.

My Lord,
I need only one Boon from You:
I wish to sing my heart-songs
Right at Your Feet
For Eternity.

3235.

Where do I live?
I live in the Compassion, Affection
And Protection-Lap
Of my Lord Beloved Supreme.

3236.

My Lord,
Your Eye is my path,
Your Heart is my journey's
    Destination.

3237.

My Lord is so pleased with me
Because I keep my heart open
To His constant Silence-Whispers.

3238.

Eternity's Silence-Eye
Gives birth
To Infinity's sound-life.

3239.

Have a new mind and an old heart
Every day
To please your Lord Supreme.

3240.

Is there anything
That does not come
From Silence?

3241.

Is there anything
Humanity cannot accomplish
With a silence-heart?

3242.

Sleeplessly and breathlessly
I climb up
To see the Eye
Of my Lord Beloved Supreme.

3243.

I dive deep
To place my very existence
At the Feet
Of my Lord Beloved Supreme.

3244.

Enlightenment is a far cry
For the self-imposed
Solitary confinement-seeker.

3245.

God's temporary absence
From my heart
Literally kills me.
I do not know what will happen
If ever I shall have to brook
His long absence.

3246.

Far away, far away,
O my restless mind,
I shall keep you.
I shall become
My heart's nectar-silence-delight.

3247.

O where is my dream-boat,
O where is my dream-boat-Pilot,
    where?
O where is my purity-heart's
Ever-blossoming garden?

3248.

O my Father Lord Supreme,
Today I shall worship Your Feet
With my tearful eyes and cheerful
    heart.
Today I shall definitely please You
In Your own Way.

3249.

Total transformation
I want from my life.
Therefore, sleepless prayers
And breathless meditations
I need.

3250.

I am entering into the silence-
    clime,
I am.
Smiling, I long to please
Each and every citizen of the
    world.

3251.

You have just come back
From visiting God.
How is it that your face and eyes
Are still the same?
Alas, you carry the message
Of the unchangeable!

3252.

When we strive for
God the Creator,
God the creation
Thrives for us.

3253.

You can easily remain close to God
If you want to,
Even if you are in confusion-mart.

3254.

Let me ask God for His Help
In everything that I do and say.
If He does not help me,
Then who can and who will?

3255.

If you do not put an end
To your anxieties, worries,
Fears and doubts,
Then you will get an invitation
From the despair-confines.

3256.

A spiritual Master is he
Who assures his disciples
That their inner progress
And outer success
Can be made much faster.

3257.

Every day God comes to us
With a new supply of happiness.
But alas, we pay no attention!

3258.

When his ego
Was totally smashed,
He started singing
Devotion-flooded heart-songs.

3259.

When life faces realities,
It is all tragedy.
When life stays in
The dreamland and moonland,
It is all comedy.

3260.

God wants us to quench His Thirst
And feed His Hunger
With our gratitude-heart-
    blossoms.

3261.

It is absolutely useless
To repent our past blunders.
We must go forward, fly upward
And dive inward
If we want to place ourselves
At the Feet of God.

3262.

We must quench our God-thirst
With our heart's
Blossoming smiles.

3263.

My life, come back from
Your self-styled retirement.
Let us try once more
For satisfaction-enlightenment.

3264.

God can easily take a body
And walk among us.
But where is our heart's
Sleepless and breathless inner cry
To recognise Him when He
    comes?

3265.

Even our happiest days
Are no match
For God's Fondness-Smile.

3266.

When the body, vital and mind
Are invited by God,
Even God is shocked
By their wild misbehaviour.

3267.

When the disciples deeply miss
The physical presence of their
    Master,
The Master unmistakably misses
The inner presence of his
    disciples.

3268.

May all my heart-songs
Have only one note:
Devotion.

3269.

Parting sorrows
Are more powerful
Than welcoming joys.

3270.

The mind displays
A wide variety of tricks
To get God-Attention.

3271.

When the doubting mind
Wants to enter into your heart,
Immediately, unmistakably
And categorically
Say "No!"

3272.

The more I understand
Why my life
Is fettered by ignorance-bondage,
The more I blame
My world-possession-desire-life.

3273.

Each uncomely thought
Is a most serious stumbling block.
This is what our aspiration-life
Must unmistakably realise.

3274.

Readiness, willingness, eagerness
And self-givingness:
These four virtues
Are the relay runners
In our spiritual life.

3275.

We are asking the outer world
To give us peace,
Which it does not have at all,
Instead of entering into our
Prayer and meditation-life,
Which definitely has and is peace.

3276.

I can be happy and perfect
Only by reminding myself
All the time
That I belong only to God,
And never to myself.

3277.

The power of my aspiration-heart
Always protects me
From my disobedience-attacks.

3278.

My aspiring heart
Is always at home
In the inner world.
Therefore, my Lord's Joy
Knows no bounds.

3279.

My desiring mind
Is always out
Roaming the world
Of temptation-frustration.
Therefore, my Lord Supreme
Is doomed to disappointment.

3280.

No matter how long
We have been in the world
Of our self-chosen ignorance-
    night,
We are never, never God-forsaken.

3281.

When I devotedly appreciate,
    admire,
Adore and love my Lord's
Compassion-Forgiveness-Feet,
My Lord says, "My child,
I now definitely can claim you
As My own."

3282.

When I go to God's Palace
With my streaming devotion-
    tears,
God Himself opens up
His own Heart-Gate.

3283.

Each and every
God-obedience-thought
Is, indeed, indomitable.

3284.

My Lord,
There is only one thing of Yours
That frightens me,
And that is Your Indifference-Eye.

3285.

My Lord repeatedly tells me
That I must not surrender my life
To my confusion-dissatisfaction-
    mind.

3286.

The faith-blooms in my mind
And gratitude-blossoms in my
    heart
Are satisfying my Lord Supreme
Far more than I could ever
    imagine.

3287.

An ideal disciple
Cheerfully and self-givingly
    places
The heaviest burdens
Of his past, present and future
At his Master's feet.

3288.

My Lord, forgive me!
I do not remember
Why I called You.
"My child, you called Me
To replace your desire-life
With an aspiration-heart."

3289.

It pains my Lord so severely
When I pray to Him to come to me
With His Compassion-Heart,
And to go
To the rest of the world's citizens
With His Justice-Mind.

3290.

My Lord Himself has shocked my
    mind
And sealed my mouth
So that I can enjoy the beauty
Of His Infinity's Silence-Light.

3291.

If you believe in your Inner Pilot
And can listen to His Dictates,
Then you do not have to cross
    oceans
To find an outer Master.

3292.

When I do not pray and meditate,
My indifference to Mother Earth
Does not allow me to know
What is going on with her.
But when I pray and meditate
Regularly and devotedly,
I see and become the bleeding
    heart
Of Mother Earth.

3293.

God tells me
That my life will attain perfection
If I can juggle prosperity's smiles
And adversity's tears
At the same time.

3294.

If there is an actual contest
Between the doubting minds
And the aspiring hearts,
In most cases the doubting minds
Will win a sweeping victory.

3295.

Two dividing minds
Challenge each other
And strangle each other.

3296.

Two aspiring hearts
Embrace each other
And need each other.

3297.

If you have soaring aspiration
In your heart,
Then your outer life will be filled
With glowing elation.

3298.

When I am my desire-life,
I see right in front of me
And all around me
God's Concern-Eye,
But God's Satisfaction-Heart
Is nowhere to be found.

3299.

Our heart's indomitable courage
Is definitely meant for the
   illumination
Of our mind's ignorance-night.

3300.

Today I have kept
My heart-door wide open
To welcome
All God-fulfilling promises.

3301.

If we do not practise detachment
In our day-to-day life,
Then our eyes shall not be able
To escape streaming tears.

3302.

Life on earth is shorter than the
   shortest.
Then how is it
That we take upon ourselves
Unnecessary burdens?
Only one responsibility we have:
God-satisfaction for God's sake.

3303.

There is no end to our folly!
We pride ourselves on our
   physical,
Vital and mental achievements.
Do we not know that these
   achievements
Will invariably mingle with the
   dust?

3304.

I pray and pray
Only to dance the dance
Of God-satisfaction
In my aspiration-heart.

3305.

If you want to offer unalloyed love
To your Lord Supreme,
Just use your heart,
And keep your head at the farthest
    corner
Of the globe.

3306.

Every day
My heart and my Lord's Heart
Write love letters to each other.
My heart overflows.
I am sure His does, too.

3307.

My Lord's Compassion-Eye
Never stops,
Not even for a fleeting second.

3308.

My rejection-mind
Never stops.
Ceaseless it is.

3309.

My mind-meditation
Sadly
Stops and stops.

3310.

My heart-meditation
Bravely
Soars and soars.

3311.

My mind-prayers work so hard
To receive favours from God,
Yet God remains heedless.

3312.

My heart-prayers work
    spontaneously,
Effortlessly and selflessly
To receive favours from God.
Answers come immediately
In the affirmative.

3313.

The mind wants to live
Independent of everything,
Including God.

3314.

The heart wants to remain
Independent of everything,
Save and except God.

3315.

God wants me to feel
His Oneness-Heart
And not understand
His Vastness-Mind,
Never!

3316.

I want God to understand
My misunderstood mind
And feel my neglected heart.

3317.

Heaven smilingly touches
Earth's heart and says,
"Stop crying!"

3318.

Earth devotedly touches
Heaven's Eye and says,
"Start smiling!"

3319.

I ask God if He still remembers
When we met for the first time,
Since I have totally forgotten.

3320.

God tells me that He also
Has completely forgotten
When we met for the first time,
But He is more than eager
To have another meeting.

3321.

I pray to God
To give me the capacity
Forever to remain
At His Forgiveness-Feet.

3322.

God tells me
That He is willing to sanction
My prayer,
Provided I pray in a different way.
He wants me to pray
To please His Compassion-Heart.

3323.

Alas,
So many unnecessary problems
Orbit around
Our ego-mind.

3324.

When you write God
Your love-devotion-surrender-
    letters,
Do not edit them.
Your heart's first, spontaneous
Aspiration-cries
Are of paramount importance.

3325.

In a true seeker's life,
A moment with God
Is an experience
That forever lasts.

3326.

Have you heard the latest news?
Peace
Has been unanimously elected
As ruler of the mind-world.

3327.

God lives happily and proudly
Inside my soul's smiles
And my heart's tears.

3328.

God loves to play everywhere,
Even inside
Our unsearching mind.

3329.

Alas, for such a long time
I have been trying to illumine
My heart's darkness-despair-
    night.

3330.

God employs
Each and every heart
To work lovingly and soulfully
Inside His Heart-Garden.

3331.

The world-responsibility
That you accept cheerfully
Is preparatory to a higher
And deeper life.

3332.

I am so excited and delighted
That God Himself has chosen me
To be a preschool student
In His own Heart-School.

3333.

O seeker, can you not see
That God the Inner Runner
Is waiting for you to start the race?
If you just start,
He will happily and proudly
Do the rest
To complete the race for you.

3334.

O my mind's insincerity,
O my heart's impurity,
O my life's disobedience,
Do you think I am blind?
Do you think I am deaf?
Do you think I am dumb?

3335.

Poor God!
He resorts to love
When the mind
Deliberately misbehaves.

3336.

If you have a prayerful
And soulful life,
Then you can always
Accompany truth everywhere.

3337.

My heart's real friend is faith.
How I wish my mind also
To have the same friend!

3338.

Your heart's genuine aspiration
Must never surrender
To your mind's wild desperation.

3339.

All you do is pretend
That you are excellent in
   everything
That you say and do.
Poor God is working so hard
To inject sincerity
Into your heart, mind and life.

3340.

My heart's love
Of God
Is absolutely real.

3341.

My mind's deliberate rejection
Of God
Is most painfully real.

3342.

O my mind,
God has come so many times
To visit you,
But you always hide.
This is really making Him angry.

3343.

O my sleeping body,
O my strangling vital,
O my doubting mind,
O my fearing heart,
You stupidity incarnates!
How long do you think
God will wait and wait
And wait for you?

3344.

Like my heart,
My mind also has to be
A fountain of prayers
Before I can dream of placing
    myself
At the Feet of my Lord Supreme.

3345.

By every means,
I must stop for good
My life's attachment-journey.

3346.

Today I am so proud
Of my mind, vital and body,
For they all have bowed
To my Lord Supreme most
    devotedly.

3347.

Instead of pretending
That you know everything
And you are everything,
Just start attending
God's Compassion-Heart-School.
Soon you will really know
    everything,
And really become everything.

3348.

My Lord, if I have a greatness-
    mind,
A goodness-heart
And a selflessness-life,
Will that be enough?
"My child, more than enough,
More than enough!"

3349.

Now I know why God
Has never accepted the prayers
Of my mind.
They are all full of insincerity
And impurity.

3350.

The outer school gives us
Machine-made
Mind-diplomas.

3351.

The inner school gives us
God's own Heart-made
Pride-diplomas.

3352.

I do not intend
To give up groping
For the Truth —
Never!

3353.

God does not want
To give up hoping
That I will find the Truth —
Never!

3354.

The spiritual life,
Which is God's own Life,
Is not for the weak
And the unwilling.

3355.

Once God starts pouring
His Compassion-Light into
     someone,
His philosophy
Does not allow Him to stop.

3356.

Nobody can escape
The battlefield of life.
Therefore, the wise thing to do
Is to fight hard and gloriously
     win.

3357.

I pray to God
To bless me
With His Universal Oneness.

3358.

God prays to me to give Him
My sincere readiness,
My sincere willingness
And my sincere eagerness.

3359.

I am absolutely sure
That my life-river
Will one day rush
Into my soul's illumination-sea.

3360.

My Lord, I am fully prepared
To lose the world,
As long as I can accompany You,
Only You.
"My child, if you really
    accompany Me,
Then you will see the rest of the
    world
Right inside Me."

3361.

Quite true, quite true, quite true:
God was, God is and God will
    forever be
For you.

3362.

Love and joy can live everywhere,
But they prefer to live
In the smiles of a sweetness-heart.

3363.

O my eagerness-heart,
Be grateful to my soul's
Fulness-height.

3364.

Mankind's transformation-life
Without a God-invocation-heart
Is simply impossible.

3365.

The gratitude-heart-committee
Has shockingly few
Members.

3366.

O Lord Supreme,
I may one day know who You are,
But I shall never know
How vast Your Forgiveness is.

3367.

God's Radiance can dance
Only in the seeker's
Devotion-heart-eyes.

3368.

As long as God has faith in me
And I have faith in God,
I do not have to worry
If the rest of the world
Has faith in me.

3369.

Today, O my Lord Supreme,
I really feel
That You are my Eternity's All.
"My child, look what I am doing!
I am dusting off
Your ignorance-dirt
Blessingfully, happily and
    proudly."

3370.

Today my soul has given me
Two new names:
Obedience-beauty
And surrender-fragrance.

3371.

My Lord,
Let me love You only,
Let me serve You only,
Let my aspiration-flames
Fly only towards You.

3372.

Today both my inner life
And my outer life
Are thirsting for the fount
Of God-Satisfaction.

3373.

It is we who decide
Whether we shall arrive at God's
    Feet
Through countless mistakes,
Or through the path of faith,
    obedience,
Love, devotion and surrender.

3374.

We can never separate
The Master's teachings
From the immortal Delight
Of the supernal Light.

3375.

Real aspiration
Only lives
In God-gratitude-home.

3376.

Each time I cultivate a good
    thought
In my mind,
I immediately see, feel and
    become
A fountain of joy.

3377.

God's Forgiveness-Feet
And God's Compassion-Eye
Can at once be sought and caught.

3378.

My Lord asks me
To smile and smile and smile—
To smile within and smile
   without—
For He is making me
A citizen of His Heart-Country.

3379.

My Lord listens to all my prayers,
Save and except one:
"May I be worthy of
Your Leadership-Eye and Feet."
My Lord corrects my prayer
And tells me to pray to Him
For His Friendship-Hands
   instead.

3380.

I say to God:
"My Lord, Your Forgiveness-Feet
Are so beautiful."
My Lord's immediate
Compassion-Response:
"My child, your heart's aspiration-
   eyes
Are so lovable."

3381.

O God-fear, enough of you!
Today I am determined
To tear your body
Into millions of pieces.

3382.

The inner wisdom
And the outer knowledge
Must sing one, only one, mantra:
God-dependence.

3383.

There was a time
When my heart was beautiful,
My eyes were beautiful
And everything that I had was
   beautiful.
But now my life is totally empty
Of beauty
Because I have allowed my mind
To enjoy doubt-meals.

3384.

My negativity-mind faded
Into nothingness
When I invoked God
On the strength of my full
Openness-heart.

3385.

My Lord,
When You and I are talking,
May I be allowed
To change my name to gratitude?

3386.

Alas,
Why do I always see my doubting
    mind
Chasing my happiness-heart?
Can I not see something
Really inspiring and illumining?

3387.

I know I shall be perfect
Only when I cannot separate my
    mind
From the beauty of my prayers
And my heart
From the fragrance of my
    meditations.

3388.

There is only one supreme
    necessity
In my life,
And that necessity is to hasten
My Godward journey.

3389.

Blessed is he
Whose heart is an express train
Journeying towards
God-Satisfaction-Station.

3390.

A God-devotion-heart
Is made of God's
Own Sweetness-Bliss.

3391.

My meditation-eye not only sees
The Beauty of God's Face,
But also embraces
The Duty of God's Life.

3392.

There shall come a time
When my doubting mind
Will be terribly afraid
Of standing between
My climbing aspiration-heart
And my Lord's smiling
    Compassion-Eye.

3393.

My Lord,
May every morning come to me
As a beautiful, sweet
And unexpected Blessing
From You.

3394.

Life is for self-giving action,
And this action we have to offer
Devotedly
To our own Inner Pilot.

3395.

My aspiration-heart-bird
Has two special wings
With two special names:
Obedience and gratitude.

3396.

My heart asked my life
To follow.
My life followed.
Where are they now?
They are now dancing inside
God's smiling Eye.

3397.

Love, devotion and surrender
Are divine virtues
That do not have to remain always
    hidden
Inside our heart.
They can be brought to the fore
And marshalled for God-Victory.

3398.

The dream of science
Is not my problem.
No, not at all!

3399.

Scientists'
Misconduct-behaviour
Is my very serious problem.

3400.

A mind-talker
I deplorably was.
A heart-giver
I am and I shall
Forever remain.

3401.

O my life,
You and I must obey
God's Commands
Immediately, happily and
     proudly.

3402.

O my life,
You and I must disregard and
     discard
All absurd demands
Of our mind and our vital.

3403.

The soul comes to the fore
And tells the darkness-mind,
"Come home, come home!
For such a long time
I have been waiting for you."

3404.

Every day my Lord Supreme asks
     me
To keep my mind under control
And to live inside my heart,
But alas, every day I fail!

3405.

Alas, my mind-piano
Has only three keys:
Expectation, frustration and
     destruction.

3406.

Start!
You will be able to reach the
     Highest.
Stop!
You will be forced to become
A citizen of the lowest.

3407.

Doubt enters into belief
In total disguise
To ruin belief and destroy
     aspiration.
Belief enters into doubt
To illumine doubt
For God-worship.

3408.

For a heart of sincere longing,
No distance is too far
To travel.

3409.

I come to God
With my heart's
Newness-bloom.

3410.

God comes to me
With His Heart's
Fulness-Blossoms.

3411.

It is not easy,
But we must tame and train
Our old, unwilling thoughts
For a higher life
And richer achievement
In the inner world.

3412.

Your soul wants to live
Inside your heart
To illumine your heart.
But you are forcing your soul
To live behind your heart
And meet with constant
    frustrations.

3413.

I call it
My humility-mind.
God calls it
His greatest utility-instrument.

3414.

God does not want you
To imitate your soul.
He only wants you
To fly with your soul
Wherever it flies.

3415.

Without being asked,
The inner meditation
Will perfectly answer
The outer questions,
Even those unasked.

3416.

Each incarnation
Is a golden opportunity
To love
God's Lotus-Feet
And manifest
God's all-fulfilling Dreams.

3417.

Depression silences
The dynamism
Of the vital.

3418.

Depression delays indefinitely
The forward journey
Of the mind.

3419.

Depression paralyses
The life-energy
Of the body.

3420.

Each self-offering moment
Of my life
Beams with God-Delight.

3421.

Be not afraid of self-
    transcendence.
God's own breathing Life
Is smiling and singing
Inside it.

3422.

God gives me the Beauty
Of His Compassion-Eye.
I give God the tears
Of my gratitude-heart.

3423.

My aspiration-heart
Follows God's Compassion-Eye
From world to world.

3424.

God's Forgiveness-Feet
Follow my doubting mind
From world to world.

3425.

What is faith?
It is a divine achievement
Of our heart
That outlasts everything undivine
In us.

3426.

My heart has been waiting
For years and years
For my mind to enjoy
A God-surrender-moment.
And now, finally,
It has been achieved.

3427.

God wants me to collect
Only my heart's surrender-songs,
And no other songs,
To sing for Him.

3428.

Alas,
I never realised
That my life's failure-sadness
Could be so powerful.

3429.

O God,
What have I done wrong
That I am again thrown into
My mind-prison?

3430.

God tells me that every moment
Is a choice hour
For me to please Him
In His own Way.

3431.

We get angry with God
Without any rhyme or reason,
And do not want to pardon Him.
But God never abandons us.

3432.

God, since I am sincerely tired
Of thinking in my own way,
Can You not show me
Your Way of thinking?
Who knows,
Perhaps I shall be extremely
    happy.

3433.

God, the pride of my division-
    mind
Is torturing my heart ruthlessly.
I am begging You for a
    replacement:
Humility.

3434.

It seems that both God and I
Are hoping against hope.
When I think of my God-
    satisfaction,
It is nothing short of hoping
    against hope.
When God thinks of my
    perfection-life,
It is, indeed, the same.

3435.

I see fertile receptivity
In my mind-field
Only when I scatter
Some dust of my Lord's Feet.

3436.

In every way
My life becomes prosperous
When I entirely depend on God
In my inner life of aspiration
And in my outer life of dedication.

3437.

In every way
My life becomes totally disastrous
When I proudly claim to be
The owner of my life.

3438.

This morning
God came to his soul and said:
"What are you doing?"
His poor soul said to God:
"Father, I am just covering
The imperfection-holes
Of my body, vital, mind and
     heart."

3439.

When my Lord's Compassion-Eye
Appears,
My depression-vital
Disappears.

3440.

Inspiration invites aspiration
To accompany it
While it goes forward to the
     farthest.
Aspiration smilingly accepts.

3441.

Aspiration invites inspiration
To accompany it
While it flies upward to the
     highest.
Inspiration bravely accepts.

3442.

The willingness
Of the mind
Is surprisingly powerful.

3443.

The eagerness
Of the heart
Is astonishingly fruitful.

3444.

O world-beauty-face,
Where are you?
Do not deprive me
Of seeing you.

3445.

O world-purity-heart,
Where are you?
I am dying to become one with
    you.

3446.

God needs my cheerful availability
All the time,
More than anything else.

3447.

Each time I follow
The Fragrance-Footsteps
Of my Lord Supreme,
I swim breathlessly
In the sea of ecstasy.

3448.

My Lord Supreme,
You have made me an aspiration-
    tree.
Now I am offering You
My dedication-fruits and flowers.

3449.

I call it disobedience,
But God calls it danger,
Real danger.

3450.

All along,
God has been asking me
To love Him
With my aspiration-heart.
Now He is asking me
To add something.
He wants me to serve Him
As well
With my surrender-life.

3451.

God asks me
To keep my gratitude-heart
Always active and dynamic.

3452.

The more I pray and meditate,
The longer my Lord keeps
His Satisfaction-Smile.

3453.

Today I am fully resolved
To challenge the invasion
Of my God-unwillingness-mind.

3454.

Unlike my mind,
My heart always walks along
The God-fulfilment-road.

3455.

I call it
My God-hungry heart,
But God calls it
His Satisfaction-Pride.

3456.

May my aspiration-heart,
My dedication-life
And my God-manifestation-
    breath
Forever and forever
Sing their God-Victory-songs.

3457.

God smiled.
My doubting mind
Immediately surrendered.

3458.

God thundered.
My destruction-cherishing vital
Immediately surrendered.

3459.

My soul every day collects
God's teeming Dreams
And offers them lovingly and
    faithfully
To all God-seekers.

3460.

When my mind exercises
Its determination-power,
God smilingly and proudly says:
"My child, I am expediting
My choice Hour for you."

3461.

My Lord tells me, "My child,
    observe!
Observe everything and
    everybody.
Then, when the time comes,
I shall tell you what to say
And what to do."

3462.

Every day God tells me
To feel that His Satisfaction-Heart
Is more mine than His own.

3463.

Each individual has many virtues.
God tells me that in my inner life,
My best virtue is my tearful
      gratitude,
And in my outer life,
My best virtue is my blissful
      surrender.

3464.

O my prayerful mind,
Where are you?
It is high time
For you to come back to me.

3465.

O my grateful heart,
Where are you?
It is high time
For you to come back to me.

3466.

Obedience is
The secret and sacred name
Of my aspiration-heart.

3467.

Determination is
The secret and sacred name
Of my dedication-life.

3468.

O my God-gratitude-heart,
You are my light,
You are my pride,
You are my everything.

3469.

My Lord's Compassion-Eye
Smilingly travels the inner world
Every day.

3470.

My Lord's Concern-Eye
Carefully travels the outer world
Every day.

3471.

My Lord's Sadness-Eye
Tearfully travels the lower worlds
Every day.

3472.

My Lord's Satisfaction-Eye
Proudly travels the higher worlds
Every day.

3473.

My Lord,
You are my divinity-soul's
Immortality-Destination.

3474.

My Lord,
You are my humanity-life's
Daily destination.

3475.

Whatever is sleeping inside my
    heart
Has to wake up.
Why not now, this very moment?

3476.

My soul is commanding
My stubborn mind
To surrender to my soul's light
Before it is too late.

3477.

My today's aspiration-battlefield
Tomorrow I shall turn into
An aspiration-heart-garden
With the unconditional Help
Of my Lord Supreme.

3478.

I want my mind to know
What the truth
Actually looks like.

3479.

I want my heart to feel
What the truth
Actually is.

3480.

I want my life to support
Truth
And what it stands for.

3481.

Alas, God alone knows
When our outer life
Will be a perfect exponent
Of our inner life!

3482.

World-peace is a subject
We ceaselessly talk about.
World-peace is a lesson
We all needs must learn.

3483.

Our own inner light
Has to come to the fore
To illumine the darkness-weapon
That our mind uses
To maintain its supremacy.

3484.

You profess to have
The compassion, concern
And feeling of oneness
To put an end to world-conflicts
And world-sufferings.
Why then do you exhibit
So much disagreement,
Disharmony and bitter wrangling
With others?

3485.

The positive aspect of life
Is not only neglected,
But totally forgotten
By the majority of humanity.

3486.

Outer peace-promises
Are at once
Extremely hollow
And
Shockingly shallow.

3487.

Peace is
An inner achievement,
Not an outer compromise.

3488.

Compromise
Is not
A permanent solution
To any problem,
Inner or outer.

3489.

Compromise only creates
A kind of uncertain hope
For future amicability.

3490.

Compromise is like an agreement
Between two boxers
To stop fighting,
While secretly they muster their
     strength
For an imminent encounter.

3491.

Peace is first
An individual achievement.
Then it grows into
A collective achievement.
Finally it becomes
A universal achievement.

3492.

Alas, the truth
That the unaspiring human
     beings
See and feel
Is deplorably partial.

3493.

My Lord blessingfully says to me,
"My child,
I love your world-beckoning
     courage,
Your world-illumining mind
And your world-uplifting heart."

3494.

Your wisdom-flooded life
Will confidently guide the world
To a glorious God-Satisfaction-
     Goal.

3495.

When we live in the mind,
The future is so unpredictable
That it can give us
A very shocking and devastating
Experience.

3496.

My soul,
Yours is a clarion-call
That is destined to be heard
Far and wide.

3497.

When a cynic
Enters into a garden,
The first thing he does
Is look for the weeds,
And not for the beautiful flowers.

3498.

When a cynic
Looks at the moon,
Consciously and deliberately
He tries to see all its dark spots
And big holes.

3499.

A cynic thinks and feels
With utmost certainty
That spirituality's outer life
And inner breath
Are made of hollow stupidity.

3500.

A cynic feels
That he has the capacity
To size up spiritual values
And spiritual Masters
In the twinkling of an eye.

3501.

A cynic drinks nectar-delight
The moment he can criticise
And belittle
The world around him.

3502.

A cynic is certain
That everybody should be
   admitted
To a mental asylum –
Save and except him!

3503.

A cynic abhors the stupidity,
Which he calls gullible stupidity,
Of his own previous years.

3504.

A cynic feels
That his present life
Is inundated
With immeasurable wisdom.

3505.

A cynic says to God,
"Had I known before
Who You truly and eternally are,
Then I would not even
Have condescended
To enter into Your creation,
Let alone remain in Your
   creation."

3506.

A cynic's life-boat plies between
The world-sneering
And world-backbiting shores,
Regularly, punctually
And unfailingly.

3507.

Day in and day out,
A cynic has only one question
To ask God:
"Why, why, why, why?"

3508.

Poor God has only one answer
To give a cynic:
"My Game is not over,
My Game is not over,
My Game is not over,
My Game is not over."

3509.

A cynic cautions
Each and every human being:
"Do not enter into the unknown!
Do not cultivate an unfamiliar
    field!
Do not have faith in anybody else!
Muster all faith in yourself
And for yourself!"

3510.

A cynic cautions me:
"If you make mistakes on your
    own,
You will somehow be able
To save yourself.
But if you are suffering
From the mistakes committed by
    others,
Then there is no hope for you
To move forward."

3511.

A cynic has convinced himself
That he is
A self-sufficient person.

3512.

To a cynic,
The world is a costly
Farce.

3513.

To a cynic,
The inner world is wedded
To brooding confusion.

3514.

To a cynic,
The inner world is nothing
But a chimera's mist.

3515.

To a cynic,
The inner world is
A phantasmagoria.

3516.

A cynic says to humanity,
"I am a new light, the only light.
Follow me!
If you do not,
The utter futility of your life
Will eventually paralyse you,
Astonishingly and shockingly."

3517.

O cynic,
For years and years
You have been climbing
The pinnacle-heights
Of negativity.

3518.

God has unmistakably taught us
That the tenebrous night
Is not life's ultimate message.

3519.

Let us all chant
The birthless and deathless
Nectar-delight-message
Of the Vedic seers
Of the hoary past—
Tamaso ma jyotir gamaya—
"Lead me from darkness
To Light."

3520.

Let us all chant
The Immortality-flooded
World-birth-message
Of the Bible—
Lux sit—
"Let there be Light."

3521.

Many will come and many will go.
But some will definitely remain
Faithful children of the Supreme
And devotedly stay with Him
In His Boat
To reach the Destination:
The Golden Shore of the Beyond.

3522.

President Kennedy's loftiest
America-illumining utterance:
"Ask not what your country
Can do for you;
Ask what you can do for your
    country."
The Supreme's loftiest
World-illumining utterance:
"Ask not what spirituality and I
Can give to you;
Ask what you can give
To spirituality and to Me."

3523.

God loves us and needs us
Infinitely more
Than we can ever imagine.

3524.

God begs us not to house
Two most destructive
Weapon-words
In our heart-dictionary:
Negativity and cynicism.

3525.

Cast aside negativity!
Lo, you will fly and fly
In Infinity's Sky,
And God will sing and dance
In your world-illumining
And world-fulfilling achievement.

3526.

Now that you have
Completely given up
Your negativity,
I can clearly see
That you are blossoming
Most beautifully,
Like a sweet, young child.

3527.

O world,
My happiness-heart-blooms
To you I give –
Even if you do not want.

3528.

O God,
My gratitude-life-blossoms
To You I give –
Even if You do not need.

3529.

The smile of new faces I have seen,
But now I want to become
The heart of oneness-life.

3530.

Alas, will my self-doubt-
Nightmare-indulgence
Ever end in my life?

3531.

The oneness-philosophy
That your soul learnt
From God Himself
Your soul is now trying to share
With you.
But alas, success still remains
A far cry!

3532.

My Lord,
I have dragged You down
From Heaven,
But instead of getting angry with
    me,
You have placed
Your Compassion-Crown
Upon my head.

3533.

Disturbing doubts
Must be caught
By the God-searching mind.

3534.

Since God Himself is not
A frustrated humanity-lover,
How can I be one?

3535.

Your life is an unmistaken reality
When it feels that it lives
Only for the fulfilment
Of God-necessity.

3536.

Our Lord Supreme
Is never
An unpredictable investment.

3537.

Each unaspiring life
Is a fearful and tearful series
Of broken promises.

3538.

The human power-towers
Rise
Only to fall.

3539.

What is despair?
It is nothing but our unfulfilled
    desire
In disguise.

3540.

An atom of sincere aspiration
Can bring my heart to the fore
And place me at the Feet
Of my Beloved Lord Supreme.

3541.

Alas,
Human life is torn
Between the heart's fear
And the mind's greed.

3542.

A seeker must march forward
In the face of insurmountable
    obstacles,
To arrive at his supreme
    Destination.

3543.

An uncomplicated mind
Will definitely accompany
A prayerful heart.

3544.

Self-confidence
Without God-assistance from
    within
Is the height of stupidity.

3545.

Seize every moment
To transform the undivine into
    the divine,
And the divine into the perfect.

3546.

My soul asks my life
To claim my soul's enlightenment
As its own
To further its aspiration and
    dedication.

3547.

The Tears of God
Have purified my heart.
Now the tears of my heart
Must purify my mind.

3548.

O fair face of the world,
How I wish for you to have
A real heart and not a false one!

3549.

My heart has only
One desire:
It wants to touch
God's Feet.

3550.

My mind has only
One desire:
It wants to measure
God's Heart.

3551.

I am happy and fulfilled
Because I have learnt
To face life
As it is.

3552.

Our sincere aspiration
To evolve into godliness
Is God's measureless Satisfaction.

3553.

Rare is the heart
That can feel everything
As divine.

3554.

Rare is the mind
That sees anything
As divine.

3555.

God is performing His Task:
He is dreaming of me all the time.
But alas, where is my awareness?
Where is my belief?
Where is my satisfaction?

3556.

My heart-tears purify my mind
And satisfy both God's thirsty Eye
And His hungry Heart.

3557.

O seeker,
Every day make a special effort
To remain far above
Your mind's self-doubt-clouds.

3558.

You, too, can see God's Eye
And hear God's Message.
Just cultivate readiness in your
    mind
And willingness in your heart.

3559.

My heart wants me to sit
At God's Feet,
And my soul wants me to sing
A self-giving song for God.

3560.

When God sees gratitude
Inside our heart,
He asks His Smiles
To come and live with us.

3561.

Just step aside
If you do not want to be
Misunderstood
By others' minds.

3562.

Just step aside
If you do not want your heart-sun
To be eclipsed
By others' jealousy-clouds.

3563.

If we dare to brave
The inevitable,
God immediately comes
And embraces us.

3564.

When we have ceaseless faith
In our spiritual life,
Our desire-mind finally bows to
    us.

3565.

In the spiritual life,
Do not waste your time
Trying to find out facts.
It may blind your mind
And bind your heart.

3566.

As desperation knows
No tomorrow,
Even so, aspiration knows
No tomorrow.

3567.

Hope and promise
Can make us
Extremely fast runners
In our spiritual life.

3568.

Who imposed heavy loads
On you?
Look carefully within.
You will see that they are all
Self-imposed.

3569.

God's Heart waits and waits
To hear one song,
Only one song
From my gratitude-heart.

3570.

If you want to lose
Your suffering,
Then choose concern
For the rest of the world.

3571.

A small mind feels that everything
Is infinitely bigger,
And everybody is infinitely taller.

3572.

The enthusiasm of the vital
Is the dynamic energy
Of the entire body.

3573.

God asks us to do
Only one thing:
Enjoy the world
With the light of detachment.

3574.

Too much faith
Is an impossibility.
This is a foolish idea
Invented by foolish seekers.

3575.

The source of life's attachments
Is the turbulent sea
Of the mind.

3576.

The more I crave for
Earthly fulfilment,
The more I suffer from
A famished aspiration-heart.

3577.

My mind-violin
Has only two strings:
Desire-mountain
And despair-sea.

3578.

Self-indulgence-disasters
Secretly begin,
But openly end.

3579.

God's Eye observes everything,
But preserves only the things
That it chooses.

3580.

The doubting mind
Has never won
The popularity competition.

3581.

The aspiring heart
Wins the popularity competition
Without even participating.

3582.

Desire-fulfilment
Will never be in vogue
In a seeker's life.

3583.

We beg and beg greatness
To share with us
Its success-smile.

3584.

Even before we think
Of begging goodness
To share anything,
Goodness comes to share its
    breath
With us.

3585.

During our short visit to earth,
Can we not become
A long-lived self-offering
To God the creation?

3586.

Because I belong to the Supreme,
It is beneath my dignity
To make friends with ignorance-
    life.

3587.

I must convince myself
That I am
A supremely chosen instrument
Of my Lord Supreme.

3588.

My realisation
Looms large
Inside my God-conviction.

3589.

Human pride is division-
    darkness.
Divine pride is light within,
Light without
In universal oneness.

3590.

We have many undivine qualities.
Among them,
Pride is unsurpassable.

3591.

Pride secretly
Enters into our mind
And openly destroys
Our life.

3592.

Humility is the collector
Of all our undivine qualities,
Which it places at the Feet
Of our Lord Beloved Supreme.

3593.

Human pride runs and jumps,
Demanding,
"Break, break, break!"
Divine pride radiates and glows,
Urging,
"Build, build, build!"

3594.

Inside the depth of your prayer
You will find
Your soul's message-light.

3595.

God-manifestation
Is for
God-Satisfaction.

3596.

If you are praying soulfully
And meditating self-givingly,
Then rest assured you are doing
Absolutely the right thing,
And God Himself treasures you.

3597.

May I cry, smile, sing and dance,
My Lord,
Around Your Feet all the time.

3598.

God wanted me to come
And be admonished by
His Thunder-Justice-Feet.
I went, but I could not help
    kissing
His Thunder-Feet instead,
To my heart's content.

3599.

You believe in
Your ego-demonstration,
But God believes in
Your ego-demolition.

3600.

My Lord,
Since I am not worthy of
The dust of Your Feet,
May I beg You to bless me
With the dust of the dust
Of Your Feet.

3601.

His life is torn between
His mind's greed
And his heart's fear.

3602.

We must arrive at our destined
    Goal
In the face of
Insurmountable barriers.

3603.

My Lord,
My entire being aches and aches
To manifest all Your Dreams
Here on earth.

3604.

God is extremely proud
Of his heart's
Sudden magical awakening.

3605.

My uncomplicated days
Are giving my life
The golden opportunity
To make the fastest progress.

3606.

I do not care for
The mind-compromise-
Life.

3607.

I only care for
The soul-sunrise-
Heart.

3608.

My Master's blessingful smiles
Every day strengthen
My fearful heart.

3609.

My future has
Two places to live:
At my Master's lotus-feet
And
In my Master's rose-heart.

3610.

Spiritual enlightenment
Will flood the entire world.
It may take a very, very long time.

3611.

God's Compassion-Eye
Has paved the way,
O seeker,
For you to walk along
His Compassion-flooded Road.

3612.

I pray and pray to God
To demolish
My pride-mind-edifice
Once and for all.

3613.

Capture all moments,
Transform them,
Then place them at the Feet
Of your Lord Supreme.

3614.

We feel that suffering is necessary
In the spiritual life.
Our souls tell us
That this is absolutely wrong.
Our souls tell us that
From Delight we came,
In Delight we grow
And into Delight we shall retire.

3615.

His divine associations
Have brought to the fore
The very best in him.

3616.

Not by singing loudly,
But by singing prayerfully
And soulfully,
You can bring God to you.

3617.

Alas,
His life's faith-tree
Was felled
By his mind's giant doubt.

3618.

If you want to be at peace
Within yourself,
Then frighten your proud mind
And proud vital
With your heart's God-given light.

3619.

Pray to God to own nothing
In your mind-world,
So that you can gain everything
In your heart-world.

3620.

Inspiration, aspiration and
    dedication:
These three are our unfailing
    friends
When we run towards God.

3621.

My heart,
You are overjoyed in your bright
    days.
Continue aspiring;
Even brighter days are coming.

3622.

God wants you to be
A lover of the world
And not a sufferer
In the world.

3623.

My searching mind
Is a local
God-Compassion-Train-
    passenger.

3624.

My aspiring heart
Is an express
God-Justice-Train-passenger.

3625.

You, too, can see God's Eye.
You, too, can feel God's Heart.
You, too, can sit at God's Feet.
You, too, can satisfy God
At every moment
In His own Way.

3626.

When God gives us the capacity
To identify ourselves
Lovingly and self-givingly
With His entire creation,
Our division-supremacy-pride
Bursts like a balloon.

3627.

My Lord proudly smiles and
    smiles
When I measure the length of
    sincerity
In my aspiration, my dedication
And specially, my devotion.

3628.

My heart's gratitude-tears
Make my Lord Beloved Supreme
Extremely proud of me.

3629.

Illumination-shore nears us
When we do not carry
Hesitation-load in our mind.

3630.

God's Forgiveness-Willingness
And our gratitude-necessity
Should go together.

3631.

I think of God
Not because God loves me,
But because my heart
Always desperately needs Him.

3632.

Self-indulgence
And overconfidence
Are our two true enemies.

3633.

If for four hours
We repeat God's Name
Every day,
Then our life will be able
To acquire a reputation
For purity.

3634.

Temptation-desires
Must be shunned
Not only every hour
And every minute,
But every second.

3635.

Every morning we must separate
And liberate our mind
From desire-attacks.

3636.

In our spiritual life,
Needless to say,
There are many undivine forces
That we carry along with us,
And pride is the worst of all.

3637.

Eventually the mind's pride
Has to surrender
To the heart's humility.

3638.

I believe in
The magic transformation
Of life:
We can establish universal
    oneness
Through our prayer and
    meditation.

3639.

When we deliberately disobey
The Will of our Inner Pilot,
We enter into the darkest chasm
Of ignorance-night.

3640.

Out of His infinite Compassion,
My Lord has replaced
My uncertainty-mind
With certainty-promise,
And my insecurity-heart
With security-delight.

3641.

To achieve mastery over the mind
Is not an impossible task.
Many have done it.
I shall definitely join them
In the course of time
At God's choice Hour.

3642.

Where does hypocrisy come from?
Hypocrisy comes from
Our exorbitant greed
For our own happiness.

3643.

The birth of universal peace
Will arrive
From individual longing
For constant God-satisfaction
In God's own Way.

3644.

We have the mistaken belief
That we have to sacrifice
   everything
To please God in His own Way.
Pleasing God in His own Way
Has nothing to do with
   renunciation.

3645.

Our total surrender-heart
Helps our life to thrive
Far beyond our imagination.

3646.

Let us continue, my life!
Let us continue with
Our God-dedication-cries
And God-satisfaction-smiles.

3647.

We tell God
That there is no proper substitute
For His Compassion-Eye-Height.

3648.

God, out of His infinite
   Compassion,
Tells us
That there is no proper substitute
For our gratitude-heart-depth.

3649.

The loftiest pride
Of the mind
Can easily blight
The brightest achievement
Of the heart.

3650.

My heart's patience-light
Laughs and laughs
At my mind's despair-night.

3651.

Alas, there is
A most deplorable difference
Between our heart's prayers
And our mind's misdeeds.

3652.

My Master,
I shall love you deeply
As long as you do not ask me
To sit for my
Surrender-oneness-examination.

3653.

Wisdom says to patience:
My oneness-friend,
For us there can be
No permanent defeat.

3654.

God blessingfully
Invited me
To take care of
His Feet.

3655.

I have prayerfully
Invited God
To take care of
My head.

3656.

God-fulfilling opportunities
Divinely used,
We become kings
In the inner world.

3657.

God-fulfilling opportunities
Deliberately misused,
We become veritable beggars
In the inner world.

3658.

Every day
We give God
Our heart's prayerful tears.

3659.

Every day
God gives us
His Eye's blissful Smiles.

3660.

My life's surrender
To God's Will
Is the source
Of my heart's ceaseless peace.

3661.

Sleepless and breathless
    enthusiasm
Can not only shake the world,
But also transform the world.

3662.

Each positive thought
Is a step
Towards God's Delight-flooded
Palace.

3663.

O seeker,
Do you remember
That you were devotedly with God
To offer Him repeated successes?

3664.

O seeker,
Do you know
That you are self-givingly with
    God
For His complete manifestation
On earth?

3665.

O seeker,
I am sure
That you will be gratefully with
    God
Forever and forever
To please Him at every moment
In His own Way.

3666.

God tells me again and again,
Out of His infinite Bounty,
That He can and He will
Obliterate and nullify
My most deplorable past.

3667.

Rest assured,
All your good deeds
Will only be multiplied and
    multiplied
By the power of God's Grace.

3668.

I cannot believe
That God is telling me
He will be responsible
For all my misdeeds
If only I give Him
Full responsibility to be so.

3669.

God asks me to do Him
A big favour:
Either to take His philosophy
As my philosophy,
Or to stay with my own
    philosophy,
But not to unite them.
His philosophy is self-giving;
My philosophy is world-
    possessing.

3670.

God Himself has asked your
    Master
To be the golden bridge
Between you and God,
And also to be
Your absolute fate-maker.

3671.

Once you accept the spiritual life,
God-satisfaction has to be
Your inner choice
And outer voice.

3672.

Your philosophy has to be
The manifestation
Of your soul's closest connection
With God.

3673.

Your philosophy has to be
The manifestation
Of your Master's sleepless concern
For humanity.

3674.

Your philosophy has to be
To awaken the sleeping humanity
To take eternal shelter
At God's Compassion-flooded
Liberation-Feet.

3675.

If you are positive
In whatever you say and do,
Then you will be able to bring
All your divine qualities
To the fore
And have most powerful
God-satisfaction-meditations.

3676.

You are telling me
That you have lost faith in God.
I take it as your yesterday's news.
Today's news, whether you want
    to give
Or not,
God will give me on your behalf:
That you have not only regained
But multiplied
Your faith in God.

3677.

God tells me
That He does not need to see
My soul's credentials.
But He wants to see
My heart's credentials,
And He does not want
To waste His time
With my mind's credentials.

3678.

Do you not believe
That you have the capacity,
More than you need,
To manifest God's Light
Here on earth?

3679.

Is there any special reason
Why you cannot accept
God's philosophy as your own?
Is it too demanding,
Or is it too lenient?
"It is not that I do not want
To accept God's philosophy.
I want to, but alas,
My love-devotion-surrender
I myself buried
In my self-oblivion."

3680.

As long as you remain
In God's Golden Boat,
Rest assured,
Out of His infinite Compassion,
God will show you the light—
That His philosophy
Is the only philosophy
To give you joy
And to give you fulfilment.

3681.

The Highest can be reached
If we can make
Our love and gratitude
Abundantly rich.

3682.

Each time I do an excellent
    meditation,
God comes rushing towards me
To show me
His Tears of Light and Delight.

3683.

God does not want you to prove,
But it is your soul that wants you
To prove to God,
That you have convinced yourself
That God's Way is the only way
For you.

3684.

You give to your Master
What you have:
Devotion.
Your Master will give you
What he is:
An open heart.

3685.

If you are wanting
In devotion,
No satisfaction-progress
You can ever claim.

3686.

If you use your heart's devotion-
    magnet
All the time,
Then your God-approach-speed
Will simply fascinate you.

3687.

Bring to the fore
Your lost devotion.
Newness will be the name
Of your thought,
And fulness will be the name
Of your action.

3688.

Some are of the opinion
That one cannot do
The highest meditation
While walking.
I am so happy
That I am a perfect stranger
To that absurdity-founded
    philosophy.

3689.

My Lord,
Shall I take shelter
In my own highest consciousness
Or inside Your Compassion-Eye?
"My child,
How do you cleverly forget
That My Compassion-Eye
Is the source
Of your highest consciousness?"

3690.

Do not separate
Your soulful consciousness
From your real meditation.
They are inseparable,
Like a flower and its beauty.

3691.

Your meditative consciousness
Is nothing short of
Your God-nearing feet.

3692.

O seeker,
Why do you believe in
Your mind,
When it tells you that God-
    obedience
Is extremely bitter?

3693.

O seeker,
How is it that you do not believe in
Your heart,
When it says that God-obedience
Is sweetness-joy itself?

3694.

When I enter into
My aspiring heart,
I deeply enjoy
The feast of hopes.

3695.

Who says that there is no short-cut
To the Golden Shore?
From my personal experience,
I feel that devotion is definitely
The short-cut to the Golden
    Shore.

3696.

I am
My heart's
Aspiration-beauty-flower.

3697.

God is
His Eye's
Illumination-Compassion-Tower.

3698.

Negativity always
Wants and demands
To be at centre stage.

3699.

My mind's teeming doubts
Are bound to surrender to you,
O my heart.
Just wait a little more.

3700.

God asks me
Never to measure
My lethargy-devoured
Body-height,
But to measure devotedly
The length of my heart-height.

3701.

I give God my earthly life
To please Him.
God gives me His Heavenly Breath
To please me.

3702.

God's Compassion-Eye has
    planted
Peace-seeds inside my heart-
    garden.
Therefore, my entire being
Is overjoyed.

3703.

God's Concern-Eye not only has
Concern for me,
But also protects me
In every possible way
From temptation-life.

3704.

My prayerful and soulful
Gratitude-heart
Is too beautiful, too sacred
And too illumining to waste.

3705.

My Lord, I am all ready
And I am all willing
To do everything immediately
At Your Bidding.

3706.

O seeker, do not worry
About your teeming
    imperfections.
God will take care of your
    imperfections
As long as you have sincere
    oneness
With His Will.

3707.

My Lord, I am weak.
I have doubt,
Jealousy and insincerity.
Will You not take away my
    problems,
And also not forget
To take me with them?

3708.

There was a time
When he wanted to conquer
All his undivine qualities.
But now, alas, he has turned
All those undivine qualities
Into stark weapons
To use against God.

3709.

Instead of taking his weaknesses
As enemies
To be placed at God's Feet,
He has taken them as his soldiers
And become their commander
To challenge God.

3710.

My Lord,
My doubt-mind and insecurity-
    heart
Are so hurtful.
Why did You not conquer
Or give me the capacity
To conquer them?
Alas, even after so many years
I still remain the same.

3711.

You are trying and God is trying
To change your nature.
But you must realise
That nature's transformation
Is not like an instant sweet drink.
Everything takes its own time.

3712.

Alas, why are you feeding
Your weaknesses?
Do you not see that they are
    becoming
Your own self-destruction-
    strength?

3713.

It is beneath your spiritual dignity
To mix with those who are telling
    you
That there is nothing wrong
In disagreeing with God.

3714.

When you are in the heart,
You are all ready to give
All your imperfections to God.
When you are in the mind,
You either see no imperfections
In your life,
Or you feel that you can somehow
Manage your life
With all your imperfections.

3715.

If we are perfect,
Then why do we need God?
We need God
To teach us the song
Of perfection-transcendence.

3716.

You may be imperfect,
But your eagerness to be perfect
Is the very beginning
Of perfection.

3717.

As you offer your light to God,
Even so, offer your darkness
For illumination.
If you keep your darkness to
    yourself,
Then to your great sorrow and
    surprise,
Darkness will never leave you –
Even when you most sincerely
    long for
Its departure.

3718.

God never forces a seeker
To offer his ignorance.
Why? Because the seeker
May tell God,
"This is my hard-earned
    possession.
Let me keep it,
As You keep Your Light with You."

3719.

When love, devotion and
   surrender
Disappear,
We blame God,
As if our deplorable fate
Were all God's fault.

3720.

Alas, how often a seeker
Accuses God:
"God, how can You be truly happy
By keeping my life utterly
   miserable?"

3721.

The more we think we know
About God,
The less we know,
Because we have no idea
Of how God's Blessing-Plants
Will take shape.

3722.

My goal
Is to see reality
Not with my human eyes,
But with my divine heart.

3723.

Freedom we want,
But do we ever care to know
Where it comes from?
It comes from our sleepless
   oneness
With God's Breath.

3724.

When my hesitation-mind
Stands on the shore
Of the consciousness-ocean,
It only tries to count
The drops and waves
Of the ocean
Instead of becoming
The ocean itself.

3725.

My utter stupidity says to God,
"I am keeping my ignorance
To myself.
This is, indeed, what I want.
This is, indeed, what I need."

3726.

Alas,
There is no country
Here on earth
Where wisdom-light is king.

3727.

Not only his heart
But also his mind
Is astonishingly
In close touch with God.

3728.

In spirituality,
The highest award we can get
Is our constant oneness
With God's Will.

3729.

I am determined
Not to waste any more time
In the body of lethargy.

3730.

It is good to see God every day.
It is better to be near God every
    day.
It is by far the best to sit at God's
    Feet
And obey Him at every moment.

3731.

Temptation is now
Stronger than the strongest
In human life.
But there shall come a time
When temptation will not only be
Weaker than the weakest,
But will exist no more
In human life.

3732.

A ceaseless flow
Of gratitude-tears
Is the pinnacle of my spiritual life.

3733.

May my life every day
Be an epiphany
Of divine thoughts.

3734.

God chooses a special trophy
From His Heart-Room
To bless me
Each time I make a special sacrifice
For my fellow citizens.

3735.

My Lord,
Give me blind faith,
And no other faith,
So that I never surrender
To any difficulty in my life.

3736.

What does the doubt-thief do?
It secretly enters into
The belief-heart
To steal.

3737.

O my mind,
When my heart throws a party,
Stay as long as you can.
It is all for your good.

3738.

Blind and bind
Uncomely thoughts
Long before they attempt
To blind and bind you.

3739.

My mind's God-longing days
Are very,
Very short-lived.

3740.

There is only one way
To arrive at the destination:
Begin.

3741.

Do you want to be happy?
Then force your mind to be
Inside the breath of your heart.
This is the only way
To keep yourself happy.

3742.

Remember,
Your vital demands are
    innumerable,
But your Lord's Command is just
    one:
"March forward!"

3743.

Between two seeker-friends,
What God wants is a soulful
    conversation
And not a secret and hurtful
    competition.

3744.

Either gaze and gaze
At God's Lotus-Feet
Or face disaster after disaster.

3745.

If you most sincerely invoke God,
Then you cannot seriously
Provoke mankind.

3746.

Subtle desires
Have an extremely
Long life.

3747.

O seeker,
I assure you that your
God-inspiring soulfulness-songs
Will cure the deafness of
	mankind.

3748.

My Lord tells me
That the questions of my heart
Need no answers.
The questions already embody
The answers.
They need only self-revelation.

3749.

My Lord,
Ask my soul to free my mind
From its self-doubt-
	imprisonment.

3750.

My mind, pray,
Even if you do not have
Anything special to pray for.
Your prayers
Are your strongest bodyguards.

3751.

My soul tells me
That a self-offering heart
Is another name
For a God-becoming life.

3752.

Each new incarnation
Is a golden opportunity:
Either I become God's Heart
Or man's slave.

3753.

Meditation discovers
Silence-light.
Silence-light discovers
God's Delight.

3754.

Meditation
Is the liberator
Of self-limitation.

3755.

My meditation becomes one
Not only with God-Universality,
But also with God-Responsibility.

3756.

It is the bounden duty
Of willingness and eagerness
To transform the mind
Of unwillingness.

3757.

We love God the Compassion
And dislike God the Justice
In the same breath.

3758.

Not to pray
And not to meditate
Is a sheer waste
Of God-blessed breath.

3759.

My devotion
Surprisingly makes
My mind beautiful.

3760.

My devotion
Spontaneously makes
My heart sweet.

3761.

My devotion
Untiringly makes
My life perfect.

3762.

A doubting mind
Is quite apt to eclipse
The heart's
Moon-love-beauty.

3763.

Each aspiration-heart
Is
A God-satisfying song.

3764.

With the blossoming of each day,
I shall intensify
My God-search-aspiration-flames.

3765.

The mind-government
Shall always be wanting
In wisdom-light
And compassion-delight.

3766.

Self-denial
Is nothing short of
Self-styled self-indulgence.

3767.

Even the unwillingness-mind
Finally surrenders
To the eagerness-heart.

3768.

Not the powerful earth,
But the tearful earth
Compels God's blessingful
And blissful Descent.

3769.

Do not allow your mind
To cancel your heart's pilgrimage
To God's Delight-flooded
    Kingdom.

3770.

Every day
My Lord is
A Forgiveness-certainty.

3771.

No matter how many times
And in how many ways
Silence wants to give some advice
To my mind,
My mind just runs away.

3772.

My heart's excruciating pangs
Are the result
Of my being a hesitation-victim.

3773.

Day in and day out
I struggle,
Not for God's Light,
But for my supremacy supreme.

3774.

I am absolutely certain
That my God-longing voyage
Will be crowned with success
At God's choice Hour.

3775.

When my gratitude-heart and I
Look at God's Lotus-Feet,
God asks us to jump into
His Delight-Heart-Ocean
To swim and swim and swim.

3776.

Be like a child,
Act like a child.
Go from one flower to another
In your heart-garden
Until you find complete joy
And perfect satisfaction.

3777.

Think of yourself as a river
Constantly flowing at top speed.
Your mind
Will never be discouraged,
And your heart
Will never be disheartened.

3778.

In life we must never give up!
Acceptance
And self-transcendence
Should always remain our motto.

3779.

Even if there are
A great many obstacles in life,
Be like a river that continues
    flowing,
Paying no attention to all barriers.
Unmistakably it arrives at its goal:
The vastness-sea.

3780.

If we do not expect anything
Either from ourselves or from the
    world,
Discouragement cannot chase us.

3781.

Always keep in mind
That you are definitely going to
    fulfil
Your God-entrusted
    responsibility
On earth.

3782.

Muster strength
And say to yourself
That God-satisfaction
Is your birthright.

3783.

In life we are always
Proceeding forward.
God Himself is proceeding
And progressing,
So there is no such thing
As a finished product.

3784.

God does not mind
If we do not fulfil Him
According to the capacity
He has given,
But our soul,
The God-representative,
Feels extremely sad.

3785.

Let us not stop!
If we stop,
Despair is bound
To devour us.

3786.

Let us not delay our journey.
Let us not halt anywhere.
Even if we take a sidestep,
We shall come back to the right
    track
And reach our Destination.

3787.

We must never hesitate.
Today we may take short steps,
But tomorrow we may take
Long, longer, longest steps,
And the day after tomorrow
We may run and sprint
And arrive at our Destination,
Far beyond our imagination.

3788.

If you choose to be
In life's continuous flow
And in life's dynamic movement,
Despair you will find nowhere.

3789.

If you stop,
Then unconsciously, if not
    consciously,
You are proclaiming the victory
Of your deplorable and miserable
    life.

3790.

Movement is always equipped
With the capacity to destroy
The stagnant negativity
Of the mind.

3791.

O seeker, just get up
Early in the morning
To pray and meditate.
Lo, you have conquered
The pride of lethargy,
And you have won
The Smile of God.

3792.

Even if you have become
A slow train
On your life's journey,
You will get joy,
Abundant joy,
Because you are moving,
Moving forward.

3793.

If you are going
To keep the mind busy,
Then ask the mind
To study God-lessons thoroughly.

3794.

If you are going
To keep the heart busy,
Then ask the heart
To invoke God happily
And self-givingly.

3795.

All the things
That you know are good
In your aspiration-life,
Ask them to play like children
In your heart-garden.

3796.

A saviour remains a saviour,
No matter what others say about
    him.
He came into the world only to
    love God,
Serve God and manifest God,
And for nothing else.

3797.

When I say, "I am a way,
But not the only way,
And in me is my goal,"
That gives much freedom
Not only to me
But to everyone else.

3798.

If I say, "My way
Is by far the best for me,
And others' ways are best for
    them,"
Then God comes running towards
    me
To garland me.

3799.

If I say, "My path
Is a sunlit path for me,"
And if you also say the same,
Then immediately God embraces
    us
Together.

3800.

I have renounced my mind-
    kingdom.
Therefore, God has proudly
    invited me
To visit His Heart-Palace.

3801.

Once your heart is inundated
With God-Delight,
Your heart will never lose it.

3802.

At times, intellectual goals
Can be as funny
As circus clowns.

3803.

My Lord Supreme,
Do tell me
How I can run faster, fly higher
And dive deeper
At every moment.

3804.

The very nature of the unaspiring
    mind
Is to dampen the inspiration
That wants to come to the fore
From within.

3805.

When my mind is all fixed on God,
The Protection of God
I see all-where.

3806.

I pray and pray every day
To climb the tallest
God-achievement-mountain
And never to descend.

3807.

God is at once fond of
And proud of
Our ever-new beginnings.

3808.

My life's golden dawn
Is the result
Of my newly-born cries.

3809.

Smiling children are always
God's Love-distributors,
Wherever they go.

3810.

God connects our prayerful tears
With the Smiles
Of the ever-transcending Beyond.

3811.

O my heart,
You are making a serious mistake
In feeding the mind's
Expectation-greed.

3812.

My heart-flute
Is
My morning prayer.

3813.

My mind-piano
Is
My daily meditation.

3814.

God has no intention of curbing
My life,
But He is all willingness
And eagerness
To shape and mould my life
In a unique way.

3815.

Real aspiration can never be
The rejection of life.
Real aspiration is the beauty
Of life-acceptance
And the fragrance
Of life-transformation.

3816.

If it is my humility-heart,
Then God lovingly and proudly
Accepts.

3817.

If it is my arrogance-mind,
Then God deliberately and
    vehemently
Rejects.

3818.

My Lord, may my life be
As beautiful and pure
As my morning-prayer-sunrise.

3819.

Every morning, when hope
    arrives,
I feel that I can become
The possessor of a new life.

3820.

Every evening, when hope
    departs,
My sadness and loneliness
Beggar description.

3821.

Every day I pray to God
To give me the capacity
To sail my faith-boat
Speedily and safely.

3822.

Every day I pray to God
To give me the capacity
To capsize my doubt-boat
Happily and proudly.

3823.

Those who live only in the heart
Are accepted
In God's Heart-Guesthouse.

3824.

My Lord smilingly tells me
That He is more than willing
To accept my gratitude-heart
As His lifelong partner.

3825.

In his case,
Everything is under repair –
His aspiration-heart, his
    dedication-life
And his God-satisfaction-will.

3826.

A day without being blessed
By God's Compassion-Eye
Is a totally wasted day.

3827.

I want to explore my aspiration-
    heart;
I need a witness.
My Lord's Compassion-Eye
Is more than ready.

3828.

Finally,
All my worries and anxieties
Have taken shelter
In my Lord's Compassion-flooded
Heart-Sky.

3829.

My Lord, do tell me if my desire-
    hunger
Will ever come to an end.
If not, I am ready to exit
Secretly and peacefully
From spirituality's home.

3830.

The moment I remove my head
From my Lord's Feet,
My anxiety-mind runs riot.

3831.

Hope-world
Belongs
To the faithful.

3832.

Promise-world
Belongs
To the brave.

3833.

The day I forget to smile,
I deplorably fail in everything
That I do and say.

3834.

My heart's God-songs
Are saving me
From my God-doubting mind.

3835.

My meditation discovers
My Lord's Silence-Sea
Long before anything else.

3836.

My Lord,
I do not know how far away
You are from me,
But I do know that slowly, steadily
And unerringly
I am nearing Your Heart-Garden.

3837.

O my aspiration-heart,
Do tell me what you would like to
    do
With my desire-mind.
I want to burn it immediately,
Right here.

3838.

My Lord smiles His immortal
    Smile
To console my sorrowful heart
Every day.

3839.

Every day I arm myself
With God's Light
To protect myself
From uncomely thought-attacks.

3840.

I do not know
Where despair comes from,
But I do know that it destroys
Ruthlessly
My mind's freedom-smile.

3841.

Each time I offer myself
To my Lord Supreme,
He immediately blesses me
With a new promise
For His new manifestation.

3842.

God tells me that if I have
A lion-courage-heart,
Then every day He will proudly
    come
To visit me.

3843.

Compromise
Is nothing short of
False satisfaction.

3844.

O seeker,
If you truly want to be wise,
Then do not read mind-stories,
But only play heart-songs.

3845.

May my mind's inspiration-bird
And my heart's aspiration-tree
Always live together.

3846.

Everything on earth is short-lived.
My ignorance-days,
How is it that you
Do not fall into that category?

3847.

God wants me to have a purity-
    temple
Inside my mind and not inside my
    heart.
Why?
Because I already have a purity-
    temple
Inside my heart.

3848.

My soul, you have plenty of
    divinity.
How is it that I do not have
Any hunger-necessity?

3849.

My stupidity-incarnate-mind,
How is it that you so often
Dare to argue
With my Lord's Compassion-Eye
And with His Forgiveness-Heart?

3850.

If everything is said and done
With compassion, affection and
    love,
Then Heaven's earth-descent
Cannot remain a far cry.

3851.

I asked God if He could be
My Executive Director.
His immediate answer was:
"Happily and proudly, My child,
I am granting your wish."

3852.

To have an internal connection
With God's Will
Is not an impossible task.
Just apply your heart's devotion-
    magnet.

3853.

My Lord tells me to learn
Only His Heart-Songs
And not His Life-Stories.

3854.

Lord, I do not know how to thank
    You
At every moment
For what You are doing and not
    doing
To fulfil Your Mission
In and through me.

3855.

God and God's Will
Have chosen my heart
To be their most faithful follower.

3856.

O my depression-vital,
I shall prove to you
That my heart's joy
Is infinitely stronger than you are.

3857.

Every morning
My Lord enters into my heart-
    garden
And plants a new peace-tree.

3858.

Even when God is extremely busy,
He does not fail to think of me.
He sends His Compassion-Eye
And Forgiveness-Heart
To take care of my aspiration-
    heart
And dedication-life.

3859.

Lord, please make me
A supreme adorer and lover
Of each and every utterance of
    Yours.

3860.

God does not mind
If my mind does not want to be
Acquainted with God's Will,
But He does mind,
And gets extremely angry
With my heart,
When it wants to be the same.

3861.

We must always remember
That anything uninspiring
Is, indeed, a dead-end road.

3862.

Unconditionally
We must love God –
The sooner the better.

3863.

Every day, with the first rays
Of the morning sun,
I try to become closer and closer
To God's Compassion-Feet.

3864.

Each moment
Is a new
God-creation-smile.

3865.

If you want to endear yourself
To God,
Your desire-life and aspiration-life
You must give to Him
At the same time.

3866.

Desire-life leads us,
But where?
Only to the nearest graveyard!

3867.

I am absolutely sure
That the future God-Light
Is waiting to guide me and lead
    me.

3868.

My Lord's Compassion-Eye
Is the only initiation
I need.

3869.

Long ago
I gave up listening
To my mind's
Negativity-thoughts.

3870.

When you surrender yourself
To God's Will,
The Smile you receive from God
Can easily stop your sorrow-
    flooded life.

3871.

In our spiritual life,
Nothing can be more precious
Than our faith in God
And our faith in ourselves.

3872.

O seeker,
Even the morning birds
Know that they belong to God.
How is it that you do not know?

3873.

No matter how many times
God comes
To pay a visit to your human
    mind,
He is received
With a most cautious welcome.

3874.

Now that I have liberated myself
From my undisciplined days and
    nights,
My heart is sweetly drawn
To my Lord Beloved Supreme.

3875.

In my inner life,
I become much richer
Than I ever expected
By walking along the road
Of God-obedience.

3876.

Finally, my wandering mind
Has found its real home:
Silence.

3877.

O my lotus-heart, do tell me
When you are going to bloom
Beautifully,
And when you are going to
    blossom
Perfectly.

3878.

I always take
My aspiration-heart-shrine
Wherever I go,
Even when I enter into my mind's
Ignorance-cave.

3879.

Human pride
Can easily darken
The heart's
Brightest light.

3880.

The Fragrance-Heart-Smile of
    God
Every morning blesses me
Before I meditate.

3881.

He who sees the divine in
    everything
Is divinely great.
But he who sees everything as
    divine
Is supremely good.

3882.

Brave are those
Who face existence as it is.
Braver are those
Who accept the challenge to
    transform it.
Bravest are those
Who want to establish
God's permanent Victory
Inside life.

3883.

I ask my mind why it is so
    unwilling
To think of God and pray to God.
My mind says, "There is no
Particular reason.
The only thing I can think of is
    this:
I am terribly afraid of God —
Specially His Eye."

3884.

Without having a goodness-heart
    first,
We cannot grow into
A godliness-life.

3885.

"Lord, although I have failed You
Many, many times,
Please give me another chance
To love You and serve You."
In response, God gives me
An immediate embrace.

3886.

I think of
God's Victory.
God thinks of
My perfection.

3887.

God, I have only two desires:
To touch Your Forgiveness-Feet
And to claim You as my own,
Very own.

3888.

In the morning
I turn towards
God's Compassion-Eye.

3889.

In the evening
I turn towards
God's Protection-Feet.

3890.

When I look at the world,
I see the world's standard
Is too low.
I am totally disappointed.

3891.

When I look at God,
I see God's standard
Is too high.
I get terribly frightened.

3892.

Be a heart of compassion.
Humanity will sincerely
Love you.

3893.

Be a life of sacrifice.
God will immediately
Need you.

3894.

My happiness is my
God-fulfilling
Inner achievement.

3895.

Every morning
My Lord Supreme comes to me
And feeds my heart
With His Sweetness-Smiles.

3896.

Aim always
High, higher, highest
With your aspiration.

3897.

Dive always
Deep, deeper, deepest
With your eagerness-dedication.

3898.

Purity, where are you?
My mind is searching for you
Everywhere.

3899.

Security, where are you?
My heart is crying
And crying and crying
For you.

3900.

Where are the sun-smile-blossoms
Of my future life?
They are inside the Compassion-
   Heart
Of my Lord's eternal Now.

3901.

God loves us even on the days
We enjoy
Our insecurity-hearts
And impurity-minds.

3902.

Age has nothing to do
With wisdom.
Wisdom is the fragrance
Of one's inner soul-beauty.

3903.

Many highly developed souls
Have died for their beloved
   countries
Unheralded, unrecognised
And even unnoticed.

3904.

Each positive thought
Is a powerful Blessing
From our Lord Supreme.

3905.

Enthusiasm
Is an unparalleled virtue
In our inner life of aspiration
And in our outer life of
    dedication.

3906.

Enthusiasm
Is the fastest success
Of the mind.

3907.

Enthusiasm
Is the fastest progress
Of the heart.

3908.

Enthusiasm
Is the fastest satisfaction
Of life.

3909.

O my mind,
Do you really want peace?
Then shun competition-
    comparison,
World-criticism and self-criticism.

3910.

My prayers sing
For my Lord's Heart.
My songs pray
For my Lord's Feet.

3911.

How to achieve happiness?
Not by giving, not by talking,
But by being.

3912.

A doubting mind
Unmistakably means
A confusion-mart.

3913.

When God's Compassion-Eye
Scolds me,
My aspiration-heart flies
Faster than the fastest.

3914.

A friend of mine said to me:
"There was a time
When I did not care for God,
But now I am all for Him.
Why?
Because every day He feeds
My aspiration-heart
    sumptuously."

3915.

A friend of mine said to me:
"There was a time
When I immensely loved God,
But now I just hate Him,
Because He has fully fulfilled
My desire-life."

3916.

My mind's dictionary
Does not house the word
'Gratitude'.

3917.

My heart is always grateful
To God
For what it is.

3918.

O my mind,
Why do you expect
Everything from God
And nothing from yourself?

3919.

O my mind's depression,
Have you any idea
How much you have weakened
The breath of my aspiration-life?

3920.

No matter how undivine
We have become,
God's Compassion still remains
The same for us.

3921.

God, when You smile,
My whole world
Has a special meaning.
Otherwise, depression and
    frustration
Have become my roommates.

3922.

Humility is not humiliation.
No, never!
Humility is an inner light
That genuinely inspires
The rest of the divine virtues
To come to the fore
And illumine the world.

3923.

I am most sincerely
And most proudly discarding
My greatness-mind
To have a goodness-heart.

3924.

God never expects anything
From the unaspiring
Mind-students.

3925.

God expects everything,
Both in the inner world
And in the outer world,
From the aspiring heart-students.

3926.

My gratitude-heart-blossoms
My Lord treasures infinitely more
Than I can ever imagine.

3927.

My Lord tells me
That He will never pardon me
If I deliberately abandon
All my hope-dreams.

3928.

My Lord,
I want to bathe
In the Compassion-Smile of Your
    Eye
At every moment.

3929.

I need a heart
That will be marvellous
In God-qualities.

3930.

Right at the very start
Of my spiritual journey,
My aspiration-heart warned
My God-disobedience-mind.

3931.

My Lord,
I shall celebrate only one victory,
And that victory will be
My unconditional surrender
To Your Will.

3932.

God does not send invitations
To my mind,
But invites my heart quite often
To be His divine guest.

3933.

A spiritual Master can take
Even the smallness
Of a grain of sand
Most seriously
And, at the same time,
Not take the arrival of death
Seriously.

3934.

My aspiration-heart
And God's Compassion-Eye
Like to remain eternal optimists.

3935.

To me, the unwillingness
Of the mind
Is the worst torture
In my spiritual life.

3936.

Every day
I place my head and my life
On the altar
Of my Lord's Compassion infinite.

3937.

A faith-flame may be
Small in appearance,
But supremely great
In reality.

3938.

O my mind,
I shall not allow you
To end in a void.
I want you to live
In the heart of infinite Fulness.

3939.

Who wants to be a member
Of the non-accomplishment club?
Not me, not me!

3940.

The life divine
Has no room for
Why and how
In its heart.

3941.

My Lord,
I pray to You
To give me Blessings
So that I can end my life
In fulness-light
And not in an empty void.

3942.

Cry for God today,
Smile at God today,
Fly with God today,
For tomorrow never comes –
Believe me,
Never!

3943.

May my life's obedience
And my heart's gratitude
Bloom and blossom
Every single day.

3944.

It quite often happens
That my Lord's Compassion-Eye
Is struck by
Humanity's cruel criticism
And misunderstanding.

3945.

God's Heart arrives
Long before God's Feet arrive
To console the streaming tears
Of my heart.

3946.

Bury all your negativity-cynicism
Inside the dust
Beneath your own feet.

3947.

God always holds
My life's surrender-smile
Close to His own Heart.

3948.

My Lord,
You come only to go.
Please, I beg of You,
This time stay a little longer
Than ever before
To make me really happy.

3949.

O my mind's ego,
How many times I have told you,
You are no longer welcome
Inside my God-gratitude-heart!

3950.

If it is real Truth,
Then it will always remain
Fresh like the morning rose.

3951.

Every day
I want to take a new birth
With my heart's devotion-tears.

3952.

If anything remains on earth
Forever untired,
Then it is my Lord's Forgiveness-
    Feet.

3953.

God powerfully
Shakes hands with
My willingness-mind.

3954.

God proudly
Embraces
My eagerness-heart.

3955.

My Lord,
I have only one prayer:
May my aspiration-hunger
Every day increase.

3956.

May my heart-room
Remain always open
For small and great
To meet, sing and dance.

3957.

God's Compassion-Eye
Is the only thing
I see in God's creation
That remains always busy
And occupied.

3958.

God transforms
My gratitude-whispers
Into His Satisfaction-Drum-
    Sound.

3959.

If you are sincerely following
The spiritual life,
Then stop saying, "I hope."
Start saying, "I am absolutely
    certain
That I am a real instrument
Of my Lord Supreme
To manifest Him here on earth."

3960.

Nothing on earth
Is destined to last forever,
Save and except
My Lord's Love-Fountain for me.

3961.

With our outer eyes,
We see an abysmal abyss.
With our inner eye,
We can see the same thing
As beauty's rainbow-dream.

3962.

The rainbow of our inner divinity
Always rises from
Our crying and weeping hearts.

3963.

God tells me not to delay,
But to come immediately
To join His Infinity's
Vision-Manifestation-Game.

3964.

Three significant ways
My soul reveals its divinity:
Poetry, music and art.

3965.

My Lord,
Every day I wish to breathe in
Your Infinity
Inside my finite and fleeting
Heart-cries.

3966.

O my God-representative-soul-
    tree,
Please bless me
With your newness-flowers
And sweetness-fruits.

3967.

Nothing can be more inspiring,
More illumining and more
    fulfilling
Than humanity's
God-gratitude-heart-garden.

3968.

An atom of gratitude
Can unmistakably
Bring down Heaven here on earth.

3969.

Gratitude is not a mere dictionary
    word.
Gratitude is the golden link
Between man's heart and God's
    Heart.

3970.

My mind,
God alone knows
How you have become
A spirituality-authority.
To me, you are nothing but
A learned parrot.

3971.

He who has gratitude to the
    Supreme
Is bound to succeed
In pleasing the Supreme in his
    Master
In His own Way.

3972.

No matter how far away you are
From your God-realisation,
Gratitude will give you the fastest
    speed
To arrive at your Destination.

3973.

Gratitude smashes the pride
Of all the undivine qualities
That a human being
Can possibly have.

3974.

Cultivate God-gratitude,
Cultivate!
You will succeed
In the battlefield of life.

3975.

I am determined
To smash the pride
Of all the negative qualities
That torture me day in and day
    out.

3976.

A seeker who has
Gratitude-heart-blossoms
In abundant measure
Can never fail, never!

3977.

When wrong forces assail us,
We must become the living breath
Of our gratitude-heart.

3978.

Gratitude
Is our most significant
God-manifesting dream.

3979.

Let us not fail
Our Lord Beloved Supreme
In this special, very special
    incarnation.

3980.

The things that you
So eloquently utter
And so profusely advise,
You have no time to practise.
I feel sorry for you,
I really do!

3981.

If we fail God here on earth,
We shall fail Him in Heaven
And all-where.
Let us not fail Him,
Let us not fail Him!

3982.

Your inner speed
You have already shown:
Love, devotion and surrender.
Now it is time for you to show
Your outer speed:
Readiness, willingness and
    eagerness.

3983.

Let us start praying,
Meditating and self-giving
Right from this moment
For the ultimate Victory
Of our Lord Beloved Supreme.

3984.

My spiritual children
Have given me two beautiful
And powerful wings
To fly and fly
In the God-Satisfaction-Sky.

3985.

Each soulful song
Is a beautiful, fragrant flower
To illumine the seeker's heart
And purify his mind.

3986.

Now that ingratitude-height
Has become your very name,
The abysmal abyss-memory
Shall unfailingly haunt you.

3987.

In God's Heart-Garden
Are all the flowers you need
To inspire your mind
And feed your heart.

3988.

When you satisfy your own
    Master,
It is not only your Master
Who blesses you inwardly,
But also other spiritual Masters.

3989.

Your only reality is your soul,
Not your perishable
Body, vital, mind and heart.
Without your permission,
They all will leave you.

3990.

Under the influence of the
    undivine vital,
Even the heart
Can do many things wrong.
But the soul can never, never,
    never
Do anything wrong,
For the soul is a conscious
God-representative here on earth.

3991.

For the sincere seekers,
God's manifestation-creation
Is a heart-garden
Filled with thousands and
    millions
Of flowers.

3992.

God has everything brand new
Available in His Heart-Home
For the sincere seekers
To choose and take.

3993.

When I heard the Supreme's Voice
Singing Delight-Songs,
Even my stone heart melted.

3994.

My Lord,
You want me to sing
My heart-songs
Before You.
I am turning insane
With happiness and eagerness.

3995.

Every day God watches me
Affectionately and proudly
When I carry
My love-devotion-surrender
To His Peace-Altar.

3996.

I see a new world
Inside each step
That my Master takes
To lead us and guide us
Towards our Destination.

3997.

God's Compassion-Eye
And my gratitude-heart
Dream of each other
Simultaneously.

3998.

I wish to hear only one sound:
The sweetest and most profound
Soundless Sound
Of my Lord's Forgiveness-Heart.

3999.

Every day God gives me
The most beautiful flowers
And most delicious fruits
From His Light-Delight-Heart-
    Garden
To create God-hunger in me.

4000.

A God-dreamer
I was.
A God-lover
I am.
A God-server
I shall become
And forever remain.

4001.

Every single day
I wish to be hallowed
By kissing the dust
Of my Lord's
Forgiveness-Feet.

4002.

Every single day
I must cry and cry
For a God-fulfilment-heart.

4003.

The God-realisation-pinnacle-
    height
Is within the reach
Of every sincere seeker.

4004.

Every morning when I pray,
I see my heart-sky
Surrounded by rainbows.

4005.

If you go back
To your seven-year-old age,
You will see how charming,
How beautiful and how satisfying
Your life has become
In every possible way.

4006.

Prepare yourself always
For the Call
Of the Inner Pilot Supreme.

4007.

There is only one immediate
    question:
Where is God?
The immediate answer is:
God is where
My heart's love-breath is.

4008.

God blessingfully asks
Our aspiration-hearts
To watch
His world-transformation-
    Dreams.

4009.

Those who consciously and
    prayerfully
Come within the radius
Of God's Will
Will be not only protected,
But also illumined.

4010.

We can appreciate God
With our eyes,
We can appreciate God
With our hearts,
But it is only when
We appreciate God
On our knees
That we can be fully satisfied.

4011.

May my aspiration-heart
At every moment
Sing like the birds
That do not care for appreciation
And admiration.

4012.

Our hearts bloom and blossom
Most beautifully
When we unreservedly value
Others' contribution
Towards the perfection of the
    world.

4013.

God writes
Every God-lover's biography
With His Compassion-Eye-Tears.

4014.

A God-doubt-drummer
Is inconscience
Within and without.

4015.

Detachment is
Faith in God
In a very special way.

4016.

The outer history
Is based upon
Individual opinion.

4017.

The inner history
Is founded upon
The acceptance of God's Will
In God's own Way.

4018.

There was a time
When God showed me
The short success-road
In my outer life.

4019.

God is showing me now
The never-ending progress-road
In my inner life.

4020.

Attachment is a very strong
    power.
It contaminates anything
That it touches.

4021.

When I climb up
My mind-hill,
I become extremely proud of
My achievement.

4022.

When I climb up
My aspiration-mountain,
God's Pride in me
Knows no bounds.

4023.

Man's hope
Is
Sweeter than the sweetest.

4024.

God's Hope
Is
Mightier than the mightiest.

4025.

Man's hope
Flies and flies
In the sky.

4026.

God's Hope
Sings, dances and marches
Along His Eternity's Road.

4027.

Indulgence is disaster.
Unfortunately, we realise it
Too late.

4028.

So often we tell God
What to do.
To our greatest surprise,
God is unimaginably obedient.

4029.

Do not be afraid of
Tomorrow's light.
Tomorrow's light will clear
Your mind-jungle
And beautify your heart-garden.

4030.

I see no difference
Between my self-doubt
And my helplessness-life.

4031.

How I wish I could spend
My aspiration-life
Between my gratitude-heart
And God's Compassion-Eye.

4032.

My heart's aspiration-intensity
Is my life's
God-realisation-certainty.

4033.

If you want real freedom,
The freedom of the soul,
Then dive deep within.

4034.

For a desiring mind
To be free of fear
Is an impossible task.

4035.

God wants my heart
To be a self-giver
And not a world-possessor.

4036.

In the spiritual life,
Unwillingness
Is a dangerous enemy.

4037.

Man tells God,
"Perhaps You do not
Understand me."

4038.

God tells man,
"I shall understand you
Only when you really need Me."

4039.

Every day my Lord Supreme
Gives me the opportunity
To walk along a never-ending
Progress-satisfaction-road.

4040.

We must develop a new way
Of looking at things
To enjoy
The beauty of newness
And to become
The fragrance of fulness.

4041.

When the desire-bird
Tries to fly forward,
It flies backward.

4042.

The aspiration-bird
Flies only forward.
While flying forward,
It sees the beckoning Hands
Of God.

4043.

The aspiring heart
Wants to climb
And reach Heaven.

4044.

The desiring mind
Wants not only to reach
Heaven,
But to go beyond –
Without climbing.

4045.

Not where *could* I go,
But where *should* I go,
If not only to my
Lord Supreme?

4046.

To sanctify my life,
I must crucify
My ego-king-mind
First.

4047.

Be careful of
Your world-doubting mind!
It can easily betray you
As well.

4048.

God's dear son
Is
Sincerity.

4049.

God's favourite son
Is
Purity.

4050.

God's perfect son
Is
Divinity.

4051.

Any action
Without devotion
Is an emptiness-failure.

4052.

Insecurity
Has the capacity
To successfully hide pride.

4053.

An emancipation-life
Is the result of God's
Unconditional Compassion-Eye.

4054.

A divine surrender
Is
A supreme freedom.

4055.

No, not he,
But God's Compassion-Eye
Has snapped
His desire-attachment-life.

4056.

To surrender unconditionally
Is to swim across
The Ocean of Delight.

4057.

A positive determination
Can easily keep us away
From the despair-snare.

4058.

Do we actually sleep?
No, we just roam in our mind's
Desire-jungle.

4059.

God's Smile
Is my
Heart-garden.

4060.

God's Eye
Is my
Heart-gardener.

4061.

O seeker,
God wants to be reborn
In your heart-garden.
This time do not resist!

4062.

My mind is not happy
When it has to touch
God's Feet.
It is happy only when
It can touch God's Head and
    Hands.

4063.

My heart is happy only when
It can touch, feel and become
The dust of God's Feet.

4064.

May my God-worshipping
    devotion
Not look back –
Even for a fleeting second.

4065.

My Lord, do lead me
From my own fearful shadows
To Your blessingful Light.

4066.

Each gratitude-song
Is a new God-growing plant
On earth.

4067.

God always keeps
My prayer-life
And
My meditation-life
Under His golden Canopy.

4068.

God wants me only
To pray and meditate.
He will gladly
Do the broadcasting.

4069.

For my joy and satisfaction,
I must close down
My unwillingness-mind-business.
Because of it I have become
A helpless
Peace-bliss-satisfaction-beggar.

4070.

No more self-doubt-clouds
Can wrap
My morning prayer-hour.

4071.

God lovingly comes down
To share His Smile
With man.

4072.

Man fearfully goes up
To share his tears
With God.

4073.

Man is a pendulum
Between his soul-smiles
And his heart-tears.

4074.

Devotion
Is the secret key
For God-realisation-acceleration.

4075.

The smiles of my soul
Tell me
That my Lord Supreme
Is sleeplessly
With me.

4076.

The tears of my heart
Tell me
That my Beloved Supreme
Is breathlessly
For me.

4077.

A constantly climbing
Aspiration-heart
I need.

4078.

A constantly spreading
Dedication-life
I need.

4079.

When my heart becomes
Only a God-devotion-choice,
My life becomes
A sweetness-voice.

4080.

Definitely
God has given us
His own Boat,
And that Boat will not arrive
    empty
At the Golden Shore.

4081.

Once upon a time,
My life was light-flooded,
Delight-flooded
And divinity-flooded.
But now those days
Are buried in oblivion.
Alas, alas!

4082.

As long as you are walking along
The spirituality-road,
Feel that you are doing
Absolutely the right thing.

4083.

Go forward!
Kick aside the past
That gave you self-doubt
And God-doubt.

4084.

Go forward!
Go forward with the foundation
Of the past
That gave you simplicity,
Sincerity, humility and purity.

4085.

Alas, instead of conquering
Your insecurity, impurity
And pride,
You have taken them as your brave
And faithful soldiers
To fight for you.

4086.

Anything the past taught you
That is good, divine, illumining
And fulfilling,
Bring back and treasure.

4087.

If you feel the spiritual life
Was a great mistake,
Remember, there is a wide, vast
And open world
Where you can enjoy yourself once
    more
In your own way.

4088.

Multiply, multiply and multiply
The soulfulness and fruitfulness
Of your golden past.

4089.

Forget, forget and forget –
The sooner the better –
The sadness
Of your past failure-life.

4090.

There is not a single day
When spiritual Masters
Do not use occult power
In the inner world
For the betterment and
    enlightenment
Of mankind.

4091.

Thousands of years ago
The spiritual figures
Of the hoary past
Tried to transform the world.
They did not fully succeed.
Now it is your supreme task.
It is your time to continue the
    game
And complete the game
Most gloriously.

4092.

A God-worshipping prayer-song
Of the Mother Earth
Immensely increases the beauty,
Fragrance and delight
Of the Father Heaven.

4093.

Instead of making friends with
The goddess of sleep,
Make friends with
The god of dynamism
To expedite the world's
Godward journey.

4094.

When I meditate
Deep in the inmost recesses
Of my heart,
God's divine Joy and His supreme
    Pride
Know no bounds.

4095.

When a spiritual Master
    meditates,
Does humanity know
Where his consciousness is?
Will humanity ever know
What he is doing
For the betterment of humanity?
No, never!

4096.

Even in the hustle and bustle of
    life,
A spiritual Master has the capacity
To converse
With the Absolute Lord Supreme
For the full manifestation of His
    Light
Here on earth.

4097.

There was a time
When God's Way was the only way
For you.
Now you have ten ways.
Alas, alas, what has become
Of you?

4098.

God is begging and begging us
To go back to our childhood life
When we were totally ignorant
Of doubt, suspicion, negativity
And cynicism.

4099.

Pray and meditate,
Meditate and pray
If you want to go
Happily and proudly
To any corner
Of the delight-flooded Heaven.

4100.

No more fear and doubt
For him who has become
A conscious and self-giving
    instrument
Of God's Will.

4101.

An Avatar is He in whose inner life
God enjoys
His universal Sweetness
And His transcendental Newness.

4102.

Self-discovery makes you one
With the joy of God the Creator
And with the sorrow of God the
    creation.

4103.

Only when I dive deep within,
I see that my Lord's Compassion-
    Eye
Is the beauty
Of an ever-increasing Infinity.

4104.

How I wish I could write
My heart-diary
With my God-invocation-tears.

4105.

Every morning
I till my aspiration-ground-life
With my devotion-heart-plough.

4106.

My self-giving life to God,
To please God in His own Way,
Never needs ceremonies.

4107.

My Lord Supreme,
Out of Your infinite Bounty,
You are holding my life's
Surrender-breath
Close-closer-closest
To Your Heart.

4108.

May my life-boat every day
Ply between
My obedience-mind-shore
And
My gratitude-heart-shore.

4109.

One thing that is essential
On any spiritual path
Is perseverance.

4110.

I do not allow anybody
To intimidate
My determination.

4111.

I do not allow anybody
To give a discourse
On self-indulgence.

4112.

Disobedience is terribly afraid
Of one thing:
Catastrophe.

4113.

God read my negativity-mind.
Therefore
He did not care
To bless my mind.

4114.

God read my surrender-heart.
Therefore
He was all eager
To bless my heart.

4115.

When I am my gratitude-heart,
God blesses me
With His amplitude-Smiles.

4116.

When divided minds
Become united,
God immediately sheds
Tears of delight.

4117.

The title of his mind's
Frustration-lecture:
I cannot go on this way
Anymore.

4118.

The Master's body
May not be everywhere,
But his blessingful eyes
Are everywhere.

4119.

God tells me
That if I want to remain
A choice instrument of His,
Then He will not allow me to
    enjoy
Any prayer or meditation-
    vacation.

4120.

A suspicion-mind
Will never feel
The real happiness
Of life.

4121.

What is suspicion,
If not a voracious devourer
Of God's Compassion-Light?

4122.

O my mind,
Do not try to explain the truth.
You will gain nothing.

4123.

Only a genuine God-seeker
Can compel destiny
To surrender.

4124.

I always keep
My gratitude-heart-door
Wide open.

4125.

Is there any hour,
Any minute, any second
When God's Compassion-Eye-
    Feast
Is not needed by humanity?

4126.

I have been living for years
On my hope-beauty
And on my promise-fragrance.

4127.

The mind that does not want
To understand,
The heart that does not want
To love,
The life that does not want
To care
Will never be able to arrive
At the Golden Shore.

4128.

The satisfaction of life divine
Lives far beyond
The horizon.

4129.

Because of a devotee's immense
And intense love,
God manifests Himself on earth.

4130.

The unaspiring mind
Can never grasp
The Infinite.

4131.

The aspiring heart
Can not only grasp
But also clasp
The Infinite.

4132.

A life of humility
Is the abode
Of teeming virtues.

4133.

Every day I live in the heart
Of my life's
Transformation-hope.

4134.

The spiritual Masters
Descend on earth's stage
To remove all its miseries.

4135.

May my heart be strengthened
Every day
By the inner assurance
That I shall definitely realise God
In this lifetime.

4136.

The seeker's purity-heart
Is his life's
God-satisfaction-joy.

4137.

God's Compassion-flooded Eye
Is beckoning me.
I cannot and I shall not fail.

4138.

My only desire
Was
To realise God.

4139.

My only desire
Is
To become another God.

4140.

My only desire
Will be
To make every human being on
    earth
Realise God.

4141.

There was a time
When he was drowning
In worldliness.
Now he is desperately longing
For aloofness.

4142.

There shall come a day
When he will realise that
Neither worldliness nor aloofness
Can make him truly happy.
To be happy, what he needs
Is a oneness-heart.

4143.

The real seeker
Does not want to know
What tomorrow will bring him.
He is only concerned about one
    thing:
What he can do to heighten
The standard of humanity.

4144.

God is fond of those
Who sincerely
Love Him.

4145.

God is more fond of those
Who sincerely and prayerfully
Love Him.

4146.

God is most fond of those
Who sincerely, prayerfully
And self-givingly
Love Him.

4147.

Faith is what tells me
That God is lovable, approachable
And attainable.

4148.

Do you think that God
Will indefinitely wait for you
In the background
Of your desire-life?
No, never!

4149.

When inspiration-tide ebbs,
No human being
Can achieve anything laudable.

4150.

When you are grounded
In the God-obedience-soil,
Then there is nothing
That you cannot accomplish.

4151.

My Lord,
May I have the capacity
To congratulate
Each and every human being
On their each and every success,
No matter how trivial it is?

4152.

O seeker,
Bring back your devotion
Once more
To increase the beauty and light
Of your lacklustre heart.

4153.

My seeker-friend,
How can you succeed
In your outer life
And how can you proceed
In your inner life
If you do not keep
Our Lord Beloved Supreme
All the time in mind?

4154.

We are rank fools
If we always take
God's Compassion-Flood
For granted.

4155.

How is it that
We do not take advantage
Of our wisdom:
On our aspiration-road,
There is no speed-limit?

4156.

Our inner hunger
Can be satisfied
Only by God's Satisfaction-Smile.

4157.

I must bring back
My prayer-heart
And
My aspiration-breath
To be once more
A choice instrument
Of my Lord Supreme.

4158.

O my mind,
How is it that you
Do not believe me
When I tell you
That you were born
To do something divinely great
For God?

4159.

O my heart,
It pains me deeply
When you do not see
Eye to eye with me:
You were born to do something
Supremely good
For the betterment
Of the entire world.

4160.

Do you want to be happy,
Really happy?
Then just think
Of your outer life less,
A little less,
And live more,
A little more,
In your inner life.

4161.

Fate is not indomitable,
But faith is –
Also indispensable.

4162.

Give up once and for all
Treasuring ignorance.
To your great surprise,
Ignorance will also
Do the same.

4163.

My eyes tell me
That my obstacles
On the way
Are insurmountable.

4164.

My heart tells me
That on the way
There is no obstacle
That cannot be bravely challenged
And defied.

4165.

With my book-knowledge,
I may go to the other end
Of the world.

4166.

With my heart-wisdom,
I can unmistakably bring
The whole world to me,
Plus its Creator.

4167.

If I really obey God's Will,
Then the whole world
Will one day gladly approve
Of my inner and outer actions,
Plus derive benefit from them.

4168.

Alas, I cannot imagine
How my own creation-thoughts
Can stand in my way
All the time
When I prayerfully and soulfully
Make attempts to arrive
At God's Heart-Garden-Gate.

4169.

I prayerfully gave my heart
To God.
God immediately said to me:
"Claim My Love as your own
As much as you want to."

4170.

I reluctantly gave my mind
To God.
God said to me:
"I am gladly accepting you,
My child, to tame you
And to please Me eventually
In My own Way."

4171.

If your aspiration-heart
Is wanting in tears,
How can you even imagine
Running towards God?

4172.

What is your heart for,
If it is not solely meant
To love God the Creator?

4173.

What is your life for,
If it is not solely meant
To serve God the creation?

4174.

Awaken your mind
To appreciate sincerely
The magnificent beauty
Of the world.

4175.

Widen your heart
To include the four corners
Of the globe
In your own life.

4176.

O my mind,
How do you say
That you have love
In abundant measure,
When you do not have even an iota
Of forgiveness-capacity in you?

4177.

Do I love God enough?
According to God,
I do.
But my heart says:
"Definitely not!"

4178.

The outer beauty
Grows old,
But the inner beauty
Has made friends
With Immortality.

4179.

Unlike the outer hero,
The inner hero
Is always supremely humble.

4180.

We must defy the buffets
Of world-suspicion
If we want to offer
Something sublimely good
To humanity.

4181.

I do not want
The hour of power,
But the love
Of the entire day.

4182.

Adamantine will-power
Is what we need
If we really want to please God
In His own Way.

4183.

The depression of the mind
Has the power to kill
All our divine virtues.

4184.

Not my sorrowful eyes,
But my tearful heart
Has freed me
From my mind-prison.

4185.

After having a long, beautiful
And soulful meditation,
When I go to sleep,
My Inner Pilot watches me
With utmost Compassion-Light-
    Delight.

4186.

O pleasure-enjoyer,
Can you not see
The quagmire of the mind
Is chasing you?

4187.

Each prayerful and soulful
    moment
Embodies Eternity's tears
And Infinity's smiles.

4188.

I need a heart
That will not only make me see,
But also make me become
Divinity's Reality.

4189.

Awake! Awake!
O my body, awake!
You know your soul
Is waiting for you
With a morning rose
To greet you.

4190.

God wants me to walk only
On my heart-road,
Which He Himself has paved.

4191.

What I need is
A life-evolution
And not
A mind-revolution.

4192.

My Lord,
I may pray to You for retirement
From my earthly activities,
But I shall never, never pray to You
For my heart's gratitude-
    retirement.

4193.

Alas, how stupid we are!
We cannot appreciate
The illumination-music
Of the Universal Silence.

4194.

May my mind
Every day
Set new records
In the God-given sincerity-
    contest.

4195.

May my heart
Every day
Set new records
In the God-given purity-contest.

4196.

May my life
Every day
Set new records
In the God-given surrender-
    contest.

4197.

Everything we desperately need
In the outer life
Breathes secretly
In our inner life.

4198.

A seeker without a lofty vision
Is in no way better than
An ordinary human being.

4199.

A seeker with a supreme vision
Is, indeed,
A planetary citizen
Of the world.

4200.

If my heart becomes
A fountain of goodness,
Then my mind
Will invariably become
A mountain of greatness.

4201.

Today I call it
My heart-aspiration.
Tomorrow that very thing
I shall call
My God-possession-satisfaction.

4202.

There is only one journey —
The perpetual
God-fulfilment-journey.

4203.

If the outer prosperity
Is not founded upon
The inner divinity,
Then the outer prosperity
Is nothing short of
An added burden
In the spiritual life.

4204.

The more I expand
My endurance-life,
The more I receive from God
His Assurance-Delight
In my self-discovery.

4205.

God accepts our blunders
Unconditionally,
But our mind enjoys a proud
    hesitation
In believing it.

4206.

My Lord Supreme tells me
That what I need
Is faith-expansion
And not faith-expression,
Not to speak of faith-
    demonstration.

4207.

When we tell God
That we love Him only,
God in silence speaks:
"A real joke."

4208.

Since God is omnipresent,
Omniscient and omnipotent,
Can He not take care of you?
He easily can.
But you have to give Him the
    chance.

4209.

When God tells us
That He always thinks of us,
The divine in us says,
"It is absolutely true."
The human in us says,
"Possible."
The animal in us says,
"Ridiculous, absurd."

4210.

If we love God only,
Then our progress will definitely
    be
Faster than the fastest,
Far beyond our imagination's
    flight.

4211.

True, we may have fear, doubt,
Jealousy, insecurity and
    ignorance,
But one thing we must never
    forget:
Inside all our imperfections
The Compassion-Eye
Of our Lord Supreme resides.

4212.

O truth-seeker and God-lover,
Always remember:
What your heart needs
Is God's Love.
What your life needs
Is God's Compassion.

4213.

We invariably see
A yawning gulf
When we compare
Your molehill-life
With your Himaloy-high
Preachings.

4214.

If we really love God only,
We will have no time
To look around to see
Who is better and who is worse.

4215.

If we really love God only,
Then we shall work only for God
In our aspiration-world
And in our dedication-world,
And our only desire
Will be to please God
In God's own Way.

4216.

Each spiritual Master can write
    down
Not thousands, but millions of
    pages
Of his heart-crying
And soul-smiling stories.

4217.

The inner life of each
God-realised soul
God's own Heart-Breath treasures.

4218.

God the Beggar
Comes to my stupidity-mind.
God the Emperor
Invites my wisdom-heart.

4219.

No matter what you have done
For the world,
Humanity will say:
"Nothing. You have done
    nothing.
We expected much, much, much
    more
From you."

4220.

Even if you have not finished
God's task,
God will say: "My child,
You have done infinitely more
Than I expected."

4221.

To deliberately deceive your
    Master
Is to become
A distasteful disgrace-life.

4222.

While you are praying,
While you are meditating,
You are bound to get God-
    Messages,
Once you become totally
    conscious
Of your inner life.

4223.

Your soul is dreaming, dreaming
And dreaming
To give you God-Messages.
But alas,
How often you turn a deaf ear!

4224.

You may not believe it,
But it is absolutely true
That you are afraid of
Your soul's messages.
You feel your soul's messages
Will be impossible for you to
    execute
Here on earth.

4225.

Is there anybody on earth
Who can say
That he has never disobeyed
His soul's will?

4226.

O my mind,
Because you are heartless,
You have lost everyone,
Including God,
The Fountain-Delight.

4227.

As long as you have
    embarrassment,
Hatred and fear in your nature,
God-realisation will remain
A far cry.

4228.

You may think that your Master
Is strict, very strict,
But just enter into the inner
    world.
Then what will you see?
You will see that God
Is infinitely stricter
With your Master.

4229.

A God-realised soul receives
God's sleepless, thunderous
    Command
With divine pride.

4230.

My Lord, do make me
Always worthy
Of Your Commands and
    Demands.

4231.

I know, I know,
My Lord's Command is flooded
With Affection,
Sweetness and Fondness.

4232.

My Lord Supreme
Never asks me,
"My child,
Do you think you can?"
He always tells me,
"Just do it!"

4233.

On very rare occasions,
When I ask my Lord Supreme,
"My Lord, is it Your Request?"
He immediately tells me,
"No, My son,
This is My Command Absolute."

4234.

When you regularly practise
Clever deceptions,
Your Master becomes
A helpless victim
To your ruthless torture.

4235.

When you enter into
God's Heart-Temple,
What does God do?
He does only one thing:
He begs you and begs you
Only to smile.

4236.

Believe me, O seeker,
When you smile,
All your negativity-poison
    disappears
In the twinkling of an eye.

4237.

Believe me, O seeker,
When you give a soulful smile to
    God,
You get the strength of ten lions,
Roaring and roaring to devour
Your depression-frustration.

4238.

God tells us that when we do not
Prayerfully and soulfully smile
At Him,
Then we are third-class
Or even no-class seekers.
But when we give Him a prayerful
And soulful smile,
Then immediately we become
His first-class disciples.

4239.

O vital, just look in the mirror
And smile and smile and smile.
This is the spiritually sick seeker's
Best medicine.

4240.

You may think that you do not
    have
An iota of haughtiness.
Just dive deep within.
To your deep surprise,
You will see haughtiness in your
    mind
In abundant measure.

4241.

When you smile and smile
In all sincerity,
Soulfully and prayerfully,
Lo and behold,
Your haughtiness has
    disappeared.

4242.

In how many ways
You have exploited
The compassion-flooded heart
Of your Master,
God alone knows!

4243.

You have no idea
How easily and how effectively
You can get rid of your worst foe:
Despair.
Smile, prayerfully smile,
Smile, soulfully smile,
Smile, self-givingly smile.

4244.

If your smile comes from
The very depth
Of your aspiration-heart,
Then definitely it can devour
All the negativity of your mind.

4245.

I assure you,
If you think you have
A number one enemy,
Then it is your pride
And nothing else.

4246.

Look at your pride.
It has made you utterly helpless.
When you say something
In a positive way,
Out of nowhere pride appears.
When you say something
In a negative way,
Again out of nowhere pride
    appears.
Alas, how helpless you are.

4247.

It is only our prayers and
    meditations
That can tame the circus animals
Of our life:
Pride and haughtiness.

4248.

O seeker,
Whether you are first-class
Or third-class,
Keep pride always under
Your immediate control.

4249.

Proudly you quote
From the ancient scriptures.
Secretly you vote
For ignorance-night.

4250.

Is there anybody on earth
Who is not inwardly,
If not outwardly proud of his
    existence?
Either negatively
He is proud of his existence,
Or positively
He is proud of his existence.

4251.

My Lord Supreme
Has repeatedly told me
That of all our undivine qualities,
Our pride is undoubtedly and
    absolutely
The worst.

4252.

Alas, instead of playing
The oneness-heart-game,
We enjoy playing daily
Either the division-game
Or the comparison-game.

4253.

How can we smash our pride,
How?
We can smash our pride
When we see and feel deep within
The existence of beauty's
Oneness-heart-garden.

4254.

If you express your pride
In season and out of season —
How great you are, how good you
    are —
To me, you are enjoying foolishly
A slow poison.

4255.

Soulful, devotional singing
Is, indeed, a part of our deep
And real meditation.

4256.

The more we misuse and enjoy
Our outer freedom,
The sooner we dig our own graves.

4257.

O seeker,
Always take your spiritual life
With utmost seriousness.
If not, God's Golden Boat
Is not meant for you.

4258.

May I become
The delight
Of my God-surrender-hour.

4259.

Right now
God does not expect from me
A perfection-life.
He expects from me
Only an aspiration-heart.

4260.

When our life's enthusiasm dies,
The blue bird in our heart-sky
Stops flying.

4261.

O gossip-spreading mind,
Your untold punishment-days
Are fast approaching.

4262.

To me,
An unwillingness-mind
Is, indeed,
A ruthless torture.

4263.

Each day
We can have a new heart
With God-satisfying melodies.

4264.

Heaven wants peace and has
    peace.
Earth thinks
It can manage somehow
Without peace.

4265.

What does ego
Actually want?
It wants only praise
And adulation –
Nothing else.

4266.

God's Compassion-Eye
And my heart-tears
Live together.

4267.

Eventually,
Somehow God's Justice-Light
Catches us.

4268.

May my aspiration-heart-door
Remain open
To all God-children
All the time.

4269.

When I pray,
My dear Lord Supreme
Is within my earshot.

4270.

When I meditate,
My sweet Lord Supreme
Is within my eyeshot.

4271.

When I desire,
My Lord Supreme
Is nowhere to be heard
And nowhere to be seen.

4272.

The souls that are speeding
   towards
God-manifestation
Are the chosen God-
   representatives
On earth.

4273.

Man betrays God
Again and again.
Yet God gives man
Chance after chance
To give up his betrayal-nature.

4274.

Negativity comes
From the darkness-mind
And returns also
To the darkness-mind.

4275.

The excuses
Of our clever mind
Can never satisfy God.

4276.

My Lord,
I do not want to know
The Heights of Your Will
And
The Depths of Your Will.
I just would like to be one
With Your Will.

4277.

Each soul has
A special fragrance-light
To inundate the aspiration-world.

4278.

May my mind's willingness
And my heart's eagerness
Forever remain invincible.

4279.

I am not only hopeful,
But also confident
That one day
God's Light divine
Will illumine my mind-jungle
At His choice Hour.

4280.

No power on earth
Can dare to challenge
God's Compassion-Fulfilment-
    Hour.

4281.

When I am in
A divine consciousness,
I see and feel
That even God's Justice-Light-
    Mind
Is sweeter than the sweetest.

4282.

In each and every seeker's life,
Doubt-demolition
Is of utmost necessity.

4283.

O stupid human mind,
Opportunity is not for parade,
But to take full advantage of.

4284.

If your heart swims
In the sea of devotion,
Then your mind cannot have
A dull moment.

4285.

O my mind,
Let us sincerely inspire
Each other
At every moment.

4286.

O my heart,
Let us soulfully aspire together
For God-realisation.

4287.

O my life,
Let us self-givingly
Serve God together.

4288.

When God comes and knocks
At your heart-door,
Your hesitation is the beginning
Of your self-destruction.

4289.

My heart tells my mind
That it most sincerely
Loves my mind.
But my mind
Never believes.

4290.

My heart lovingly tells my mind
A few inspiring things.
But my mind
Immediately rejects.

4291.

The money-hungry mind
And
The God-hungry heart
Remain perfect strangers
To each other.

4292.

God values the smile-beauty
Of our oneness-heart
More than we can ever imagine.

4293.

Each good thought
Is, indeed, a special blessing
From Heaven.

4294.

Do not escape
The mind's battlefield.
God wants you to be
The victor supreme.

4295.

God needs
My immediate availability,
And not my capacity.

4296.

God does not need
My mind's self-styled
Rich capacities.

4297.

To fear God's Eye
Is to become a member
Of the mind's stupidity-club.

4298.

I sincerely welcome humiliation,
If needed
For my perfection-life.

4299.

O seeker,
Your God-necessity
Must defy
All your mind-barriers.

4300.

The more I am sincere,
The clearer it becomes to me
That I speak of God
For my own glorification
And not
For God's Glorification
And Satisfaction.

4301.

When we follow
Our inner guidance,
We truly feel
The Breath of God's Love.

4302.

Surrender to God's Will.
God will transform
Your loneliness
Into His complete Fulness.

4303.

To cover the full distance
Of desire-life
Is, indeed, a ridiculous
And absurd task.

4304.

The mind has to be
Totally flexible
To abide by God's Will.

4305.

Self-doubt
Dwarfs
Our inner heights.

4306.

Jealousy-indulgence
Is a most destructive
Inner ailment.

4307.

Art
Gives joy
To my searching eye.

4308.

Poetry
Gives joy
To my crying heart.

4309.

Music
Gives joy
To my dreaming soul.

4310.

A self-giving seeker
Knows no limits
In his goodness-attainment.

4311.

The heart that loves
Is as beautiful, fresh,
Charming and inspiring
As a morning rose.

4312.

Inner freedom will shine
Bright, brighter, brightest
When we stop singing
"My" and "mine" songs.

4313.

My Lord,
May I be blessed by You
Every morning
With a rocket-aspiration-height.

4314.

O world, believe me,
In so many ways
I am trying to love you,
Serve you and please you.
Alas, I never succeed.

4315.

To please ourselves,
We use our hearts
To praise
God's Compassion-Height.

4316.

To please ourselves,
We use our minds
To blame
God's Justice-Light.

4317.

My purity-heart
Is God's
Smile-Beauty.

4318.

When my heart is empty
Of aspiration-cries,
I am forced to become
A friend of empty days
And empty nights.

4319.

My God-adoration-bird
Has God-charming
And God-pleasing wings.

4320.

Be a Divinity-lover
Before you become
A humanity-server.

4321.

With secret steps
I enter into my Lord's
Sacred Heart-Room.

4322.

God-discovery
Is Infinity's
Delight-festival.

4323.

He is at once
A visible student-mind
And
An invisible teacher-heart.

4324.

God-discovery
Is at once the Way
And the Goal.

4325.

How can you be
A God-intoxicated singer
Without singing devotion-songs?

4326.

My God-dream-heart
Brings me
Closer than the closest
To God's Heart.

4327.

My God-expectation-temptation
Takes me
Farther than the farthest
From God's Feet.

4328.

Where the heart's eagerness
Is strong, very strong,
Life's obstacles
Are weak, very weak.

4329.

The God-believer in you
Deliberately wants to remain
A perfect stranger
To your mind's counterfeit
    sincerity.

4330.

You force yourself
To swim in a sea of tears
When you bring your heart
To God
With counterfeit devotion.

4331.

My God-devotion-heart
Does not need
Any God-existence-life-proof
On earth.

4332.

We do know
That it is very unpleasant
To work with doubts, fears,
Worries and anxieties,
But alas, we do not know
Why we continue.

4333.

Heaven smiles
And smiles
At my ever-blossoming
Heart.

4334.

As we carry
Perfect heart-melodies,
Even so
We must endeavour to carry
Perfect mind-melodies.

4335.

Insecurity disappears
The moment the light of the soul
Enters into the heart.

4336.

An unaspiring mind
Cannot house supernal ideals —
No, not even lofty ideas.

4337.

The unaspiring mind
May not know
Or even may not want to know
That it weakens
The aspiring heart.

4338.

The mind never thinks
That the heart also can have
A way of its own.

4339.

Heaven laughs
And laughs
At my arrogance-stubbornness-
   mind.

4340.

Never allow your doubting mind
To shatter
Your faith in humanity.

4341.

Ever examine the aspiring heart.
Its self-giving
Will not only surprise you,
But also inspire you
To become
A good citizen of the world.

4342.

My Lord,
May Your blessingful Choice
Be my immediate voice.

4343.

Every morning
My God-obedience-heart
And my God-service-life
I carry and place
At the Feet
Of my Lord Beloved Absolute
   Supreme.

4344.

Blunders do not dare
To touch me
When my life clings
To God's Feet.

4345.

The God-reluctance-mind
Is
Inhuman.

4346.

My prayerful breath,
With quenchless thirst,
Clasps my Lord's
Blessingful Feet.

4347.

My soulful breath,
With multiplying tears,
Washes my Lord's
Bountiful Feet.

4348.

Peace-manifestation on earth
Is a unique
Dream-joy-creation.

4349.

My faith
In God's Forgiveness
Is my firmly rooted happiness.

4350.

There is every likelihood
That a computer-mind
And confusion-life
Will collide, clash
And crash together.

4351.

If you are a God-dreamer,
Then at every moment
Hope will blossom
Inside your heart-garden.

4352.

God tells me
That He has watched my life
Very carefully for a very long time.
Now He wants me to play with
    Him
His Dream-blossoming Reality-
    Game.

4353.

God is always ready
To row your boat,
But alas, you are not available.

4354.

A major change
You want in your life?
Then increase
Your God-surrender-eagerness
At every moment.

4355.

O seeker,
Self-doubt has blighted your
    mind.
Out of sheer embarrassment,
Your poor soul has gone into
    hiding.

4356.

Sometimes I wonder
If this world of ours
Will ever be ready
For the descent of peace.

4357.

May my disobedience-mind
    disappear
With the break
Of my heart's dawn.

4358.

Each heart-boat has to leave
The earth-bound moorings
To arrive at Heaven's Shore.

4359.

My heart's gratitude-tears
Are only for the Forgiveness-Feet
Of my Lord Beloved Supreme.

4360.

God's Compassion-Eye
Is blessingfully and sleeplessly
    ready
To console our broken hearts.

4361.

When my willingness-mind
And my eagerness-heart
Sit at God's Feet,
I swim and swim
In the ecstasy-sea.

4362.

As a humanity-server,
Alas, my eagerness
Is deplorable.

4363.

As a Divinity-lover,
May my sleepless eagerness
Forever last.

4364.

God the Justice
And
God the Compassion
Always consult each other
Before they execute anything.

4365.

Alas, how many hours a day
I spend in begging my mind
To love my heart!

4366.

I must never, never
Follow the footsteps
Of my negativity-mind.

4367.

Every day God whispers
His Transcendental Truth,
And every day
Humanity rejects it.

4368.

The Boatman
Devotedly loves
The life-river.

4369.

My life-river-boat and I
Prayerfully and proudly treasure
Our Boatman.

4370.

My Lord,
Your very Glance
Is my delight-thrill.

4371.

The moment I look
At my Master's compassion-eye,
I return
To my Eternity's Heart-Home.

4372.

I know,
My God-possession-disease
Can be cured
Only by God-Compassion-
    Medicine.

4373.

I have stopped
Giving ignorance joy.
Therefore, ignorance
Has left me for good.

4374.

The best eyewitness
Of God's Compassion-Eye
Is my heart's cry.

4375.

My Lord tells me
That I must feel every day
An inner cry
For an outer change.

4376.

God kindles
My heart-lamp
To transform it
Into His own Heart-Lamb.

4377.

God tells me
That He is really tired of watching
Cosmic tragedies.
God wants to enjoy
Cosmic comedies
For a change.

4378.

If we do not kneel
At God's Throne,
We shall remain
Ignorance-intoxicated.

4379.

God blessingfully comes to me
And my heart
To show us His Infinity's
Peace-Horizon.

4380.

God's Peace-Heart
Welcomes all –
The higher than the highest
And
The lower than the lowest
Human beings.

4381.

What we need
Is an ever-transcending progress
And not a fixed
Himalayan height-progress.

4382.

The unforgivable boldness
Of the mind
Does not deny,
Does not apologise.

4383.

May my gratitude-heart-flower
Remain available
Only at the Feet
Of my Lord Supreme.

4384.

My heart is so grateful to God
For asking my soul
To give my heart spiritual lessons
Every morning.

4385.

Alas, God Himself
Comes to my mind
To teach every morning,
But my mind refuses to learn.

4386.

Is the world so unbearable?
No!
What we need is only
A little more love
For the world.

4387.

God's every
Whisper-Request
Saddens
My aspiration-heart.

4388.

God's every
Thunder-Command
Gladdens, illumines
And fulfils my entire being.

4389.

Only inside the heart
Of silence-depth
Resides Heaven's starry sky.

4390.

Desire-forest
Cleverly tempts
Humanity's mind.

4391.

Aspiration-mountain
Smilingly inspires
Humanity's heart.

4392.

Just a sweet whisper
From my compassion-soul
Has saved my life
A great many times
From grave dangers.

4393.

There was a time
When I enjoyed being
A God-Compassion-seeker.

4394.

Now I enjoy myself
By becoming
A God-Compassion-Smile-
    devourer.

4395.

When my expectation-mind
Loves God,
It is sheer torture.

4396.

When my surrender-heart
Loves God,
It is all rapture.

4397.

My Lord,
Every morning I need
Your special Protection
To discontinue my friendship
With ignorance-night.

4398.

My Lord,
My difficulty is this:
I know You will not forget
Every morning to wake me up,
But will I respond
To Your Compassion-flooded
    Call?

4399.

My gratitude-heart to God
Is the only thing
That gives my soul
Boundless joy and pride.

4400.

Alas, he is such a fool
That he confines God
Only to his Master.

4401.

My mind has been ruling my life
For a long time.
I am begging and begging
My illumination-soul
To take over.

4402.

Doubt-fighting
Is, indeed,
An honourable and admirable
    task.

4403.

Every day my soul comes
To my heart
With the astonishing beauty
Of a new dream.

4404.

Opportunities want to bloom
Here, there and everywhere.
Alas, we give them no chance.

4405.

May my
Unwillingness-mind-bank
Immediately go bankrupt.

4406.

O doubting world,
When I talk about God-
    manifestation,
There is a no-nonsense objective
Behind it.

4407.

Each aspiring seeker knows
The value
Of a non-partition-life.

4408.

What I already have
Is a God-certified heart.
How I wish to have
A God-certified mind, too!

4409.

God's Patience
Is His Eternity's
Full-time task.

4410.

God's special
Love-Message-Light
Is only for God-surrendered souls.

4411.

How stupid the human mind is!
It does not mind dancing
With brooding disasters.

4412.

Imagination-manifestation
Is the beauty
Of poetry's breath.

4413.

With comatose aspiration
And dedication,
Nobody will be able to arrive
At God's Delight-flooded Palace.

4414.

Today's compromise-satisfaction
Can give birth to
Tomorrow's competition-rivalry.

4415.

Alas, the fear of constant failure
Has paralysed
His inspiration-mind
And aspiration-heart.

4416.

There was a time when I was
An incessant
God-talker-mind.
Now I have become
A sleepless and breathless
God-lover-heart.

4417.

O unaspiring mind,
Poor God expects only
    pleasantness
From you,
And nothing else.

4418.

Today's divinity-torn heart
Will give birth to
Tomorrow's divinity-born life.

4419.

Humility and pride
Never believe
In friendship.

4420.

A mind of wisdom-light
Does not believe in binding
The world-citizens.

4421.

My mind, everybody sees and feels
    one
With my heart's tears.
How is it that you have a category
Of your own?

4422.

A blooming heart
Carries with it
A radiance-smile.

4423.

God keeps a special seat
At His Feet
For my prayerful heart.

4424.

I am so fortunate
That my gratitude-life
And my receptivity-heart
Are inseparable friends.

4425.

May my entire life become
A God-pleasing
Soulfulness-heart-song.

4426.

A silence-heart
Is the home
Of a tension-free mind.

4427.

Readiness, willingness
And eagerness:
These are three choice
    instruments
Of God.

4428.

A true sage loves to live
In God's
Compassion-Protection-Heart-
    Cage.

4429.

My heart,
Instead of leaving me,
Help me to fight against
A wrong thought-attack.

4430.

Every morning I build my heart
And break my mind
To be a choice instrument of God.

4431.

My hesitation-mind starves
My aspiration-heart
To death.

4432.

An unwillingness-mind
Is
A spirituality-famine-life.

4433.

Self-doubt
Is the very beginning
Of self-destruction.

4434.

We can conquer
The impossibility-hurdle,
If we become one
With our all-illumination-soul.

4435.

I shall not allow
My God-satisfaction-heart
To be stolen
By brooding self-doubts
And world-doubts.

4436.

What is meditation?
The beauty and fragrance
Of heart-education.

4437.

Make a bold and immediate
    decision:
God-satisfaction-hunger
Or
Man-adulation-thirst.

4438.

God the Compassion-Eye
And
God the Forgiveness-Heart
Have not only solved
All my major problems in life,
But have also dissolved them.

4439.

Do not think of a reward
For what you have done
For the world.
God's choice Hour
Will definitely do it for you.

4440.

When our unaspiring mind
Makes a bad decision,
Helplessly our aspiring heart
    cries.

4441.

May my hesitation-mind
Surrender sooner than the soonest
To my aspiration-determination-
　　heart.

4442.

Without a cheerfulness-mind,
The willingness-heart
Cannot go very far.

4443.

O my Lord Supreme,
I need only one favour:
Do banish my worries and
　　anxieties
From my helpless mind.

4444.

If you have
A God-surrender-heart,
Then you can have
A rainbow-life.

4445.

My Lord, Your Compassion-Touch
My heart and I cherish.
My Lord, Your Forgiveness-Touch
My life and I treasure.

4446.

God wants us to participate
In His Cosmic Drama,
Keeping aside
The expectation-snare.

4447.

If we are really sincere
In our aspiration-heart
And dedication-life,
Then the hustle and bustle
Of desire-life
Cannot frighten and strangle us.

4448.

The desire-life
Eventually burns
Our very being.

4449.

Pay no attention to the dark
　　tunnel
Inside your mind,
If you want to be inundated
With light eventually.

4450.

If you cannot believe
What your Inner Pilot says to you,
Then your doom
Is fast approaching you.

4451.

Pure devotion
Is
A totally illumined emotion.

4452.

I know, I know
That long before the end
Of my earth-journey's close
I shall once again meet with
The Compassion-Eye, Concern-
    Heart
And Forgiveness-Feet
Of my Lord Beloved Supreme.

4453.

For a seeker,
Wisdom-delight is founded upon
His God-reliance-light.

4454.

My Lord assures me again and
    again
That my ignorance-life will before
    long
Fade into a nothingness-zero.

4455.

God wants me to sing
My gratitude-heart-songs
Not only for Him,
But also for each and every
Human being.

4456.

All that my heart longs for,
I see in the Compassion-Eye
Of my Lord Supreme.

4457.

My soul tells me that it is high
    time
For me to be on the way
To my Supreme Lord's Palace.

4458.

I know I came into the world
With a sole purpose:
To be an unconditionally
God-surrendered will.

4459.

What I needed,
I now have:
A self-transcendence-will.

4460.

My mind,
You are so worthless and useless.
It takes you such a long time
To turn aside from your desire-
    life.

4461.

My Lord,
May Your Silence-Beauty-Eye
Hypnotise my entire being.

4462.

God wants me to sing
One by one
All the surrender-songs
That I have so far learnt.

4463.

When I prayerfully value
My Lord's Compassion-Eye,
He immediately invites me
To visit His Heart-Garden.

4464.

Unimaginable, but true—
Even my restless vital
Is enamoured of
My Lord's Nectar-Delight-
    Messages.

4465.

Alas, I do not know
How and why
I have become
A God-dissatisfaction-mind.

4466.

What is the main characteristic of
    ego?
Ego is something that never wants
To learn anything from anybody.
It feels that it is always
Self-sufficient.

4467.

I call it
My obedience-life.
God calls it
His Hope-Heart.

4468.

Every morning God blesses me
With a new supply of thirst and
     hunger
To be a supremely choice
     instrument
Of His Heart.

4469.

I am so fortunate to have
Two real friends:
My faith-fountain-heart
And
My obedience-service-life.

4470.

I need only two things in my life:
A heart of gratitude
And a mind of peace.

4471.

I need an illumination-heart
To disentangle
My confusion-mind.

4472.

I tell God
That if He really loves me,
Then He has to keep my pride-
     mind
Always under His Thunder-Feet.

4473.

Falsehood is afraid of him
Because of his sleepless devotion
To his Lord Supreme.

4474.

You cannot expect
Each and every path in life
To be strewn with roses.
Choose the rose-path.

4475.

A doubting mind
Is
A self-damaging life.

4476.

A happiness-heart
Makes very fast progress
In the realm of spirituality.

4477.

A mind without flexibility
Cannot walk very far
Along the road of true spirituality.

4478.

The mind's idleness
And the body's uselessness
Are inseparable.

4479.

May my God-gratitude-heart-
     river
Never, never
Run dry.

4480.

O my mind,
I want you to dive deep within
     every day
To discover
That once upon a time you were
A God-fulfilment-promise-maker.

4481.

God,
When You bless me
With Your express Command,
I swim in the ecstasy-sea.

4482.

Each human being
Can hear
The God-Fragrance-Messages,
If he at all wants to.

4483.

A smiling child
Is
The fast ascent of earth-hope.

4484.

A smiling child
Is
A God-Satisfaction-bloom.

4485.

A smiling child
Is
A God-Heart-shoplifter.

4486.

A crying child
Is
Heaven's immediate delight-
     bringer.

4487.

A crying child
Is
The hope-bridge-builder
Between earth and Heaven.

4488.

A crying child
And a singing bird
Are twins.

4489.

My gratitude-tears
Are
God-Compassion-Eye-drawing
    magnets.

4490.

My soul has only two requests to
    make:
It wants me to conceal
My frustration-mind
And reveal
My aspiration-heart.

4491.

If God is your only desire-breath,
Only then can you be a real seeker
For the real spiritual life.

4492.

Today, my Lord, I have a strong,
Extremely strong desire.
I want to bury my very earth-
    existence
In the dust beneath Your Feet.

4493.

Each unaspiring man
Loves to live
Within his self-made boundaries.

4494.

I do hurt God's Eye
When I do not worship and
    treasure
God's Feet
Inside my heart-temple.

4495.

My Lord,
May I be the beauty
Of an obedience-life
Every morning.

4496.

My Lord,
May I be the fragrance
Of a gratitude-heart
Every evening.

4497.

Detachment
Is a very special kind of faith
In God.

4498.

The oneness-heart-tower
Only rises,
And never falls.

4499.

My Lord Supreme,
Do allow me to remember
Only one thing:
The Forgiveness-Touch
Of Your Lotus-Feet.

4500.

We need a heart of purity
To convince ourselves
That God loves us
    unconditionally.

4501.

If you are fully determined to love
    God
In God's own Way,
Then 'how' and 'why' cannot exist
In your mind-dictionary.

4502.

Since our Father Lord Supreme
Is the supreme Optimist,
We needs must be the same.

4503.

God invites me and my heart
Every morning.
How is it that my heart and I
Fail to invite God
Every evening in return?

4504.

I want my disobedience-mind
To be a stranger
To my obedience-heart.

4505.

No special procession,
No, not even a special occasion,
Is needed to please my Lord
    Supreme.

4506.

My Lord,
I want to be a perpetual student
In my selfless service to You.

4507.

My God-loving songs
Are the results of
My God-longing tears.

4508.

My doubtful mind
And
My fearful heart,
I do not want to be
In your company anymore.

4509.

May my mind remain
An open book
To my Lord Supreme,
Exactly the way my heart is.

4510.

To expand my heart-sky,
I need only one thing:
A birthless and deathless cry.

4511.

A self-giving life
Is always blessed with
A God-singing heart.

4512.

If you love and treasure
The uncomeliness of your mind,
Then you are bound to lose
The beauty of your heart.

4513.

O my vital,
Suppression is not desire-
    rejection,
Never.

4514.

Suppression
Is ever
Wisdom-annihilation.

4515.

My sleepless God-surrender
Does not live in the vicinity of
    Heaven.
It lives in the complete
Satisfaction-Heart of God.

4516.

This world of ours is perfect,
Absolutely perfect,
If we see it through
God's constant Compassion-Eye
And Forgiveness-Heart.

4517.

If death does not take us seriously,
We are also under no obligation
To take death seriously.

4518.

We must accomplish everything
That we are supposed to
Here on earth,
Long before death knocks
At our life-door.

4519.

When I sail with my Lord
   Supreme
In His Boat,
In a twinkling we vanish
Into His Infinity's Light.

4520.

My Lord,
I have only one prayer:
May my surrender-beginning
Know no end.

4521.

Alas,
The greatness of the human mind
Vehemently ignores
The goodness of the divine heart.

4522.

Every time God visits me,
My heart prays to Him
To lengthen the time.

4523.

Every time God visits me,
My mind unwillingly listens
To Him.

4524.

Ego,
I needed you to wake up,
But I need only surrender now
To run my fastest.

4525.

My Lord,
May my gratitude-heart
Always remain as busy
As Your Compassion-Eye.

4526.

The love that the heart
Cannot trust
Can never last.

4527.

There is only one
Trouble-shooter in my life:
God's Compassion-Eye.

4528.

My Lord Supreme,
My heart and my breath
Are really tired of
Earthly demands
And Heavenly commands.

4529.

Alas!
I really do not know
How I have become
Lethargy's lifeless life.

4530.

Every day
My Lord Supreme advises me
To devour His Light
To lose my ignorance-weight.

4531.

Each time I self-givingly serve
God the creation,
God the Creator asks
The angels of delight
To dance for me.

4532.

Self-improvement
And self-aggrandisement
Are two perfect strangers.

4533.

You can be a perfect instrument
Of God
If God-obedience is the only item
On your life-agenda.

4534.

The country that does not
Believe in God
Is a perfection-satisfaction-
Failure-country.

4535.

Stay away!
Not as often as possible,
But all the time,
From the ferocious desire-tiger.

4536.

I pray for Divinity's Delight.
God says to me,
"Keep your heart-door open
A little wider."

4537.

I am my stupidity-mind,
Therefore, I have postponed
So many times
God's Hours.

4538.

If the whole world
Rejects you,
You lose nothing,
Absolutely nothing.

4539.

If God accepts you,
You not only gain everything,
But also become
The beauty
Of God's outer world
And the fragrance
Of His inner world.

4540.

O seeker-friend,
Do you know why you are making
The fastest progress?
Because you are impervious
To the arrows of world-criticism.

4541.

God's Heart-Door-entrance
Is denied to you
Because you do not knock
At God's Heart-Door
Prayerfully and soulfully.

4542.

Your soul goes into hiding
When your mind
Does not want to play
The oneness-fulness-game.

4543.

A child's joy
May be short-lived,
But not his heart-cry.
Never!

4544.

We brave the inevitable
To become the Smile
Of our Lord Supreme.

4545.

Finally, I have joined God
To see and feel everything
With love.

4546.

My obedience
Is a short-cut
To my God-satisfaction.

4547.

The God-doubt-shouter
Is, indeed,
A producer of empty words.

4548.

The attachment-mind-train
Arrives at
Frustration-pain-station.

4549.

Just wait and see!
Your mind's doubt-mountain
Will eventually surrender
To your heart-faith-fountain.

4550.

God's Compassion-Eye
Shows me rainbows.
I see them
Even from my mind-abyss.

4551.

O my ego,
Why are you not sensitive?
Can you not see
That you are no longer welcome?

4552.

Outer complacency
Is the sure beginning
Of inner death.

4553.

The vision of a seer-poet
Is
A Heaven-excellence-splendour.

4554.

Your mind-credit card
Is always unacceptable
In the aspiration-world.

4555.

March on!
March on!
Perfection-satisfaction
Is beckoning you.

4556.

I am determined
To liberate my mind
From confusion-captivity.

4557.

My soul
Sleeplessly soars
On wings of universal love.

4558.

Yesterday I believed in faith.
Today I believe
In God's Compassion-Gaze.

4559.

A new and illumining beginning
Always blossoms
Far beyond the horizon.

4560.

Every morning
My Lord comes and plays
With my infant-sweetness-heart.

4561.

Surely I was not born
For God-dissatisfaction.
I was born
Only for God-satisfaction
At every moment
In every way.

4562.

Ask the immediate question:
Do you really love God?
Discover the immediate answer:
You really do not know.

4563.

If you are in a position
To serve God,
Then God will definitely
Be in a position
To embrace you.

4564.

Eternity's atom
And Eternity's Infinity
Have the same source:
God's Vision-Eye.

4565.

God is always hungry
For the smile
Of oneness-hearts.

4566.

Do not be afraid
Of God's Eye.
God's Eye is a Compassion-Ocean,
And not a destruction-volcano.

4567.

A God-lover's heart
Is empty of inferiority-tears
And superiority-smiles.

4568.

My poor heart
Every day suffers
From an endless succession
Of frustrations.

4569.

May my obedience, readiness,
Willingness and eagerness
Form a God-dedication-team.

4570.

Neither the voice
Nor the choice of the mind
Knows what happiness is.

4571.

My mind tells me
That God is only
For the chosen few.
This is, indeed,
A foreign concept to me.

4572.

My mind
Takes tremendous pride
In the outer speed.

4573.

My heart
Takes special pride
In the inner speed.

4574.

My soul
Takes divine pride
In God-manifestation-speed.

4575.

God tells me
That a compromising mind
Is a failing joy.

4576.

O my cluttered mind,
You are fully responsible
For my heart-joy-bankruptcy.

4577.

Even God,
Who is not tired of anything,
Is totally tired
Of my absurd excuses.

4578.

The unwillingness
Of the mind
Is, indeed, a fatal disease.

4579.

Disobedience
Faithfully obeys its master:
Disaster.

4580.

My heart's tearful letters
Get an immediate reply
From my
Absolute Lord Beloved Supreme.

4581.

When my mind shines bright,
I see tenebrous night
Nowhere.

4582.

God has always ample time
To read our aspiration-heart-
   letters,
But He has no time
To read our frustration-mind-
   letters.

4583.

Patience and perseverance
Are of supreme importance
On any spiritual path.

4584.

What my mind wants
Is a marathon satisfaction
From tiredness.

4585.

What my heart prays for
Is an inexhaustible
Energy-sea.

4586.

Every morning
My soul's silence-sea
Invites my mind.
Alas, a negative response
It invariably receives.

4587.

May my heart
Always remain a stranger
To aspiration-vacation.

4588.

The mind-explanation
Of truth
Is empty of illumination.

4589.

My soul was definitely born
When God's
Light-manifestation on earth was
    born.

4590.

Prayers and meditations
Are of supreme necessity
If you want to dine with God
Every day.

4591.

O seeker,
Are you so blind
That you cannot see
God's Compassion-Eye
Beckoning you?

4592.

I offer my Lord Supreme
My heart-tears
For His Heart-Smile to embrace.

4593.

If your mind has fixed ideas,
Then God-realisation
Will remain a far cry.

4594.

May the world's inner love
Be the source
Of the world's outer beauty.

4595.

Possession-greed
Is
Emptiness-feast.

4596.

Divinity's Love,
And not human pretense,
Is my heart's immediate
And only choice.

4597.

The human in me
Cries for
God's Attention-Light.

4598.

The divine in me
Longs for
God's Satisfaction-Delight.

4599.

I am extremely proud
Of my
Aptitude-mind.

4600.

God is transcendentally proud
Of my
Gratitude-heart.

4601.

My heart's gratitude-tears
Are only for the Forgiveness-Feet
Of my Lord Beloved Supreme.

4602.

Each aspiration-heart
Is God's
Newness-Fulness-Promise-Song.

4603.

God's Forgiveness-Heart
And God's Compassion-Eye
Are the most prominent citizens
In my heart-land.

4604.

A spiritual Master is the heart-
    lover
And the mind-teacher
Of his students.

4605.

What else is a miracle,
If not the closest association
Of the Master's highest height
With the ignorance-abyss
Of the disciples?

4606.

If you want to remain happy,
Always follow the starlit footsteps
Of your soul.

4607.

No music can ever be
As haunting, illumining
And fulfilling
As the footstep-whispers
Of the soul.

4608.

The divine Love
Loves human limitations
So that the human limitations
Can unmistakably be
    transcended.

4609.

The human mind finds it
Extremely difficult to believe
That God the creation can be
God the Satisfaction as well.

4610.

The mind offends God
Carelessly, callously
And deliberately.

4611.

The heart defends God
Immediately, stoically
And self-givingly.

4612.

God is proud of my eagerness
Only when it serves God
Prayerfully and soulfully,
And not loudly and proudly.

4613.

The soul's all-illumining
Inner poise
Knows no disturbing mind.

4614.

The soul's all-illumining
Inner poise
Knows no decaying heart.

4615.

The soul's all-illumining
Inner poise
Knows no dying life.

4616.

The unwillingness-mind
Is spirituality's
Unproductive sleep.

4617.

My life is not
A holiday-fun.
My life is
An adventure-run.

4618.

May my life grow into
A rainbow-promise
To manifest God's Victory-Light
On earth.

4619.

Where is the promised land,
If not inside the dedication-breath
Of my heartbeat?

4620.

My mind is extremely proud
Of my
Thunder-success.

4621.

My heart is extremely fond
Of my
Lightning-progress.

4622.

In the spiritual world,
The mind's sovereignty
Is the mind's
Deplorable hallucination.

4623.

God immensely suffers
When unwillingness-hands
And unaspiring hearts
Are in collusion
Against God's Will.

4624.

O stone-dry intellect-world,
You have no idea
How my mind and I
Enjoy your absence!

4625.

Bravely
I accept
My Lord's Justice-Light.

4626.

Prayerfully
I offer my Lord
My life's ignorance-night.

4627.

My heart's peace
Is dependent on
My life's surrender-smiles.

4628.

God has two special guests:
My sleepless aspiration-heart
And
My breathless dedication-life.

4629.

Alas, a very limited time
Is granted to the mighty souls
To perform the mightiest
God-manifestation-tasks
On earth.

4630.

My soul urges my heart
Never to miss
Any God-company-opportunity.

4631.

God sends
One of His representatives
To collect
My mind's smile-flames.

4632.

God Himself comes
To collect
My heart's teardrops.

4633.

In the morning,
I love to enjoy
The beauty of an angel.

4634.

During the day,
I love to feel
The heart of an angel.

4635.

In the evening,
I love to be
The breath of an angel.

4636.

At night,
I want my angel-life
To sing with God the Creator
And dance with God the creation.

4637.

The seeker in me
Tells the world
That my real God-realisation
Was a tremendous task.

4638.

The seeker in me
Tells the world
That my full God-manifestation
May not be an accomplished task.

4639.

The more humanity enjoys
Restlessness-freedom,
The farther humanity is
From God-satisfaction.

4640.

I clearly see
That my outer insecurity
Is nothing other than
My inner pride.

4641.

The outer pride
Is the unconscious revelation
Of the inner insecurity.

4642.

My Lord, the Forgiveness-Beauty
Of Your Compassion-Eye
Is a feast for my hunger-heart.

4643.

With uncomely thoughts
We starve ruthlessly
The divine in us.

4644.

With comely thoughts
We climb up
To our own divinity's
Highest height.

4645.

A self-contradiction-mind
Is a veritable
God-manifestation-failure.

4646.

I must intensify
My aspiration-heart,
I must.

4647.

I must beautify
My dedication-life,
I must.

4648.

Humanity's colossal pride
Depends on my
Heavenward march.

4649.

I sleeplessly love
God's Heart,
I do.

4650.

I breathlessly need
God's Feet,
I do.

4651.

It is extremely difficult
For a secret mind
To make friends with
A sacred heart.

4652.

My Lord,
I really do not want
To remain any longer
The cause of Your Sadness-Heart.
This time do trust me.

4653.

God blesses us
With infinitely more
Than we actually need
To please Him in His own Way.

4654.

My thirsty eyes
Are not enough.
My hungry heart
Is also needed
To realise God
And fulfil God.

4655.

An aspiration-heart
And a surrender-life
Have a large amount of credit
At God's Bank.

4656.

Long before I do anything
For mankind,
I take sanction
Not only from God's Eye
But also from God's Feet.

4657.

Every day
My heart desperately tries
To mingle
With God's Compassion-Smiles.

4658.

Every day
I desperately try
To kiss the dust
Of my Lord's Lotus-Feet.

4659.

The music of my heart
Is the progress-smile
Of my life.

4660.

A negativity-mind
Always turns its deaf ear
To the heart's
Happiness-music.

4661.

The quicker we lose ourselves
To our inner life,
The more we grow
In our divinity.

4662.

Each divine thought
Embodies the beauty
And fragrance
Of God's Love.

4663.

My soul knows
What my Master is.
My heart has
A very tiny glimpse.
My mind is not interested
In my Master's heights
And depths.
It only wants from the Master
Freedom, endless freedom.

4664.

O doubting world,
I have all along been inside
My Master's heart-kingdom.

4665.

I am begging and begging my
    Master
To allow me to be a member
Of his feet-kingdom
To get more joy
And more fulfilment.

4666.

I came to break my Master's heart
With my deplorable spiritual life.
To my greatest joy and relief,
I see that my Master
Has already melted my heart.

4667.

Before,
Peace was a dream-bloom.
Now,
Peace has become
A reality-blossom
In my God-aspiration-heart
And God-dedication-life.

4668.

When I am one with God's Will,
I see a vast sun
Inside my tiny aspiration-flame.

4669.

O seeker, do not give up
If your first attempt
At aspiration-height
Is not successful.
Patience and perseverance
Are of supreme importance.

4670.

Self-aggrandisement-laughter –
No! No! No!

4671.

Self-improvement-smiles –
Yes! Yes! Yes!

4672.

The very thought
Of my Master's happiness-smile
Carries me far beyond
My life's sadness-river.

4673.

Nothing carries certainty
As does
A heart of peace.

4674.

I stole,
I am stealing,
I shall always steal
The nectar-dust
From the Feet
Of my Lord Supreme.

4675.

If we ceaselessly offer
Peace-prayers to God,
Then God will allow us
To claim His Infinity's Delight
As our own.

4676.

My Lord, I do not need hours,
But just a few moments
To be at Your Compassion-flooded
    Feet,
For my life's illumination.

4677.

I must never forget
That God's Compassion-Eye
Originated my aspiration-heart.

4678.

Yesterday
My heart was the beauty
Of streaming tears.

4679.

Today
My life is the freedom
Of soaring smiles.

4680.

My Lord Supreme,
Will I ever be worthy
Of Your ever-forgiving Heart?

4681.

A peace-dreamer
My soul was.

4682.

A peace-lover
My heart is.

4683.

A peace-giver
My life shall become.

4684.

When God wants me
To hide inside His Eye,
I carry with me
My aspiration-tears.

4685.

When God wants me
To hide inside His Heart,
I carry with me
My dedication-smiles.

4686.

When God asks me
To hide inside His Feet,
I carry with me
Everything that I have
And everything that I am.

4687.

My mind's motto:
A birthless and deathless
"No!"

4688.

O my mind,
I really do not know
How you can appreciate,
Admire and love
Your own self-styled
Unhappiness-creation.

4689.

When I live in my heart,
I pray for my Lord's
Supreme Victory.

4690.

When I live in my mind,
I pray for my mind's
Constant victory.

4691.

When I live in the world,
I completely forget
My prayer-life.

4692.

Only when I become
A hope-harvest,
Satisfaction becomes
My name.

4693.

I cheerfully, bravely
And unconditionally
Obey my Lord's spokesman:
My soul.

4694.

I see the world
Through
My frustration-mind.

4695.

God wants me
To see the world
With His Satisfaction-Heart.

4696.

Like my heart-room,
May my mind-room also become
The newness-blossom of hopes.

4697.

He whose life is full of God-
     dreams
Will definitely be
A God-manifestation-hero
On earth.

4698.

Challenge,
Challenge your mind's
Frustration-strength.

4699.

Challenge,
Challenge your heart's
Insecurity-length.

4700.

The human mind feels safe
And secure,
Alas, even inside an abysmal
     abyss.

4701.

God tells us not only
To share our smiles,
But also to care for
Others' tears.

4702.

O Compassion-Eye
Of my Lord Supreme,
Will You not take me
As I always am:
An ingratitude-life?

4703.

Since you do not listen
To your heart's dictates,
You are bound to fall.

4704.

There is no comfort
That can ever satisfy
A genuine God-seeker.

4705.

Once you are totally
God-oriented,
No earthly pleasure
Can ever fulfil you.

4706.

A wise seeker
Does not harbour
Future miseries.

4707.

My heart every day,
Out of sheer compassion,
Goes to visit my mind-jungle
For its transformation.

4708.

God-Compassion is at once
My life-protection
And
My heart-satisfaction.

4709.

God has given you the capacity
To run along His Road.
Why do you limp?
Is it because you want
Extra attention from humanity?

4710.

A complication-mind
Must be rejected
Right from the very beginning.

4711.

A God-disobedience-mind
Does not realise
That an inevitable blow
Is imminent.

4712.

You must not neglect
Your daily morning walk
Along God's Love-Road.

4713.

Everything is
Easier than the easiest
If I sit at the Feet
Of God's Will.

4714.

The retaliation of the mind
Is a foolishly useless
Waste of energy.

4715.

I call it
My gratitude-heart-tears.
God calls it
His Satisfaction-Heart-Smile.

4716.

My heart's peace
And
My mind's unwillingness,
Alas,
Fail to meet together.

4717.

God the Compassion-Eye
Leads
His choice instruments.

4718.

God the Protection-Hand
Follows
His choice instruments.

4719.

A negativity-mind
Hurts the God-loving heart
More than we can ever imagine.

4720.

Anything deep, illumining
And fulfilling
Cannot be adequately measured.

4721.

If God has changed your life,
Then God can and will
Change the world-life
As well.

4722.

Every morning I clear
My mind's negativity-dust
From my heart-garden.

4723.

I call it
A sophisticated life.
God calls it
His exasperated Breath.

4724.

With each step I take forward,
I multiply
My Lord's Confidence
In me.

4725.

I easily breathe
When I prayerfully repeat
God's Name.

4726.

I freely breathe
When I soulfully pray
To God.

4727.

I perfectly breathe
When I deeply meditate
On my Absolute Lord Supreme.

4728.

An Avatar's
World-illumining Light
Endures throughout Eternity.

4729.

Spirituality-knowledge
Is good,
But spirituality-practice
Is infinitely better.

4730.

The self-giving seekers
Are always
In short supply.

4731.

Love:
The unparalleled wisdom-light
Of the heart.

4732.

The breath of spirituality
Can be used
Not only every day,
But also every hour,
Every minute
And every second
For God-manifestation
On earth.

4733.

A willingness-mind,
An eagerness-heart
And
An enthusiasm-life
Can easily defy age.

4734.

The happiness of the soul
Eventually conquers
And transforms
The sadness of the heart.

4735.

Bury the deplorable past
At once.
No sigh you have to heave.

4736.

My life's sadness-cries
Are being transformed
Into my heart's
Gladness-flights.

4737.

Purify your wild senses.
Your life will need
No strong fences.

4738.

Frustration is heavier
Than the heaviest
When self-modification
Is weak.

4739.

Do not bind
Your aspiration-heart
And dedication-life
With your
Doubt-suspicion-mind-cord.

4740.

My mind loves to walk
On my
Arrogance-paved road.

4741.

My heart loves to walk
On my
God-obedience-paved road.

4742.

The outer strength disappears
When the inner power
Goes to sleep.

4743.

I was utterly stunned
By the panoramic view
Of my stupendous
God-representative-soul!

4744.

Stop your lethargy-life.
A new supply of energy
Will immediately be yours.

4745.

Humility purifies his mind,
Illumines his heart
And fulfils his life.

4746.

The aspiration-heart
Is a piece
Of inner music.

4747.

Spirituality is not meant
For those who are addicted
To the path of pride.

4748.

Purity runs in his veins.
Therefore
Everybody loves him.

4749.

Simplicity, sincerity
And purity:
These three are
The most faithful members
Of the soul's family.

4750.

In his outer
And desiring mind,
He is a divided man.

4751.

In his inner
And aspiring life,
He is a united heart.

4752.

Lamentation
Does not cure lethargy,
But enthusiasm does.

4753.

My Master
Is the only God-singer
In my heart.

4754.

I sit at my Master's feet
Because his eye
Is the compassion-beauty
Of God's Smile.

4755.

Look forward
And run your fastest!
Your yesterday's failure-life
Will not be able to chase you.

4756.

God repeatedly tells
Each human soul
That he is destined
For a higher life.

4757.

God's own Divinity
Comes to play with me
When silence descends on me.

4758.

My disobedience-life,
How cruel you are
To force me to come
To my destruction-tear-
     destination.

4759.

This morning my soul
Unsealed my heart's
Illumination-treasure.

4760.

Each self-giving thought
Is a most exemplary
God-representative
On earth.

4761.

Every day my prayer-heart
And my meditation-life
Flow into the sea of silence.

4762.

The tears of my aspiring heart
Are always enraptured
By the Footprints
Of my Lord Supreme.

4763.

God is ready to hear
Only when my heart speaks,
And also
As long as my heart wants to.

4764.

My gratitude-heart
Is my God-blessed
Godward march.

4765.

A suspicion-mind
Is, indeed, a havoc
To its own self.

4766.

Humanity is divided
Into diversity
So that each human being
Can have the opportunity
To play a unique role
In God's Cosmic Drama.

4767.

From your purity-heart,
God knows how strong
Your spirituality-foundation is.

4768.

My self-importance
Is another name
For my self-torment.

4769.

Each and every time,
My Lord Supreme has listened
To my prayerful heart-whisper.

4770.

What I desperately need
Is a remote control
For my unruly mind.

4771.

My joy knows no bounds
Because my obedience-heart
Was my predecessor
And my surrender-life
Is my successor.

4772.

The desire-life
Is frightened
By the touch of vastness.

4773.

The aspiration-life
Is enlightened
By the touch of vastness.

4774.

My confidence-heart
Is
My God-obedience-life.

4775.

Thinking is becoming.
Therefore, be extremely careful
In your thinking.

4776.

God asks me to be
Divinely brave
And ceaselessly brave.
He is all ready
To make me His choicest
World-manifestation-light-hero.

4777.

I know
My desire-choice-mind
Is a quenchless thirst.

4778.

Anything divinely illumining
And fulfilling
Is duty-free.

4779.

God's Transcendental Meditation
Is His immediate
Universal Expansion.

4780.

God wants me
To be happy
By forgiving my life
And forgetting my mind.

4781.

God wants me to love
His fleeting Breath
And His eternal Life
Equally.

4782.

My service-life
Is
My heart-satisfaction
And not
My mind-servility.

4783.

My anxiety-mind
Is
My self-imposed torture.

4784.

My relief-heart
Is
My God-bestowed rapture.

4785.

Beautiful, more beautiful
And most beautiful
Are my gratitude-heart-tears
When they prayerfully wash
The Lotus-Feet
Of my Lord Supreme.

4786.

God does not play the game
Of partiality.
He gives each child of His
His Whole.

4787.

My regularity
Is my spirituality's
Heart-beauty.

4788.

My punctuality
Is my spirituality's
Soul-fragrance.

4789.

God does not want me
To take any rest
Until I have arrested
All evil forces.

4790.

Humanity,
I serve your life
And become
God-perfection.

4791.

Divinity,
I love Your Eye
And become
God-satisfaction.

4792.

When I powerfully enjoy
Ignorance-sleep,
Even God's own alarm clock
Does not succeed.

4793.

A most difficult task, indeed,
Is to become
A citizen of sincerity-kingdom.

4794.

How I wish I could breathe in
At every moment
The Nectar-Breath
Of my Lord's Compassion-Feet.

4795.

Although we are all
Temporary world-residents,
We can accomplish
A good many things
For the betterment of the world.

4796.

God is extremely proud of him
Because he thrives
On his mind's willingness
And his heart's eagerness.

4797.

My soul teaches me every day
How to fly
On God-surrender-wings.

4798.

Each good thought
Can be not only the beginning
But also the continuation of joy.

4799.

Frustration-pressure
Quite often chases
Expectation-pleasure.

4800.

O seeker,
If you carry unnecessarily
The heavy load of your doubting
    mind,
No fulfilment-destination for you.

4801.

Be not afraid of telling the world
That at God's choice Hour
You will definitely be able
To realise God.

4802.

A doubting mind
Is, indeed,
An unhappy life.

4803.

From God-surrender only,
Self-discovery
Is possible.

4804.

The difference between the mind
And the heart is this:
My mind majestically commands;
My heart affectionately pleads.

4805.

The mind
Wants to be the expression
Of speed-pride.

4806.

The heart
Wants to be the embodiment
Of God-cries.

4807.

The desiring mind
And an endless succession
Of frustrations
Cannot be separated.

4808.

My prayer
Is
My God-climbing tear.

4809.

My meditation
Is
My God-descending Smile.

4810.

My Lord,
Will You protect me
Whenever I am in danger?
"My child,
Danger gives no warning.
Start immediately running
Towards Me."

4811.

We do not need a visa,
Not even a passport,
To enter into God's
Heart-Kingdom.

4812.

Silence can spread everywhere.
It can even spread inside
The doubting and suspicious
    mind.

4813.

No patience, no perseverance,
The outer success and the inner
    progress
Will remain a far cry.

4814.

Only a deep meditation
Can silence
The mind-doubt-storms.

4815.

Peace may hide
From a doubting mind,
But not from a blossoming faith,
Never!

4816.

A narrow mind has to remain
A perfect stranger
To happiness-fulness.

4817.

My self-giving heart,
Your inner name is
My divinity's beauty,
Your outer name is
My divinity's responsibility.

4818.

With an impure mind,
Nobody can purify
His heart-shrine.

4819.

Lethargy-enjoyment
And success-fulfilment
Never meet.

4820.

Each opportunity
Is
A success-progress-harbinger.

4821.

God will be highly pleased
If you immediately unburden
All your anxieties
At His Lotus-Feet.

4822.

God-company means
The negation
Of failure-destiny.

4823.

God is at once fond
And proud of
My heart's devotion-tears.

4824.

My love of God
Is
My brightness-life.

4825.

My devotion to God
Is
My sweetness-heart.

4826.

My surrender to God
Is
My fulness-earth-existence-smile.

4827.

My cleverness-mind
Is not a God-authority,
But my purity-heart is.

4828.

A sleepless God-lover
Is
Imperfection-exempt.

4829.

Our aspiration-heart-flames
Can solve and dissolve
All our problems.

4830.

What I need
Is an immediate decision:
My fame or God's Name.

4831.

What is my meditation?
My meditation is
My sleepless God-education.

4832.

The mind loves and serves
Only one
Particular nation.

4833.

The heart serves
The United Nations —
All the nations.

4834.

Eternity is long,
Endlessly long,
Only for the unaspiring mind.

4835.

Each time my heart cries,
My life
Immediately rises.

4836.

O my seeker-friend,
How long will you enjoy
Your romance
With your doubting mind?

4837.

Each time you are absent
From your heart-home,
You totally become a useless life.

4838.

If you dare to play
With your troubles,
They will fail to torture you.

4839.

Each time I try,
My devotion-cry becomes
Stronger and stronger.

4840.

Have you forgotten your promise
To God?
Do you not want anymore
To become a choice instrument
Of God's Will?

4841.

My Lord, is there any special way
To run fast, faster, fastest
In the spiritual life
Without aspiration-tears?
"My child, there is none,
And there will be none."

4842.

O seeker, smile spontaneously,
Smile easily
And smile self-givingly.
Lo, your destination
Is within your easy reach.

4843.

Only a God-realised person
Can tell you how far you are still
From the God-realisation-clime.

4844.

God wants me to go forward,
Only forward,
To receive from Him
His Life's signal award.

4845.

How unfortunate and deplorable
His life has become.
Even God's repeated Visits
Have failed to gladden his heart.

4846.

An enthusiasm-mind
And a dynamism-vital,
Without fail, can fulfil
Their God-manifestation-
    promises.

4847.

A self-giving life definitely
    receives
God's Compassion-Blessing-Sea
At God's choice Hour.

4848.

Once you sincerely and seriously
Enter into the spiritual life,
God Himself will keep you away
From the hustle and bustle
Of the desire-life.

4849.

Only a spiritual Master
Of the highest height
Can tell you where you are,
How far you will go
And how long it will take you
To arrive at your final Destination.

4850.

If you want to be
Unimaginably happy,
Then be an unconditional
Smile-giver.

4851.

My heart-shrine is only
For God-worship,
And for nothing else.

4852.

I gaze in utter amazement
At my Lord's smiling Eyes
And forgiving Heart.

4853.

Intensity can illumine
The confusion
Of the mind-jungle.

4854.

I need patience
More than anything else
For the birth of a new dawn
In my aspiration-heart.

4855.

God laughs and laughs
When my mind
Tries to conceal something
From Him.

4856.

God smiles, sings and dances
When my heart
Wants to reveal something.

4857.

May my
Desire-mind-elevator
Never function.

4858.

Each divine thought
Has the capacity
To help us reach the length
Of God's Infinity.

4859.

May my aspiration-heart
And my dedication-life
Grow into the beauty
And fragrance
Of perfect perfection.

4860.

My life's service-road
May be too long,
But it is never wrong.
It will definitely take me
To my long-cherished
God-realisation-destination.

4861.

Each day I long for
A new heart-blossom
In my aspiration-life.

4862.

My God-submission-life
Is
My God-satisfaction-heart.

4863.

A tireless toil
Is my life's
Progress-satisfaction-soil.

4864.

Be fearless.
Never allow your doubts
To invade your mind.

4865.

Delay not
In inviting divinity's
Perfection-poise.

4866.

The God-doubting mind
Will never be able to keep pace
With the God-satisfying heart.

4867.

God wants to illumine me.
Therefore, He repeatedly tells me
Not to tremble at His Justice-
    Door.

4868.

What we need
Is a marathon hope
In our spiritual life
To please God in His own Way.

4869.

Sincerity is not enough.
A determined intensity is needed
For fastest progress in the inner
    life.

4870.

Hearts without aspiration-breath
Are tolerated,
But never cherished by God.

4871.

When all the mind's complexities
Leave us,
We find ourselves in the proximity
Of God's Heart-Palace.

4872.

I shall never be satisfied
Until my meditation
Has full mastery
Over my entire being.

4873.

There is only one world
Inside the unaspiring mind:
The world of ever-increasing
Attachment.

4874.

I feel I am useless
If I cannot climb up
The aspiration-mountain
And if I cannot swim across
The dedication-ocean.

4875.

Alas,
At times the thundering pride
Of certain world leaders
Deafens the inner world.

4876.

Every day, in vain,
I try to persuade my mind
To study the art of self-giving.

4877.

Alas, I do not know when
I shall be able to run
And sit at the feet
Of my own ancient wisdom-soul-
    tree.

4878.

Pay no attention to the mind.
Even the body and the vital
Receive more light than the mind.

4879.

If we can illumine the mind,
By virtue of our prayers
And meditations,
Its capacities will be
    unimaginable.

4880.

Before illumination,
The doubting mind is really
Our ruthless enemy.

4881.

Fear, doubt, anxiety, suspicion –
Is there any negative force,
Alas,
That the mind does not gladly
    welcome?

4882.

Along with tremendous
    soulfulness,
What we all need
Is the freshness-breath of devotion
For our fastest progress.

4883.

Like fresh flowers
That charm us and give us soulful
    joy,
Every morning we need fresh
    devotion
To please our Beloved Supreme.

4884.

Even if your Master
Is in a different world during
    meditation,
He sees clearly the activities
Of your desiring mind
And your aspiring heart.

4885.

If I look deeply into God's Eye,
I see that He is both
Compassion-Mother-Tear
And
Wisdom-Father-Smile.

4886.

Ask your soul.
Your soul will tell you
How many millions of times
God has told you
That unconditional surrender
Knows no equal.

4887.

Even if God tells me
Something unpleasant,
I know it is only
For my own perfection-progress-
      delight.

4888.

O God-manifestation-eagerness-
      servers,
For you, only for you,
God's Blessing-Sky
And His Pride-Ocean.

4889.

We can show our outer sympathy,
But the real inner help,
Consolation-illumination,
Must come from the Supreme.

4890.

If you serve your Master
Sleeplessly and breathlessly,
In one incarnation you can get
The most astonishing results
Of one hundred incarnations!

4891.

Every day we are nearing
Our God-realisation
On the strength
Of our surrender-delight.

4892.

When a mantra rings like a bell,
My whole world
Quivers with joy.

4893.

The very name
Of your spiritual Master
Must give you
Infinity's joy and fulfilment.

4894.

All the outer creations
Of a spiritual Master
Are no match
For his inner achievements.

4895.

Not the fame-power,
But the name-tower
Of a spiritual Master
Shall forever remain the tallest
In the aspiration-hearts
Of his disciples.

4896.

The leaves and flowers of the God-
    Tree
Give the feeling
Of a universal oneness.
The topmost branch of the God-
    Tree
Gives the feeling
Of a transcendental uniqueness.

4897.

God the creation
Is the Universal
Beloved Supreme.

4898.

God the Creator
Is the Transcendental
Absolute Supreme.

4899.

God the Creator
Soars,
God the creation
Spreads.

4900.

To me,
God the Creator is always perfect.
But as soon as I look at God the
    creation,
It is nothing but imperfection.

4901.

My philosophy tells me
That God is inside my giant mind.
My spirituality tells me
That God is inside my tiny heart.

4902.

I always feel
That as a creator
I am perfect.
But alas, not my creation.
Never.

4903.

My name will remain infinitely
    higher
Than what I have achieved for
    myself
And what I have soulfully offered
To humanity.

4904.

In my heart-to-heart
    conversations
With God,
I see that there are so many ways
I am deeply hurting God.

4905.

God always wants me to know
Who I am—
Not what I have
And not what I give.

4906.

When you think of God,
Do not think
Of all His attributes.
Just think of His Compassion-Eye.

4907.

When you pray to God,
Do not think of all the questions
That you have.
Just ask yourself one question:
"Am I ready?"

4908.

True disciples need not depend
On their Master's outer
    achievements,
But they must depend
On their heart-connections.

4909.

The name of their spiritual Master
Is enough for his true disciples.
What he did or achieved in the
    outer life
Can give them outer happiness,
But not God-realisation.

4910.

It is also true that
A spiritual Master's achievements
Are his disciples' inspiring
And fulfilling opportunities
To love God the Creator
And serve God the creation.

4911.

God wants the spiritual Master to
    create.
God wants his disciples to
    lovingly offer
His creation to the world.

4912.

Sri Ramakrishna had.
Vivekananda distributed.
The world accepted,
Unreservedly accepted.

4913.

The spiritual Master
Is the soaring bird.
The disciples
Are the spreading wings.

4914.

My Lord, You are so smart.
You are far beyond
The attachment-detachment-
    domains.
But it seems that You do not care
    for
My freedom from attachment-
    snares.

4915.

The height of your prayer
And the depth of your meditation
Give you the capacity to claim God
Unmistakably as your own, very
    own.

4916.

For centuries and centuries
And centuries
You did not care consciously
For spirituality.
Yet you think that God Himself
Is delaying your God-realisation.

4917.

God cannot imagine how real
    seekers
Can take sabbatical leave
From the spiritual life.

4918.

A seeker's vacation from the
    Supreme
Cannot last forever,
For his soul will not
Remain indulgent to him
For a long time.

4919.

When a seeker meditates
On God's supreme Victory,
God Himself
Keeps his heart-door wide open
For humanity.

4920.

By this time,
Your Master has proved
To your aspiring heart
In thousands of ways
Your soul's birthless and deathless
Connection with him.

4921.

If I do something wrong,
Unless some higher forces
Come to my rescue,
Definitely I will be ruthlessly
   caught
By the law of karma.

4922.

I do not have any problem with
   my soul,
The divine representative of God.
Only my mind and my vital
Are the real problems!

4923.

My Lord Beloved Supreme,
My only prayer
Is to remain at Your Feet.
"My child,
May My adamantine Will-Power
Be your new name."

4924.

I know, I know,
Nothing is as sweet,
Nothing is as illumining,
Nothing is as fulfilling
As my heart's devotion-tears.

4925.

If you have a sleepless
Devotion-heart,
Love and surrender
Are bound to follow.

4926.

Every day you are having
A new desire-life.
Every second you demand
Ten things from poor God.
Ask yourself
If you are doing the right thing.

4927.

You are entitled to expect
Only two things from God:
God-realisation and God-
   manifestation.

4928.

If you indulge in depression
And frustration
Day after day, week after week,
Month after month, year after
    year,
Even God will not be able
To look at your face.

4929.

God sees your constantly guilty
    mind,
But His Compassion and
    Forgiveness
Always prevail.

4930.

When God talks to me,
How often my mind ignores
And my heart adores.

4931.

To preserve your life's simplicity
And your mind's sincerity,
Always take the positive side of
    life.

4932.

I know you always keep God
Inside your heart.
Can you not keep God also
Inside your mind?
Try, you will definitely succeed.

4933.

The higher you go,
The simpler and sweeter you
    become,
Like a child playing
In Eternity's Heart-Garden.

4934.

Try to have an illumined mind.
God will highly speak of you.
God will speak through you
To the world-nations.

4935.

The soul is learning from God.
The heart is learning from the
    soul.
Now the mischievous monkey-
    mind
Must learn from the gracious,
Self-giving heart.

4936.

I do not believe in
Earth-bound time,
Like my Lord Beloved Supreme.

4937.

God wants me to make
An immediate choice:
My frustration-mind
Or
My aspiration-heart.

4938.

Every day
My Lord's Compassion-Eye
Encourages me to equal Him
In everything.

4939.

I am fully determined
Not to ever take
An aspiration-dedication-
  vacation.

4940.

I shall never allow my mind
To be fettered
By uninspiring thoughts.

4941.

He who thinks that he has
A monopoly
On God's Compassion and
  Affection
Is, indeed, a stark fool.

4942.

There is only one short-cut
To our divine fulfilment
And God's supreme Satisfaction:
Our sleepless and breathless
Devotion-cry.

4943.

God's Heart is infinite.
Therefore, God does not mind
If each and every human being
Desires to monopolise His Heart.

4944.

My Lord Supreme, please tell me
Which is absolutely the best place
For me to grow and glow
At every moment.
"My child,
Your gratitude-heart-garden."

4945.

I shall not permit
Even an iota of self-doubt
Or God-doubt,
Even in the most remote corner
Of my mind.

4946.

As my Lord's Compassion is
    infinite,
Even so
I want my self-transcendence-life
To be unlimited.

4947.

True, God's Compassion-Light
Is unconditional,
But you must never take it for
    granted
At any moment.

4948.

God has come to congratulate
My aspiration-world
On its perfection in self-offering.

4949.

Today I am so happy
And proud of myself
For being a member
Of the ignorance-demolition-
    team.

4950.

We make so many mistakes so
    often,
But we must never make
One particular mistake:
We must never miss our
    appointment
With our Lord Beloved Supreme.

4951.

God is extremely proud of me
Because He does not have to wait
Even for a fleeting second
In the background of my
    aspiration-life.
I am keeping Him to the fore
Sleeplessly and breathlessly.

4952.

Unless we constantly keep
Our Lord Supreme in mind,
How do we expect Him to make us
His choicest instruments?

4953.

My Himalayan-height-greatness
Makes my Lord laugh and laugh.
My ocean-vast goodness
Makes my Lord smile and smile.
My sleepless and breathless
Selflessness
Makes my Lord happy, satisfied
And fulfilled,
Far beyond the flight
Of my imagination.

4954.

O my God-searching mind,
God is asking you to minimise
Your thinking of yourself,
But He never, never asks you
To think ill of yourself.
He also tells you
That you are destined
To be a choice instrument
Of His
At His choice Hour.

4955.

I shall have peace when my mind
Stops hearing everything.
I shall have peace when my heart
Starts loving everything.

4956.

I deeply long to ply my life-boat
Between my joy of loving
The God-Shore
And my joy of serving
The God-Shore.

4957.

Let us not be fools.
There is no law against
Our fastest inner progress.

4958.

What we need is the beauty
Of constant God-remembrance
And the fragrance
Of sleepless God-service.

4959.

Every day my Lord wants me
To ascend from earth-life
To Heaven-Heart.

4960.

Be careful of your desire-life.
What you desperately desire
    today,
You may ultimately become.

4961.

Each day comes to us
As a golden dream
To transform our hearts
Into our soul-delight.

4962.

God thinks of me.
Therefore
I am able to climb up
The aspiration-mountain.

4963.

God thinks for me.
Therefore
Perfection is
My outer name,
And satisfaction is
My inner name.

4964.

When I become
My aspiration-choice,
God beckons me to come
And hear the Destination-Voice.

4965.

God will allow me to participate
In His Cosmic Game
If He sees that my heart-breath
Is made of sincerity and eagerness.

4966.

The jealousy of the mind
And the insecurity of the heart
Can never see the Beauty of
God's Face.

4967.

God compassionately corrects
My outer life.
God proudly directs
My inner life.

4968.

No! Never be tempted
To study
At God-disobedience-school.

4969.

Who tells the whole world
That my heart-river
Will never be able to run into
The Heart-Ocean of God?

4970.

O world,
Enter into the spiritual life,
If you want to claim the Beauty
Of God's Eye
And the Fragrance
Of God's Heart
As your own, very own.

4971.

A positive life
Is
A God-inspiration-heart.

4972.

O my heart, be not earth-bound.
Be Heaven-free
And live on the highest branch
Of the aspiration-tree.

4973.

Even after the full enlightenment,
There is no such thing
As retirement.

4974.

We shall definitely be successful in
    life,
If we take each outer difficulty
As an inner opportunity.

4975.

A surrender-smile of the heart
Is by far
The best prayer.

4976.

Incessant
Is God's Love
For His creation.

4977.

Not even intermittent
Is the creation's love
For the Creator.

4978.

Not only the power,
But also the luminosity
Of the inner voice
Can never be described.

4979.

I tell God
That His Smile-Blossoms
Are breathtaking.

4980.

God tells me
That my tear-blooms
Are equally breathtaking.

4981.

My life is thrown into chaos,
Not because I ignore God,
But because I never think of God.

4982.

God secretly whispers a word
In your listening ear:
"Do not lend your ear
To the suspicion-mind-speech."

4983.

Disobedience is afraid
Of God's Will.
Therefore, it cleverly avoids
God's Will.

4984.

God does not want you to choose
The most attractive
Or the most secretive path.
He wants you to choose only
The self-offering-path.

4985.

If you start your morning life
With a negative thought,
Rest assured the rest of the day
You will become a complete
Failure-story.

4986.

Nobody cares for your
    nightmares.
Nobody!
Nobody cares for your
    temptation-snares.
Nobody!
But everybody cares for
Your self-offering-smiles.

4987.

Alas, how is it
That I do not realise
That my mind's eye
Is always misleading?

4988.

If our aspiration-heart
Is always on time
To please God in His own Way,
Then God-realisation has to be
Within our easy reach.

4989.

The world-transformation-
   capacity
Lives inside
The willingness-intensity.

4990.

O God-criticising mind,
Be careful.
O God-loving heart,
Be blissful.

4991.

I fly and fly in happiness-sky
When God Himself plays the role
Of my life's decision-maker.

4992.

Realise God.
Claim once again that you are
His supremely chosen child.

4993.

May my life's hope-star
And my heart's promise-star
Succeed in manifesting
My Lord Supreme
Here on earth.

4994.

When we aspire most intensely,
We feed all the world-souls,
Who value us infinitely more
Than even we can dare to imagine.

4995.

God tells me that I have done
Many good things for Him.
Therefore, He wants to give me
A special award.
I say to God, "Please give me
Only this award:
Constant obedience-achievement-
   award."

4996.

My inspiration-friend tells me
To wake up.
My aspiration-friend tells me
To start flying.
My dedication-friend tells me
To never stop singing
God's Victory-Songs.

4997.

When I brought prayer
Back into my life,
God gave me His most beautiful
And most powerful Smile.

4998.

When I brought meditation
Back into my life,
God did not wait, even for
A fleeting second,
To come and embrace me
With His greatest Satisfaction.

4999.

Mind-training
Gives us strength
Indomitable.

5000.

Heart-training
Gives us peace
Infinite.

5001.

My Lord,
You do not have to knock
At my heart's door.
Just come in!
I shall embrace Your Feet
Immediately.

5002.

My Lord,
You always tell me
That You love me dearly.
If so, give me the joy
Of serving You sleeplessly.

5003.

Please, my Lord, please,
Do not delay anymore
In giving me
A mind that will adore You,
A heart that will love You
And
A life that will serve You
Unreservedly.

5004.

I am saved,
My life is saved
Because God's Compassion-Hands
Are unconditionally
Holding us taut.

5005.

How charming it looks
When the tears of my heart
And the smiles of my soul
Play hide-and-seek.

5006.

God, not only happily
But also proudly,
Counts my heart-happiness-baby-
    steps
Towards Him.

5007.

With my heart's tears
My Lord Supreme is building
A rainbow-bridge
Between earth and Heaven.

5008.

When God wants us
To fly towards Him,
He blesses us
With His Wisdom-Light-Wings.

5009.

My Lord,
You are the only reason
I live on earth,
Believe it or not.

5010.

My Lord, Your Feet embody
Not only all the things
That I believe in,
But also all the things
That I love.

5011.

My Lord, I feel my existence
Is real and true
Only when I place
My gratitude-heart-garland
At Your Feet.

5012.

My Lord,
You do not have to call me.
Just allow me only to think of You.
The very thought of Your Heart
Thrills my entire being
With delight.

5013.

We must brave and conquer
The inevitable,
So that no darkness-night
Can prevail over us.

5014.

In the unaspiring life,
Ambition is
Of supreme importance.

5015.

In the aspiring heart,
Ambition is
Nothing short of self-destruction.

5016.

We actually do not compromise.
We just cleverly pretend
To compromise.

5017.

No inner peace,
No outer detachment.
Never.

5018.

To judge others
Is to sadden
God's all-loving Heart.

5019.

My God-surrender-heart
Is
My world-oneness-light.

5020.

To my extreme delight,
I have received
The aspiration-heart-award
From God.

5021.

Alas,
I have no idea
If ever I shall receive
My transformation-life-award
From God.

5022.

Every day
God wants my life to be
A cheerful and self-giving server.

5023.

O my mind,
When are you going to discard
Your competition-compulsion-
    desire-life?

5024.

Within
A purity-heart.
Without
Two beauty-eyes.

5025.

I get tremendous joy
By telling the world
That God does not love me.

5026.

My soul tells the world
That my soul's only motto is:
"God for God's sake."

5027.

God the Compassion teaches us
Sleeplessly
How to love the world
Unconditionally.

5028.

Man the frustration
Deliberately
Does not want
Illumination.

5029.

He who intensely longs
For God's Compassion-Light
Is enormously fortunate.

5030.

Do you really love God?
Then the moment I utter
The Name of God,
You must show me
Your heart's uncontrollable thrill.

5031.

What has ignorance-night
Done to me?
It has at once
Sumptuously fed my ego
And starved my humility
To death.

5032.

My Lord,
Your Heart-Beauty's Eye
Sweetly awakens my heart
To fulfil You in my life.

5033.

God's Compassion-Eye
Called me.
My aspiration-heart
Immediately answered.

5034.

What is disobedience?
Disobedience is
My conscious, deliberate
And malicious
God-separation-pleasure.

5035.

What is my immortality,
If not my permanent residence
Inside God's Compassion-Eye
And His Satisfaction-Heart?

5036.

Only my gratitude-heart knows
In how many ways
My Lord wants to make me happy
And keep me happy.

5037.

The sole purpose
Of my desire-life
Is to unmistakably possess God.

5038.

The sole purpose
Of my aspiration-heart
Is to devotedly become
God's cheerful Choice.

5039.

The human in me
Wants God
To smile at me only
And constantly.

5040.

The divine in me
Wishes God
To smile at His own creation
Lovingly, blessingfully
And ceaselessly.

5041.

If you can remain
All the time
Inside your aspiration-heart,
Then your progress-life
Shall be not only permanent,
But ever-transcending.

5042.

When expectation-sweetness
Leads me,
I meet with frustration-bitterness
As my destination.

5043.

When my mind makes God
Really happy,
God immediately becomes
My mind's unconditional Slave.

5044.

My detachment-life
Not only liberates me,
But also enlightens
The whole world.

5045.

My human mind
Is an information-collector.
My divine heart
Is an aspiration-climber.

5046.

Knowing perfectly well
That God has done everything for
    me
And will also do everything for
    me,
How do I get malicious pleasure
In making complaints
Against God?

5047.

Long ago
My heart became a member
Of God's Happiness-Circle.
Alas, even now
My mind does not care at all
For God's Happiness-Circle.
My mind wants happiness
In its own way.

5048.

I am looking out
For God's Compassion-Feet.
God is looking out
For my aspiration-heart.

5049.

My aspiration-heart
And my dedication-life
Are studying most seriously
At 'self-transcendence' school.

5050.

What is Heaven?
The Compassion-flooded Eye
Of my Lord Supreme.

5051.

Where is Heaven?
Heaven is inside
The Beauty and Fragrance
Of my Lord's Forgiveness-Heart.

5052.

There was a time
When my heart desired to see
God's Victory-Banner.
But now my heart desires to
    become
The divine pride
Of God's Victory-Banner.

5053.

Everything
May eventually desert us,
But not our Beloved Lord's
Compassion-Eye.

5054.

My Lord,
Do bless me with the capacity
To say something really kind
Even to those
Who are extremely unkind to me.

5055.

My Lord,
Will You not give me
The blessingful capacity
To burn my gratitude-heart-
    candle
Every morning and every
    evening?

5056.

Finally, I was able to sing proudly
The farewell song
For my doubting mind.

5057.

Alas, there is no reason
Why I love my mind's
Complication-confusion-jungle.

5058.

God is not only ready and willing
But also eager
To keep my monkey-mind
   occupied
So that it does not create
Any serious problem.

5059.

My God-faith
Is a daily companion
Of my devotion-heart.

5060.

May I live between
My heart's gratitude-tears
And my life's surrender-smiles.

5061.

The mind-room
Is always empty
Of aspiration-cries.

5062.

The heart-room
Is always full
Of God-Satisfaction-Smiles.

5063.

The heart of an Avatar
Is
A God-Love-feast.

5064.

Alas, each human life
Has to swim
Against the attachment-waves
Of the shoreless ocean.

5065.

It seems that the temptation-
   expectation
Is extremely difficult
To avoid.

5066.

The happiness we discover
In our tranquillity-mind
Is an unparalleled achievement.

5067.

My Lord Supreme says to me:
"My Divinity's child,
How could you have surrendered
To ignorance-night?
How could you?"

5068.

To have a good thought
Is to enter
Into God's Heart-Palace.

5069.

To become a good thought
Is to become
A real member
Of God's immediate Family.

5070.

I call it
My unconditional surrender.
God calls it
My soul's ecstasy-dance.

5071.

God wants to prove to us
That nothing is impossible.
Lo, my doubting mind
Is begging my God-loving heart
For forgiveness.

5072.

The readiness of the life,
The willingness of the mind
And
The eagerness of the heart
Together grow, together glow
And
Together flow.

5073.

May my gratitude-heart
One day be worthy
Of my Lord's
Compassion-Ocean.

5074.

My oneness-heart
Has finally challenged
And defeated
My aloofness-mind.

5075.

If anybody asks me
What my immediate need is,
I shall tell him
That my immediate need is
God's Forgiveness-Feet
And not
God's Compassion-Eye.

5076.

My Lord,
Is there anything special
That You want me to accomplish
Every day?
"Yes, My child.
I want you to renew
Every morning
Your surrender-life
And gratitude-breath."

5077.

An unaspiring mind
Even unconsciously
Does not need God.

5078.

An aspiring heart
Desperately and constantly
Needs God.

5079.

A surrendering life
Dearly and carefully treasures
God's Compassion-Eye
And
God's Forgiveness-Feet.

5080.

My faith in God
Is at once
My God-Protection-Fort
And
My God-Destination-Port.

5081.

Beautiful is my heart's
Hope-dawn.
Powerful is my mind's
Promise-morning.
Fruitful is my soul's
Smile-day.

5082.

I have two homes
To live in:
My obedience-mind-home
And
My devotion-heart-home.

5083.

Can you imagine!
I was quite happy
In my mind-prison.
Can you imagine!
I am not proud
Of my heart-palace.

5084.

It is impossible for me to separate
My heart's happiness
From my life's progress.

5085.

My knowledge-mind
Cautions me always.
My wisdom-heart
Illumines me always.

5086.

My determination-mind
Is the beginning
Of my success-life.

5087.

My God-surrender
Is the beginning
Of my progress-life.

5088.

Aloofness does not
And cannot conquer
Life's immeasurable problems.

5089.

A truly aspiring heart
Cannot believe
In enmity.

5090.

My heart sings and sings
And plays and plays
Right in front of
My smiling soul.

5091.

Simplicity-living
And sweetness-feeling
Are oneness-friends.

5092.

A seeker's
God-manifestation-journey
Begins with
Unlimited possibilities.

5093.

Each aspiring life
Is a masterpiece
Of God's Art.

5094.

A clarity-mind
Is the supreme revelation
Of Truth.

5095.

A purity-heart
Is the absolute manifestation
Of Truth.

5096.

To accept any situation
Willingly
Is to fly in God's Satisfaction-Sky
Indefinitely.

5097.

My mind's
Constant frustration
My life was.

5098.

My mind's
Surprising fascination
My life now is.

5099.

If your heart chooses kindness,
Then your life becomes
God's immediate usefulness.

5100.

Not long ago
I was
A self-centred mind.

5101.

I now am
A God-centred heart.

5102.

You are not
Your yesterday's
Mind-frustration-life.

5103.

You are
Your tomorrow's
God-satisfaction-heart.

5104.

Behold,
My heart's devotion-tears
Have reached
The Golden Shore.

5105.

Each smiling child
Embodies
Humanity's high hopes
For God-manifestation
On earth.

5106.

My soul-garden
Is a perfect stranger
To weeds.

5107.

The stillness of the inner Divinity
Has the power
To challenge and conquer
The pride of time.

5108.

My attachment-mind
Binds me
Ruthlessly.

5109.

If you do not aspire,
Naturally you are going to fall
Upon the sidewalks
Of your spiritual life.

5110.

Every morning
My soul inspires my heart
To board the progress-flight
To a new destination.

5111.

Do not underestimate
The destruction-power
Of your impurity-mind!

5112.

If you enjoy the comedy of life,
Then you should be prepared
To suffer the tragedy of death.

5113.

Every day
God plants new hope-trees
In my heart-garden.

5114.

My heart says to God,
"Please correct me immediately
If and when I am wrong."

5115.

My mind says to God,
"Father, since I am never wrong,
Why do You hesitate
To give me my due reward?"

5116.

Use your heart's joy;
Do not keep it,
If you really want God
To be extremely proud of you.

5117.

If you want to see God
Smiling at you
Most powerfully and most
    proudly,
Then cast off
All shackles of pride.

5118.

When I aspire
Most self-givingly,
The world sees my heart
In my eyes.

5119.

God is always ready
To hear me singing,
Whether I sing
The songs of joy
Or the songs of sorrow.

5120.

I travel uphill
With the beauty and fragrance
Of my aspiration-heart.

5121.

I travel downhill
To enjoy
My confusion-mind.

5122.

A dreaming heart
God proudly cradles.

5123.

A sleeping mind
God deliberately avoids.

5124.

Gratitude flies
Faster than the fastest
To sit at God's
Protection-Satisfaction-Feet.

5125.

Devotion
Without an immediate obedience
Is of no avail.

5126.

When my heart is unhappy,
My doubting mind becomes
Stronger than the strongest.

5127.

God wants me
To feel His Heart,
But I prefer
To touch His Feet.

5128.

My life will be incomplete
If my heart is empty
Of tears
And my soul is empty
Of smiles.

5129.

There is no special way
To satisfaction.
The way itself
Is stupendous satisfaction.

5130.

Simplify your life-temple.
Purify your heart-shrine.
Lo, your Lord Beloved Supreme
Is singing and dancing
With enormous joy and pride.

5131.

God laughs and laughs
When He hears the world
Calling His lover
Stupidity incarnate.

5132.

Stay, my Lord Supreme, stay!
I promise
I shall never betray You
Anymore.

5133.

Each divine thought
Is a blossoming progress-smile
Of my heart.

5134.

My silence-heart
Is my matchless
Meditation-companion.

5135.

I call it
My gratitude-heart.
God calls it
My perfection-acceleration.

5136.

O my temple-purity-heart,
May my tears and smiles
Play hide-and-seek
Inside you.

5137.

Only when I pray and meditate,
I see the Beauty of God's Smile
In my heart-garden.

5138.

Each smiling child
Is God's new satisfaction-promise
On earth.

5139.

Humanity cries.
Divinity descends.
Infinity smiles.

5140.

In the morning I pray for
A mind-illumining life.
In the evening I pray for
A heart-fulfilling breath.

5141.

When we pray,
We carry our hopeful heart
To God.

5142.

When we meditate,
God comes to us,
Carrying with Him
His bountiful Heart.

5143.

Not my Master's polite request,
But his express command
Energises me, illumines me
And fulfils me.

5144.

Each new self-giving thought
Is
A new oneness-peace-harbinger.

5145.

Finally, I am happy and fulfilled,
For now I can stand in between
My rainbow-devotion-tears
And
My Lord's Satisfaction-Sun-
    Smiles.

5146.

Alas, I do not know
Who can and who will rescue me
From my
Drowning depression-frustration-
    life.

5147.

Even the very thought
Of my unaspiring mind
Compels me to feel
That I am a catastrophic failure.

5148.

My soul is teaching my heart
How to carry
God's Peace-Manifestation-Light
From horizon to horizon.

5149.

Just one doubtful thought
Is enough to paralyse
The joy of an aspiration-heart.

5150.

No matter how brave I am,
I still find it impossible
To disentangle myself
From my confusion-mind.

5151.

Day in and day out
I spend my time
In watching my Lord's
Forgiveness-Happiness-Rainbow.

5152.

To achieve the flexibility of the
    body
May take a very short time,
But to achieve the flexibility of the
    mind
Is, indeed, a most arduous task.

5153.

If you still want to keep your
    pride,
Then place it at your Master's
Forgiveness-feet.

5154.

How can you be attached to
    falsehood
When your heart
Is all devotion to please God?

5155.

Not God's Justice-Light,
But His Compassion-Delight
Is travelling the whole world.

5156.

My God-obedience-heart
Will definitely fulfil
My God-fulfilment-promise.

5157.

My dream of Infinity abides
Inside the reality
Of my God-surrender-life.

5158.

My soul, my heart and I
Are rising high, higher, highest
On a new God-satisfaction-wave.

5159.

My God-obedience-heart
And
My God-manifestation-hope
Are my only two friends.

5160.

A spiritual Master's voice
Has the capacity to garner
Not only sweetness
But also fulness.

5161.

My mind's readiness,
My life's willingness
And
My heart's eagerness
Are constantly supporting
My God-manifestation-promise
    on earth.

5162.

My ignorance-life expires
Only when
I feel that I belong
Only to God's Satisfaction-Heart.

5163.

Hard is it for depression
To find anything satisfying,
Even in God.

5164.

My Lord, You ask me
And immediately I do.
What do I do?
I sing Your Light-Manifestation-
    Song.

5165.

My God-worship
Has to be constant
And not frequent.

5166.

When my gratitude-heart
Implores God for anything,
God immediately responds.

5167.

My only prayer to God:
"My Lord,
Do take full control of my life
At every moment."

5168.

Anything that makes me closer
To my Lord Supreme
Is invaluable.

5169.

My broken heart can be healed
Not by mere affection and love
From humanity,
But by sheer oneness
With God's Will.

5170.

When I look at the Beauty
Of my Lord's Eye,
I am all enchanted
And I sleep no more
Ignorance-sleep.

5171.

When I look at the Power
Of my Lord's Feet,
I am all energised
And I serve Him more.

5172.

A heart of genuine aspiration
Can never
Be kept down.

5173.

My aspiration-heart
Is the fragrance
Of my pilgrim-soul.

5174.

Every hour
Is a God's choice Hour
For us to realise,
Reveal and manifest God.

5175.

He who has a measurable goal
Cannot make
Immeasurable progress.

5176.

What else is the source
Of my world-encouragement,
If not my self-enlightenment?

5177.

Because of my limitation-mind,
My aspiration-heart sees no escape
And no recourse.

5178.

You want to succeed –
But where is
Your patience-heart?

5179.

You want to proceed –
But where is
Your surrender-life?

5180.

My Lord, let me chase
Your Compassion-Eye
And You chase
My ignorance-life.

5181.

We struggle and struggle
Because our mind's faith
In our Lord Supreme
Is not sufficient.

5182.

We suffer and suffer
Because our heart's
Surrender to God
Is incomplete.

5183.

The ignorant
World-enjoyment-thirst
I had.

5184.

The wise
World-service-hunger
I am.

5185.

Every day
My Lord wants me to increase
My world-acceptance
Readiness, willingness and
    eagerness.

5186.

Alas,
We do not know
And we shall never know
How compassionate
And how self-giving
Our Lord Beloved Supreme
Really is.

5187.

My sweetness-life-smiles
Expedite and multiply
God's Affection for me.

5188.

My gratitude-heart-tears
Expedite and multiply
God's Compassion for me.

5189.

My surrender-oneness-breath
Expedites and multiplies
God's Satisfaction in me.

5190.

My Lord, once upon a time
I gave You a headache
Because of my great love for
    ignorance.

5191.

My Lord, now is the time
For me to show You
How sincerely my heart aches
For Your Love.

5192.

My Absolute Lord's
Omnipotence-Eye
Frightens my mind.

5193.

My Beloved Lord's
Omnipresence-Life
Enlightens my heart.

5194.

I am happy and I am perfect
Only when God's likes and
    dislikes
Guide my aspiration-heart
And dedication-life.

5195.

My Lord,
When I tell You that I have
    stopped
Expecting and demanding,
Do not believe me –
I must confess my insincerity.

5196.

O seeker,
Do not look at others' outer
    prosperity.
It may sadden your mind.

5197.

O seeker,
Look at others' inner prosperity.
It may intensify your God-hunger.

5198.

My Lord,
Do use Your Heart only one time
And see how quickly
My heart and I perish
Without Your Love.

5199.

When I pray soulfully,
I love to enjoy
God's blessingful Presence.

5200.

When I meditate deeply,
God loves to enjoy
My blissful presence.

5201.

Even death
Has no use
For our dry mind.

5202.

Every day
My God-realisation-hope
Is getting stronger and stronger.

5203.

Dark mind, dark thoughts,
Dark face and dark eyes
Are fond of one another.

5204.

God-manifestation-
    responsibilities
Are meant only for
God-chosen instruments.

5205.

My Lord, there was a time
When my mind and I
Craved only
Name and fame.

5206.

My Lord, my heart and I
Are craving only
Your Compassion-Eye.

5207.

If you cannot meditate
On your Goal,
Try to dream of your Goal
At least.
It will be of great help
To you.

5208.

My mind-turbulence
Frightens
My heart.

5209.

My heart-tears
Inspire
My mind.

5210.

In the desire-world,
Sooner or later
We shall all be devoured
By helplessness.

5211.

I shall no longer
Remain chained
To my mind's choices.

5212.

From now on
I shall remain chained
Only to my Lord's Compassion-
    Eye
And His Forgiveness-Feet.

5213.

God wants us to cut
The bondage
Of worldly attachment
And not world-affection.

5214.

Where else can God be,
If not inside
Our sincerity-mind?

5215.

Where else can God be,
If not inside
Our purity-heart?

5216.

Where else can God be,
If not inside
Our simplicity-life?

5217.

True love of God
Knows no
Reciprocity-desire.

5218.

O my mind,
Seek not, avoid not.
Take whatever comes.
Peace will be all yours.

5219.

Be pure in mind,
Be pure in heart,
Be pure in thought and speech
And stand aside.
Allow God to work for you.
He will do it,
Gladly and proudly.

5220.

Only two things I need:
A prayerful heart
And a self-giving breath.

5221.

What am I doing?
I am celebrating my mind's
Final doubt-demise.

5222.

Even the lower than the lowest
    mind
Is never a non-entity
In God's Compassion-Eye.

5223.

O my mind,
How many times
Do I have to tell you
That doubt and suspicion
Are untouchables?

5224.

From perfection-height
When I look,
Everything is perfection
    incarnate.

5225.

During my prayer,
I clearly see God
Ushering in
Divinity's newness.

5226.

During my meditation,
I clearly see God
Ushering in
Immortality's fulness.

5227.

May my purity-heart-garden
Never lose even an iota
Of its divinity's beauty.

5228.

He who does not aspire
Will be consumed
With a self-doubt-hunger.

5229.

I never knew that
My frustration-mind-friend
Would be so dangerous
And so destructive.

5230.

Perfection and satisfaction
Are always
In short supply.

5231.

My Lord, do tell me
How I can ever endure
A long spell of indifference
From You.

5232.

A doubt-demolition-mind
Is
A progress-promotion-life.

5233.

May each and every deed
Of my life
Become a climbing delight
Of my heart.

5234.

I call it
My aspiration-advancement.
God calls it
His proudest achievement.

5235.

An aspiration-hungry heart
Is a special satisfaction
Of God.

5236.

God's Sweetness-Compassion-
    Smile
Loves everything,
Even my mind's desire-hunger.

5237.

My morning God-surrender-
    breath
Sumptuously feeds
My entire day.

5238.

When I sing for God,
My heart resonates
With God's Fulness-Dreams.

5239.

I cry to see God,
Not in my eyes,
Not even in my heart,
But only
In my ever-blossoming tears.

5240.

I find my divinity
Only in the community
Of God-surrendered souls.

5241.

My soul embraces
Divinity's Beauty
To enjoy
Infinity's Fragrance.

5242.

An unconditional surrender
Is just one farther stride
To Heaven.

5243.

Jealousy-mind
And insecurity-heart
Together live.

5244.

To my greatest surprise,
My Lord's Compassion-Eye
Has smashed asunder
All my attachment-ties.

5245.

The transformation of life
Begins with a soulful smile
Of the heart.

5246.

Mankind's oneness-dream
Was founded upon
God's ever-transcending Reality.

5247.

Even through my mind's
Thickest and heaviest fog,
My heart is proceeding
Towards God.

5248.

God is all ready
To edit my life-book.
Alas, will I ever be inspired
To write?

5249.

My God-searching mind
Has always room
For obedience.

5250.

Disobedience-temptation
Is an open door
To hell.

5251.

Self-destruction
Is the mind's
Breathing room.

5252.

God-satisfaction
Is the heart's
Breathing room.

5253.

Conquer insecurity.
God the Pride
Shall beckon you.

5254.

I shall treasure only
My God-obedience-achievement-
    award
And nothing else.

5255.

O God-disobedience-life,
I really do not want to know
Where you live and what you do.

5256.

The complexities of worries
Each human mind
Is fully aware of.

5257.

What the heart desires,
Eventually the mind,
Vital and body become.

5258.

Where do I live?
I live inside my heart's
Sincerity-cries.

5259.

Where shall I live?
I shall live inside my soul's
Divinity-smiles.

5260.

At God's choice Hour,
Each old dream
Becomes a new reality.

5261.

My God-Destination-choice
I made
With my heart's tremendous
    courage.

5262.

My name is adamantine
    determination
To pull my days and nights
Out of their vagabond
    aimlessness.

5263.

The beauty
Of my illumination-soul
Is changeless.

5264.

The fragrance
Of my illumination-soul
Is fathomless.

5265.

Only a God-surrender-heart
Knows
What God-ecstasy is.

5266.

What have I drowned?
I have drowned my life's
Ignorance-night
In my heart's aspiration-flood.

5267.

A spiritual life
Without love-devotion-surrender
Is worth next to nothing.

5268.

The aspiration-heart
Does have the capacity
To answer
All the complicated questions
Of the mind.

5269.

May my life be guided
At every moment
By my soul's lightning-
    illumination.

5270.

May my mind be shaped
By my heart's
Thunder-determination.

5271.

My heart
Is extremely fond of
My soul's
Wisdom-light-tree.

5272.

God does not like the idea
Of my calling Him
Only in case of emergency.

5273.

God is compelling my mind
To study my heart-lessons
Every day, without fail.

5274.

God knows
What not to do:
He does not demand.

5275.

I know
What not to do:
I do not expect.

5276.

I had not the slightest idea
That my aspiration-cries
And my devotion-tears
Would be so beautiful.

5277.

A relaxation-mind
I desperately need.

5278.

An intensity-heart
I sleeplessly need.

5279.

Knowledge-information
My mind has.
Useless.

5280.

Wisdom-illumination
My heart needs.
Here and now.

5281.

Disobedience means
God-Will-avoidance.

5282.

Choose the most attractive path;
I mean,
The path of the heart.

5283.

Widen
Your mind's eye
To include everything.

5284.

Widen
Your heart's eye
To become everything.

5285.

Widen
Your life's eye
To enjoy everything.

5286.

Negative thought
You cherish,
Destructive deed
You become.

5287.

A true dedication
Is a perfect stranger
To vacation.

5288.

The beauty of his eyes
Lives inside
The purity of his heart.

5289.

O my mind,
Still there is plenty of time
For you to destroy
All shackles of pride.

5290.

May my heart-tears
Mount high-higher-highest
At every moment.

5291.

May my soul-smiles
Spread all-where
Every day.

5292.

Today my aspiration-heart
Has become the bliss
Of the farthest shore.

5293.

O doubting mind,
The waves of world-criticism
You have to brook.

5294.

Alas, when will I be able to declare
My final readiness
To accept God in His own Way?

5295.

Each time I pray
To God,
I become a new personality.

5296.

Each time I meditate
On God,
I grow into a new divinity.

5297.

Each time I say to God,
"I have,"
God corrects me:
"No, My child,
You are."

5298.

My Lord, my heart is dying
To have from You
The breath of an unconditional
Surrender.

5299.

My God-obedience-number
I can
Easily count.

5300.

My God-disobedience-number
Defies
My counting capacity.

5301.

When I walk towards God,
God Himself
Counts my baby steps
Most proudly.

5302.

In the morning
I soulfully watch
The beauty of the dawn.

5303.

In the evening
I self-givingly watch
The silence of the sky.

5304.

The child that smiles
Is the Beauty
Of God's Dream.

5305.

The child that cries
Is the Compassion
Of God's Reality.

5306.

The doubting mind itself
Is
A confusion-market-torture.

5307.

The God-loving heart
Is
The exquisite thrill
Of God's own Heart.

5308.

The outer speed
Fascinates
The human mind.

5309.

The inner speed
Originates
A new creation.

5310.

Be not afraid
Of telling the world
That your mind can aspire,
Your heart can love,
Your life can serve
And you can become
God's choicest instrument.

5311.

When I am
My aspiration-lover,
God becomes
My decision-maker.

5312.

My Lord,
How I wish I could hear
Your Footsteps
Inside my heart-cries.

5313.

Peace
Is the flower of love
And the fruit
Of detachment.

5314.

I sing my heart's
Oneness-song
For God.

5315.

God compassionately strikes
His Fulness-Gong
For me.

5316.

Slowly, steadily
And unerringly
You must climb up
Your life's progress-ladder.

5317.

I pray to God
In silence.
But God loves to amplify
My prayer.

5318.

Each God-lover
Is a unique
God-heart-fragrance.

5319.

My Lord,
Only for Your Feet
My heart's rainbow-colours.

5320.

Life is bound to remain
Incomplete
Without perfection-smiles.

5321.

The happiness of the heart
Supplies us with the wings
To fly
In God's own Heart-Sky.

5322.

No true outer freedom
Can ever be achieved
Without inner peace.

5323.

Faith is
The life-beauty-supplier.

5324.

We must all obey God
In the heart-temple
Of self-offering.

5325.

There is only one way
To realise God,
And that way is
Constant surrender-oneness
With God's Will.

5326.

Alas,
How many times
My mind has not cared
For God-appointed hours.

5327.

My God-realisation knows
That anything that is limited
Can be made unlimited
By virtue of
God's Compassion-Rain.

5328.

As there is no fixed hour
For us to move forward,
Even so, there is no fixed hour
For us to arrive
At our destined Goal.

5329.

The beauty
Of my heart's hope
Is pure.

5330.

The fragrance
Of my soul's promise
Is sweet.

5331.

My devotion-tears
Every night
Lull me to dream
Blissful dreams.

5332.

Love and surrender
Always shine
On the altar of devotion.

5333.

I see God's Eye
Every day
Inside the temple-purity
Of my heart.

5334.

The soul's realities
Are totally different
From our mind's concepts.

5335.

God wants each and every
Opportunity of my life
To be a tremendous outer success
And inner progress.

5336.

No, it is not true
That the human doubt
Is stronger
Than the divine belief.
It is definitely the other way
    around.

5337.

My openness-heart
Expands
God's Fulness-Life.

5338.

Most beautiful
Are my heart's
Gratitude-tears.

5339.

Sweetest
Are my Lord's
Satisfaction-Smiles.

5340.

My mind, tell me how long
You will deceive yourself,
How long you will ignore my
    heart,
How long?

5341.

How can we really
Love our mind,
Without forgiving
Our mind first?

5342.

The inner peace
Knows not
The power of death.

5343.

It is not that we are not warned
By God's Will;
We just do not pay any attention
To it.

5344.

May my life live
Between
My mind's thunder-progress
And
My heart's lightning-perfection.

5345.

Fastest is my aspiration-speed.
How?
I have cleaved asunder
My mind's disobedience-
   mountain.

5346.

My soul-seed
Struggled to sprout—
But succeeded.

5347.

My heart-bud
Is struggling to blossom—
But I am sure it will succeed.

5348.

God Himself fought for me
Against my mind's doubt
And won,
And gave me victory's crown.

5349.

My heart and I have heard
Many different kinds of music,
But the sweetest music
Is my Lord's fast-approaching
Footsteps.

5350.

God's Footstep-Whispers
Immediately
Send me to Heaven.

5351.

When the eagerness of my heart
Speaks soulfully to God,
God's Joy knows no bounds.

5352.

God wants my life
To be
His Peace-Triumph-Banner.

5353.

The inner peace-fire
Does have the capacity
To radiate
In all directions.

5354.

Each heartbeat definitely
    embodies
The beauty and fragrance
Of the Promised Land.

5355.

My soul has only one question
To ask me:
When will my mind be ready
To love God?

5356.

What a great relief,
Now that I have taken my work
As my life's playground!

5357.

Bravely
I collect doubt-thorns
From my mind-jungle.

5358.

Bravely
I sow my heart's faith-seeds
In my mind-jungle.

5359.

The mind's negativity-deafness
Has to be cured
By the heart's peace-music.

5360.

O doubting mind,
Are you so blind
That you cannot see and feel
You are passing from
Joy-starvation-station
To joy-starvation-station?

5361.

Tomorrow's truth-victory-bell
Is ringing
In my today's aspiration-heart.

5362.

I can meet with Infinity's Peace
Only at my life's
Unconditional surrender-shore.

5363.

How I wish my mind
To be fully acquainted
With my Lord's Feet,
As is my heart.

5364.

My heart's teardrops
Are so sacred
That God Himself
Collects them.

5365.

My heart's cheerfulness
Every day receives
A special invitation
From my Lord Supreme.

5366.

Only an unconditionally
Surrendered soul
Can have a free access to God's
Seventh Heaven of Delight.

5367.

May my God-eagerness-heart
Consume
My entire being.

5368.

May I be prayerfully
And devotedly conscious
All the time
Of my life's sacred
God-manifestation-duty.

5369.

God tells me
That He will be more than willing
To bless me
With His Ecstasy's Flood
If I just make a solemn promise
To Him
To break my doubting head.

5370.

I have given my heart
A most thrilling task:
Every day
My heart steals the golden dust
From my Lord's Golden Feet.

5371.

Where is my God-faith?
It is inside
My blossoming heart.

5372.

Where is my God-faith?
It is inside
My glowing eyes.

5373.

Where is my God-faith?
It is inside
My streaming tears.

5374.

Where is my God-faith?
It is inside
My beaming smiles.

5375.

When you start your journey,
Only look for the stars
In your own heart-sky.

5376.

A low consciousness
Precedes
Our spirituality's downfall.

5377.

As falsehood
Does not become truth,
Even so, hatred
Cannot become love.

5378.

Today's God-disobedience
Will turn into
Tomorrow's life-depression.

5379.

I am going back
To my Beloved Supreme
With my renewed hope-heart.

5380.

I am going back
To my Lord Supreme
With my mind's
Renewed determination.

5381.

God is ready
To wipe away your heart's tears,
But where are they?

5382.

Only your heart's love for God
Will carry you home
To God's Compassion-Nest.

5383.

God does not know
Whether He will cry
Or smile or laugh
When He sees my heart's
Microscopic faith.

5384.

For my puny dedication,
Alas,
I expect a giant congratulation
From my Lord Supreme.

5385.

The Compassion-Heart
Of my Lord Supreme
Does not believe in placing
An embargo
On my mind's blind and wild
Unwillingness.

5386.

Love God more, infinitely more,
Or love God more, a little more.
You will be able to bring
All your mind's fears and doubts
To a standstill.

5387.

God comes and asks us
To show Him
Our dynamic aspiration.
To His great surprise,
We cannot show Him
Even our static aspiration.

5388.

An insecurity-heart
And a narrowness-mind
Love each other
Most sincerely.

5389.

The heart must needs have
Adamantine inner strength
To overtake
The mind's stormy decisions.

5390.

I give myself a hearty laugh
When I remember
That I was a passenger
On a non-stop ignorance-train.

5391.

I thought it was an impossible
   task
For me to reclaim God's trust in
   me.
To my greatest joy,
My Lord's Compassion-Eye
Has made the impossible possible.

5392.

My illumination-soul
And my aspiration-heart
Used to live in adjoining rooms,
But now they prefer to live
   together
In the same room.

5393.

I never thought
That it would be so easy for me
To say adieu to doubt.
Now I see that God's Compassion-
   Eye
Has performed an unconditional
   miracle
For me.

5394.

When I pray and meditate,
Renunciation
Is easier than the easiest.

5395.

When I do not pray and meditate,
Possession-hunger
Is my only preoccupation.

5396.

God-realisation you want
Sooner than the soonest.
Do you not know where
Your aspiration is?
Your aspiration is at its lowest.

5397.

There are limitless ways to please
   God.
But alas,
When will my heart discover
Even one way?

5398.

I wish to see God smiling
Every day.
Therefore, every morning
I shall embark
On a new project.

5399.

To surmount ignorance-barrier,
I must develop an unquenchable
    thirst
For God's Compassion-Eye.

5400.

My heart declined the invitation
From my desire-mind,
And I have become now
The happiness-prince.

5401.

Alas, my outer success-life
And
My inner progress-heart
Are not permanent.

5402.

O seeker, be careful!
It does not take even a second
To lose everything
That is inspiring and illumining.

5403.

My Lord,
Even one fleeting moment
Away from You
Seems to me longer than Eternity.

5404.

My Lord, do take me back.
This time I assure You
I shall never disappoint You
In any way.

5405.

My Lord,
No matter what befalls me,
I shall sing Your Victory-Song
While walking along Eternity's
    Road.

5406.

My Lord, I love You.
Love means self-giving.
How is it that I hesitate to give You
All that I have and all that I am?

5407.

There is no proper substitute
For God-realisation-delight.

5408.

My Lord,
Two kinds of fear torment me:
The fear of displeasing You
And
The fear of Your withdrawal from
   me.

5409.

My Lord, I would like You to know
Only one thing:
How sad I feel when I withdraw
From Your Compassion-Eye.

5410.

My Lord, there is no joy
In displeasing You.
Yet why do I continue doing it
Day after day, week after week,
Month after month?

5411.

My Lord's Forgiveness-Feet
And my gratitude-heart
Together have made meteoric
   progress.

5412.

Divinity's self-giving
Is far beyond
Humanity's receptivity.

5413.

My Lord, do believe me.
Not only my heart,
But even my mind is crying
To please You in Your own Way.

5414.

I know, I know
That I am attached
Only to one thing:
My Lord's Sweetness-Heart.

5415.

O seeker, protect and preserve
Only what God has secretly
And blessingfully
Kept inside your aspiration-heart.

5416.

God is so strict with me
That He never expects
Any explanation from me
When my consciousness descends.

5417.

My Lord,
How I wish I could remain
As a permanent infant
In Your Compassion-flooded
     Nursery.

5418.

In eager anticipation
I love to wait only for one thing:
My Lord's
Compassion-Forgiveness-Arrival.

5419.

A mind
Of world-detachment
Is what I need.

5420.

A heart
Of God-attachment
Is all I need.

5421.

My Lord,
I do know that
You are waiting for me.
I do know that
I shall swim
In Your Infinity's Vastness-Sea.

5422.

A self-conscious mind
I was.
A God-conscious heart
I now am.

5423.

The more
I have You, my Lord,
The more
I must please You.

5424.

My Lord called.
My heart answered immediately,
Happily, devotedly and self-
     givingly.

5425.

When I am in my animal
     consciousness,
I feel that I have loved God
More than He deserves.

5426.

When I am in my human
     consciousness,
I feel that I have loved God
As much as I should.

5427.

When I am in my divine
    consciousness,
I feel I must love my Lord
    Supreme
Infinitely more.

5428.

I say to God, "My Lord,
I am all ready
To think of You constantly."

5429.

God says to me, "My child,
I am also all ready
To give you Myself completely."

5430.

Innumerable chances
My Lord has given me.
Alas, yet I do not know why
I am still missing His Golden
    Boat.

5431.

An obedience-heart
And a surrender-life
Will never stumble
On the way to God-realisation.

5432.

I shall never allow
My aspiration-heart
To be in the company
Of my desire-mind.

5433.

A God-doubter
Is
An abysmal abyss-enjoyer.

5434.

A spiritual Master
Equally enjoys
The breath of an atom
And
The Life of Infinity.

5435.

Alas, will humanity's
World-attachment-train
Ever stop functioning?

5436.

How can the music of silence
Be appreciated by someone
Who does not have a prayer-heart?

5437.

If you are a heart-smiler,
Then eventually you will become
Your mind-barrier-breaker.

5438.

Be serious. Be brave.
You can easily become
A frustration-devourer.

5439.

God-days must start
In the small hours
Of the mornings.

5440.

My Beloved Supreme
Every day comes to me to measure
My heart-height.

5441.

My Lord Supreme
Never comes to me to measure
My mind-length.

5442.

A God-lover's every breath
Is God's
Sweetness-Thrill.

5443.

My obedience
Purifies
My God-searching mind.

5444.

My obedience
Intensifies
My God-loving heart.

5445.

My obedience
Expedites
My God-manifesting days.

5446.

The heart-room of love
Always remains
Empty of question.

5447.

If you speak ill of God's
Compassion-Eye,
Your mind-prison-torture
You will not be able to escape.

5448.

God tells me that
My heart's gratitude-tears
Are His most precious treasures.

5449.

There was a time
When I greatly admired
My mind's ego-sermons.
But those days are buried in
    oblivion.
I now only admire and love
My heart-songs.

5450.

May the beauty
Of my obedience-mind
And the fragrance
Of my gratitude-heart
Forever remain inseparable.

5451.

An aspiration-heart-nest
Is
God's Dream-Manifestation-
    Reality.

5452.

God enfolds
Each and every truth-seeker
And peace-lover
At His choice Hour.

5453.

Sleep
Is not rest.
Sleep
Is energy-gathering wisdom.

5454.

The past failures
Do not take as real.
The future promises only
Are real in our spiritual life.

5455.

If we look with the mind's eye,
We shall see and feel no happiness
In this world.

5456.

Since you do not have
Even a grain of aspiration,
Why and how are you blaming
    God
For delaying your God-
    realisation?

5457.

My morning meditation
Does not deal with
Yesterday's frustration.
It deals only with
Tomorrow's illumination.

5458.

The outer environment can be
    perfect
Only when
The inner environment cares only
    for
God-satisfaction.

5459.

Each uncomely thought
Can easily blight
Our heart-smiles.

5460.

Divinity's infinite Joy
Is found only
In the temple of silence.

5461.

Let my illumination-soul
Smile
Through my aspiration-heart.

5462.

Let my aspiration-heart
Cry
Inside my doubting mind.

5463.

Let my doubting mind
Feel guilty
And take a new way of life.

5464.

How do I love humanity?
I love humanity through
My soul's inner happiness.

5465.

How do I serve humanity?
I serve humanity through
My heart's inner concern.

5466.

His soul's rich smiles
He is sharing with
Poor and suffering hearts.

5467.

Feel for others' minds
The way you feel for
Your own heart.

5468.

Each spiritual Master
Is a lighthouse
For those who are lost
In ignorance-sea.

5469.

The mind's volcano-anger
Is no match for
The heart's fountain-love.

5470.

How I wish I could be
A source of inspiration
And strength
For those who think
That they are total failures.

5471.

If you take pride
In being humble,
Then you are a humility-clown.

5472.

He who develops inner strength
Through outer discipline
Will last long.

5473.

If you utilise only your leisure-
        moments
To think of God,
Then you are a useless seeker.

5474.

No matter how strong
The ignorance-mind-fort is,
It can easily be destroyed
By my God-oneness-will.

5475.

The mind's excitement-
    exploration
I dearly loved.
The heart's illumination-
    perfection
I now am.

5476.

Without a very rich heart,
How can you have
A peaceful mind?

5477.

Every day I pine
To grow into
The beauty and fragrance
Of my heart-rose.

5478.

In the outer world,
God's number one choice
Is my sleepless surrender-life.

5479.

In the inner world,
God's number one choice
Is my breathless gratitude-heart.

5480.

How beautiful is
The morning
Of God's Love-Light.

5481.

How peaceful is
The evening
Of God's Silence-Delight.

5482.

The fear of my mind
Can be replaced
Only with my heart's sleepless
    faith
In God.

5483.

O seeker,
If God's Love-Weapon
Cannot conquer you,
What else will conquer you?

5484.

Every day
Mankind is aiming
Its dissatisfaction-arrows
At God.

5485.

Do you want to be perfect?
Then feel for others
The way you feel for yourself.

5486.

I feel deeply honoured
When my Master scolds me
In season and out of season.

5487.

In the morning,
The God of Love
Tells me what to do.

5488.

At noon,
The God of Joy
Tells me what to do.

5489.

In the evening,
The God of Peace
Tells me what to do.

5490.

Each seeker has to realise
That he is a special spark
Of the Infinite.

5491.

If you have an aspiration-heart,
Then either today or tomorrow
Your heart will smile
Through your eyes.

5492.

Unimaginable
When my soul smiles
Through my dedication-life.

5493.

On the altar of peace,
Inner silence speaks, sings
And dances.

5494.

God's infinite Grace does not
    allow me
To see anymore
My old, ancient ignorance-face.

5495.

God tells me that
I can be perfect,
If ever I can resign myself
Unconditionally
To His divine Consciousness
And supreme Love.

5496.

If you really love God,
Then God wants you to prove it
By loving all.

5497.

It is God's Compassion-Eye
That does not allow any negative
    force
To blight
My inner smiles.

5498.

When prosperity comes,
Grow into an extra expansion
Of gratitude-heart-smile.

5499.

My aspiration-heart
Needs no mind-inspiration
For interpretation.

5500.

To the greatest joy and satisfaction
Of my Lord Supreme,
I am now all ready to become
A new aspiration-heart
And
A new dedication-life.

5501.

If we cannot transform
The ingratitude-mind-dragon,
Then we shall not have
Abiding happiness
In our life.

5502.

Alas, for a long, long time,
A growing pain of emptiness
Inside my heart
Has been disturbing my inner
    poise.

5503.

To say that I can fathom
God's Compassion-Eye
Is to say that I can exhaust
The inexhaustible.

5504.

Every day God wants us
To come and enjoy
His magical Prayer-Grace.

5505.

We can swim against the stream
Of our deplorable deeds
If we can arm ourselves
With God's Compassion-Light.

5506.

There are so many divine things
To see and become
When we go beyond the horizon
Of the known.

5507.

We should not try
To dampen the spirit
Of the discontented.
We should only increase and
    increase
The satisfaction-flames
Of the contented.

5508.

Each time we have a deep
    meditation,
God invites us to feast
On the Nectar-Bliss of His divine
    Love.

5509.

My morning prayer to God is this:
"My Lord, do give me the capacity
To soar
On my heart-dream-bird-wings."

5510.

My gratitude-heart is the smile
That lights my entire life
And welcomes my Lord Supreme.

5511.

Excruciating pangs
Dig holes
For Divinity's Joy
To fill.

5512.

My soulful prayers
Enjoy the breathtaking,
Divine spectacle
Of God's Heart-Garden.

5513.

Nothing is lost
By discarding the uncomely
    thoughts
Of our God-searching mind.

5514.

Every seeker must try to deserve
At least one Gift
From our Lord Beloved Supreme.

5515.

Every morning God comes
To affirm our inner strength
And praise our outer efforts.

5516.

Your endeavours will not end
In disappointment
If God is what you want
In all your actions.

5517.

One word that wakes
All humanity:
Love, love, love!

5518.

If we love the spiritual life,
It is God who will tell us
When to start, how to start,
Why to start and where to end.

5519.

When God smiles,
His Smile is for everybody's heart
To clasp.

5520.

Either you do the right thing
To soar,
Or you do the wrong thing
To sink.
It is you who have to decide.

5521.

No matter how hard we try to
    deny it,
There shall come a time
When we will be bound to hear
God's clarion Call.

5522.

When our faith becomes
   immortal,
There will be nothing difficult
For us to accomplish for God.
Everything will be
Easier than the easiest.

5523.

An impurity-mind-river
Will never be able to run
Into a peace-sea.

5524.

Even if you dream of postponing
The Hour of God,
When that Hour strikes,
Immediately wake up, look
   around
And run straight towards
Your destination.

5525.

There is an instant recovery
From your mind's impurity-
   ailments.
That instant recovery is your
   entrance
Into the beauty-purity
Of your heart-garden.

5526.

My clever mind takes me
Into the whirlpool of confusion
And tells me that this is
The perfection-satisfaction-hope
Of illumination.

5527.

If you do not enjoy
Your journey's start,
A sad failure will be
All yours.

5528.

At times the outer victories
Prove to be a veritable defeat
For our inner aspiration-life.

5529.

When I want to speak to God,
He tells me:
"Come and see Me
At My old, illumining Vision-
   Home."

5530.

God is always ready
To free us
From the noise of our mind
And take us into
Our self-transcendence-heart.

5531.

God created us
Only to provide
His own Happiness-Chariot.

5532.

Do not surrender to your mind's
Mortal desires,
But surrender to your soul's
Immortal aspirations
Every day and every hour of your
    life.

5533.

Keep your heart's faith-fountain
Always
In cheerful and self-giving action.

5534.

How can we develop our love for
    God
If we do not consciously try to feel
His boundless Compassion
And boundless Concern for us
At every moment?

5535.

Obedience
Is the secret and sacred key
To open up
God's Satisfaction-Heart.

5536.

You have not come into the world
To see the number of your years.
You have come here
To become the tears of your heart
And the smiles of your soul,
To become consciously
And inseparably one
With God's Love-Will-Power.

5537.

When my heart smiles,
God sees another God
Inside me.

5538.

The silence of the mind
Has to go beyond all reasons
And beyond all understanding.

5539.

Pour goodness and not greatness
Into your aspiration-life
To please God in His own Way.

5540.

We must compel
The mind's sun to set
On both stupidities and trickeries.

5541.

The blossoming heart
We see
Only when the heart is armed
With surrender-light.

5542.

When my mind lived in a
    monastery,
It became God-forgetfulness-
    misery,
Plus mockery.

5543.

We must never allow ourselves
To drown in depression's abysmal
    abyss
If we have even an iota of love for
    God.

5544.

If we constantly calculate
Each and every move of ours,
Then we are heading towards
A dead end.

5545.

Close your eyes
To miss your doubt-strangers.
Close your ears
To miss your doubt-
    acquaintances.

5546.

I am more than satisfied
In breaking my old ties
With my fear-doubt-friends.

5547.

My Lord,
As soon as You see me,
You take the possession-greed
Out of me
And replace it with aspiration-
    need.

5548.

We must have a field
Where we can sow the seeds
For God's Love, Blessings
And Compassion,
But we shall not sow expectation-
    seeds.

5549.

Is there anything
That enthusiasm cannot conquer
In our life
And thus bring about satisfaction?

5550.

My Lord, I would like to have
At least one purity-page
In my entire life-book.

5551.

Man's perfection
Is God's Goal
For mankind.

5552.

Our heart-cries are not sincere
    enough,
Loud enough or pure enough
For God to hear.

5553.

God is asking me to tell Him
My progress-promise
Every day.

5554.

Slowly, steadily, gradually
And unerringly
We must move forward
Towards the beauty and delight
Of our Goal.

5555.

I am happy only when
I sincerely invoke
My Lord's Forgiveness-Feet.

5556.

Give and take, give and take;
But give more, give more
To make the divine in you
Extremely happy
And extremely proud of you.

5557.

We must not delay in capturing
All our mind-jungle-animals:
Pride, fear, doubt, self-
    complacency,
Insincerity and impurity.

5558.

Every day God asks me to come to
    Him
And sing a new heart-song
To inspire Him
For His full manifestation on
    earth.

5559.

Finally I have decided that I must
    join
An ignorance-weight-loss
    programme
To make myself happy and
    perfect.

5560.

My Satisfaction-God
Never wants
My surrender-voyage
To end.

5561.

Your self-discovery is not a secret
    thing.
It is a sacred thing,
And also it is something
That God Himself treasures.

5562.

God's Compassion wanted me
And my God-longing tears
To discover Him.

5563.

When we do not march alongside
Our fellow seekers,
God feels that we are not ready
For the Path.
It is one family.
He wants all the members
To march along together.

5564.

Every time my Lord examines me,
He expects me to pass my
    examination
With flying colours.

5565.

My unconditional surrender
Has received Heaven's highest
    award:
Immortality's Smile!

5566.

Always keep your vital under
    control.
Do not allow it to be tempted
By dark, darker, darkest desires.

5567.

My Lord, relieve my heavy
    burden!
"My child, I have already relieved
    you
Of your burden of ignorance-
    indulgence.
See it and believe it!"

5568.

In the inmost sanctuary of silence,
I hear my Lord singing,
I see my Lord dancing.

5569.

If you can roar
With God-satisfaction-
    determination,
Then definitely one day
You will be able to satisfy God
In His own Way.

5570.

O seeker,
If you want to run faster than the
    fastest,
Do not hide behind the walls
Of self-importance, arrogance
And pride.

5571.

Alas, how difficult it is to find
One's long-lost
God-invocation-capacity.

5572.

I do not need
A larger than the largest hope-
    boat
To save me.
Even the tiniest hope-raft can save
    me
And save my all.

5573.

Each human being arrives on
    earth
With a very special plan
Given by God Himself.

5574.

God blessingfully invites me
Every day
To come and sit at the summit
Of my aspiration.

5575.

We must ignite the fire
Of self-giving love
To please our Lord Supreme
In His own Way.

5576.

When you sing a sweet melody
Flooded with purity,
Then God will be right beside you.

5577.

What I need,
What I needed
And what I shall always need
Are two God-service-arms.

5578.

My Lord is blessing my heart once
    again
With my childhood's
Sweetness-fragrance.

5579.

Ignorance-night and wisdom-
    light
With equal happiness
Course through me.

5580.

My Lord,
Let me find myself
With You, in You and for You
Once and for all.

5581.

The moment I hear
The Heartbeat of my Lord
    Supreme,
I immediately follow.

5582.

My Lord's unconditional
Compassion-Smiles
Are piloting my life-boat
Towards His Infinity's Golden
    Shore.

5583.

It is a foregone conclusion
That truth
Eventually prevails.

5584.

Pay no attention
To your animal instincts.
Pay all attention
To your divine intuition.

5585.

Be not predisposed to guilt-
    thoughts
If you want to succeed in your
    outer life
And proceed in your inner life.

5586.

My Lord,
How I wish I could be fed every
    day
By the Smiles of Your Fragrance-
    Eye.

5587.

Alas, I do not know why I still
    cherish
Disposable thoughts in my mind
And disposable feelings in my
    heart.

5588.

Those who want to live
On the island of expectation
Ultimately live in frustration-
    desert.

5589.

When I do not want to serve
God the creation,
God the Creator denies me
    admission
To His Heart.

5590.

Each human being must realise
That this world needs only smiles
And not frowns from him.

5591.

A genuine God-lover
Must not spend even one minute
In worthless and useless
    fascination
With the past.

5592.

If we do not purify and illumine
The mind,
We are bound to develop
A spiritual cancer
In our aspiration-heart.

5593.

If you have a strong belief
In God's Omnipresence-
    Existence,
Then God will bless you
With His own Breath.

5594.

We want to enjoy
Our journey's completion-
    celebration
Long before our journey's start.

5595.

Harmony and peace:
These two friends are always ready
To give us a very long life
For God-realisation
And God-manifestation.
But alas, we deliberately do not
    take
Their assistance.

5596.

To cure humanity's lifelong
    ailments,
Every day God uses
His Forgiveness-Remedy.

5597.

The mind-lecturer has lectured
For a long time.
Now I would like the heart-singer
To sing for me.

5598.

When we grow into
The Universal Consciousness,
Infinity's Fulness comes
And embraces us.

5599.

The heart faces problem after
    problem
When the mind constantly
    changes
Its opinion of God.

5600.

A sleeplessly self-giving heart
Uniquely shines
In the galaxy of divinity.

5601.

Alas, I never knew
That my intelligence-greed
Would bury my wisdom-hunger.

5602.

Every day I voice forth
My praise for angels
For their eagerness for the
    manifestation
Of God's Light on earth.

5603.

If you want to receive from God
His highest Praise,
Then immediately surrender
Your individuality's shameless
    face.

5604.

May my God-hungry heart
Every day bloom and blossom
With mystical dreams.

5605.

Whenever my undivine mind
Gets an opportunity,
It steals away my heart's God-
    dreams.

5606.

My Lord tells me
That He will not accept
My pitiful pleas,
But He will only accept
My cheerful invitation.

5607.

No matter how sincere and deep
My heart's gratitude is,
It will never match
My Supreme Lord's Compassion-
    Eye.

5608.

There was a time
When my desire-bound mind
Was repelled by divinity.
But now the same mind
Is attracted by divinity.

5609.

If you have compassion,
You must express it
To make it more effective
And more perfect.

5610.

The outer enemies
Are dangerous.
The inner enemies
Are treacherous.

5611.

My Lord tells me
That He loves my affection-heart
And my gratitude-heart
Far more than I can ever imagine.

5612.

How easy to do the right thing!
Yet we enjoy doing
The wrong thing.

5613.

God's Smile
Charms my heart
And disarms my mind.

5614.

When you invite attachment,
You do not realise that misery
Also follows.

5615.

Quite often we are afraid of
Our mind's warnings,
But not those from God.

5616.

Catch the underlying thought
In your mind
Before it catches you.

5617.

In our spiritual life,
The speed of the doubting mind
Is never registered.

5618.

How cleverly and powerfully
The doubter in me
Exercises its ego-power.

5619.

The mind enjoys
World-information-food.
The heart enjoys
God's Compassion-Eye-Food.

5620.

God's Compassion-Eye can
    transform
Even the lowest sinner-mind
Into the highest sage-life.

5621.

God has made
Each soul
His own Divinity's masterpiece.

5622.

At every moment
You must fight and fight
Against the strongest ignorance-
    current.

5623.

Alas, how often our mind
Houses
Life-destruction-thoughts!

5624.

God is waiting
For me to fly,
And I am waiting
For God to smile.

5625.

There are many places
For my soul to live,
But it prefers living inside
My heart's aspiration-flames.

5626.

Cover immediately
Your foolishness-mind,
And enjoy at every moment
Your openness-heart.

5627.

Wisdom can speak perfectly,
But it begs God
To speak in and through it.

5628.

Divine dreams hold reality
Not only very dear
But also very near.

5629.

Alas, in vain I have been trying
To come out of my mind's
Nightmare-mire.

5630.

My mind, I need no more
Explanations from you.
I need only one thing from you:
Expansion.

5631.

To enjoy a rapid inner ascent,
We must empty our mind
Completely.

5632.

Every day we must ignore
Our temptation-vital
Dauntlessly and ruthlessly.

5633.

Too much, too much, too much!
My mind thinks too much.
My heart feels too much.
I hate my life too much.

5634.

When my mind is fast asleep,
What does my heart do?
My heart enjoys playing
God's Compassion-Flute.

5635.

The moment a dreamer of peace
Visits God's Compassion-Palace,
He immediately receives
A sweeter than the sweetest
Smile from God.

5636.

Do not say that you want to
    surrender
Ultimately,
But declare that you want to
    surrender
Immediately, plus completely.

5637.

My insecurity does not miss
Any opportunity
To take away my heart-joy.

5638.

His God-surrender-joy
Permeates each and every action
Of his.

5639.

Today's climbing prayer
Will tomorrow reach
God's Illumination-Tower
Without fail.

5640.

A oneness-lover
Has an ever-expanding heart
And an ever-widening mind.

5641.

My patience is my revealed
God-manifestation-
Determination-promise.

5642.

I do not long for
God's Love-Height,
But I do long for
God's Forgiveness-Depth.

5643.

I live on my heart's
Helpless tears.
I live on my Lord's
Nectar-Smiles.

5644.

When my mind does not obey
    God,
I am forced to live in a bed
Of hurtful thorns.

5645.

May my mind always
Live in the land of inspiration.
May my heart always
Live in the land of aspiration.
May my life always
Live in the land of dedication.
May I always
Live in the land of self-
   purification.

5646.

To adorn my life's shrine,
I need both my heart-tears
And my God-Smiles.

5647.

O my mind,
Every morning you take
A full breath of optimism;
O my heart,
Every morning you take
A full breath of dynamism –
To please my Lord Supreme
In His own Way.

5648.

My Lord has blessed me
With sleepless heart-tears
And what do I see in Him?
His all-embracing, self-giving
   Heart.

5649.

My seeker-friend,
You are destined
Not only to discover God,
But also to become another God
At God's choice Hour.

5650.

O my sleepless God-hunger,
You are the only hero in my life
Whom I adore.

5651.

Each time we embark on a new
   project
For God-manifestation,
God blesses us
With a most powerful Smile –
Long before we place our victory
At His Feet.

5652.

When I ask my Lord to wake up
And talk to me, He tells me:
"My child, when did I go to sleep?
It is you who are fast asleep
And not talking to Me!"

5653.

O forces of failure,
Do you think I will give you
    satisfaction?
Never.
Not even an iota of satisfaction!
I shall definitely be crowned
With success.

5654.

Yesterday I thought God was
    upstairs.
Today I see God is not only on my
    floor,
But also in my room, inviting me
    to play
Hide-and-seek with Him.

5655.

God tells the sincere seekers
That He does not approve of
Their slightest postponement.

5656.

God does not want to frighten us.
He just wants to enlighten us
In His own Way.

5657.

The smallest act
Of self-offering to God
Can easily smite
Our mind's doubt-tree.

5658.

God knows no preferences.
But He does know the excellence
Of God-seekers
Who definitely deserve His
    Closeness
And Nearness.

5659.

When impatience assails us,
We blindfold our eyes
And see not the arrival of light.

5660.

If you fail to subdue your passion,
You will not be able to remove
Your mind-clouds.

5661.

Can you not see, O seeker-friend,
That your iron self-discipline of
    the past
Has made your life infinitely
    easier
While you are walking along the
    road
Of perfection and satisfaction?

5662.

Do not blame your circumstances
If your own aspiration-seed
Is lying indefinitely dormant.

5663.

It is not a bad thing
To stimulate your curiosity,
But you must not stop
At curiosity.
You have to go further and further
To enter into
Your God-necessity-sincerity.

5664.

God's Grace descended,
And the uncomely thoughts of his
    mind
Disappeared like storm clouds.

5665.

In the clear space
Between my surrender-life
And my gratitude-heart,
I see my Lord smiling, singing
And dancing.

5666.

Cheerfully and self-givingly
He bends his all
To the Will of God.

5667.

Do not turn your back on God.
He is your Friend,
Your true Friend
And only Friend.

5668.

When I enter into my mind,
What I invariably see
Is a huge wave of restlessness.

5669.

When I enter into my heart,
What I immediately see, feel
And become
Is a sea of peacefulness.

5670.

Yesterday I flew in my mind-sky
On wings of imagination.
Today I am flying in my heart-sky
On wings of inspiration.
Tomorrow I shall fly in my soul-
sky
On wings of God-realisation.

5671.

What an undivine mind we have!
We see that God is waiting,
waiting,
Waiting for us,
But we have no affection for Him,
We have no concern for Him.
We live in our self-indulgence-
pride.

5672.

Choose your spiritual Master
wisely,
If you decide to choose.
Give yourself entirely to him,
If you at all want to give.

5673.

Only God's unconditional Grace
Can do this for me:
I keep meeting His Compassion-
Eye
Wherever I go today.

5674.

How fortunate I am!
Today God is chasing away
My mind-thief and my vital-
culprit.

5675.

If you have the power of love,
Use it time and again
As long as you want to.
But if you have the love of power,
Do not manifest it.

5676.

There is always a divine choice:
Either we shall pay all our
attention
To God's Miracles
Or
To God's Compassion.

5677.

In the inner world
They ask me
Not what I have done,
But whose I am.

5678.

We do not know why we enjoy
Not only strange necessities
But also
Worthless and useless necessities.

5679.

No matter how undivine and
    hostile
A human being is,
There cannot be a total eclipse
Of his soul.

5680.

When we live
Only in past happiness-days,
We double our present pain.

5681.

When my heart
Wants to feel something,
I get joy.
When my mind
Wants to doubt something,
I get joy.
Alas, why do I accept
Both positive and negative aspects
Of my life?
My life should be only for the
    positive!

5682.

What is human life,
If not the union
Of bombastic words
And empty talk?

5683.

Your life shall blossom
Like roses in your heart-garden,
If you kindle the flames
In your aspiration-heart-temple.

5684.

My mind's darkness,
No matter how thick it is,
Has to give way to my heart's
    light,
However little it is.

5685.

My mind's confusion-thunder
Is frightening the angels
In my heart-garden.

5686.

God tells me that He treasures
My life's simplicity,
My mind's sincerity
And my heart's purity.

5687.

What indefinitely delays
My God-realisation?
My mind's volcano-pride!

5688.

God loved you.
You loved God.
God continues to love you,
But you have withdrawn your love
From God.
God will remember this;
God will remember this!

5689.

When I enter into God's Heart-
    Boat,
I immediately see
That God has replaced
His Greatness with His Goodness.

5690.

If you want to have an infinite
    series
Of God-experiences,
Then each moment of your life,
Dedicate yourself unconditionally
To God's Will.

5691.

Emotional detachment has to be
    valued
If we want to strengthen
Our devotional attachment to
    God.

5692.

Can you not see
What you have in your mind?
You have a destructive speed-
    demon
That will devour you before long.

5693.

If your heart-eye is streaming
With tears of devotion,
God-realisation will not remain
A far cry.

5694.

May my life be flooded
With aspiration-dedication-
    promises
To fulfil God the Creator
And God the creation
As soon as possible.

5695.

May my aspiration-heart
And dedication-life
Remain bent all the time
To touch the Lotus-Feet
Of the Lord Supreme.

5696.

No ear can ever be as deaf
As a disobedience-ear
To God's Compassion-flooded
Message-Light.

5697.

In the spiritual life,
A seeker always has to feel
That his life is permanently
    endorsed
By God's divine Presence.

5698.

My life has value
Only when it sings
Soulful joy-songs
At the Feet of my Lord Supreme.

5699.

My Lord Supreme,
I have been praying to You
To open my heart's silence-door
To welcome Your Silence-Smiles.

5700.

God's magic Touch
Can transform
Even the desert-mind
Into an aspiration-fountain-heart.

5701.

God tells me
That He wants to live only on
My self-giving to His universe.

5702.

Who else will be able
To uproot the deep-rooted
Ignorance-life-tree,
If not the God-seekers?

5703.

I tell my doubt-mind
That it is an unwelcome
Travelling companion.

5704.

May my life stand between
The beauty
Of my God-realisation
And the fragrance
Of my God-manifestation.

5705.

If we all cherish
Our life's ingratitude-mind,
Then it will be an unimaginable
    loss
For our God-hunger.

5706.

I want to see
The smiling and dancing child
In my heart-garden.
But alas, what do I see?
A devouring dragon-frown
Inside my mind-jungle!

5707.

My Lord,
Your Scolding creates
A genuine hunger
For Your Smile.

5708.

When I am in the physical
    presence
Of my Master,
His greatness tells me
What I shall eventually become,
And his goodness tells me
What I eternally am:
His Eternity's choice instrument.

5709.

My mind-jungle
Is the last place to look
For my soul's smile.

5710.

You are not conscious of the fact
That the great illusion
Has closed your eyes
With your permission.
Remember this.

5711.

My heart cries and cries with
    gratitude
When God's Smiles come down
To feed my heart.

5712.

My Lord, before I even offer You
My heart-gratitude-flower,
You bring me Your Heart's
Satisfaction-Fruit.

5713.

With an eager heart
I have been waiting
For my mind's transformation.
With a smiling heart
I shall continue to wait
Until my mind's transformation
    dawns.

5714.

We cannot believe
That God's Compassion-Eye
Is attracted to our helplessness.

5715.

O my heart, wake up, wake up!
Can you not see that our Lord
    Supreme
Is waiting for you to learn
An ever-new soul-song and soul-
    dance
From Him?

5716.

I wanted to show my Lord
    Supreme
My heart-cottage.
My Lord Supreme told me:
"My child, first come and see
My Heart-Palace,
Which is your real home, only
    home."

5717.

When I take my spiritual life
Seriously,
God increases His Love for me
Immeasurably.

5718.

Alas, meaningless thoughts
And worthless ideas
Are ruling the entire world.

5719.

The earth-bound time
Is ceaselessly crying
For the Heaven-free hour
In vain.

5720.

Man creates disaster after disaster
For himself.
What does God do?
God tries to save man
Each and every time.

5721.

When we love God
With our heart's gratitude-tears,
God tells us:
"My child, My Infinity's Smiles
Are for you.
They are all yours!"

5722.

Before you go to sleep,
You must pray to God
For a prayerful, cheerful
  awakening.

5723.

When we pray and meditate,
We feel a new life
And hear a new message
With each breath.

5724.

Be careful!
Do not cut jokes
With disobedience-darkness.

5725.

God's Compassion-Eye
Has transformed my volcano-
  mind
Into my peace-flower-heart-
  garden.

5726.

A seeker's most sacred possession:
The dust-atoms
Of his Master's feet.

5727.

Do not be unnecessarily involved
In others' problems,
But be immediately involved
In others' sorrows.

5728.

Every day I invite my mind
To come and play
With my oneness-heart,
But my mind deliberately
And pointedly refuses.

5729.

Whether you look upward or
    inward,
You are bound to see
The same Sunshine-Smiles
From God's Eye.

5730.

It seems that each human life
Is a victim
To intermittent
Depression-frustration-showers.

5731.

If you are planning to advance
Each step in your spiritual life
With great hesitation,
Then your Goal will always
    remain
A far cry.

5732.

We are tortured ruthlessly
Even by the smaller than the
    smallest
Doubt-dragon.

5733.

God literally begs His children
To make all possible attempts
To amuse Him every day.
But alas, somehow we do not
    succeed!

5734.

If your heart becomes a devotion-
    flower,
Then your mind will not suffer
Long spells of spiritual dryness.

5735.

There can be no spiritual life on
    earth
That is beyond correction
And beyond perfection.

5736.

Every day, with bated breath,
I long for my Lord's
Clear and unmistakable Presence
Inside my heart-garden.

5737.

My mind is finally ready
To be fully awakened,
Like my God-oneness-heart.

5738.

Every day
You must compel your mind
To avoid
Disobedience-highway.

5739.

Practise every day
Readiness, willingness
And eagerness-exercises
To become the strongest soldier
In God's Army.

5740.

God is really fond
Of your heart-hope
More than anything else.

5741.

When I meditate on the sunset-
    silence,
I see that God's Peace-Boat
Is sailing towards me
Fast, very fast.

5742.

If you have a suspicion-mind
In your spiritual life,
Then you are bound to feel
That you have nowhere to live
And you have nowhere to go.

5743.

At the very start of my spiritual
    journey,
God told me that there would be
No station-stop,
Because the journey itself
Is ever-inspiring, ever-illumining
And ever-fulfilling.

5744.

As long as we do not protest
The mind's leadership,
We are bound to miss the ecstasy
Of our fountain-heart.

5745.

My Lord, may my heart-tears
Be as infinite
As Your Heart-Smiles eternally
    are.

5746.

O my heart, look, look!
Sweet thoughts are descending
From Above
To revive you from your amnesia.

5747.

My Lord tells me
That His Compassion-Eye
Will enable me
To transform my desire-elephant
Into an aspiration-deer.

5748.

Perfection will dawn
Only when all human beings
Sing, play and dance
In unison.

5749.

Your God-dreams
Will save you
From all your mind-disasters.

5750.

A true seeker will definitely
Be helped by God
To disperse his life's mist.

5751.

Look at the world
Prayerfully, soulfully and
    affectionately
If you want the world
To make progress.

5752.

We must serve our Lord Supreme
With sterling devotion
To make the fastest progress.

5753.

My Lord Supreme
Is far away from me
Precisely because I claim
My superiority over others.

5754.

Always long for speed.
If not, the slow death of
    stagnation
Will capture you.

5755.

My Lord,
At every moment of my life
I shall fulfil
Your supreme Command.

5756.

The culmination of aspiration
Is God-realisation.
The culmination of God-
    realisation
Is God-manifestation.
The culmination of God-
    manifestation
Is humanity's total
    transformation.

5757.

You can stand far above
The dictates of morality.
But you must never dare
To stand far above
The dictates of spirituality,
For spirituality is inseparable
    oneness
With God's Will.

5758.

What determines our rebirth?
God's Vision-Eye
And our soul's God-acceptance-
    delight.

5759.

When we become absolutely one
With God's Will,
Imperishable and infallible truths
Become ours.

5760.

I do not pray
For a man-made palace.
I pray
For a God-made heart-cottage.

5761.

Every day,
Either consciously or
    unconsciously,
So many human beings
Are starving their souls.
Yet their souls continue to forgive
Their body, vital, mind and heart.

5762.

The more we enjoy expectation,
The heavier becomes
Our mind's frustration.

5763.

Desire-prompted actions
Are nothing other than
Himalayan blunders.

5764.

Happy are those
Who follow their Master.
Happier are those
Who follow and love their Master.
Happiest are those
Who follow, love and surrender
Their very existence to their
    Master.

5765.

My Lord,
You have been leading my soul
For millennia.
Will You not lead my body, vital,
Mind and heart from now on?

5766.

Opportunity beckons us
Quite often,
But we do not pay any heed to it.

5767.

We can bury all our problems
If we strengthen our faith in God
And multiply our love for God.

5768.

We do not have to understand
The power of the Goal.
We just have to become one
With the beauty and perfection
Of the Goal.

5769.

The wisdom of the ancients
Was self-discovery.
The wisdom of the moderns
Is science-mastery.

5770.

What is pride?
It is something that will
    eventually
Trample its possessor.

5771.

You want to go out
And see the world.
God wants you to come home
And become the world.

5772.

Instead of trying to demolish your
     life,
You must face life
And make it infinitely better
By bringing down God's Grace.

5773.

Happiness
Is an inner journey
From one world to another.

5774.

Aspiration
Is the pride of religion.
Dedication
Is the pride of science.

5775.

Although our questions about
     God
Are faulty,
We all expect proper answers.

5776.

What does it take
To have a self-giving life?
It takes a combination
Of determination and patience.

5777.

Every day
I must look at the world
With the freshness
Of my Lord's Eye
And with the fulness
Of my Lord's Heart.

5778.

How breathtaking it is
To see my heart
Playing, singing and dancing
With the morning rainbow-
     beauty!

5779.

Every day
My soul is helping my heart
To climb to God's Satisfaction-
     Summit.

5780.

Not God's Justice-Mind,
But God's Compassion-Eye
Sleeplessly guards the border
Between earth-cries and Heaven-
     Smiles.

5781.

O seeker,
Do not forget that each new day
Is a golden God-Arrival-
    opportunity-day.

5782.

We all live
In the mind-world of earning.
But God wants us to live
In the heart-world of learning.

5783.

My heart does not have to prove
That it lives in God.
But my mind has to prove
At every moment
That it lives in God.

5784.

God sheds uncontrollable Tears
When He sees
That I leave no stone unturned
To dwarf all my
Aspiration-dedication-friends.

5785.

My Lord Beloved Supreme
Has repeatedly told me
That I do not have to knock
At His Heart-Door
To come in.
He has said to me:
"My child, you have a free access
To My Heart.
I am always eager to greet you
Happily, blessingfully and
    proudly."

5786.

My ceaseless self-discovery-
    hunger
Has silenced
My storm-tossed, sleepless days
And nights.

5787.

Aspire, seeker, aspire!
Breathlessly aspire!
Do not allow
Your God-manifestation-dream
To expire.

5788.

A sleeplessly self-giving life
Is very close
To the summit-height of Heaven.

5789.

A God-surrendered mind
Is not afraid
Of even an avalanche of thoughts.

5790.

My smiles conceal
The human in me.
My tears reveal
The divine in me.

5791.

Every morning and every evening
My soul teaches me
How to listen
To its soundless sound-whispers.

5792.

Neither God's tall Order
Nor His sorrowful Pleas
Can change
My ignorance-addicted mind.

5793.

God dearly treasures
Even my fleeting oneness
With His Will.

5794.

When my mind and I
Live together,
We live in the land of talkers.

5795.

When my heart and I
Live together,
We live in the land of self-givers.

5796.

I am not as simple, as sincere
And as pure as my ancestors of old.
Nevertheless, my Lord tells me
That I shall manifest His Light
Infinitely more than my ancestors
    did.
What else is my Lord's
Compassion-Miracle-
    Performance?

5797.

No more my mind
Shall disobey God.
No more my vital
Shall deny God.
No more my body
Shall delay God.
No more my life
Shall starve God.

5798.

God comes not
To brick-stone-temples.
He frequents only
Heart-devotion-breath-temples.

5799.

When I invoke God
With my heart's love-tears,
He immediately starts running
His fastest towards me,
His Destination,
To give me His proudest Embrace.

5800.

My gratitude-heart-river
I have offered to my Lord
    Supreme.
Every morning He comes
And enjoys fishing.

5801.

My Lord Supreme,
Your Forgiveness-Heart
Is my happiness-kingdom.

5802.

God's Smiles melt
My heart.
They do not break
My heart.

5803.

My Lord,
Your Eye brightens my hope
And
Enlightens my promise.

5804.

When God the Compassion
    invites you,
Receive His Invitation
    immediately
And
Do not forget to take with you
Your silence-mind.

5805.

My life-boat plies
Between my heart's streaming
    tears
And
My soaring smiles.

5806.

What this world needs
Is a constant peace-dreamer
And sleepless God-lover.

5807.

My Lord,
How I wish at every moment
Your Forgiveness-Magnet
Would pull my heart.

5808.

My Lord,
I have become
The dust of Your Feet.
What more do I need?

5809.

Your aspiration is high
And
Your dedication is sincere.
Therefore, Eternity's ocean
And Infinity's sun
Shall welcome you.

5810.

My Lord,
Keep me always inside
Your blessingful and powerful
    Dream.

5811.

Does God live close enough to
    you?
If He does not,
Cry like a child,
Smile like a child.
Lo, God is available everywhere
    for you.

5812.

I always listen to
My Lord's
Oneness-heart-spokesman.

5813.

The God-dividing mind
Will never be invited
By the angels
To come to God's Palace.

5814.

God definitely wants you
To harvest
Your heart's hopes.

5815.

When I feel that
God is pleased with me,
I keep all my thoughts
Clinging to His Feet.

5816.

My soul is helplessly alarmed
At my life's
Sadness-sigh.

5817.

My heart-hunger's only feast
Is my Lord's
Compassion-Eye.

5818.

God's Satisfaction-Feet
Have given me a free ticket
To enter into the heart
Of Infinity's Bliss.

5819.

A river of enthusiasm
Is carrying my life
To Infinity's ocean,
Singing, "Yes, yes and yes."

5820.

I am so happy
That my heart-house
Is full of
Blossoming hopes.

5821.

The modern world
Thinks that it can live
Without the deepening depth.

5822.

The modern world
Thinks that it cannot live
Without the conquering breadth.

5823.

God is God's
Loving Presence-Response
When my prayer's name
Is soulfulness.

5824.

Pray and meditate!
Pray and meditate!
Your mind is not meant for
Uncomely thoughts.
Your mind is meant to be
A choice instrument of God.

5825.

May my aspiration-heart
Be anchored
To the highest planet.

5826.

In every fibre of my soul,
God's Compassion,
God's Protection
And
God's Satisfaction I feel.

5827.

If a seeker's life is empty
Of God-dreams,
Then he cannot succeed.

5828.

I am desperately trying to revive
My God-sweetness-memories
Long past.

5829.

Each God-realised soul
Happily, proudly and self-givingly
Endorses God's Dream
For the sorrowful earth.

5830.

Challenge complacency
If you want to include
An extra supply of God-energy
In your life.

5831.

God's secret and sacred Whispers
Show us the way
To God's Ecstasy.

5832.

I never have a sense of
    completeness
In my life
When I miss
God's inner Presence.

5833.

Deep meditation means
God-satisfaction
Lovingly, soulfully and self-
    givingly.

5834.

May my heart's happiness-breath
Become a choice instrument
Of my Lord Beloved Supreme.

5835.

If you cannot conform your will
To God's Will,
You are bound to fail miserably
In your spiritual life.

5836.

There was a time
When I was caught
In the meshes of the mind,
But now I am a citizen
Of my heart-delight.

5837.

God asks you to pay
Sleepless and breathless attention
To your heart's inner cry.

5838.

My mind,
Keep your thoughts silent.
Keep your words silent.
Keep everything that you have
And you are silent
To make me and my heart
Extremely happy.

5839.

If you do not welcome
God-ordained humiliation,
Then how can you make
The fastest progress?

5840.

May the storm of the senses
No more dare to near
My aspiration-heart.

5841.

Be brave!
Do not allow yourself
To be at the mercy
Of torrential thoughts.

5842.

The doubting world
Must not stop you
On your way to God's Palace.

5843.

God assures me
That my heart's inspiration-bird
Will return
And fly again once more
In my soul-sky.

5844.

The small "i" enjoys
Its stubbornness.
The big "I" enjoys
Its God-oneness and world-
    oneness.

5845.

Be always fluent
In your heart's
Love-devotion-surrender-
    languages.

5846.

The finishing touch
Is called
A God-satisfaction-surrender-
    breath.

5847.

God never says that it is easy
To unload human problems.
But He says that human problems
Can definitely be surmounted
If patience can be all the time
Available.

5848.

Poor God is surprised
To see
The mind's self-aggrandisement-
    ability.

5849.

Self-doubters obstruct
God-aspiration
And
God-dedication-speed.

5850.

Receptivity-durability
Has to be increased
In every human being
In every way.

5851.

If you are armed
With boundless peace,
You can please God
In every way single-handed.

5852.

God does not allow
A sincerity-heart
To make repeated mistakes.

5853.

God wants me to serve Him
Sleeplessly and breathlessly
Before I can claim
A safe seat at His Feet.

5854.

Alas,
My God-satisfaction-cries
Are so feeble, plus so late.

5855.

O my pride-mind,
Have you any idea
How foolishly you waste
Your time?

5856.

Only when God feeds
My hunger-heart
Am I fully satisfied.

5857.

March forward
Like a supreme hero
With a God-manifestation-drum.

5858.

God tells me
That what I was before
Is of no consequence.
He tells me
That what I am now
Is a matter of supreme
    importance.

5859.

God-realisation-victory
Is, indeed, a very slow
And
Steady process.

5860.

God wants me to sing
All the time,
Whenever I am with Him,
His Heaven-manifestation-song
    on earth.

5861.

My devotion-heart pleases God
More than anything else
That I have.

5862.

Finally
Lethargy, insecurity and impurity
Have found a new host.
They have left me
To remain all by myself.

5863.

My heart hopes for
A brighter future.
My soul promises
A more God-fulfilling
    manifestation.

5864.

To free yourself
From the shadow of doubt
And fear,
Climb up the aspiration-height
Accompanied by God's Eye.

5865.

God wants me to grow and glow
In the aspiration-heart
Of the New Millennium.

5866.

How can God be pleased with you
And proud of you
If you live in the thick
Of a disobedience-hurricane?

5867.

My God-searching mind
Rises and rises,
And
God secretly smiles and smiles.

5868.

My world-doubting mind
Sinks and sinks.
Nobody comes to its rescue,
Not even God.

5869.

What my life needs
Is nothing short of
A constantly flowing aspiration-
    river.

5870.

O aspiration-determination-
    lightning,
Please do not forget
My mind anymore.

5871.

Ignorance forces
My Godward path
To be narrower than the
    narrowest.

5872.

A clear mind and a strong faith
Can be of tremendous help
For humanity's fastest progress.

5873.

O my unwillingness-mind,
You are destroying
My life's God-service-blossoms.

5874.

My devotion-heart
And
My Lord's Compassion-Eye
Are extremely dear to each other.

5875.

My disobedience-life
Is destroying my heart's
Rainbow-dawn.

5876.

Sweeter than the sweetest,
Purer than the purest
Are
My gratitude-heart-tears.

5877.

An aspiration-heart
Is
Its own fountain-life-joy.

5878.

What I was,
Was for my personal use.
What I am now
Is only for God's personal Use.

5879.

Alas, will I ever have
An opportune moment
When I shall be able to explore
All my divine dimensions?

5880.

To dismiss the ignorance-prince
Is not the most difficult task.
Many have done, many will do.
What is wrong with you?
You can try and you will succeed.

5881.

God has appointed my heart
To collect the devotion-letters
From my mind, vital and body
And
Submit them to God Himself
On a daily basis.

5882.

The evolution of mankind
Is upward –
High, higher and highest.

5883.

God says He will never agree
To give up on
Any human being.

5884.

My heart's songs
Are all made of
My life's prayer-tears.

5885.

My soul's breath
Is created by God the Creator
To be of service to God the
    creation.

5886.

He who has accepted spirituality
Wholeheartedly
Will not sigh.
It is only the half-hearted seekers
Who are bound to sigh.

5887.

Purity, purity, purity!
It will save you
From many hostile attacks
In the inner world.

5888.

We are thinking of offering
Our gratitude-hearts to God.
God is thinking of
How He can make us happy.

5889.

The mind-clown
Will never be able to enjoy
The ecstasy of silence.

5890.

The stupidity-mind says
To the wisdom-heart:
"You are a hopeless case."

5891.

He who is my heart-friend
Shall endlessly
Care for me.

5892.

Fly, fly, O my mind,
Upward towards
The summit-height-bliss.

5893.

At last I know the way,
The only way:
My heart's self-giving way.

5894.

O golden eye of silence-light,
My aspiration-heart loves you
And
My dedication-life needs you.

5895.

O my doubting mind,
My heart sleeplessly loves
My Lord Supreme.
Are you not ashamed of
What you are doing?

5896.

No more shall I roam
Inside my confusion-mind-
   jungle,
No more.

5897.

No mind's
Transformation-light,
No heart's
Satisfaction-delight.

5898.

My life is a secret
And sacred
Descendent of God.

5899.

I have smashed asunder
The ramparts
Of my illusion-delusion-mind.

5900.

When prosperity smiles
At your life,
Slowly, steadily and unerringly
Use it.

5901.

My God-surrender-life is
    complete.
Therefore God Himself rings
My freedom-heart-bell.

5902.

An unconditional life
Is a supremely monumental
Life-performance.

5903.

Be not enamoured
Of possession-mind,
But of renunciation-life.

5904.

At every moment
I try to elevate my mind
To God-good thoughts.

5905.

No rest
Is ever needed
Along God's Way.

5906.

God never wants
Love-power
To have any equal.

5907.

Meditation
Means
Fragrance-blossom-heart-petals.

5908.

Without a rich heart,
Wealth
Is a pathetic life.

5909.

In the morning of love-light
My prayer reaches
The highest height.

5910.

In the evening of peace-bliss
My meditation reaches
The deepest depth.

5911.

My heart's implicit faith in God
Has given me
The most powerful shelter
From my mind-storms.

5912.

My God-surrender-heart
Is my life's
Fastest progress-track.

5913.

Precious is
The renunciation-life
Of my aspiration-heart.

5914.

Ferocious is
My earthly
Mind-aggression-possession.

5915.

No seeker must tolerate
His mind's
Aspiration-unwillingness.

5916.

Every morning my Lord
Blessingfully commands
My aspiration-heart-ascent.

5917.

An inspiration-mind
Needs
No explanation.

5918.

An aspiration-heart
Needs
No interpretation.

5919.

O stupidity-mind,
Can you not see
That you are prolonging
The reign of ignorance-monarch?

5920.

An acceptable
Indulgence-life
Is a joke number one.

5921.

No more my heart
Shall remain
A dim aspiration-flame.

5922.

Only inside my heart-garden
Dwells
My aspiration-redolence.

5923.

I shall not permit
Anything in my life
To grow taller and larger
Than my humility.

5924.

Infinity's Satisfaction
Is the Alpha and Omega
Of God's Will.

5925.

God is extremely proud
Of my
Willingness-sincerity-mind.

5926.

God is extremely fond
Of my
Eagerness-intensity-heart.

5927.

My mind's God-willingness
Has transformed my life
Immeasurably.

5928.

Insecurity destroys
The life
Of the mind.

5929.

Impurity destroys
The breath
Of the heart.

5930.

God-obedience
Is the completion
Of my self-education.

5931.

My God-satisfaction-heart
Is far beyond
My mind's longitude
And latitude.

5932.

Needed: a sincerity-mind-bud
To enter into
The outer temple.

5933.

Needed: a purity-heart-blossom
To enter into
The inner temple.

5934.

Humanity's God-obedience
Is humanity's
Only salvation.

5935.

God's Heart does not allow
God's Eye to examine
My mind's closets and cabinets.

5936.

The impurity-mind threatens
The purity-heart
All the time.

5937.

God's Power-Presence
My mind
Strongly desires.

5938.

God's Compassion-Presence
My heart
Sleeplessly desires.

5939.

God wrote His Peace-Book
Not only for my heart
But for my mind as well.

5940.

A dryness-mind
Is not allowed to study
At God's inner School.

5941.

A soulfulness-heart
Is not only allowed but invited
To study at God's School.

5942.

God's Forgiveness-Heart-Office
Remains open
Twenty-four hours.

5943.

The narrowness-mind-eye
Sees Partiality-God
Everywhere.

5944.

The wideness-heart-eye
Sees Equality-God
Everywhere.

5945.

My gratitude-heart
Is a newcomer
To my Lord's Heart-Home.

5946.

Alas, why do I not believe God
When He tells me that
He is always ready to defend me
Against ignorance-night?

5947.

No earth-bound life
Can ever
Battle time.

5948.

To be perfect,
God asked me to smile
At His creation.
I did it immediately.

5949.

My heart's streaming tears
Are intimately related
To my Lord's Lotus-Feet.

5950.

My God-devotion
Knows
No failure-life.

5951.

An ignorance-cherishing life itself
Is its own
Imminent doom.

5952.

Mine is
An everyday
God-satisfaction-cry.

5953.

Mine is
An everyday
Man-transformation-aspiration.

5954.

My faith has given me
Its beauty's heart
Unreservedly.

5955.

My faith gives me
Its God-manifestation-
    responsibility
Confidently.

5956.

A godless man
Is his own
Mind-forest-fear-torture.

5957.

My soul wants me to be
A God-Destination-adventure-
    hero
Supreme.

5958.

My Lord Supreme comes to me
To navigate
And not to investigate.

5959.

Unwillingness,
You are your own
Tragedy within
And tragedy without.

5960.

Willingness,
You are your own
Life-kingdom's master-key.

5961.

God draws my devotion-heart
To His ever-illumining
Compassion-Heart.

5962.

Every day my Lord Supreme
Expects my searching mind
To know better.

5963.

Every day my Beloved Supreme
Expects my aspiring heart
To climb up higher.

5964.

The unaspiring mind
Is negativity's
Argument-dexterity.

5965.

May my heart's
Be this goal:
To love the unloved.

5966.

Humiliation
Chases pride
And succeeds.

5967.

What do you want
To see in me?
God the Power?
Impossible.

5968.

What do you want
To see in me?
God the Surrender?
Behold,
Here He is.

5969.

Where do I want to go?
My heart-home
And nowhere else.

5970.

My heart's ever-blossoming purity
Is my passport
To God's Kingdom.

5971.

What have I discovered?
I have discovered
God's Fountain-Bounty.

5972.

Mine is the bounden duty
To bring dead hopes
To life.

5973.

My mind, not you,
But all your doubts
I condemn to death.

5974.

The God-aspiring heart
Always outruns
The God-doubting mind.

5975.

Do not avoid trials and
    tribulations.
Face them.
Lo, they are in the land of
    nowhere.

5976.

May my mind be
A perfect foreigner
To any doubt-industry.

5977.

May my mind be
A perfect foreigner
To any fear-colony.

5978.

Every morning
I expect my mind to be
A newness-vision.

5979.

My Beloved Lord,
Do tell me,
When will be the proper time
For me to unlearn
All that my mind has taught me?

5980.

I love and love
Peace-dream within
And
Bliss-reality without.

5981.

I love God
Unreservedly.
God fulfils my dreams
Unconditionally.

5982.

Needless to say,
Each human being
With no exception
Is totally free in his spirit.

5983.

Gone
Are my emptiness-insecurities,
Gone, totally gone.

5984.

My Lord,
I am all gratitude to You
For blessing me
With Your Delight-flooded Heart.

5985.

A negativity-mind
Is, indeed,
A dead-end road.

5986.

All-where
Disobedience is
An uninvited guest.

5987.

My heart is all eagerness
To kiss the dust
Of God's Footsteps.

5988.

O my mind,
Just mount and ride
My heart's aspiration-horse.

5989.

Out of His infinite Bounty,
Today God is planting peace-trees
Inside my heart-garden.

5990.

What am I doing?
I am just having a short talk
With my Lord Beloved Supreme.

5991.

My mind, keep always
A longer than the longest distance
From ignorance-night.

5992.

My heart's satisfaction-smile
Is my Lord's
Number one choice.

5993.

Smile powerfully.
Cry soulfully.
Hearken, God's Thunder-
    Applause!

5994.

Fly, fly non-stop upward.
God the Eye
Is secretly waiting for you.

5995.

Dive, dive non-stop inward.
God the Heart
Is breathlessly waiting for you.

5996.

My Lord, do bless me
With a very special Promise:
You will always have the last word
In my aspiration-life.

5997.

The mind's philosophy is:
Give not happiness,
But expect happiness.

5998.

The heart's philosophy is:
Give happiness.
Become happily and proudly
What God wants you to be.

5999.

The soul's philosophy is:
Give happiness constantly,
Give happiness unreservedly,
Give happiness unconditionally.

6000.

God has chosen
My God-realisation-soul
To rock this world
In His Peace-Cradle.

6001.

When my heart received
An invitation from God,
My soul danced and danced
With ecstasy.

6002.

To create a supreme atmosphere
On earth,
Each human being
Must grow into a soulful prayer
And fruitful meditation.

6003.

Every day, every hour, every
    minute
We must pay utmost attention
To God's bountiful
Silence-Messages.

6004.

Every day
We must make a special effort
To bring to the fore the inner sun,
Which is all-illumining
And all-fulfilling.

6005.

Your mind must think
The way your heart wants
Your mind to think,
For your heart is in direct touch
With the all-illumining soul.

6006.

My heart whispers.
God's Compassion-Ear
Leans low.

6007.

My mind and I
Like to know
All about God's
Secret days.

6008.

My heart and I
Love to feel only God's
Sacred moments.

6009.

My life and I
Prayerfully treasure
God's longest Eternity.

6010.

The doubting mind
Does not hesitate even to doubt
God's Compassion-Eye.

6011.

Every morning I pray to God
To bless me with
A singing heart-bird.

6012.

God's Compassion-Height
I sleeplessly
Love.

6013.

God's Justice-Light
I unmistakably
Need.

6014.

God's Will-Fulfilment
Is my heart's
Greatest thrill.

6015.

A selfishness-mind
Suffers
A loneliness-life.

6016.

My eagerness-heart
Runs along
God's Fulness-Road.

6017.

I know not where
My Lord's Compassion-Eye
Is unavailable.

6018.

Our desire-life
Is not interested
In our heart's
Beauty-fragrance-garden.

6019.

God's choice children
Are those who see God's Will
As their own, very own.

6020.

Alas, my mind is limping
For extra attention
From God.

6021.

I am my mind's
Tallest
Ignorance-tower.

6022.

God is God's
Sleepless
Forgiveness-Shower.

6023.

God is God's
Forgiveness-Heart.
I am my life's
God-gratitude-breath.

6024.

When God is God's
Sorrow-Eye,
I know that I am doing
Something wrong.

6025.

When God is God's
Smile-Face,
I know that my life
Is God-Satisfaction.

6026.

My God-unwillingness-mind,
You have no idea to what extent
You are torturing my heart.

6027.

O my unwillingness-mind,
You will never succeed
In hiding.

6028.

O my eagerness-empty heart,
You will never succeed
In hiding.

6029.

Do not demand.
God is not at your feet,
But He is inside your heart.

6030.

My heart's inspiration-flood
Has destroyed
My lethargy-body's
Unending life.

6031.

Day in and day out,
My Lord is my
Aspiration-dedication-supplier-
    multiplier.

6032.

My love, my devotion
And my surrender
Every morning congregate
At my Lord's Lotus-Feet.

6033.

In my outer life
I love God's
Forgiveness-Heart.

6034.

In my inner life
I love God's
Compassion-Eye.

6035.

My aspiration-heart
Is my
Prayerful choice.

6036.

My realisation-life
Is God's
Bountiful Choice.

6037.

My mind,
Do not be lost in your
God-acceptance-hesitation-fog.

6038.

Desire-life leads.
But where?
Only to the ever-ready grave.

6039.

The mind's negativity-fort
Astounds
Even God the Compassion.

6040.

My Lord tells me
That my heart-tears
Are sweeter than the sweetest.

6041.

My heart,
Once more you must make
Your God-satisfaction-efforts.

6042.

My aspiring heart
Loves and loves God
With no expectation.

6043.

My doubting mind
Never loves God,
But it constantly expects
God's Love.

6044.

May I be a heart
That is sleeplessly
God-yearning.

6045.

My God-surrender-heart
Is
A God-Satisfaction-Pride.

6046.

An aspiration-heart
Makes the life
Younger.

6047.

My mind,
You can easily settle
Your God-surrender-question.

6048.

Man is man's
Peace-rejecting
Face.

6049.

God is God's
Peace-offering
Embrace.

6050.

An Avatar will never be
    understood.
This story will be learned
From generation to generation.

6051.

If your heart cheers God,
Then only will your heart be able
To hear the Message of God
The way your soul does.

6052.

Mourn not for those
Who are spiritually dead.
God knows how
To take care of them.

6053.

I just love and love and love
God's every
World-transformation-Thought.

6054.

My mind,
God is infinitely more inspiring
Than you can ever imagine.

6055.

My heart,
God is infinitely more forgiving
Than you can ever imagine.

6056.

My life,
God is infinitely more fulfilling
Than you can ever imagine.

6057.

God will definitely fulfil
All the promises
That our soul has made
To Mother Earth.

6058.

Mother Earth and Father Heaven
Dearly love my heart's
Love-devotion-surrender-tears.

6059.

Everybody must walk
Through the heart-temple
To arrive at God's Palace.

6060.

May my heart-temple-bell
Ring every day
As loudly as possible
To awaken my dormant inner life.

6061.

O my disobedient mind,
You are bound to shed bitter tears
In the very near future.

6062.

God is extremely proud
Of His self-giving
Seeker-hearts.

6063.

My Lord expects
Only one thing from me:
My God-realisation-hunger-cry.

6064.

To live a God-protected life,
One must long for
A God-satisfaction-heart.

6065.

My Lord does hear
My heart's sleepless cries,
But He has His own Time
To make me happy
In His own Way.

6066.

Stop thinking, stop thinking,
My mind,
If you really feel the need
Of God's Blessing-Light
And Delight.

6067.

My only aim
Is to reach the highest
In my aspiration, dedication
And surrender-life.

6068.

Look, look what is happening!
Heaven's Gate,
My Lord's Golden Gate,
My Lord Himself is opening.

6069.

Never hold back
Your heart's
Gratitude-fragrance-tears —
Never!

6070.

My doubting mind
Always tries to break off
All the communications
With my aspiring heart.

6071.

Every morning
I place my life's surrender-smiles
On my heart-shrine.

6072.

How can the idleness of the body
And the narrowness of the mind
Ever find God?
Impossible!

6073.

The human life
Is God's ever-blossoming
Dream-beauty.

6074.

Music and poetry
Are the giant branches
Of my life's aspiration-tree.

6075.

Pay no attention
To the utter indifference
Of the world
While you are serving God
In His creation.

6076.

I know
My God-manifestation-promise-
    life
Is bound to succeed.

6077.

Peace
Is not to be found
In the mind's territory.

6078.

To fly in the firmament
Of God's Vastness-Sky,
I do not need wings.
I only need implicit faith
In my Lord Supreme.

6079.

Happiness is not
A matter of chance.
We must cultivate happiness
By virtue of our prayers
And meditations.

6080.

Each divinely inspired dream
Is the precursor
Of a divine fulfilment.

6081.

The earth-bound life
Is full of ups and downs.
The Heaven-free life
Is full of blooming light
And blossoming delight.

6082.

Be not a fool!
Nobody can solve
Either the inner problems
Or the outer problems
Without God's express Help.

6083.

Surrender, surrender, surrender!
All your dreams
Will eventually ripen
Into fulfilment-realities.

6084.

I do not know
If I will ever be able to separate
The doubting mind
From the confusing and confused
    life.

6085.

A seeker's heart
Must live in between
His inner aspiration-life
And his outer inspiration-life.

6086.

My Lord never comes to me
Alone.
He brings with Him
His all-encouraging Smile.

6087.

If meditation is properly done,
Then we reach
Higher than the highest heights
And deeper than the deepest
    depths.

6088.

Miracles do happen.
But if we want to learn something
From the miracles,
Then we must believe in them.

6089.

Always be on the alert!
Your golden dreams
May fly away.
Catch them and manifest them
For God-Satisfaction
Here on earth!

6090.

I have done many more
Strange things
Than I have ever seen.

6091.

Each heart-dream
Of mine
Rises high above the stars.

6092.

May my heart become
A regular
Peace-dream-lover.

6093.

Your soul is punishing you.
Why?
Because your soul is extremely
    Disappointed in you.

6094.

True, you have many enemies,
But why do you not value
Your inner Friend, only Friend,
And why do you not claim Him
As your own, very own?
Do you not know who He is?
He is your Eternity's
Lord Beloved Supreme.

6095.

My heart does at once
What it is told by my soul
To do.

6096.

A godless mind
Is, indeed,
A helpless, hopeless and useless
    life.

6097.

My soul is asking all the members
Of its immediate family –
Heart, mind, vital and body –
To look high, higher, highest
And see the God-promised day
That is blooming fast, very fast
On the horizon.

6098.

Sorrows not only deepen
But also strengthen
Our heart-power.

6099.

The lost paradise
Can be regained.
Just increase immeasurably
Your love of God.

6100.

Because of my unfailing
Rainbow-hope,
I shall succeed in my life.

6101.

When tears arise
From the gratitude-heart,
God's Compassion-Feet descend.

6102.

What I need
Is
A never-tiring heart-cry.

6103.

What I need
Is
A never-ending soul-smile.

6104.

What I need
Is
An ever-willing and ever-
    sacrificing
Life-breath.

6105.

He who cherishes
His doubt-suspicion-mind
Is infinitely worse
Than my enemy.

6106.

My Lord blessingfully invites me
To come to His Heart-Home,
But I prefer to roam and roam
In my mind-territory.

6107.

Finally my stormy mind
Is surrendering to
My peace-blossoming heart.

6108.

My Lord Supreme,
My desire-possession-love for You
Is extremely painful.

6109.

My Lord Supreme,
My aspiration-surrender-love for
    You
Is unimaginably blissful.

6110.

My Lord, do give me the capacity
To please You in as many ways
As You want me to.

6111.

Alas, what I need
Is a permanent
Progress-satisfaction-heart
And not a permanent
Success-glorification-life.

6112.

Any promise I make to God
And fail to keep
Is, indeed, a tragedy of tragedies.

6113.

Alas, the mind-doubt-shocks
Know not
What compassion is.

6114.

A proud mind
Is prone
To a divine life collision.

6115.

O human life,
Be always on guard;
At any moment,
God-Justice-Court
Can be in session.

6116.

God wants my soulful heart
To whistle
His Delight-Music.

6117.

The universal Harmony
And the transcendental Delight
Are twins.

6118.

God's Justice-Line
Can at times be busy,
But never His Compassion-Line.

6119.

On earth nothing is permanent—
No, not even my Lord's
Compassion-Forgiveness-Smiles.

6120.

I must love
My Lord Beloved Supreme
Infinitely more
With every breath of mine.

6121.

Our faith in God
Has only one destination:
God-Satisfaction.

6122.

What I need is a life
Immersed in sleepless
And breathless God-longing.

6123.

My heart's only friend
Is my Lord's
Compassion-flooded Smile.

6124.

Do you know what God is doing
For me?
Every morning He shows me
His smiling world-illumining
        Face.

6125.

There was a time
When my mind was
Nothing short of
God-oblivion.

6126.

God has now
Made my mind
A doubt-empty champion.

6127.

When my awakened heart sings,
I see Paradise all-where
In my heart-sky.

6128.

Suffering
Is the slogan
Of the human body.

6129.

Renunciation
Is by far the best
Ignorance-night-destroyer.

6130.

My Lord,
May I come to You
With my devotion-ocean-heart
And not
With my gratitude-mind-bubbles.

6131.

Wisdom knows
No fear, no doubt
And no failure.

6132.

If you do not pull out
Your mind's ego-weeds,
How will God appreciate
Your heart-garden?

6133.

Once you see God,
You become
God's own lion.

6134.

Once you become God,
You become
Another lamb.

6135.

May my effulgence-mind
And
My sweetness-heart
Always live together
To sing God's Victory-Songs.

6136.

My desire-life
Does not know
What God-Reality is.

6137.

My aspiration-heart
Does not know
What the world-unreality is.

6138.

A heart of peace
Can easily set at rest
The question in mind.

6139.

When I am in my deep
    meditation,
I see clearly God carrying
Inside my heart
His own lighted Lantern.

6140.

Pure God-love
And
Sure world-desire
Can never mix.

6141.

It seems that suffering
And the body
Cannot be separated.

6142.

My Lord,
I shall never pray to You
For my world-healing herbs,
Never!

6143.

My Lord,
I shall always pray to You
For a worshipping heart-flower.

6144.

My Lord says to me,
"My child, My child,
Give Me quickly, quickly
Your mind-thorn
And
Take from Me quickly, quickly
My Heart-Rose."

6145.

If you renounce world-
    temptation,
Then God-satisfaction
Is all yours.

6146.

Every day
My meditation-eye
Feasts on
Nature's God-beauty.

6147.

Be not afraid of Heaven.
Heaven is empty of justice-hands.
Heaven is all compassion-heart.

6148.

God is preparing your heart.
Do you know why?
For His own Satisfaction-
    manifestation.

6149.

The streaming tears
Of my heart
Purify my mind-impurities.

6150.

My happiness-life
Is in my heart's
Aspiration-field
And nowhere else.

6151.

God wants my meditation-wings
To accompany
His ever-blossoming Dreams.

6152.

May my mind
Become the possessor
Of a wisdom-magnet.

6153.

May my heart
Become the possessor
Of a surrender-service-life.

6154.

In appearance,
God-lovers may be
Stupidity incarnate.

6155.

In reality,
God-lovers are
God's choicest prides.

6156.

Alas,
A desire-doom-life
I was.

6157.

An aspiration-heart-bloom
I now am.

6158.

My Lord,
Do come and feed
My inner loneliness.

6159.

My Lord,
Do give me the capacity
At every moment
To feel the Breath of Your Love.

6160.

When I do not pray and meditate,
I am at war
With myself.

6161.

If we do not aspire,
Then our own body, vital, mind
And heart
Are bound to misunderstand
One another.

6162.

We must be aware of
The nature of trees:
Sacrifice, sacrifice, sacrifice –
From the very foot
To the highest height.

6163.

You must love
The human in you
For its transformation.

6164.

You must love
The divine in you
For its manifestation.

6165.

Do not think ill of yourself.
Do not waste your God-given,
Precious time.

6166.

My mind,
Be not attached
To the world-attachment-illusion.

6167.

There is no other journey
As inspiring as
Peace-manifestation-journey.

6168.

My Lord,
I do not have to understand You.
Just allow me to love You
Sleeplessly and breathlessly.

6169.

When I am in the desire-world,
My Lord's Justice-Eye
Frightens me.

6170.

When I am in the aspiration-
    world,
My Lord's Compassion-Eye
Beckons me.

6171.

Only a divinely wise man
Makes his anxieties, worries,
Fears and doubts obsolete.

6172.

Unlike the journey without,
The journey within
Is birthless and deathless.

6173.

My Lord, do dictate.
My heart-pen
Is all ready.

6174.

When I soulfully pray,
God sends His Heart
To me.

6175.

When I unconditionally meditate,
God breathlessly runs
Towards me.

6176.

My Lord,
May my mind be a monkey-brain
To amuse You.

6177.

My Lord,
May my heart be a devotion-dog
To follow You.

6178.

I do not believe in
Tomorrow's rainbow-beauty.
I believe only in
Today's God-fulfilment-duty.

6179.

Without the God-lovers,
This world would be
A haunted house.

6180.

It is our love of Divinity
That keeps us
Still sane.

6181.

My Lord,
I do not hide from You anymore.
Why?
Because I have conquered my
      pride.

6182.

The surrender-life
Gets the highest degree
In God-love.

6183.

What is obedience,
If not something
That dances with God
The Beautiful?

6184.

My Lord Supreme
Replaces my aching heart
With His Rainbow-Dreams.

6185.

This moment
We live in humour,
And the next moment
We live in rumour.
Alas, this is what human life is.

6186.

You are
Your inner cry.
God is
God's brighter Smile.

6187.

How do you expect to fly
In the realisation-sky
With no meditation-wings?

6188.

God loves you unconditionally:
The depth
Of His Goodness.

6189.

You value God's creation
    sincerely:
The height
Of your greatness.

6190.

May my God-faith
Stand upon
The rock of Eternity.

6191.

My unconditionally surrendered
    life
To God
Is the zenith
Of my aspiration-happiness.

6192.

My mind says to God:
"You can leave aside everybody
    else,
But raise me."

6193.

My heart says to God:
"My Lord, do not leave anyone
    aside.
Raise us together,
For we are Your Oneness-Joy."

6194.

I call it
My meditation.
God calls it
His Heart's Magic Lamp.

6195.

If we want to succeed
In our spiritual life,
We needs must unmask
The mind.

6196.

Unlike our birthdays –
Once a year –
God's Birthday is at every
    moment.

6197.

God never writes
"I love you, My child.
I need you, My child.
We shall be fulfilled together, My
    child"
With invisible ink.

6198.

My mind says:
"I think of myself constantly.
Therefore, I am."

6199.

My heart says:
"My Lord loves me at every
    moment.
Therefore, I am."

6200.

The doubting mind
And the domineering vital
Are nothing but two time-bombs.
God alone knows
When they will explode.

6201.

My soul and I are happy
Only when
We try the impossible.

6202.

My heart,
Wake up! Wake up!
God is waiting for you to join
His World-Illumination-
    Symphony.

6203.

Just dive deep within.
You will be the discoverer
Of God
The Beloved Supreme.

6204.

In your own eye
You may not be important,
But in God's Eye
You are His indispensable child.

6205.

The stormy life can be braved
Only by the heart's
Sunny meditations.

6206.

To realise God means
You will become at once
God's Heart-Choice
And God's Life-Voice.

6207.

O my stupid mind,
Delay not;
My wise heart is already on its way
To reach the Golden Shore.

6208.

The searching mind
Has to go to God.
God comes
To the crying heart.

6209.

My heart is a surrender-bird.
Therefore,
My life has freedom-wings.

6210.

My doubting mind
Wants to commit suicide.
There can be no better news.

6211.

The God-surrender-students
Have
No vacation.

6212.

Pay soulful homage
To our Lord Supreme
Here and now.
Do not wait for tomorrow.

6213.

Our God-service
Is the fragrance
Of our inner beauty.

6214.

Your ego's misdeeds
Have destroyed your heart-flower
Completely.

6215.

My negativity-mind
Is chased by
My Divinity-hunger.

6216.

When the soul supervises us,
Our inner progress and outer
    success
Are guaranteed.

6217.

Sincerity and purity
Are the two main pillars
Of my climbing aspiration-heart.

6218.

Every morning
I practise devotedly
My God-surrender-game.

6219.

God does not need
A big performance from me
To transform my life.
He can and will do everything
Unconditionally.

6220.

Experience and realisation
Are not free;
They have to be paid for.

6221.

We must climb up
The inner peaks of life
To arrive at our Goal.

6222.

What am I doing?
I am waiting for my Lord Supreme
In a corner
Of my heart-room.

6223.

Every morning
God expects to hear from me
Inspiring and encouraging news.

6224.

Everybody's life
Every day sails along
The coast of hope.

6225.

May my God-fulfilment-eagerness
Remain
Constantly busy.

6226.

There are many ways and means
To fight against
Ignorance-night.

6227.

No more
Shall I allow ignorance
To shadow my life.

6228.

May self-giving
Be my heart's
Passion.

6229.

My aspiration-heart
Eagerly listens to
My Lord's Nectar-Whispers.

6230.

My mind, I beg of you,
Do not take any more advice
From desire-night.

6231.

Where do I take shelter?
I take shelter beneath my Lord's
Compassion-Forgiveness-Feet-
    Dust.

6232.

The unaspiring mind
Can easily be prone
To dangerous self-doubt-
    avalanches.

6233.

When I tell God that I am not
    ready
For His manifestation-light
On earth,
He immediately blesses me
With roaring laughter.

6234.

Is there anybody who does not
    have
A free access
To God's Forgiveness-Heart?

6235.

Do not close your aspiration-heart
To God's Will,
Even for a fleeting second.

6236.

May my earth-existence
Be thoroughly acclimatised
To my Lord's
Compassion-flooded Will.

6237.

It seems that the appearance
And disappearance of gratitude
Are quite sudden.

6238.

At every moment
We must do the right thing
So that we can keep the Tears
From God's Eye.

6239.

My heart has taught me
To be always eager
To do what God tells me.

6240.

As my love of God
Is sleepless,
Even so, His Pride in me
Is limitless.

6241.

The prayer of the centuries
Is for the flowering
Of a oneness-peace-heart-world.

6242.

Negativity's mind and face
Are
Always ugly.

6243.

The cheerfulness of the heart
Has to put an end to
The miseries of the mind.

6244.

My God-gratitude-heart
Is at once
Speechless and breathless
With joy.

6245.

My heart's inner pilgrimages
Are extremely sacred, illumining
And fulfilling.

6246.

God has not given up
And will never give up on me,
No matter what I say and do
Against Him.

6247.

To keep the mind pure
And illumining,
Every day you must take in
God-Satisfaction-breaths.

6248.

May each day of my life
Be
God-obedience-fragrance.

6249.

I treasure each and every
God-Touch-moment
In my life.

6250.

Readiness, willingness
And eagerness
Must extend themselves
To serve God sleeplessly.

6251.

Alas, every morning,
Why do I not avail myself
Of the clearness-mind-sky?

6252.

The spiritual life
Is moment to moment
God-fulfilment-lessons.

6253.

My soul blows out
At every moment
The desire-dust
From my mind.

6254.

God-obedience knows
How to pave the way
For the arrival
Of ecstasy-flood.

6255.

God always loves playing
His Oneness-Satisfaction-Game
With His children.

6256.

Correct your mind;
Perfect your vital.
Lo, satisfaction
Is your life.

6257.

A self-giving hero supreme
Is the pride of Heaven's soul
And the pride of earth's heart.

6258.

Every moment
My soul is desperately trying
For a reconciliation
Between my demanding mind
And my crying heart.

6259.

Each day I am being blessed
With the rising sun
Of my God-Satisfaction-dream.

6260.

Do you want to be perfect?
Then unmask the truth
In everything.

6261.

Nothing gives me as much joy
As the sailing boat
Of my silence-heart.

6262.

Needless to say,
My aspiration-heart is the
    birthplace
And nursery
Of world-peace.

6263.

Break the tradition of millennia:
God-realisation can be achieved
Sooner than at once!

6264.

God is sincerely pleased with me
When I do not want to measure
   time,
But to go beyond time.

6265.

You have been on the path,
O seeker, for so many years.
How is it that your spiritual
   progress
Is now in reverse?

6266.

God's Compassion-Eye
And Forgiveness-Heart
Always finance my inner journey.

6267.

Only a happy heart
Finds God's blessingful Presence
Everywhere.

6268.

God always loves
To say everything to me
In a Sweetness-Whisper.

6269.

Alas, how desperately
I am trying once again
To make my way back
To God's Will.

6270.

My Lord,
May I be a leaf
Of Your Eternity's
Vision-Manifestation-Tree.

6271.

This time
I am absolutely determined
To conquer
My pride-doubt-suspicion-mind.

6272.

If there is no optimism,
Opportunity
Is of no avail.

6273.

It is not true
That life is made of
Failure-sorrows.

6274.

When I do not aspire,
I am
My sleeper-body.

6275.

When I aspire,
I am
My leaper-soul.

6276.

My outer obedience
Results from my heart's
Inner gratitude-tears.

6277.

I have made
My God-manifestation-promise
Here on earth
Sleepless and breathless.

6278.

My life may not be
Spiritually fertile,
But my feelings definitely are.

6279.

When I am exceedingly happy,
My Lord tells me that my life
Is nothing short of perfection.

6280.

Poetry, music and art
Are the members
Of God's immediate Family.

6281.

My Lord,
May my aspiration-heart-machine
Never be out of order.

6282.

I hearten God
When I am all concern
For the suffering humanity.

6283.

Alas,
Nobody wants to carve
My mind-stone –
Not even God.

6284.

God wants me to do
Only one thing:
He wants me to plant
The seed of satisfaction
In my mind.

6285.

Each good, inspiring
And aspiring thought
Is, indeed,
A masterpiece of God.

6286.

An unconditional surrender-soul
Rockets satisfaction
To Heaven.

6287.

Fame is glorious,
But often
It is poisonous.

6288.

Every day
Divinity's peace tiptoes
Into my aspiration-heart-room.

6289.

Inspiration sings
In my
God-searching mind.

6290.

Aspiration dances
In my
God-loving heart.

6291.

What is my life doing?
My life is crusading sleeplessly
For God-manifestation on earth.

6292.

How can I face tomorrow
If my heart does not have
Hope-dreams?

6293.

I do not allow God to embrace me.
I just kneel down
Before His Forgiveness-Feet
And
Kiss them to my heart's content.

6294.

Each divinely great idea
Is
My outer eye-opener.

6295.

Each supremely good deed
Is
My inner eye-opener.

6296.

When I obey God,
I am able to stretch my mind
Measurelessly.

6297.

When I devote myself entirely to
    God,
I keep my heart-door open
    smilingly
Twenty-four hours a day.

6298.

Neither God's Forgiveness
Nor His Compassion
Can ever be duplicated.

6299.

A smiling child
Is the owner
Of a rainbow-heart.

6300.

A God-realised soul
Knows no bounds
Either on earth or in Heaven.

6301.

Be not afraid
Of any shadow.
This includes your own.

6302.

The unconditional surrender-
    moment
Is a never to be forgotten
Moment.

6303.

My heart's streaming tears
Are my life's
Bosom friends.

6304.

May my earth-life
Remain always
Beautiful.

6305.

May my soul-life
Remain always
Bountiful.

6306.

I clearly see
That my Lord's Compassion-Eye
Is closer than my own breath.

6307.

O my mind, wake up!
It is high time for you to see
Your own heart's sunrise.

6308.

The call of the inner sunrise
Is so charming, illumining
And fulfilling.

6309.

No more amusement-life,
No more.
An enchantment-heart more,
Ever more.

6310.

God wants my emptiness-heart
To make friends with
His Compassion-flooded Heart.

6311.

To end your sorrowful life,
You needs must have
A prayerful heart.

6312.

Kindle peace, kindle bliss,
O my self-giving life,
In every heart.

6313.

My Lord,
Your Forgiveness-Heart
I shall most faithfully follow
Everywhere.

6314.

The compromise of the mind
Does not stop
The turmoil of the heart.

6315.

My God-surrender-life
Is the only open book
Of all the secrets of Divinity.

6316.

An indulgence-mind
Does not have the capacity
To endure anything.

6317.

At every moment
May my surrender-breath
Be at God's beck and call.

6318.

My life is torn between
My mind-train-frustration-
    destination
And
My heart-train-illumination-
    destination.

6319.

Satisfaction, O satisfaction,
How I wish you would accompany
    me
Every day, everywhere.

6320.

My life is my Lord's
Forgiveness-Smile
Twenty-four hours a day.

6321.

Never forget
That your first God-task
Is to aspire, and nothing else.

6322.

God dearly loves
My life's
Self-transcendence-call.

6323.

My little soul-bird
Tells me a secret:
God's unconditional Love for me
Breathes Eternity's Breath.

6324.

A heart of devotion
Is
An ever-green life.

6325.

Do not live like
An outer hermit,
But live like
An inner prince.

6326.

Everything that you have
And are
Is an unripe fruit.

6327.

God's bountiful Love
And my cheerful faith
Together sing and dance.

6328.

Make your doubting mind
A perfect slave
Of your ever-climbing
Aspiration-heart.

6329.

The body of greatness
Definitely
I have.

6330.

The heart of goodness
Unmistakably
I need.

6331.

If you do not live
Your God-dreams,
Then who will and who can?

6332.

My God-realisation-anniversary
My Lord Beloved Supreme
Every year smilingly, lovingly
And proudly observes.

6333.

Be not
An empty promise-life,
But live
In your heart-shrine.

6334.

O Heaven,
Be not indifferent
To my heart-cries.

6335.

O earth,
Be not afraid
Of my soul-smiles.

6336.

No more, no more
My mind shall wallow
In ignorance-pleasure-life.

6337.

Keep your heart's
Ever-new progress
A top secret.

6338.

The heart-purity
And the mind-patience
Must protect my life-fort.

6339.

You must realise
That misfortunes follow
In the wake of your consciousness
    low.

6340.

True God-lovers
Are always
In short supply.

6341.

The mind's eye misleads us
More than we can ever
Know and feel.

6342.

Every day my life-boat plies
Between my soul-ecstasy-shore
And my heart-sorrow-shore.

6343.

May my aspiration-heart
Be a pilgrim of Eternity
To arrive at Infinity's Shore.

6344.

Be not a fool.
You cannot extinguish
The burning aspiration-heart
Of any seeker.

6345.

I sighed and sighed
At the sight
Of my God-unwillingness-mind.

6346.

Every morning
My heart admires, adores and
    loves
My soul's wake-up call.

6347.

Day in and day out
God will pull you forward
If you agree to push yourself
    forward
To arrive at His Heart-Palace.

6348.

Alas, I do not know why
I tolerate my failure-life
Every day.

6349.

No matter how inclement
The outer weather is,
My devotion-mail
Always goes through.

6350.

No, not every day,
But at every moment,
My soul sweeps out
My doubt-mind-dust.

6351.

Alas, is there any day
That I am not ashamed
Of my intolerance-mind?

6352.

Deep, very deep,
I have buried
My mind's confining past.

6353.

My surrender-smile-heart
God uses to broadcast
All His Views.

6354.

To be a top-seeded God-lover,
I must keep my heart-door
Sleeplessly open.

6355.

God tells me that soon
He will allow my aspiration-heart
To feast upon His Infinity's
   Delight.

6356.

To me,
A most sublime achievement
Is to sing every day
A oneness-world-heart-song.

6357.

O seeker, if you do not fell
Your mind's jealousy-tree,
Your life cannot swim
In ecstasy-sea.

6358.

Be careful of your doubting mind.
It is expert in impairing
Your heart's God-response.

6359.

A passive surrender-life
Is the worst possible
Failure-experience.

6360.

My morning dawns.
New possibilities replace
My old impossibilities.

6361.

Left to myself,
I become one with
My heart's orphan tears.

6362.

The moment I recognised my
   Master,
He blessed me with his heart-
   wings
To soar in Infinity's Sky.

6363.

How do you expect
God-Satisfaction-Smile
If you are unwilling
To subordinate your will
To God's Will?

6364.

Cultivate flexibility in the mind
If you want to experience the
     beauty
Of the Ultimate Height.

6365.

To my illumination-soul
There is no such thing
As a foreign thought.

6366.

May the fulfilment
Of God's absolute Will
Be my own absolute priority.

6367.

Like God,
God wants me to be
My soul's bravest light
To challenge
My mind's blackest night.

6368.

O my Lord of unchanging Love,
Do give me the capacity
To be an all-ranging heart.

6369.

My heart, I urge you
To sing the song
Of the ever-transcending Beyond,
And not of nothingness-beyond.

6370.

Needless to say,
My heart is always
Ahead of my mind
In everything divine.

6371.

My heart treasures its friendship
With my soul.
My mind, never!

6372.

Determination always finds
The way to solve
Any problem.

6373.

Take a break
From compulsion.
Take a break
From frustration.
But never take a break
From compassion.

6374.

My soul is excited to see
My heart, my vital and my body
Playing the oneness-game.

6375.

When God saw me last,
His Message-Light for me
Was only one word:
Gratitude.

6376.

If you walk with your heart,
God is bound to come
And talk with both of you.

6377.

My God-realisation-soul
Will inspire
My earth-dedication-life.

6378.

Keep your gratitude-smile
In your heart-garden,
And not in your mind-jungle.

6379.

Unwillingness
Eventually proves to be
A total unworthiness.

6380.

My Lord, I am crying, I am dying.
I prayerfully implore:
Do give me another chance
To fulfil You and please You.

6381.

Every morning
I pray to my Lord Supreme
To connect my heart
With His Forgiveness-Feet.

6382.

O seeker,
If you are ready to leave
Your doubting mind,
Then come and join
My aspiring heart.

6383.

Comatose aspiration
Will be chased
By frustration-demon.

6384.

Resolute determination
Is what we need
To increase our speed
In everything we do.

6385.

There was a time
When I was an incessant
God-talker.

6386.

I am now
A sleepless
God-lover.

6387.

There shall come a time
When I shall become
My God-promise-manifestation-
    fulfiller.

6388.

An uncompromising loyalty
To God's creation
Can alone make this world
    perfect.

6389.

My heart-divinity
Can never be butchered
With my mind-knife.

6390.

When the mind is clear,
Divinity's Satisfaction
Has to be extremely near.

6391.

Before you seek fame,
Can you not see shame
Is standing right in front of you?

6392.

Finally
I have made my life
A God-gratitude-heart-song.

6393.

I measure
My heart-smiles
With my surrender-life-cup.

6394.

The mind is
Its own helpless
Confusion-life-boat.

6395.

The confusion-mind
Sees the Golden Shore
Nowhere.

6396.

The aspiration-heart
Not only sees
But also grows into
The Golden Shore.

6397.

I am commanded by my Lord
  Supreme
To recharge my readiness-mind,
My willingness-life
And my eagerness-heart
Every single day, without fail.

6398.

Your purity-mind
And
Your heart-fragrance
God needs
To fulfil
His World-Transformation-Task.

6399.

Each human life
Is definitely
A Heaven-sent God-Song.

6400.

When I fly
On the wings of my heart-tears,
Infinity's Heart embraces me.

6401.

May my aspiration-heart
Never be
Without obedience.

6402.

What is a frustration-mind?
A frustration-mind is something
That always mistrusts humanity.

6403.

No aspiration-heart
Will ever accept
The mind's negativity.

6404.

My heart's aspiration-cry
Every day
Circles the universe.

6405.

I really do not know
If I will ever be able
To express adequately
The beauty
Of gratitude-heart-tears.

6406.

If you can hold the creation
In your heart,
You will see everything beautiful,
Everything fruitful,
In your inner life and your outer
    life.

6407.

If you are afraid of
Your ignorance-darkness-mind,
Who will challenge it,
And who will conquer it?

6408.

Each soul-bird sings
On top of life's
Aspiration-tree.

6409.

He is so happy that finally
He is able to dig the grave
Of his depression-vital.

6410.

May my heart travel far,
Very far,
And learn from each country
The message of the beauty
And fragrance
Of God's creation.

6411.

The desiring mind
Is apt to falsify
Everything.

6412.

God loves
Most proudly
My aspiration-heart-whispers.

6413.

Ignorance-mind
Is, indeed,
A most powerful sword.

6414.

Every day I beg my soul
To end my mind's
Disobedience-disgrace.

6415.

Try with your heart's smile-power
To change the world.
You will succeed.

6416.

We shall chant God's Name
Prayerfully, soulfully and self-
     givingly
Plus sleeplessly
To satisfy our inner divinity.

6417.

Lethargy-legs and relaxation-
     chairs
Are lowering the standard
Of human aspiration.

6418.

The soul becomes ecstatic
When it hears
God's Alarm.

6419.

O seeker,
To sing a peace-song
Every day
Is of paramount importance.

6420.

My aspiration-heart
Has most devotedly accepted
The God-manifestation-task
Here on earth.

6421.

To make great strides
In spirituality,
We must love God the creation
The way we love God the Creator.

6422.

God Himself has shown my heart
How to forget
All its deplorable misdeeds.

6423.

What am I doing?
I am spreading and spreading
My heart's peace-dove-wings.

6424.

What I constantly need
Is a hope-blossoming
Inner sun.

6425.

My mind, I beg of you
To stop enjoying
Your ignorance-blanket-comfort-
    sleep.

6426.

My aspiration-heart
Is stunned by its own
God-satisfaction-devotion.

6427.

If you are highly developed
In your spiritual life,
Then your heart's cry
Will definitely be able to melt
Your stone-mind.

6428.

We usher in the New Millennium
To grow into
Its beauty and fragrance
Infinite.

6429.

The desiring mind destroys
Its own ears
With its thunder-drum.

6430.

The sweetness-smile of my heart
Is part and parcel
Of my inner divinity.

6431.

Alas, why do I have
An austere inflexibility-mind?
Why?

6432.

The mind and the heart
Must renew their friendship
To please their Lord Supreme.

6433.

Obedience is
The sweetness-delight
Of our aspiration-heart.

6434.

If you do not befriend mankind,
Then you will be found
In the loneliness-cave.

6435.

You must never relax
Your discipline-mind
So that you can swim
In Divinity's Ecstasy-Sea.

6436.

Until every day
Is a God-dedication-day,
I shall never be satisfied
With my life.

6437.

Indeed, each day can be
An unprecedented
God-satisfaction-opportunity.

6438.

If the mind refuses
To play the oneness-game,
Then the mind will be
Sentenced to ruthless loneliness.

6439.

Every day billions pass by
God's Heart-Door.
He accepts only those
Who are unconditional.

6440.

I shall never, never
Enter again
Into my mind-attachment-
    territory.

6441.

Everything
My Lord Beloved Supreme does
Is a Delight-flooded experience
For me.

6442.

Self-hatred
Is, indeed, almost
An incurable disease.

6443.

Every day the human mind
Enjoys watching
Its fantasy-movies.

6444.

No Heavenly joy
On earth
Shall remain unattained.

6445.

My hopeful heart
Forever shall breathe in
The Fragrance of my Lord's
Bountiful Heart.

6446.

O star-studded sky,
My aspiration-heart
Is prayerfully longing
For your company.

6447.

When I take God
As my sweet Lord Beloved
    Supreme,
He cannot remain unknowable.

6448.

When I take God
As my Lord Absolute Supreme,
He definitely remains
    unknowable.

6449.

I tell my Lord Supreme
That His Road
Is extremely arduous.

6450.

My Lord Supreme tells me
That His Road
Is bountifully prosperous.

6451.

Both my Lord's Face
And His Grace
Are intoxicatingly beautiful.

6452.

My life's ultimate goal
Is to be my Lord's
Slave eternal.

6453.

At long last
I am enjoying the power
Of my willingness-mind.

6454.

At long last
I am enjoying the ecstasy
Of my eagerness-heart.

6455.

Adversity's life
Can easily be smashed
By a sleepless God-oneness-heart.

6456.

My sweet Lord,
Do You know my real name?
My real name is a broken heart.
And who else is responsible,
If not You,
Your cruelty-flooded Mind?

6457.

O my heart,
You have become
The living breath of Truth.
God is all pride in you.

6458.

My Lord Beloved Supreme,
I am more than willing
To lose the beauty of my eye
To increase the beauty of my
      heart.

6459.

The illumining soul
Most eloquently speaks
God's Philosophy.

6460.

The aspiring heart
Most devotedly
Listens.

6461.

What does the ego do?
The ego rules its own
Tinier than the tiniest kingdom.

6462.

Each aspiring heart
Is an endless
Peace-bliss-pilgrimage.

6463.

Not only my outer hope
But also my inner conviction
Is that today's world will be
    flooded
With Divinity's peace
In the distant future.

6464.

My Lord, do tell me
When I will be my heart's
Sleepless and deathless cry.

6465.

When I say I can change
The fate of the world,
I immediately see
My divinity's mighty form.

6466.

When I say that God
Has blessingfully appointed me
To serve the world for its
    transformation,
My life becomes a mighty God-
    Victory.

6467.

Inside the visible,
God's Divinity looms large.
Therefore, we do not have to be
Enamoured of the invisible.

6468.

When God's Greatness
Presides over my life,
I get terribly frightened.

6469.

When God's Goodness
Presides over my life,
I am immediately enchanted
Plus enlightened.

6470.

On the road to God-realisation,
If we stop halfway for a rest,
Then we are bound to fail.

6471.

May each second
Of my life be
A God-fulfilment-certitude-
    promise.

6472.

There can be no peak
That cannot be climbed
With my heart's
God-blossoming hope.

6473.

Alas, my poor desire-life
Does not recognise
That it is captive
In its own net.

6474.

God wants my outer life
To be armed with
A doubt-free mind.

6475.

God wants my inner life
To be armed with
An ever-blossoming peace.

6476.

Each self-giving life
Is a perfect ambassador
Of God's Heart-Country
To mankind's mind-country.

6477.

Someday the mind and the heart
Will be found in a fond embrace,
And that day is fast approaching.

6478.

My heart and I came into the
    world
Not to measure the Divinity
Of my Lord Beloved Supreme,
But to treasure His Divinity.

6479.

My good news is this:
Soon I shall be able to bless my life
With the dust of my Lord's Lotus-
    Feet.

6480.

God's good news is this:
Soon, very soon, He will turn me
Into another God.

6481.

If we are afraid of giving God
Our life-reins,
How can God's Compassion-Rain
Descend on us?

6482.

Morning meditation
Is the beauty and divinity
Of our inner flames.

6483.

All things flower in time.
That does not mean
I must enjoy my Eternity's sleep.
That means I must start
Sailing my life-boat immediately.

6484.

My stupidity and I
Will no longer play
With the doubting mind.

6485.

My wisdom and I
Are all ready to slay the pride
Of the doubting mind.

6486.

My soul and I are on
The long, high road to
    timelessness,
And our joy is Infinity's
    Immortality.

6487.

The moment I prayerfully
Raised the head of my aspiration,
I met with God's Smile-flooded
    Eye.

6488.

My aspiration-heart-book
Is the only book
That I need to study
To realise God.

6489.

Mine is
The world-dedication-service-
    smile
That spans Heaven and earth.

6490.

God's Compassion-Eye
And His Forgiveness-Heart
Never believe in rest.

6491.

May each thought of mine
Come from the aspiration-purity
Of my heart-country.

6492.

O my stupidity-mind,
Is there any justifiable reason
Why you cannot surrender
To God's Will?

6493.

All God-realised souls
Are of one opinion:
God-manifestation
Is not an easy target.

6494.

To see the Face
Of my Lord Supreme
And to feel the Heart
Of my sweet Beloved,
I only need a shorter than the
    shortest
Breath of time.

6495.

The heart-land is where
The aspiration-trees
Are unimaginably tall.

6496.

Your heart-sufferings will be
Excruciating in the long run
If you continue to avoid
God's divine Sermons.

6497.

As I have dedicated my life,
Even so I shall dedicate my death
To the Will
Of my Lord Beloved Supreme.

6498.

When my heart became
An unconditionally surrendered
    life,
My Lord's Heart throbbed
And His Pulse quickened
With His Infinity's Delight.

6499.

All work has to be
The adoration of life
And the worship of the heart.

6500.

God does not care
For my mind's success-mountain.
He cares only
For my life's progress-fountain.

6501.

Nobody teaches the mind
How to doubt.
The mind itself
Is a self-taught doubter.

6502.

A smile
From the aspiration-heart
Is an amazing miracle-cure.

6503.

No matter what I say,
I am my Lord's
Sheltered life.

6504.

No matter what I do,
I am my Lord's
Treasured heart.

6505.

God and I
Take turns in flying
In Infinity's Sky.

6506.

God and I
Take turns in swimming
In the sea of tears.

6507.

When I am
My heart's devotion,
God becomes
His Life's ovation.

6508.

When faith is gone
From the heart,
Life becomes an empty gong.

6509.

When God speaks,
The mind needs
Translation.

6510.

When God speaks,
The heart becomes
Immediate identification.

6511.

The heart-telescope
Sees only Divinity's beauty
Inside the moon.

6512.

My soul smiles and smiles,
But it does not want to know
Why it smiles.

6513.

My heart cries and cries,
But it does not want to know
Why it cries.

6514.

My mind doubts and doubts,
But it does not want to know
Why it doubts.

6515.

My vital fights and fights,
But it does not want to know
Why it fights.

6516.

My body sleeps and sleeps,
But it does not want to know
Why it sleeps.

6517.

My life sighs and sighs,
But it does not want to know
Why it sighs.

6518.

I cannot believe
That anyone can have
A God-acceptance-heart
And a life-denial-mind.

6519.

My life feels
That Heaven is
A taskmaster.

6520.

My life feels
That earth is
A kinder than the kindest master.

6521.

Who breathes in us and for us
When we sleep,
If not our Lord Beloved Supreme?

6522.

The life-commotion
Does not dare to enter into
The heart-ocean.

6523.

My heart-songs I sing,
Not for Heaven's Smiles,
But for earth's tears.

6524.

God is always ready
To whisper His Infinity's Secrets
To anyone who is going to listen.

6525.

Why wait,
My heart?
Just radiate.

6526.

Why wait,
My mind?
Just meditate.

6527.

My mind,
Do you not have anything better
    to do
Than repeating day and night
Your God-denial-mantra?

6528.

If you want to run the fastest,
The first thing you have to do
Is bury your old hesitation-mind
And frustration-vital.

6529.

A God-preacher
Most of the time
Does not believe in anybody,
Including himself.

6530.

A God-believer
Not only believes in God,
But also believes in everyone
And everything.

6531.

Alas, human receptivity
Is always
In short supply.

6532.

Alas, God alone knows
When man's evolution
Will rise straight,
High, higher, highest.

6533.

It seems that
Human life fear-threat
Is looming large.

6534.

God will never give up on man,
No matter how long
He wants to live
In stark bondage-night.

6535.

It is the obligation
Of our prayer and meditation
To safeguard our mind's sincerity,
Heart's purity and life's humility.

6536.

O God, I pray to You,
Do think of clearing
The thought-jungle
Of the human mind
Once and for all.

6537.

Every day
What I need
Is experience-illumination.

6538.

To turn the mind's brooding
    doubts
Into teeming beliefs
Is not an impossible task.

6539.

My heart was created by God.
Do you know why?
For His Self-Enjoyment.

6540.

We can undo
Doubt-damage,
We certainly can!

6541.

Each time I have
A deep meditation,
My Lord blesses me
With a newly born smile.

6542.

The soul can definitely tame
Its combative
And destructive vital.

6543.

There are two roads:
A thorny road to reality
And a sunlit road to reality.
O seeker,
You are given the chance
To choose.

6544.

If gratitude we lose,
Then there is nothing meaningful
For us to offer to God.

6545.

The higher world-inspiration
Is at once illumining
And fulfilling.

6546.

The lower world-instigation
Is not only unproductive
But also destructive.

6547.

The good-hearted human beings
Whisper in their evening years,
"Alas, so little is done,
So little is accomplished,
So little have I offered
To the heart of humanity."

6548.

Do not stand near
The mind-doubt-entrance.
You may well be caught
Immediately.

6549.

Some may call it
Ego-nonsense.
I venture to say that
It is nothing short of
Ego-nuisance.

6550.

What do you want?
A decent and abiding
Solution to life
Or
A timid and cowardly
Escape from life?

6551.

The aspiring heart
Accepts everything
For the glorification
Of God.

6552.

The doubting mind
Suspects everything
To declare
Its own supremacy.

6553.

God wants you to entertain Him
With your soulful songs
And not with your boastful
    stories.

6554.

No matter how tall
Your proud mind is,
In the long run
It will be compelled to surrender
To Divinity's humility.

6555.

Be not a fool!
Your long-lost paradise
You can regain
By virtue of your prayers
And meditations.

6556.

Once you accept the spiritual life
And then give up,
You will be haunted
By your own shattered dreams.

6557.

When we do not aspire,
We are bound to be assailed
By dun desires.

6558.

Can there be anything
As fragile as human love?
The God-seeker wonders.

6559.

Every day my soul creates
A new God-hunger
In my aspiration-heart.

6560.

The God-devotion-bliss
Of humanity's aspiration
Shall one day
Illumine the entire universe.

6561.

In the morning,
When God asks me
To come and visit His Eye,
He receives an unfortunate "No."

6562.

At noon,
When God asks me
To come and visit His Heart,
He receives a shocking "No."

6563.

In the evening,
When God asks me
To visit His Feet,
He receives an immediate "Yes."

6564.

My Lord's Compassion-Heart
Has the habit of appealing
To my Lord's Justice-Eye
On behalf of humanity.

6565.

When we pray to God
And meditate on God,
God gives us
A little pocket money
To buy peace.

6566.

It seems that God the Justice
Has only one mantra
Before granting God-realisation:
"One more final test."

6567.

God has found a new occupation
For me:
A sleepless world-service-life.

6568.

We must be part and parcel
Of the ups and downs
Of the spiritual life.

6569.

God has long been planning
A oneness-meeting
Of my heart, mind, vital and body.

6570.

How does God spend His time?
God spends His time by
   entertaining –
This moment earth
And next moment Heaven.

6571.

My Lord,
I cannot believe how You can
   ignore
The world's bleeding heart.

6572.

My Lord tells me that
My self-giving life
Will soon be
His direct representative
Here on earth.

6573.

Mankind's eyeless mind
Has decisively refused
To commit itself
To God's Will.

6574.

God has given each divine
   thought
Permission to play
In the fields of Heaven
As long as it wants to.

6575.

Where does my peace-dream
Come from?
It comes from the Love
Of God's own Heart.

6576.

When I live inside my vital,
I immediately feel the breath
Of a world-frightening storm.

6577.

Of all my offerings,
God accepts
My surrender-offering first.

6578.

Peace lives next door
To my unconditional
Surrender-life.

6579.

What does my heart desire?
My heart desires to accompany
My Lord's Will
All-where.

6580.

The seekers have no idea
How carefully God examines
Their progress-life report.

6581.

I shall be perfect
Only when there is no difference
Between
My Lord's Fulness-Will
And my oneness-joy.

6582.

A genuine aspiration-heart
Eagerly feeds
On God's Will alone.

6583.

Alas, will my mind ever be able
To have
Tranquillity-treasure?

6584.

Even an iota of self-doubt
Is
A dead-end life.

6585.

The mind is certain
That the heart
Is always wrong.

6586.

The heart hopes
That the mind will one day
Have the capacity to tell
Right from wrong.

6587.

Every effort is inevitably needed
To be an eventually perfect
    instrument
Of God.

6588.

I need only one qualification
For my mind:
Willingness, constant willingness.

6589.

The understatement
Of the present century:
God is Compassion.

6590.

The overstatement
Of the present century:
God is Dictatorship.

6591.

The correct statement
Of the present century:
God is all Forgiveness.

6592.

Alas, I do not know
How long my aspiration-life
Will remain in its cradle.

6593.

A very large supply of aspiration-
    ink
I need
When I use my inner heart-pen.

6594.

My Lord's Compassion-Eye
And His Forgiveness-Heart
Are heralding
A new age of delight.

6595.

God is God's boundless Love,
In spite of man's
Constant reluctance-mind.

6596.

God is God's boundless Love
In spite of man's
Ingratitude-heart.

6597.

God is God's boundless Love
In spite of man's
Unreceptivity-life.

6598.

It is only our stupidity-mind
That can think and feel and
    declare:
"Peace has gone out of fashion."

6599.

What do I want?
I want my negativity-mind
And my criticism-mind
To fight and destroy each other.

6600.

God's Compassion-Eye
Is always ready
To give God-lessons
To all those
Who sincerely want to learn.

6601.

God's Forgiveness-Heart
Knows
No appointed hours.

6602.

God loves my mind's
Positive thoughts,
Positive ideas,
Positive ideals
More than I can ever express.

6603.

Now or never,
Select either
God the Power
Or
God the Love.

6604.

Even on my last day on earth,
My gratitude-heart and I shall
   sing,
To give joy to both
Mother Earth and Father Heaven.

6605.

What am I thirsty for?
I am thirsty only for
God's ever-descending Delight.

6606.

Each time I meditate well,
My Lord blesses me
With a special Smile-Gift.

6607.

We can never bribe
Either God-Justice-Light
Or
God-Compassion-Height.

6608.

Here, there and everywhere
I am looking for
God's Thunder-Feet
To transform my life.

6609.

Not for a minute,
But for Eternity,
I shall sleeplessly
And
Breathlessly cry
For my Lord's Satisfaction-Heart.

6610.

Unlike my mind,
My heart knows and feels
That it is quite easy
To satisfy God.

6611.

When my heart draws
Nearer to God,
Eternity's Peace
And
Infinity's Bliss beckon me.

6612.

My life is between
My Lord's first and last Requests:
Aspiration-Request being first,
Realisation-Request last.

6613.

Hesitation is my mind's
Slower than the slowest
Stumbling pace.

6614.

My heart's compassion-face
And
My life's service-hands
Are offering tremendous joy
To my Lord Supreme.

6615.

The mind and the vital:
This moment they wrestle,
The next moment they embrace.

6616.

May my aspiration-heart
Always be ignorant of
My doubting mind.

6617.

Where has my despair-vital gone?
Where?
I see it no more.

6618.

I have totally renounced
My long-standing servitude
To negativity.

6619.

We cannot separate God's Will
From striking
And illumining surprises.

6620.

Only an angel-heart
Has the capacity
To bow its head in humility
Before God the creation.

6621.

God is
Not at all interested
In my mind-mathematics.

6622.

God is
All interested
In my heart-songs.

6623.

Alas,
How true it is to see
God-gratitude dying
Before it is born.

6624.

God begs us
Only for one thing:
A smile —
A constant smile
And
A self-giving smile.

6625.

No human being
Will ever be exempt
From the God-satisfaction-test
Before God-realisation.

6626.

My heart-beauty's dream
Sings and dances
In every human heart.

6627.

Is there anything
That my love of God
Will not accomplish
For a Smile from God?

6628.

We beg God
To give and give
And give.

6629.

God begs us
To smile and smile
And smile.

6630.

The mind-bird
Is apt to fly
From one thought-tree
To another.

6631.

Where do I live?
I live between my life's heights
And my heart's depths.

6632.

Each moment
Comes with
God-fulfilment-promise-
    determination.

6633.

Falsehood never dares
To breathe,
Even for a second,
In my heart-shrine.

6634.

My self-giving life
Is my soul's
World-illumining companion.

6635.

My aspiration-heart
Has exiled doubt
From its world-service-life.

6636.

The crying heart
And
The smiling soul
Sleeplessly work together
For God-manifestation
On earth.

6637.

To reach God's starlit Sky,
I have renounced
All my earth-bound ties.

6638.

Gratitude has made this earth
Beautiful, soulful, prayerful
And Godful.

6639.

My Lord does not want me
To come to Him
In my mind-car.

6640.

My Lord wants me
To come to Him
As soon as possible
On my heart-feet.

6641.

My Lord gives chance after chance
To my mind
To divinely bloom
And
Supremely blossom.

6642.

When my Lord is my mind's
Only inspiration,
I become my life's
Inspiration-bird-flight.

6643.

When my Lord is my heart's
Only aspiration,
I become my life's
Ecstasy-heart-swimmer.

6644.

The seeker who fears pain
Never gains
God's Compassion-flooded Smile.

6645.

The desire-mind
Starves
For God's attention.

6646.

The aspiration-heart
Starves
For God's Affection.

6647.

The self-giving life
Starves
For God's Satisfaction.

6648.

Only when God is a reality
That our earth-existence
Is not a triviality.

6649.

God has no time
To visit
My darkness-mind-cave.

6650.

Every day
God happily and proudly
Visits me
In my heart-home.

6651.

My tearful heart,
I wish to be
Your lifelong friend.

6652.

My blessingful soul,
I wish to be
Your Eternity's student.

6653.

My faith
Is my Lord's
Fragrance-heart-flower.

6654.

Can Eternity help us
To enter into
Infinity's Immortality?
Certainly, it can and it shall.

6655.

God unburdens my mind.
But my stupidity-mind
Does not allow it to last.

6656.

When our heart flies
Towards Heaven,
Time stands still.
It does not interfere.

6657.

My heart does two things
At the same time:
It implores and it explores.

6658.

When the mind has its own
Clarity-light,
Insecurity, jealousy and impurity
Cannot blemish it.

6659.

Fly, fly high,
O seeker,
On your ever-spreading
Love-devotion-surrender-wings.

6660.

The only life worth living:
An unconditional
God-surrender-life.

6661.

The only name worth chanting:
God
The Forgiveness-Heart.

6662.

To feel the breath of the universe,
I must remain in tune with my
    soul
At every moment.

6663.

My depression
Is nothing other than
My life's failure-confession.

6664.

I trust
My only doctor:
God the Concern.

6665.

God cares only for
My heart's
Progress-fountain.

6666.

My sweet Lord,
You are telling me that
You have a pleasant surprise for
    me.

6667.

My Lord,
Do feel the depth
Of my curiosity-heart.

6668.

Humanity's permanent
God-gratitude
Is a miracle par excellence.

6669.

The outer electricity
Brings light into darkness.
The inner electricity
Transforms darkness into light.

6670.

When I am my heart's
Burning enthusiasm,
My Lord's Lightning-Satisfaction-
    Speed
Touches my breath.

6671.

The surrender-joy of the mind
Is almost an impossible task
To achieve.

6672.

A true disciple
Has only one choice:
His Master's voice.

6673.

My Lord,
Do make me a perfect stranger
To possession-mind
And desire-life.

6674.

Look more carefully.
God's Forgiveness-Heart
Is around the corner.
So is His Compassion-Eye.

6675.

My Lord's Compassion-Eye
Is my life's
Running coach.

6676.

Heaven I do not need,
But my Lord's Satisfaction-Heart
I always need.

6677.

There is no special time
For my Lord's Compassion-Eye
To descend
Into my aspiration-heart.
At any time it can.

6678.

A loving heart
And
A serving life
Shall always succeed.

6679.

There is
Only one winner:
God's Compassion-flooded Eye.

6680.

I wish to have a mind
As tranquil
As the bottomless depths
Of the ocean.

6681.

I awake
And what do I see?
I see God's two embracing Arms.

6682.

Everything is bound to exist
In the Light, with the Light
And for the Light
Of the Supreme.

6683.

Each luminosity-soul expands
To fill in the vastness
Of the sky.

6684.

During the day
God strictly examines
My doubting mind.

6685.

At night
God carefully examines
My aspiring heart.

6686.

Each progress-smile
Of my life
Is an advance march of humanity
Towards God.

6687.

My Lord,
Please smash and crush
My division-loving mind.

6688.

To start with,
We must fulfil the demands
Of the tradition-mind.
Then go far beyond the
    expectation
Of the tradition-mind.

6689.

I pray to my Inner Pilot
To nullify the stark failures
Of my past life.

6690.

The less we need
From the material world,
The more blessings we shall
    receive
From the higher worlds.

6691.

Insecurity, jealousy
And impurity
Are ever-recurring problems.

6692.

My prayer-life knows
What to receive
And how to receive blessing-light
From the higher worlds.

6693.

My meditation-heart knows
What to give
And how to give my service-life
To the outer world.

6694.

May my aspiration-heart
And dedication-life
Never be found
Where disharmony reigns.

6695.

When my mind touches
God's Feet,
God says to my mind,
"Ah, how soothing is your touch."

6696.

When God touches
My mind,
My mind says to God,
"What is it? What are You doing?
Do You not have anything better
    to do?"

6697.

The beauty and the fragrance
Of my God-duty
Forever shall remain inexplicable.

6698.

I cherish my heart's
Sunrise-aspiration
More than anything else.

6699.

May my heart become
The fastest climber
Of life's tallest tree.

6700.

May each thought that I create
Be a progress-promise
To my Lord Supreme.

6701.

I embrace
Each and every possibility
Of my God-satisfaction-thought.

6702.

The doubting mind
Spends the entire day
Looking for trouble –
Here, there, everywhere.

6703.

The height of our stupidity:
God is wanting
In Concern.

6704.

My Lord wants from my life
Self-illumination-flood
And not
Self-glorification-blood.

6705.

Nothing can be more obvious
Than my heart's genuine love
For my Lord Beloved Supreme.

6706.

What I need
Is the fulfilment
Of my God-ordained duties
And not
My self-imposed responsibilities.

6707.

If you want to succeed
In your outer life,
Then you must always hold fast
To your inner beliefs.

6708.

Alas, world-peace-lovers
Are misunderstood
And even scorned
By ignorance-consumed
    humanity.

6709.

A doubting mind
Is
A self-torture-life.

6710.

God wants excellence
From your life
At every moment.
Therefore,
Mediocrity does not become you.

6711.

Each moment sings
Its own unique heart-song-tune
To please the Lord of the universe.

6712.

True, no book can give us
God-realisation.
But it is equally true
That an aspiration-flooded book
Can be of immense help
In our spiritual life.

6713.

Death will not forever remain
An essential necessity
In life's experience.

6714.

My Lord says to me,
"My child, why do you
Not come to Me anymore?
Why?"

6715.

My Lord says to me,
"My child,
Why do you not come to sing
Inside My Heart-Garden
    anymore?
Why?"

6716.

My Lord says to me,
"My child, I am really waiting
For you to come and play with Me
The way you used to.
Why do you not come
To play with Me anymore?
Why?"

6717.

My Lord says to me,
"My child,
Why do you not like to be
Exactly like Me?
Why?"

6718.

My Lord says to me,
"My child,
You may not love Me.
But not only do I love you,
But also I need you at every
    moment
To be My Eternity's friend,
My Infinity's hope
And
My Immortality's promise."

6719.

O my gratitude-heart-tears,
Let us go to our Lord's Palace.
He will blessingfully
And lovingly welcome us.

6720.

What do I mean
When I say that I love God only?
I mean my sleepless and
    breathless
Faith in Him.

6721.

My Lord,
May I not have the same
    conviction
As my soul has:
That You will never forsake me?

6722.

During the day
My heart and I swim
In the cradle of Eternity's tears.

6723.

At night
My soul and I swim
In the cradle of Infinity's smiles.

6724.

For God-realisation,
I must never swerve from the path
Of God-satisfaction.

6725.

O my ecstasy-flooded soul,
Never allow me to leave you
And be in the land
Where Infinity's tears flow.

6726.

I am burying
Powerfully and proudly
The memories
Of my life's past blunders.

6727.

My Lord,
The way You claim Your own
    Vision,
Exactly the same way I wish to
    claim
Your Manifestation-Promise on
    earth
As mine.

6728.

My Lord,
Do You mind if my heart and I
Remain in touch with You
Quite often?

6729.

When I try to explain God,
I confuse the outer world
And I distance myself
From the inner world.

6730.

In the morning
The golden sunrise-inspiration
Awakens my life.

6731.

In the evening
The golden sunset-peace
Shelters me.

6732.

Cast aside your mind-attachment-
    life.
Immediately accept the invitation
From the highest heights
And the deepest depths.

6733.

Sweet is my Lord.
Sweeter is my Lord's
Compassion-Heart.
Sweetest is my Lord's
Forgiveness-Breath.

6734.

God wants you to walk the way
Of self-mastery
And never the way
Of self-denial.

6735.

My Master
Blessingfully welcomes
My heart's tearful voice.

6736.

My Master
Compassionately tells me
What I can do for God
And not what I must become.

6737.

What is the miracle of miracles
In my life,
If not my mind's sincere
And cheerful acceptance
Of my heart?

6738.

No simplicity-life,
No sincerity-mind,
No purity-heart—
Yet the whole world says
That it loves God only.

6739.

What can disobedience do?
It can shatter our aspiration-heart
And dedication-life
Easily.

6740.

Both God and I
Are doing the same thing:
We are trying to surprise each
    other.

6741.

Both God and I
Are becoming the same thing:
The fulfilment of our hopes.

6742.

When I choose God,
He helps me see
That I had no fall.

6743.

There is only one obstacle
In my life,
And that is my conscious
    separation
From God's Will.

6744.

Whom I seek
Is always within me.
What I seek
Is always around me.

6745.

God tells us
That we came into the world
Not to command Nature,
But to obey Nature.

6746.

Tell me, O evening stars,
How do you embody so much
    peace?
How?

6747.

Each new day
Is a new awareness
Of Divinity's Presence
Inside my being.

6748.

O my mind,
Hold nothing against the world.
Just shake hands with the world
And smile and smile.

6749.

Everything will be fine with me
If my heart basks
In the sunshine of my soul.

6750.

When we have an undivided
    mind,
Everything that we see and feel
Is complete and perfect.

6751.

The inner world
Accepts me
With no expectation.

6752.

The higher world
Expects me,
But never demands.

6753.

Yesterday was today's
Failure-tears.
Tomorrow is today's
God-blossoming dream.

6754.

My outer life is
My constant
God-expectation.

6755.

My inner life is
My constant
God-revelation.

6756.

My perfection is
My Lord's
Unconditional Love-
    manifestation.

6757.

Non-attachment
Is the freedom
Of real love.

6758.

Smash asunder the back of pride,
If you want to enjoy
A God-oneness-ride.

6759.

Previously,
The dust of my Lord's Feet
I tasted reluctantly.

6760.

The dust of my Lord's Feet
I now devour
Readily, willingly and eagerly
Plus breathlessly.

6761.

God the Doctor's only fee
Is our heart's
Sweetness-gratitude-smile.

6762.

Each and every heart
Is a sweet
Flower-fragrance-smile.

6763.

What a tragic experience I get:
The deeper I think I know God,
The further away He is from me.

6764.

The mind's obedience
And
The heart's perseverance
Together can accomplish
Everything they want to.

6765.

Choose God!
He at once becomes
Your heart the perpetual cry
And
Your soul the perpetual smile.

6766.

Alas,
My love of God
Has a very short life.

6767.

Alas,
My God-oblivion-mind
Lasts for a very, very long time.

6768.

Any action,
Inner or outer,
Without devotion
Is totally empty.

6769.

The seer-poet in me
Never desires to prove his
    existence.
He only wants to enrich
My entire being.

6770.

Do not wrestle with ignorance
Twenty-four hours a day.
Just invoke more light,
Infinitely more light
Than you have ever invoked,
To accomplish
Your God-manifestation-task.

6771.

No earthly anguish
Can ever help me succeed
In any field of my life.

6772.

To my extreme surprise,
My desire was summoned by
The light-flooded higher worlds.

6773.

When my poetry and my heart
Long for each other,
I become Divinity's colossal pride.

6774.

What is my divine love,
If not my Lord's
Infinite Energy?

6775.

What is divine love?
It is something that gives us
Absolute assurance.

6776.

Divine love knows
No disagreement-separation.

6777.

With our heart-attitude
We shall be able
To change the world
And not
With our life-plenitude.

6778.

My Lord Supreme,
Do illumine me,
My heart, my life and my all,
Under Your Compassion-Canopy.

6779.

When I pray and meditate,
I become the sun-garden
Of my Lord's Love.

6780.

My Lord,
In the sanctuary of Your Love
May I breathe, smile and dance.

6781.

It is all right when you
Absent yourself from God.
But when God absents Himself
    from you,
You die for His justification.

6782.

Because of the self-givers,
God is coming closer and closer
To humanity's life.

6783.

God has made my heart
A very special flame
Of His Love
To love my friends and enemies
    alike.

6784.

Each thing I hope for
Descends from the Compassion-
    Eye
Of my Lord Supreme.

6785.

Each promise I make
Is being fulfilled
By the unconditional Heart-Love
Of my Lord Supreme.

6786.

An angel of God-Hope
My aspiration-heart was.

6787.

An angel of God-Promise
My dedication-life is.

6788.

When my prayer
Comes from my mouth,
I lose my heart's inner beauty.

6789.

When my prayer
Comes from my heart,
I increase my life's God-prosperity.

6790.

My mind's ignorance-reality
Is no match for my soul's
Illumination-descending dream.

6791.

My soul's love-smile
I always express
Through my heart's
Affection-tears.

6792.

My Lord Supreme,
You have already imprinted
Your Blessing-Smile
On my heart.
Please do the same
On my head as well.

6793.

Anything special
In the spiritual life
Requires vigilant care.

6794.

As a tree is known by its fruits,
Even so a seeker is known
By his self-giving capacity.

6795.

To transcend the body-idea,
We must live in the light
Of the soul-ideal.

6796.

Your philosophical bent of mind
Is a real hindrance
To your God-seeking heart.

6797.

False belief-leaves
Will definitely drop
From your life-tree
If you daily cultivate
God-faith and self-faith.

6798.

When surrender is complete
In our inner life and outer life,
God embraces us
With His Confidence-Delight.

6799.

God wants each man
To be ready for
A fast, very fast evolution.

6800.

Earth
Is a place for
Constant God-awareness.

6801.

Heaven
Is a place of
Constant God-readiness.

6802.

My soul and I
Would like to be
Constant God-fulness.

6803.

Our heart's good intentions
Are definitely
Sacred.

6804.

You can climb the cliffs of life
If you can take
God's Compassion-Eye
As your only assistance.

6805.

Despite present hostility
Between the doubting mind
And the strangling vital,
I am sure one day
Abiding peace will descend on
     them.

6806.

I came into the world
Not to entertain illusions,
But to ascertain illumination.

6807.

Our mind's silence
Is the soundless sound
Of our soul's tranquillity.

6808.

Despite my mind's
Vehement resistance,
My heart can love
God's entire universe.

6809.

Every human being
Takes birth
In the heart of God's Hope.

6810.

God's Love
Is not a surprise.
God's Affection
Is not a surprise.
Even God's Fondness
Is not a surprise.
But God's withdrawal
Is, indeed, a real surprise.

6811.

"Movement forward,
Movement inward,
Movement upward"
Must be the incantation
Of mankind.

6812.

My life,
Nobody forced you to enrol
In the university of adversity.
It is your self-creation.

6813.

My mind's negativity
Has turned my heart's eagerness
Into futile nothingness.

6814.

My eyeless mind,
Come back to your God-readiness.
Enjoy retirement no more.

6815.

My soulless heart,
Come back to your God-eagerness.
Enjoy retirement no more.

6816.

My careless life,
Come back to your God-
        willingness.
Enjoy retirement no more.

6817.

I am coming back
To my God-awareness.
Retirement-enjoyment no more.

6818.

My Lord, do remind me
When my pride-mind hinders
My heart-service to Your creation.

6819.

My life and I know
That God loves us
Deeply.

6820.

My heart and I feel
That God is extremely intimate
With us.

6821.

My mind and I
Do not even care to know
Where God is
And what God does.

6822.

The calculating mind
Is doomed
To the tiniest circle-prison-life.

6823.

May my every action,
From morn to eve,
Be filled with
My God-gratitude-breath.

6824.

Each soulful smile
Of my aspiration-heart
Takes me nearer to God
Than all my mind-prayers.

6825.

My illumination-soul
Every day
Conveys to my aspiration-heart
A new ambrosial Message
From God.

6826.

My fame-hungry mind
Every day
Desires to climb the tallest ladder
Of celebrity.

6827.

My aspiration-heart
Every day
Devotedly, soulfully and self-
        givingly
Awakens to
My Lord's Clarion-Call.

6828.

My mind,
There are so many beautiful places
On earth
For you to move around.
Why do you want to remain
        standing
On your pride's high pedestal?

6829.

God's Satisfaction-Heart
Approaches us fast, very fast,
When we give everything
        unconditionally
To humanity
And expect nothing in return.

6830.

To my extreme joy,
Every day my aspiration-heart
Outgrows my old and false
Bondage-beliefs.

6831.

To my extreme sorrow,
The fear of my mind
Clouds my heart's
Golden opportunities.

6832.

My meditation-heart
Is the sole producer
Of my life's excellence.

6833.

Indeed,
Today we are all human beings.
Indeed,
Tomorrow we shall become
Part and parcel of our divine
    belongings.

6834.

My Lord Supreme
Commands my mind
To be absolutely still
Before He accepts any service.

6835.

If one wants to love humanity
Self-givingly,
There is plenty of love on earth.

6836.

If one wants to serve humanity
Unconditionally,
There is plenty of service on earth.

6837.

God the Father-Soul
May not always be yours for the
    asking,
But God the Mother-Heart
Always is.

6838.

Newness, oneness and fulness –
These three songs
The Heavenly angels every day
    sing.

6839.

May my heartbeat sail
Through Eternity's
Deep ocean.

6840.

When I look at
My Master's eyes,
I see his eyes are brighter
Than the sun.

6841.

When I look at
My Master's heart,
I see his heart is sweeter
Than the moon.

6842.

Do you want to be loved more,
Infinitely more by God?
Then immediately expand
Your purity-heart.

6843.

An unconditional surrender
Is the only valid passport
To enter into
God's Nectar-flooded Kingdom.

6844.

Since our very cradle,
Eternity
Has fondly embraced us.

6845.

Self-indulgence
Is, indeed,
Our worst enemy.

6846.

My Lord,
You took me.
My Lord,
You are moulding me.
My Lord,
You will eventually make me
All Yours.

6847.

My Lord Supreme,
May every heartbeat of mine
Remind me of
Your Compassion-Eye
And
Forgiveness-Heart.

6848.

Hope is the strongest pillar
That protects
The entire world.

6849.

O my self-giving life,
When everything is darkness-
   flooded,
Unlike others,
You can still see the stars.

6850.

O my heart, be not a fool!
Do not accept my mind's
   invitation.
The mind will give you, definitely,
A bumpy ride.

6851.

My heart-room
Knows that
It is eternally pure.

6852.

My mind-house
Thinks that
It is eternally significant.

6853.

Not my heart-compass,
But everything else
Needs to discover God.

6854.

Every time I lose
In the battlefield of life,
I am determined to choose
The breath of freedom-delight.

6855.

Who cares if my mind
Does not trust?
My safest harbour
Is my Lord's Compassion-Eye.

6856.

An unconditional surrender-
   seeker
Is not even a hair's breadth away
From God's Satisfaction-Heart.

6857.

So near, so close –
How can we ever miss
Our Lord Beloved Supreme?

6858.

My heart-feelings
Are always
God-oriented.

6859.

My mind-house
Either nobody cares to visit
Or nobody dares to visit.

6860.

A man of prayers
Can easily see the stars
Inside the darkest night.

6861.

Do not waste time!
If you want to discover God,
Dive deep within
Dauntlessly and self-givingly.

6862.

A heart of hope
Can never
In ignorance grope.

6863.

I do not calculate
Happiness.
I only cultivate
Happiness.

6864.

O my mind, be not stupid!
You must trust
Your blossoming hopes
And never
Your brooding fears.

6865.

Since it is infinitely easier
To smile than to frown,
How is it that I do not smile
At every moment?

6866.

Do not allow ignorance
To intimidate you.
Never!
You may not understand
    everything,
But you can easily and bravely
Illumine yourself.

6867.

My Supreme Lord's Eye
Sees
The road ahead.

6868.

My Beloved Lord's Heart
Clears
The road ahead.

6869.

Fear not
Your ignorance-pride.
Bravely and sleeplessly
Illumine it.

6870.

I can forgive everything,
But not
My misunderstanding-mind.

6871.

Patience, perseverance
And God-surrender:
These three friends are always
Found together.

6872.

My mind,
Do not disappoint God!
An unimaginable hope-sun
He has for you.

6873.

No possession
Can be as great
As self-renunciation.

6874.

My Lord,
I knew, I know
And I shall forever know
That without Your blessingful
    Feet
I cannot exist on earth.

6875.

When you play
Love-devotion-surrender-game,
Doubt, worries and anxieties
Should be onlookers
And not participants.

6876.

Every day
I faithfully empty my mind
And
Devotedly leave all its contents
At my Lord's Lotus-Feet.

6877.

A faith-claiming heart,
Indeed, deserves
A God-fulfilling smile.

6878.

The mind,
Consciously or unconsciously,
Is a strong supporter
Of stark stupidity.

6879.

My devotion-heart
Paves the way for me
To arrive at my Lord's Heart.

6880.

Killing time means
Killing God's
Fountain-Heart-Joy.

6881.

Enlightenment of thought,
And not abandonment of thought
We strive for.

6882.

May my aspiration-heart
Take every day
As a God-appreciation,
God-admiration,
God-adoration
And
God-devotion-day.

6883.

An aspiration-abundance-heart
Will definitely be treasured
By God's own universal Heart.

6884.

There will always remain
A prayerful room for me
In God's Heart-Palace.

6885.

Nobody can force me
To enjoy the bombardment
Of my ignorance-thoughts.
Nobody!

6886.

My aspiration-eye
And
My meditation-heart
Enjoy anonymity.

6887.

I have forced my mind
To come out of its long-cherished
Disobedience-grave.

6888.

Every heart
Is
A God-blossoming dream.

6889.

What does an unaspiring mind do
All the time?
It enjoys its self-assertion-pride.

6890.

My Lord Supreme sings and
    dances
To my life's
Inner awakening.

6891.

A purity-face is, indeed,
A work of Divinity's
Unconditional Grace.

6892.

Fight, fight, indomitably fight
Against your mind's
Disobedience-days and nights.

6893.

My poor heart, from now on
I shall be always with you.
You will no more remain
Isolated and rejected.

6894.

When nothing goes right,
That is the time to increase
The intensity of our devotion.

6895.

I have wandered
From birth to birth.
I do hope it is not all in vain.

6896.

This world
Is flooded with
Unconcerned smiles.

6897.

Affection-flames
Can melt
Any heart.

6898.

My mind,
Why have you drawn me
Into the whirlpool of self-hatred?
Why?

6899.

My Lord tells me that
He does not mind
If I extol myself to the skies.

6900.

My Lord tells me that
He does mind
If I disparage others
Even for a fleeting minute.

6901.

Since we take our birth
In perfect harmony,
Can we not depart from this world
In exactly the same way?

6902.

To me, expectation-fulfilment
Is nothing short of
My mental hallucination.

6903.

You may allow anything you want
    to,
But do not allow desire
To storm your life.

6904.

If you take your mind
Too seriously,
You are bound to suffer.

6905.

If you take your life
Too indulgently,
You are bound to suffer.

6906.

My Lord Supreme always
    demands
Originals from me
In everything I do for Him.

6907.

My Lord Supreme,
The song You sing,
My heart shall become.

6908.

I am all determined
To throw myself into
My Lord's Compassion-Sea.

6909.

May my heart every morning
Be on fire
For God-realisation.

6910.

Do not give up!
It is only believing
That keeps us alive
And inspires us to look forward.

6911.

When I live inside the Heart
Of my Lord Supreme,
Suffering is a totally foreign
    language.

6912.

Frustration-fight
I want to be
And not
Frustration-flight.

6913.

At times,
Duties enjoined by religion
Are utterly ridiculous.

6914.

Alas,
Outer observances we admire,
Inner significances we neglect.

6915.

How can an invalid body
Have the capacity to know
The strength
Of a dynamic mind?

6916.

My Lord Supreme wants me
To treat the world gently
And not punish the world harshly.

6917.

When my Lord Supreme
Sees my smiling face
At a distance,
He asks me to come to Him.

6918.

When my Lord Supreme
Sees my smiling heart
Even from
The farther than the farthest
    distance,
He comes running towards me.

6919.

He who does not listen
To the voice of Nature
Will never be my Lord's
Choice instrument.

6920.

A doubting mind
And a strangling vital –
These two evils are always
In collusion
To destroy the loving heart.

6921.

If yours is
A desire-bound life,
Then yours will be
A shameful death.

6922.

An aspiring heart,
Once it starts blossoming,
Can definitely continue.

6923.

Do not suppress your
    shortcomings.
Your shortcomings have to be
    accepted,
Perfected
And finally emancipated.

6924.

Everybody's mind
Has to be brave enough,
Everybody's life
Has to be brave enough
To encounter the onslaught
Of death-fear.

6925.

An enduring happiness-mind
Is
An unbelievable story.

6926.

An enduring happiness-heart
Is, indeed,
A God-loving song.

6927.

Alas, my poor failure-life
Is all due to
My doubting mind.

6928.

A gratitude-heart
Needs constant protection
From an ingratitude-mind.

6929.

I do hope that frailty
In human life
Is not an everlasting experience.

6930.

A dreamer of good,
A thinker of good
And
A doer of good
Are God's most affectionate
    children.

6931.

Alas,
We try to purify others' minds
Long before we have purified
Our own hearts.

6932.

What can poor unbelief and
    disbelief do
When God-miracle-performances
Overwhelm them?

6933.

May my heart-light
Every day shine brighter
To welcome
My Lord's Compassion-flooded
    Feet.

6934.

In the presence of God
Our complaints lose
All their strength.

6935.

My Lord,
Already You have made me
Your Hand-flute.
Do make me now
Your Heart-violin.

6936.

When you have a spiritual Master,
You can immeasurably increase
Your God-ready opportunities.

6937.

The false reports of the mind
About the inner life
Must end where they began.

6938.

A God-realised soul
Is, indeed,
The common property
Of everybody's heart.

6939.

You are telling me that
You have nothing important to do
    today.
May I suggest you do only one
    thing:
Cast away your pride,
At least for a day?

6940.

It is the self-giving hearts
That are keeping the universe
From insanity.

6941.

My Lord,
May my life listen only
To Your Compassion-Heart-
    Songs.

6942.

Only the soul of silence
Has the capacity
To unite the aspiring heart
With the serving life.

6943.

God has an easy access
To every place,
Specially to our heart-temple.

6944.

The doubting mind
Knows
How to oscillate.

6945.

The aspiring heart
Knows
How to levitate.

6946.

The illumining soul
Knows
How to accelerate.

6947.

The desiring life
Knows
How to hesitate.

6948.

When I make
God-manifestation-promises,
My Lord Supreme most
   compassionately
Takes care of them.

6949.

My self-doubt
Is extremely afraid of
My Godward march.

6950.

God has appointed
My surrender-heart
To be His representative
On earth.

6951.

My aspiration-heart,
Do make a solemn promise to me
That you will energise
My lethargy-body.

6952.

My aspiration-heart,
Do make a solemn promise to me
That you will correct
My shameless vital.

6953.

My aspiration-heart,
Do make a solemn promise to me
That you will illumine
My eyeless mind.

6954.

My aspiration-heart,
Do make a solemn promise to me
That you will transform
My prayerless heart.

6955.

My aspiration-heart,
Do make a solemn promise to me
That you will outlast
My godless life.

6956.

A gratitude-heart
Is, indeed,
A transcendental blessing
From God.

6957.

Humanity's heart
Is made of
Eternity's hopes.

6958.

Every day,
May my heart be
A new rainbow-promise
And
New God-manifestation-promise
To God.

6959.

The right place
For a temptation-frustration
To live
Is a nothingness-land.

6960.

May each thought of mine
Live inside
Tranquillity-trance.

6961.

Only a child-heart-seeker
Gives an immediate response
To God's Will.

6962.

I need infinitely more Grace
Than I ever thought
To be a genuine God-seeker.

6963.

Stop, stop, immediately stop
The wheel of madness-thoughts.

6964.

We must break asunder
Our mind-prison-fetters
And never think of
An ignoble escape.

6965.

To control the thought-waves
Of the mind,
We must beg our heart
To patrol our mind.

6966.

My searching mind
Needs
Illumination.

6967.

My serving life
Needs
Transformation.

6968.

My aspiring heart
Needs
My God-satisfaction.

6969.

My illumining soul
Needs manifestation,
Constant God-manifestation.

6970.

My compassion-flooded soul
Does not dethrone
Even my suspecting mind
And
My domineering vital.

6971.

Alas,
I do not know why
I am so attached and indulgent
To my mind's
Hallucination-illumination.

6972.

I want You, my Lord,
Not my periphery-self,
Never!

6973.

I beg my God-representative-soul
To be the sole pilot
Of my life.

6974.

Alas,
I am in between
My mind-fumbles
And
My mind-stumbles.

6975.

If you have the capacity
To have pride,
Then you have the capacity
To hide or destroy it as well.

6976.

Every morning
The rising sun blessingfully looks
At my life.

6977.

Every evening
The setting sun compassionately
    cries
With my heart.

6978.

God wants you to keep open
The gate of your heart
And not the door of your mind.
Never!

6979.

Our lives
Can be full of
Earth-tragedies.

6980.

Our hearts
Are armoured with
Heaven-God-comedies.

6981.

My prayerful thoughts
Are always cradled
In the petals of rose-beauty.

6982.

My soul always wants
My heart, mind, vital and body
To be in the temple
Of selfless activities.

6983.

The Sweetness-Heart of God
Tiptoes
Only in a prayerful
And self-giving heart.

6984.

A God-realised soul is he
Who spreads
Divinity's sunshine-goodwill
Everywhere.

6985.

My prayer
Is my life's
God-invocation-thirst.

6986.

My meditation
Is my heart's
God-manifestation-hunger.

6987.

My wheel of life
Is always out of order.
Therefore God's Will never works.

6988.

I am not my mind's
Curiosity-starvation.
I am my heart's
God-aspiration-banquet.

6989.

If you can keep illumining
The temple within,
God will blessingfully
And proudly
Broadcast your name.

6990.

Everybody is endowed
With a free choice,
But only the seekers
Want to be endowed
With a God-choice.

6991.

Forgiveness
Is a most sacred Boon
From Above.

6992.

If you cultivate calmness of mind,
You will find God
In every corner of the world.

6993.

I wish to enter into
God's Light-flooded Kingdom
That has no frontiers.

6994.

Only Love divine
Can slake
Our heart's God-hunger-pain.

6995.

May my gratitude-heart-songs
Become inseparably one
With Eternity.

6996.

May my answer be always
"Yes,"
To fulfil my Lord's Command
    divine.

6997.

The hearts that selflessly serve
    God
And never care for sleep
Are the chosen, supremely chosen
Instruments
Of our Lord Supreme.

6998.

My heart-bird is soaring
Towards the Heavens
To feed on God's Compassion-
    Delight.

6999.

To travel is to live.
To live is to serve.
To serve is to be perfect –
Perfection within, perfection
    without!

7000.

My Lord,
My every heartbeat
Is a signal proof
Of Your Compassion, Love
And Blessings.

BIBLIOGRAPHY

SEVENTY-SEVEN THOUSAND SERVICE-TREES (50 VOLUMES)

SRI CHINMOY:

—*Seventy-seven thousand Service-Trees, part 01,* New York, Agni Press, 1998.
—*Seventy-seven thousand Service-Trees, part 02,* New York, Agni Press, 1998.
—*Seventy-seven thousand Service-Trees, part 03,* New York, Agni Press, 1998.
—*Seventy-seven thousand Service-Trees, part 04,* New York, Agni Press, 1998.
—*Seventy-seven thousand Service-Trees, part 05,* New York, Agni Press, 1998.
—*Seventy-seven thousand Service-Trees, part 06,* New York, Agni Press, 1998.
—*Seventy-seven thousand Service-Trees, part 07,* New York, Agni Press, 1998.
—*Seventy-seven thousand Service-Trees, part 08,* New York, Agni Press, 1998.
—*Seventy-seven thousand Service-Trees, part 09,* New York, Agni Press, 1998.
—*Seventy-seven thousand Service-Trees, part 10,* New York, Agni Press, 1998.
—*Seventy-seven thousand Service-Trees, part 11,* New York, Agni Press, 1999.
—*Seventy-seven thousand Service-Trees, part 12,* New York, Agni Press, 1999.
—*Seventy-seven thousand Service-Trees, part 13,* New York, Agni Press, 1999.
—*Seventy-seven thousand Service-Trees, part 14,* New York, Agni Press, 1999.
—*Seventy-seven thousand Service-Trees, part 15,* New York, Agni Press, 1999.
—*Seventy-seven thousand Service-Trees, part 16,* New York, Agni Press, 1999.
—*Seventy-seven thousand Service-Trees, part 17,* New York, Agni Press, 2000.
—*Seventy-seven thousand Service-Trees, part 18,* New York, Agni Press, 2000.
—*Seventy-seven thousand Service-Trees, part 19,* New York, Agni Press, 2000.
—*Seventy-seven thousand Service-Trees, part 20,* New York, Agni Press, 2001.
—*Seventy-seven thousand Service-Trees, part 21,* New York, Agni Press, 2001.
—*Seventy-seven thousand Service-Trees, part 22,* New York, Agni Press, 2001.
—*Seventy-seven thousand Service-Trees, part 23,* New York, Agni Press, 2001.
—*Seventy-seven thousand Service-Trees, part 24,* New York, Agni Press, 2002.
—*Seventy-seven thousand Service-Trees, part 25,* New York, Agni Press, 2002.
—*Seventy-seven thousand Service-Trees, part 26,* New York, Agni Press, 2002.
—*Seventy-seven thousand Service-Trees, part 27,* New York, Agni Press, 2002.
—*Seventy-seven thousand Service-Trees, part 28,* New York, Agni Press, 2002.
—*Seventy-seven thousand Service-Trees, part 29,* New York, Agni Press, 2002.
—*Seventy-seven thousand Service-Trees, part 30,* New York, Agni Press, 2002.
—*Seventy-seven thousand Service-Trees, part 31,* New York, Agni Press, 2003.
—*Seventy-seven thousand Service-Trees, part 32,* New York, Agni Press, 2003.
—*Seventy-seven thousand Service-Trees, part 33,* New York, Agni Press, 2003.
—*Seventy-seven thousand Service-Trees, part 34,* New York, Agni Press, 2003.

–*Seventy-seven thousand Service-Trees, part 35,* New York, Agni Press, 2004.
–*Seventy-seven thousand Service-Trees, part 36,* New York, Agni Press, 2004.
–*Seventy-seven thousand Service-Trees, part 37,* New York, Agni Press, 2004.
–*Seventy-seven thousand Service-Trees, part 38,* New York, Agni Press, 2004.
–*Seventy-seven thousand Service-Trees, part 39,* New York, Agni Press, 2004.
–*Seventy-seven thousand Service-Trees, part 40,* New York, Agni Press, 2004.
–*Seventy-seven thousand Service-Trees, part 41,* New York, Agni Press, 2004.
–*Seventy-seven thousand Service-Trees, part 42,* New York, Agni Press, 2005.
–*Seventy-seven thousand Service-Trees, part 43,* New York, Agni Press, 2005.
–*Seventy-seven thousand Service-Trees, part 44,* New York, Agni Press, 2005.
–*Seventy-seven thousand Service-Trees, part 45,* New York, Agni Press, 2006.
–*Seventy-seven thousand Service-Trees, part 46,* New York, Agni Press, 2006.
–*Seventy-seven Thousand Service-Trees, Part 47,* New York, Agni Press, 2007.
–*Seventy-seven Thousand Service-Trees, Part 48,* New York, Agni Press, 2007.
–*Seventy-seven Thousand Service-Trees, Part 49,* New York, Agni Press, 2008.
–*Seventy-seven Thousand Service-Trees, Part 50,* New York, Agni Press, 2009.

Suggested citation key: ST.

POSTFACE

Publishing principles

This edition of *The works of Sri Chinmoy* aims to obey the Author's wish: scrupulous fidelity to his original words, use of typographical style by him selected, specific spelling choices, end placement of any editorial content (i.e. not written by Sri Chinmoy himself), particular treatment of some personal nouns in special cases, etc.

Textual accuracy

The text of this edition has been checked to ensure faithful accuracy to the originals. Although much effort has been put in proofreading and comparing different versions of the text, this print may still present a few lingering errors.

The Publisher would be grateful to be apprised of any mistypes via postal mail or facsimile, possibly with scan of the original page where the text is different. Please use original books only, specifying the year of publication. Online versions may be not as accurate and should not be considered authoritative.

Acknowledgements

The Publisher is very grateful to the late Professor Lambert and his équipe for his invaluable advice. For many decades Prof. Lambert conducted a small publishing house specialising in hand-made prints of philological edition of the classics. The standard of this edition would not have been the same without his scholarly advice.

The Publisher is also grateful to the international team of collaborators that spent countless hours proofreading and checking the current text against the originals.

Our deepest gratitude to Sri Chinmoy. His living presence can be felt breathing throughout his writings. It is a privilege to be involved with his works, in any form.

Citation keys

Citation keys are used throughout *The works of Sri Chinmoy* to allow accurate cross-reference of texts across titles and editions. Examples: EA 13, ST 50000, UPA 7.

Sri Chinmoy Canon

We could not use better words than Professor Lambert's, who kindly offered the name *Sri Chinmoy Canon*:

> «By defining Sri Chinmoy's first editions as *editio princeps* we chose to follow classical scholarship criteria, not because we consider Sri Chinmoy's work antique, but because we believe it is among the few post ‹classical antiquity› works to rightly deserve to be considered a *classicus*, designating by that term *superiority, authority* and *perfection*.

> «The monumental work Sri Chinmoy is offering to mankind is awe-inspiring and supremely pre-eminent in proportions and quality. It is manifest that Sri Chinmoy's work — which we feel right to call *The Sri Chinmoy Canon* — will be of profound help and source of enlightenment to anyone seeking a higher wisdom, truth and reality supreme.»

[Translated from French by M. G.S.]

TABLE OF CONTENTS

Composition typographique par imprimerie
Ab Academia Aoidon, Paris & Lyon.

Un grand merci à Prof Knuth pour
l'utilisation avancée de TₑX.

A LYON, LE 13 OCTOBRE LXXXVII Æ.G.

Ingram Content Group UK Ltd.
Milton Keynes UK
UKHW021113030523
421135UK00012B/109/J